Subduing Satan

The Fred W. Morrison Series in Southern Studies

Subduing Satan

Religion, Recreation, and
Manhood in the Rural South,
1865–1920

Ted Ownby

The University of North Carolina Press

Chapel Hill and London

© 1990 The University of North Carolina Press

The paper in this book meets the guidelines for permanence and
durability of the Committee on Production Guidelines for
Book Longevity of the Council on Library Resources.

Printed in the United States of America

94 93 92 91 90   5 4 3 2 1

Library of Congress Cataloging-in-Publication Data
Ownby, Ted.
   Subduing Satan : religion, recreation, and manhood in the rural
South, 1865–1920 / Ted Ownby.
      p.   cm.—(The Fred W. Morrison series in Southern studies)
   Includes bibliographical references.
   ISBN 0-8078-1913-1 (alk. paper)
      1. Southern States—Social life and customs—1865–   .   2. Southern
States—Popular culture—History.   3. Men, White—Southern States—
History.   4. Evangelicalism—Southern States—History.   5. Southern
States—Religious life and customs.   6. Violence—Southern States—
History.   I. Title.   II. Series.
   F215.O87   1990   89-48578
   306'.0975—dc20   CIP

To my parents, Bill and Mary Ownby

Contents

Illustrations

Tables

Preface

WHITE men and women in the South today must be troubled by the apparent contradiction between two of the more powerful images of what it means to be a Southerner. One image is that of a fighter. Young Southerners today know little of the Civil War except that their ancestors fought long and hard and somehow they are supposed to take pride in that fact. Early in life Southerners learn from television, from their elders, from the movies, and, more than ever before, from the music of their own region that they live in a part of the country where people are willing to fight if the situation seems to call for it, and they learn to be somewhat belligerent when criticized. Fully as powerful as this perception of the region is the image of the religious South. Most Southerners are very conscious—some are very proud—that they live in the so-called Bible Belt. Southerners come to believe at an early age that people in their region take religion more seriously and experience it on more of a "gut level" than most other Americans. This book examines the relationship of those two images—the fighting white South and the religious white South—and the evolution of each.

The late nineteenth century provides a fruitful period for studying the relationship between these two disparate images. Charles Reagan Wilson has argued that the psychological consequences of military defeat intensified the commitment of Southern whites to their religion. And church membership, as Samuel S. Hill has shown, increased dramatically in the late nineteenth century.[1] The violent side of Southern culture also reached new extremes in those decades, as the popularity of the Ku Klux Klan and the rise of lynching demonstrated. This book, however, examines not those dramatic manifestations but the more mundane, recreational ways in which Southern men proved themselves to one another.

My study concludes in the 1910s, when the South was beginning to feel the effects of an evolving national mass culture. It has become almost an industry in recent years for scholars to write about whether or not the South is losing, or has lost, its distinctiveness as a region. I hope this study helps to show that national culture did not overwhelm Southern life but that it intensified many of the tensions within the

South. We need to turn our focus away from the question of whether the South in the twentieth century has become more or less like the rest of the country and examine instead the often ambiguous ways in which Southerners have interpreted and responded to national developments.

I have tended to de-emphasize the diversity of cultures within the South, largely ignoring the Appalachian region and completely avoiding the predominantly Catholic sections of Louisiana, Mississippi, Maryland, and Kentucky. My goal is not to suggest that those regions were not part of the South but rather to concentrate more clearly on the great majority of white Southerners. I also have not explored the critically important growth of factories in the postbellum decades. Several works have described the enormous changes in the lives of farm people who went to work in the factories. The interaction of religion and recreation embodied in mill sports teams and mill churches is a subject worthy of more consideration. But for most Southerners, life around the turn of the century was still decidedly agricultural, and historians should never overlook what was most common in searching for what was new.

The publication of this book allows me the opportunity to thank the people who have helped along the way. Bill and Mary Ownby deserve the most thanks. They provided all the support for my education and endured the typically sullen moments of a graduate student. My grandmother, Dora Williams, kept up a strong interest in Southern history. I am proud to quote from her published reminiscence in chapter 7, and I wish she were alive to read the book.

My intellectual debts are great. By far the greatest is to John Higham, whose enthusiasm for imagination has been a good antidote to my tendency to stay on familiar ground. His openness to different approaches to history encouraged me to explore unusual sources and to try lines of argument I otherwise might never have attempted. Satisfying his standards was difficult; impressing him with an occasional insight or amusing him with a piece of evidence was a pleasure.

Timothy Smith and Jack Green exposed me to new methods of studying religious and social history. Timothy Smith was surprised to find the autobiography of his own aunt, Bertha Smith, quoted in chapter 7. His reading of the manuscript saved me from a couple of ridiculous errors. Two undergraduate professors deserve my thanks as well. Wayne Cutler was the first to suggest I might attend graduate school. Paul Conkin supervised my undergraduate thesis and set a standard for clear thinking that I could spend a lifetime trying to reach. Bertram Wyatt-Brown and Edward Ayers significantly improved the manuscript, helping me turn a somewhat disorganized series of chapters into a book. At The University of North Carolina Press, Lewis Bateman has been as patient as he has been helpful, and Pamela Upton has clarified many of my worst sentences.

A number of colleagues have helped with my revisions. At Western Washington University, Amanda Eurich and August Radke read the manuscript and offered encouragement, and Harry Ritter gave advice about chapter 4. At Central Michigan University, George Blackburn, Susan Conner, Eric Johnson, David Macleod, and Helen Schwartz helped me clarify my arguments in chapters 2 and 9. I have made my final revisions at my new home, the history and Southern studies departments at the University of Mississippi. Charles Wilson has helped me make a few last-minute changes, and a casual remark from Robert Haws led to my reference to Elvis in chapter 10.

Historians should never tire of acknowledging the work of the staffs at archives. I owe even more thanks than most because I frequently showed up unannounced at an archive and called in an enormous amount of material within a brief time. Special thanks go to the people at the Southern Historical Collection of the University of North Carolina at Chapel Hill, the Special Collections Division of the Louisiana State University Library, and the Manuscripts Department of the University of Georgia Library. I spent several months at each location. Thanks also to the staffs of the Library of Congress, the Alabama Department of Archives and History, the Disciples of Christ Historical Society, Perkins Library at Duke University, the Special Collections Division of the Robert Woodruff Library at Emory University, the Florida State Archives, the Georgia Department of Archives and History, the Georgia Historical Society, the Historical Foundation of the Presbyterian and Reformed Churches, the Methodist Publishing House Library, the Mississippi Department of Archives and History, the National Agricultural Library, the North Carolina Collection of the University of North Carolina at Chapel Hill, the Southern Baptist Library and Archives, the South Carolina Historical Society, the Tennessee State Library and Archives, the Special Collections Division of the Howard-Tilton Memorial Library at Tulane University, the William Stanley Hoole Special Collections Library at the University of Alabama in Tuscaloosa, and the South Caroliniana Library at the University of South Carolina.

Practical assistance has come from many sources. Sharon Widomski, Annette Davis, Beth Allen, and Doris Jones have helped type different versions of the manuscript, and Mary Ownby, David Nelson, and Gregory Hospodor helped with the proofreading. A grant from the Faculty Research and Creative Endeavors Fund of the Central Michigan University helped me complete the manuscript and locate the photographs. One of the pleasures of being on the road doing research was staying with friends throughout the South. I owe many thanks to hosts David Bruce, Dave Burge, John Cribb, Warner Cribb, Scott and Heather Jared, Bob and Sarah Lane, Joe Keith Robbins, Dan Sullivan, and Dave and Wendy Williams.

Five days after I finished the first draft of this work, thus ending one part of my life, I met Amanda Eurich, thus beginning another.

Subduing Satan

Introduction:
Home Sentiment
and Male Culture

Woman is oftener found on the
side of right than man.
—Robert Toombs DuBose

THERE was a certain highly charged quality about everyday life in the nineteenth-century and early twentieth-century South. The region's saints were more saintly, its sinners more sinful than those in most of the Anglo-American world. White Southerners were deeply concerned, and some were obsessed, with personal righteousness and sinfulness. More than fearing that mankind's sinful nature would never allow men and women to live up to Christian ideals, they had real fears of actual sins of commission. They had good reason for those fears, for when Southerners sinned, they sinned with a vengeance. As W. J. Cash described the nineteenth-century Southern white man, "To stand on his head in a bar, to toss down a pint of raw whisky in a gulp, to fiddle and dance all night, to bite off the nose or gouge out the eye of a favorite enemy, to fight harder and love harder than the next man, to be known eventually far and wide as a hell of a fellow—such would be his focus."[1] The opposites of aggressive, fun-loving male impulses and a deep evangelical piety worked to intensify each other. If some Southerners raised hell to dramatic heights, others felt a special need to bring heaven down to earth on a very personal level.

Subduing Satan examines how those opposites operated in the recreations pursued by white men and women in the rural South in the decades after the Civil War. It takes a broad approach to recreation, examining many leisure activities that were pursued not simply for pleasure but as expressions of important cultural meanings. Group

I

prayer and church attendance, for example, were forms of cultural expression we do not typically consider as leisure activities, but they were important group experiences. Shucking corn and hunting were productive activities, but both had cultural meanings far beyond their importance in putting food on the table. This study concentrates heavily on place. People act differently in different places, and they go to diverse places to enjoy themselves in special ways. The behavior that prevailed in the home and the church might be radically altered on trips to the country store or to certain sections of the town. A concentration on the places in which various behaviors were sanctioned allows us to examine cultural tensions in action, as people in those places acted out a whole array of often conflicting cultural impulses.

Historians are beginning to realize that it is impossible to understand the sacred without understanding the secular, or the secular without the sacred. By examining both, the study of recreation can illuminate some of the most powerful tensions within a culture. Recreation takes place within systems of oppositions. When they are enjoying themselves, people express not only who they are, but, very often, who they are not. Differences in gender, age, class, occupation, and ethnic origin, as well as simple differences in taste, are expressed, often in ways that dramatize those differences. Men enjoy some recreations that women generally avoid; the young listen to music they know their elders despise; the rich indulge in luxurious recreations that most people cannot afford; and the poor enjoy pastimes they know wealthier groups cannot understand. To identify themselves as belonging to a community, individuals must have a sense not only of being part of one group, but also of being different from another group. For example, fans of professional soccer teams in West Germany establish their opposing identities in particularly visible ways, taking separate streets to the stadia and sitting in sections partitioned by fences. Recreations very often allow people to identify their opposites, thereby giving them a firmer sense of their own group identities.

A second opposition expressed through recreation involves both those features of life that individuals wish to replicate for enjoyment and those they wish to escape, if only briefly. The study of popular recreation is often vague and unsatisfying because it is rarely clear which features of life are expressed. Does a specific sport, game, or pastime concern attitudes about work, class, gender, age, the body, or nature, or, more likely, some combination of these? Does recreation express larger individual and social mores, or does it allow a temporary escape from them? Anthropologists have taken pains to show that it can do either. A recreation can allow people, as one scholar puts it, to "transform abstract cultural values into observable behavior."[2] Unarticulated core attitudes can come to the surface, often in ways that allow people to express the depth of their adherence to certain values. On the other hand, many recreations defy the logic of everyday life. Participants in such activities rise above the boredom and dissatisfactions of mundane existence and rebel against accumulated frustrations, enjoying forms of behavior that differ dramatically from everyday norms. Certain inversion rituals in which prevailing class or gender relations are dramatically reversed reveal this form of opposition most clearly. In many cultures, during festivals men and women wear each other's clothing and assume each other's mannerisms, that is, they ridicule the respected and exalt the body.[3] The opposition thus set up is between the norm of behavior and the release from the norm, or between the recreation that dramatizes and expresses the norm and that which expresses freedom from it.

In the South, as in many cultures, recreations have been closely related to religion. Whether people escape their everyday notions of the sacred, or celebrate those notions, or do both at the same time, the suspension of everyday reality often has a decidedly religious flavor. Countless ceremonies and recreations celebrate the gods and humans' place in the gods' universe. Tributes to the gods and to the customs they demand originated in the earliest religions and continue in religious ceremonies today. In them, the behavior expected of the religious individual is celebrated; a participant leaves such ceremonies intending to do everything possible to please the gods. Other recreations violate religious norms for everyday behavior in ways that nevertheless serve religious purposes. In many inversion rituals, celebrants believe that the gods have sanctioned the temporary violation of divinely established conventions. As an anthropologist writes of a particularly dramatic Krishna "feast of love" in northern India, such rituals involve "the world destruction and world renewal, the world pollution followed by world purification."[4]

Some recreations relate to religious notions of morality only by violating them. Since religions set the standards for everyday right and wrong, many recreations provide a sense of release simply by allowing people to do wrong. Individuals indulging in these recreations are not paying homage to the gods for allowing such a release from daily norms. They are not being purified, they are sinning. As we will see, men's desire for release from a strict code of evangelical morality helps account for the emotional intensity of many male recreations in the South.

To begin to understand what Southerners expressed or rejected through their recreations, we must consider at some length the areas of their lives they considered most sacred. Here a concentration on place may be particularly helpful. In certain places people expect behavior that conforms to their conventional notions of morality, and in others they expect behavior that violates those notions. A sacred place is the center of a culture's universe, around which all else revolves. There the everyday world opens up to the divine world, and people feel the presence of something infinitely and permanently valuable in their own lives. In such places, people pursue activities that are far more significant than their lives as mere mortal beings, carrying out responsibilities that are divinely appointed and therefore deeply satisfying.[5]

In nineteenth-century Anglo-American culture, the home was a sacred place. Outside the home, individuals were exposed to sinfulness and temptations of many kinds, but home life was, in theory, safe, morally pure, and affectionate. Preaching and writing about the religious responsibilities and joys of family life, ministers and laypersons alike asserted that marriage and parenthood were religious concepts. The home was the seat of personal happiness as well as moral purity. Scholars differ on exactly when the concept of the affectionate family gained widespread acceptance, but it is clear that the real flowering of the religious notion of home life came in the nineteenth century. Middle-class families in both England and the United States began to feel, in Ann Douglas's phrase, that every day was Mother's Day. A powerful wave of sentimentality swept over the Anglo-American world in the 1830s and 1840s. The great religious revivals of the period were primarily female events. Women began to orient themselves to a changing world by rejecting most activities outside the home as threatening and sinful and by celebrating activities within the home. Religion and affectionate relations between spouses and between parents and children went hand in hand, and the home, as much as the church, became the house of God.[6]

White Southern evangelicals embraced the religious conception of family life just as fully as Northerners. Donald G. Mathews and Jean E. Friedman have shown that by the 1830s a belief in strict personal piety centered in the home was a common Southern evangelical attitude.[7] In the postbellum period, evangelical ministers constantly spoke of parents' responsibility to raise their children in a Christian environment. Parenthood was a tremendous responsibility, capable of producing real distress when children went bad and deep satisfaction when children made and lived up to Christian commitments. Being a good parent was not merely an ideal made valuable by some religious rhetoric; it was a sacred responsibility giving ultimate value to daily life.

"God, in the beginning, established the family." More important than the heavens and earth, the family was God's primary method of spreading his influence over humanity. The family was the central institution from which all other human institutions originated. In 1883 a Georgian heard her Presbyterian minister preach "that the family was the basis for the church—& the corner stone of civil government." Another Georgia Presbyterian asserted, "In the economy of God, the family is made the very foundation element of all society." South Carolina minister T. R. English considered home and church similar in many ways because the home was the first church. "It is in the family that we find at once the origin and the model of the church. As a matter of fact, the primitive church was a family. If we regard the church as originating in Eden, then it was identical with the family of Adam in membership, worship, government, and discipline." A Baptist evangelist in the 1920s said that the sacred and the sinful had battled for possession of the home since the beginning. "The chief work of the devil was to wreck the first and best home man ever had." Keeping the home morally pure was essential to keeping it happy. In an 1876 volume entitled *Our Children*, Methodist leader Atticus P. Haygood suggested, "If making our homes happy we do also make them sacred, we will have achieved for our households the utmost that is possible to us in this world."[8]

Raising children was a godly responsibility. Religious leaders urged parents to be constantly aware that they were intermediaries between God and their children. Baptist writer William Rutherford advised, "The first thing every pious parent should do is to take the new-born babe, and in solemn prayer dedicate it to God, and ask him to so control the heart of the child as to regenerate him as soon as he can understand his responsibility to God." Georgia Methodist William F. Quillian told the parents in his congregation, "You and I stand between God and our offspring, and impersonate the divine to their thought till they are lifted to the conception of the God of the skies."[9]

Skeptics might suggest that sermons and prescriptive literature did not reflect the attitudes of ordinary Southern evangelicals. But the letters of evangelical laypersons reveal a deeply felt belief that the family was a religious institution. More than being a simple feeling that parents had a role in helping their children see the virtues of Christianity and the desirability of salvation, this belief conferred religious status on the everyday responsibilities of parents and spouses. A Baptist layman in Mississippi spoke to a Sunday school group in 1897 on the duty of parents. "God's greatest gift and best earthly gift to you is children. With this great and good boon, he has imposed great obligations. On you lies the responsibility for training them for him." A man from western Tennessee prayed in 1888, "O Lord bless & own my family I have solemnly dedicated them to thee we are as far as I can put them on the Lord's side"; and Tennessean Jane Jones prayed "that our grace may be renewed so that we may train our little ones up in the 'nurture and admonition of the Lord.'" A young plantation mother in Alabama summarized with rare clarity the notion of the religious nature of affectionate parenting: "Oh my Father, guide me aright with my little ones, let Mother, home and heaven be the words dearest of all names on earth. Home—influence is the level of such vast power in the moral world, love is the magic power that can accomplish—almost—miracles."[10]

Many evangelical parents spoke of the religious necessity to do their duty. In 1859, for example, Jane Jones "heard an excellent sermon from Mr. Thompson on raising children oh that I may have grace given me to do my duty better." A Georgia woman dreaded the experience of her first childbirth, but wrote of childrearing, "God help me to discharge my duty faithfully and God help me to understand my duty perfectly." Nannie Williams, a woman on a small farm in south-central Kentucky, felt that parenthood had its sacred qualities despite its many difficulties. "There is much anxiety attending the caring for a large family, but these trials are the divinities of life, and, it is only married people that have these divinities! Then Blessed are Fathers and Mothers with their burdens!" Parenthood could be frustrating, exhausting, and rarely as satisfying as most hoped. Thinking of the trials of parenthood as "the divinities of life" was a way to make mundane daily activities rewarding by giving them a religious character. Some forms of suffering were part of the evangelical life; prevailing over the difficulties of parenthood was an achievement with religious meaning.[11]

Like being a parent, being a husband or wife was a religious joy and religious responsibility. The affectionate marriage carried a powerful religious element; a good marriage was, of all God's blessings, the most evident in daily life. On the day in 1869 when Nannie Williams became engaged, she gushed, "It seems like a dream to me that now I have a purpose in life something to live for—something that God has made woman to be, a comforter." A young Presbyterian minister in South Carolina sounded the male equivalent to this sentiment on the eve of his marriage: "I do not deserve the gift but God who has given her to me will, I trust, make me worthy of her. I have prayed his blessing most fervently upon this union." A North Carolina couple wrote a particularly illustrative series of letters on the religious joys of marriage. Calvin Wiley, a teacher and minister, mixed his love for Mittie Wiley with thanks to God in countless long and affectionate letters. "I hope & pray that God will spare us both for each other, & make us mutual supports. . . . Let our love be of a softer, more tender & sympathizing character; & remembering God's goodness & chastening, let us, hand in hand, & heart in heart, walk humbly & meekly before Him." Mittie responded in the same vein, "It seems as if I could not live without you. . . . I feel more & more thankful that I am yours, that God has given me such a loving heart to rest upon."[12]

Combining notions of eternity with hopes for a contented home life showed the depth of evangelicals' religious commitment to their family lives. A gospel song popular in the twentieth-century South proclaims, "Will the circle be unbroken, by and by Lord, by and by? There's a better home a-waiting in the sky, Lord, in the sky." The song could have spoken for countless evangelical Southerners in the postbellum period, when referring to heaven as a better home was commonplace and was more than a metaphor. Whether they spoke of their own death, the death of an acquaintance, or death in general, they referred to dying as going home. A writer in a Tennessee Methodist monthly noted that "our home is always where our affections are. . . . Very often when the eyes are closing in death, and this world is shutting off the light from the departing soul, the last wish which is made audible is 'to go home.' " A Mississippian recorded that a friend, during a long and ultimately fatal illness, "almost longed to go home to God." A North Carolinian hoped, "We will all ere long reach home, then all sorrow will be done away." A Georgian consoled herself for her young daughter's death by recalling the way the girl had prepared for the next life:

Oh! how ineffable her bliss in that glorious happy Home!! . . .
She is now enjoying the fulfilment of her sweet little Sabbath
school song "Safe in the arms of Jesus." Our dear little Pet had re-

cently learned a new hymn at Sabbath school that seemed to please her more than all others, she sang it going about the house all during the week, but especially Sabbath Evenings at home, she knew the chorus so well.

> They'll sing their welcome home to me
> They'll sing their welcome home to me
> The angels will stand on the Heavenly strand
> And sing their welcome home.[13]

What kind of lives did Southerners expect to enjoy in their heavenly homes? They foresaw a home life similar in many ways to what they had experienced on earth, with the pleasures intensified and the pains eliminated. Preachers frequently argued that if their listeners found their earthly home lives satisfying, they would discover that life in heaven was rewarding beyond description. A Methodist wrote glowingly, "Whatever there is in that place we call home—sacred, dear, restful, delightful, full of holy feelings and deathless ties, all these are predicted in a form ten thousand fold stronger and sweeter of heaven." These were homes in a conventional sense. Southerners expected to see their earthly relatives in heaven and to live with them there. For many, the only consolation for the death of a loved one was the expectation of being reunited in heaven. A young Louisiana Presbyterian echoed the song quoted above in writing of the death of a relative in 1895: "Only a few short years and we will all have passed away, then I trust our family circle may be formed never to be broken again." Some saw the moment of death as a time of family reunion. In her dying moments, a Georgia woman told her husband, "I see into Heaven. I see father and mother and many other dear friends and our two precious little children, and they beckon me over." Most spoke simply of the joys of a reunion in the next life. A Georgian consoled his cousin for his mother's death, "Oh how sweet will be the meeting in the 'better land' of so many after the long separation." A Tennessean spent a day in 1878 "thinking of my sweet babe and long to join him in that better world."[14]

A spouse's death could inspire intense longing to join the departed wife or husband in heaven. Evangelical couples did not think of themselves as marrying until parted by death; a union of Christians was eternal. Soon after his wife's death, a Georgia Methodist wrote his minister with all assurance, "I shall meet her again. I know that she is watching and waiting for me 'over there.' If you should get home first, I am confident she will greet you. Tell her I am coming—will soon be in,

The James Day family, Campbell County, Tennessee, 1890s. (Courtesy of the Looking Back at Tennessee Photography Project, Tennessee State Library and Archives, Nashville)

God helping me." A South Carolina Presbyterian minister was less certain of meeting his late wife. "Oh, if I only knew that I would know her again and that we would love each other in heaven! I believe it, but faith is not knowledge. . . . [W]ill death restore her to me? I crave it as the choicest joy that ever came to me."[15] The joy of being with family members again was always foremost in the minds of evangelicals who thought of death. In heaven the sins that threatened a peaceful home life and the disease and death that disrupted the family would be no more, and the Christian family could live in religious and domestic contentment.

Knowing that Southern evangelicals viewed heaven as the setting for an eternally satisfying family life helps us understand the power exerted by the image of the sacred home. Historians are often too quick to make rigid distinctions between myths and realities. The myth of family life stressed affection, warmth, and moral purity with a strong religious element. The reality was far more gloomy. People did not always treat their spouses or children with affection or even respect. Countless hard realities made the home a place of far less contentment than most hoped. Recreation, however, operates in an environment in which people's conceptions of themselves can be just as important as the concrete

The Robert and Sarah Ellen Yates family at their home in Chatham County, North Carolina, 1897. The boy is ready to ride away, while the youngest girl plays with a doll in preparation for domestic life. (Courtesy of the North Carolina Collection, University of North Carolina, Chapel Hill)

realities of their lives. Even though home life was not always warm and harmonious, recreations expressing home values celebrated warmth and harmony, and recreations denying home values denigrated those qualities and celebrated their opposites.

The sacralizing of the home was a common phenomenon throughout the nineteenth-century Anglo-American world. In their domestic sentiments, however, Southern whites differed from those outside the region by their constant concern about active, often lurid sins of commission. According to its historians, domesticity in nineteenth-century England and the northern United States reacted, in both its religious and secular forms, against an increasingly commercial culture. As the centers of production moved from the home into outside workplaces, the family became the sentimental alternative to a society obsessed with heartless buying and selling. The home was warm, the world outside it was cold. Those who embraced the so-called cult of domesticity believed that women felt affection more deeply than men, both in their love for other people and in their love for God. Men had to stifle their emotions to meet the cold realities of the workplace; women let their emotions flow freely in the familial and religious spheres.[16]

Southern evangelicals who extolled the religious virtues of domestic life, however, did not contrast the warm and emotional home to the cold and heartless commercial world. Instead, they pictured the opposite of the home as the hot-blooded world of male sinfulness. Life outside the home could be threatening, exciting, confusing, and tempting; recreation outside the home was more enjoyable—and usually far more sinful—than home life. And Southern men did not feel the same impulse toward upright behavior that drove middle-class men in the North. The lessons of economic morality—sobriety, thrift, and self-denial—that accompanied the development of a commercially minded Northern middle class in the nineteenth century were slow to gain acceptance in the rural South. Thus it was not leisure in general that was sinful, but specific recreations. When Southern churches condemned worldly conformity, they were referring to their members' tastes for certain entertainments, primarily drunkenness. Ministers preached unceasingly against particular amusements that violated the sacred nature of the home. A Baptist preacher in Arkansas suggested, "Drive the liquor traffic from the nation and you save the home." Condemning horse racing, a Georgia evangelist proclaimed, "I talk for home, I talk for God and native land." Of gambling, the minister of a Kentucky Christian church asked, "What does a man care for his home, when his entire mind is concentrated upon the card-table?"[17]

Central to white Southern culture was the notion that men were more sinful than women. The sinful behaviors condemned by ministers and everyday evangelicals in their sermons and letters were almost entirely those indulged in by males. Evangelicals, particularly evangelical ministers, often spoke as though women could do little wrong. Moralists repeatedly found women's outward behavior to be more virtuous than men's. In an 1899 sermon, Georgia Methodist minister Robert Toombs DuBose held that "woman is oftener found on the side of right than man. It will not do to say that she has fewer or lighter temptations. For while their temptations differ in character it is by no means proven that they differ in intensity." Evangelist Sam Jones was troubled by the realization that women were even capable of sinfulness: "I can understand how men can be wicked, and turn their backs on God, and live in sin; but the greatest moral monstrosity is a woman with the tender arms of her children around her, their eyes looking up into her eyes with innocence and love, and that mother despising God in her heart."[18]

The central values of the home—values that women embraced more fully than men—were harmony, self-control, and moderation. To enjoy a contented life as a group, family members often had to suppress their individual wills. When women discussed their own tendencies toward sinfulness, they spoke not of active sins of pleasure, but of their inability to be the level-headed near-angels that society expected. Georgian Gertrude Thomas considered a quick temper to be her "besetting sin." Fifteen-year-old Mississippian Elizabeth Wilkes displayed the same weakness when her mother asked her to wash some clothes: "I do love mother and I want to help her but I believe old Satan has power over me greater than I can resist. I try so hard to control my temper."[19] Peace in the family was far more important than the pursuit of individual pleasures; individual wills were subdued for the family's greater good. In such an environment, home life might be neither exciting nor particularly enjoyable, but it was nevertheless worthwhile and could be deeply satisfying. Most pleasures were suspect—not necessarily sinful, but always suspect. Even heaven, that eternal family dwelling, was a place for pleasures of a moderate kind. A Methodist in Georgia preached that, in the next life, "desires are to be limited, as well as appetites and passion."[20]

Ever in conflict with evangelical behavior was a complex of masculine beliefs and attitudes that historians have termed Southern honor. This tradition demanded rugged and competitive behavior that usually violated the norms of evangelical morality. Where evangelicalism demanded self-control, humility in manner, and harmony in personal relations, Southern honor demanded self-assertiveness, aggressiveness, and competitiveness. Where home life was generally quiet and peaceful, male culture was often loud and exciting.

As Bertram Wyatt-Brown has shown in detail, notions of honor helped structure numerous forms of human relationships. This work is concerned only with the intense combativeness that was evident in practically all male recreations. Wyatt-Brown describes a commitment to physical courage as one of the most important tenets of Southern honor. Southern men have always been willing to fight. Feeling a need to assert their wills over any enemy as directly and immediately as possible, they have tended to use the smallest affront as a reason for combat. Travelers in both the antebellum and postbellum South were often surprised by the importance of fighting in the region's culture. English journalist Edward King wrote in 1875 that, for poor whites in Georgia, "quarrels, as among the lower classes generally throughout the South, grow into feuds, cherished for years, until some day, at the cross-roads, or at the country tavern, a pistol or a knife puts a bloody and often fatal end to the difficulty." A related trait drew the attention of David Macrae. "In some parts of the South and South-West it seemed to me that almost everybody carried some murderous weapon." The driving impulse was not primarily a taste for blood but rather a constant readiness for confrontation. Southerners have long been quick to take offense, quick to go to war, and, when at war, quick to mount a direct assault.[21]

The swaggering, belligerent Southern man always needed to prove his worth to a group. Southern men constantly wished to earn the respect of their fellows, often by triumphing over them in some sort of competition. Legal historian Edward Ayers defines honor as "a system of values within which you have exactly as much worth as others confer upon you." Being able to put up a good fight and to answer any challenge were essential to gaining respect in the eyes of one's fellow men. A passion for the physical and a constant need for the respect of their peer group combined to give Southern men a taste for recreations characterized by action—colorful, dramatic action. The fighter's impulse enlivened almost all recreations with an air of confrontation. Men liked to see battles of many sorts, especially those with an element of chance and the possibility of danger. Honor came from winning; momentary shame came from losing; identification with the male community came from participating in the competition. As Elliott Gorn writes of the antebellum South: "The glue that held men together was an intensely competitive status system in which the most prodigious drinker or the strongest arm wrestler, the best tale teller, fiddle player, or log roller, the most daring gambler, original liar, skilled hunter, outrageous swearer, or accurate marksman was accorded respect by the others."[22] It was always necessary to have a winner and a loser. Spirited physical competition gave male recreations an element of excitement that could not be found in the self-controlled environment of family life. Male culture was a culture of intense pleasure and pain, pride and shame, all experienced far from the peace and harmony of the home.

Scholars studying Southern men have so far done little to show how evangelicalism and masculine sinfulness operated at the same time. W. J. Cash argues that the intensity of male and evangelical cultures were part of the same embrace of a life charged with emotion and immediate sensory experience. According to him, the same Southerners who loved the thrill of the drunken brawl, the cockfight, and the all-night hunt also loved the excitement of the revival meeting, and they loved them for the same reasons. In *Southern Honor*, Wyatt-Brown mentions that by the 1850s the ferocity of masculine culture was succumbing to the softening impulses of evangelical religion. Despite that realization, he is too quick to assert that religion had little effect on the daily lives of most Southern white men. Wyatt-Brown makes much of the fact that many Southerners, particularly males, did not belong to a church, that many who did belong rarely attended church, and that few church members lived up to the moral standards set by their ministers. He argues further that the manner in which evangelicals expressed themselves conformed to the standards of Southern honor; ministers, he says, wished to fight sinfulness and enjoyed combat with the forces of Satan.[23]

Both Cash and Wyatt-Brown err in neglecting the self-controlled evangelical ideal for daily home life. Those who participated in the emotional fervor of revival meetings were rarely the same people who enjoyed the hot-blooded competitions of male gatherings, unless they were men trying to renounce their sinful ways. Male culture and evangelical culture were rivals, causing sparks when they came in contact and creating guilt and inner conflict in the many Southerners who tried to balance the two. The two forces operated against each other in an emotionally charged dialectic, the intensity of each reinforcing the other.

It was the tension between the extremes of masculine aggressiveness and home-centered evangelicalism that gave white Southern culture its emotionally charged nature. Evangelicals constantly worried about the sinfulness of male culture. Summarizing the evangelical position on excessive masculinity was a Methodist sermon in 1890: "It is wonderful to see a great burly man, mostly animal, who has lived under the dominion of his lower nature and given rein to his natural tendencies, when he is born of God and begins to grow in an upward and better direction. His affections begin to lap over his passions. . . . The strong man becomes patient as a lamb, gentle as the mother, artless as the little child."[24]

Evangelicals, then, strove to bring men closer to the temperament of women and children. The familiar Christian theme that men and women must overcome their naturally sinful natures had gained a meaning that differed between the sexes. Hungers, desires, passions—the stuff many Christians had long wished to deny or overcome—had become problems that men faced far more often than women. The male was considered closer to nature and the animal need for immediate physical gratification. Evangelicals often disparaged particular men by comparing them to animals. In the eyes of one, a drunkard was "a worthless beastly nonentity"; another wrote that two drunken men were "taken home yesterday like dead Hogs." A Baptist preacher in Louisiana noted in his diary: "Man is verily an animal—sleeps like a hog—eats like an ox—and far too much forgets the source of all temporal and spiritual good."[25]

Evangelical and masculine cultures did not compete on an equal basis. Religion, after all, claimed to hold the ultimate truth and the key to eternal life; to reject it was to reject Southerners' only explanation of the meaning of the universe and humankind's place within it. Masculine attitudes toward honor and combat developed long before evangelical notions of piety and self-control. Early Virginia society, for instance, exhibited the same fighting, hard-drinking, fun-loving characteristics as the post–Civil War South, and Bertram Wyatt-Brown traces those attitudes back to the dark forests of early European civilization. But by the late 1800s evangelical Protestantism was the dominant attitude, and the great majority of young Southerners grew up with evangelical morals as their first and most important set of rules.[26] Evangelicalism, which developed in the eighteenth-century South as a religion of lower-class protest, had by the late nineteenth century become the mainstream religion. Its primary foe was no longer the dissolute planter but the fun-loving male. Evangelicalism dominated the cultural horizon of most Southerners. For some, it connected everyday life with the heavens, giving a joy and satisfaction to otherwise routine activities. For others, it set goals for behavior that were high and sometimes frustratingly out of reach. For still others, it loomed dark and threatening, inducing guilt and insecurity and working against the pursuit of pleasure. For almost all, it was an extremely powerful influence in setting the standards for personal behavior.[27]

Explanations abound for the Southern fighting impulse. Historians have attributed male tastes for toughness and personal confrontation to the region's frontier heritage, to the isolation and hard work of rural life, to the cruelty of slavery and the more general pressures inherent in a biracial society, to the chivalric traditions and ideals of the Southern upper class, to the Celtic origins of many of the plain folk, and to a climate that made hot tempers hotter.[28] My aim is not to offer yet another explanation for Southern men's combative temperament, but to show how that temperament operated in recreations. However, this work frequently stresses the important role played by racism in white Southern culture. Whatever the origins of the fighting element in Southern culture, the presence of blacks was the most influential factor in intensifying and prolonging it. Slavery showed all Southerners the significance of physical force in human relations. The opportunities for cruelty and the need for readiness in the case of slave violence affected the consciousness of almost all Southern whites, and the most extreme forms of violence in the postbellum period—lynching, night riding, and Klan violence—were directed almost exclusively against blacks. Whites' constant need to feel they had physical force superior to that of local blacks left them with a need to prove their fighting abilities both to themselves and to their fellow whites. The relations between the races created a profound tension in many phases of Southern social life, often in ways that lay just below the surface of relations among whites.

The consequences of racial conflict highlight the differences between the form taken by male culture in the South and the form that developed in the American North. A masculine subculture emphasizing sports and fitness grew up in the North in the late 1800s as men in the professional classes looked for ways to enjoy physical activity as a counterpoint to their lives of white-collar work. As Theodore Roosevelt theorized in one of his hunting narratives, "Always in our modern life, the life of a highly complex industrialism, there is a tendency to softening of fibre. This . . . is preeminently true of all occupations which cause men to lead sedentary lives in great cities. For these men it is necessary to provide hard and rough play." Organized sports allowed this release of energy in a controlled environment that stressed the same self-discipline and cooperation that professionals aimed for in their daily lives. Other male recreations developed as urban reformers searched for a safe and controlled outlet for the energies of the urban poor, especially poor boys. Finally, some male sports, such as baseball, found popularity among the urban working class largely because they allowed individual achievement while at the same time promoting teamwork. The development of what E. Anthony Rotundo calls the ideal of the "masculine primitive" was new to the period and fit the needs of the North's developing professional and industrial society.[29]

In the South, the masculine ideal was nothing new, and it did not help professional men deal with the problems of urban life. The dominant tensions in the rural South had little to do with industrial organization but much to do with questions of race and class. Southern evangelicals felt keenly the tensions within their culture because of the pressures exerted by the extremes of society. The South's upper class and its lowest class each posed tangible threats to evangelical ideals. The nineteenth-century American evangelical home was primarily a middle-class institution. Even though a number of the evangelical families studied in this book were wealthier than average Southerners, almost all identified themselves as part of the large white middle class situated between the plantation elite and the black lower class. A Methodist preacher reminded his listeners to shun the behavior of both extremes. "Society must be pure, or ignored. In social intercourse, if the wealthy be wicked, shun them; if the poor be vile, ignore them."[30] The lives of blacks and of elite planters dramatized evangelicals' fears about threats to the purity of their own homes. Those fears led to tensions within all families, tensions centered around male pleasure-seeking and female purity. Any recreations—gambling, for example, or drunkenness—that threatened the home with the roughness and near-savagery associated with black culture were, by evangelical standards, especially objectionable. Southern race relations encouraged a religious morality different from that in the rest of the country, because white men felt they had a moral obligation to be vigilant in their oppression of blacks in order to protect their women's virtue.

At the other end of the South's economic scale stood another major threat to evangelical morals. The cultural style of the richest plantations embodied an open desire for pleasure that inhabitants of evangelical homes found offensive. Evangelicals had long believed the wealthy were spending their way to damnation. Many planters enjoyed the male recreations—horse races, cockfights, all-night poker games, and drinking frenzies—that violated evangelical fears of overtly masculine pursuits. Others delighted in the great plantation balls, which demonstrated women's open desire for physical enjoyment and involved a close contact between the sexes that shocked evangelicals.

Southern men often found themselves wondering how far they could go in satisfying the demands and enjoying the pleasures of male culture without violating the standards of evangelical morality. They accepted evangelical beliefs but never felt comfortable with the accompanying moral code. Many wondered to what extent they could enjoy male recreations without too openly or drastically sinning against evangelical standards. The particular fervency with which men pursued pleasure—

almost always outside the home and out of view of the more pious gender—stemmed not only from the strength of their commitment to a hell-raising, self-proving male code of behavior but also from their need for release from the constraints of home-centered culture. The particular combination of honor and evangelicalism made the South a region of saints and sinners, and saintliness and sinfulness both showed their colors dramatically in recreational activities.

Part I
Male Culture

1

The Field

Had rare sport to-day hare-hunting.
We set fire to several broom-sedge fields
and shot the poor fellows as they rushed
out to escape the flames.
—Daniel R. Hundley

For an upcountry South Carolina man at the turn of the century, opossum hunting "gave you a wild feeling of being free, of standing alone against darkness and all the forces that bound and cramped you."[1] It was this wild freedom from the constraints of evangelical culture that made hunting the most popular sport for late nineteenth- and early twentieth-century white Southern men and boys. Southerners reveled in killing tremendous quantities of game, often by using whatever tricks and deceits they found most helpful. Until fencing and conservation laws began to impinge on hunters' freedom, the hunt worked as the Southern male's most respectable opportunity for excitement and self-indulgence.

A historian could deal with hunting in the South in a number of ways. One approach would analyze it as a productive activity important to many for simple subsistence; another would study the race relations reflected in certain hunting practices. A third possible approach would consider the aristocratic notions expressed in such practices as the Virginia fox hunt.[2] Each approach has merit, but all fail to note the extreme interest and sheer excitement with which white Southern men and boys viewed hunting of all kinds. Carolina sportsman Archibald Rutledge only slightly overstated the truth in asserting that "a deer-hunter may forget to go to church; he may forget whether he married

Grace or Glorianna; he may kiss the door and slam his secretary; but he cannot forget a big time in the woods—down to the last detail."[3] Only when it is regarded as a participant sport does the significance of the hunt as a cultural institution become clear.

If we see hunting as situated in an arena where the two extremes of Southern culture—masculine combativeness and evangelical self-control—were in conflict, we can understand the hunt's function as a respectable outlet for excitement and self-indulgence. Most men and boys wished not to reject either evangelical religion or male aggressiveness but to find a way to balance the two. Most male institutions in the turn-of-the-century South carried the taint of immorality and were hence disreputable. The churches attacked saloons, cockfights, and most sporting events for violating standard Christian practice and the order of the home. But preachers hunted, church members hunted, and, except when a Saturday event lasted into Sunday morning, no one hinted that hunting might be morally questionable. In contrast to Victorian and Edwardian England, where hunting was a symbol of gentry culture that clashed repeatedly with evangelical religion, hunting in the nineteenth-century South was a democratic pursuit accepted by all centers of moral authority.[4] In an age in which evangelicals discussed almost every feature of public behavior, very few thought to question the morality of a sport so obviously outside the boundaries of home-centered evangelical culture.

A number of features of the hunt set it apart from other aspects of Southern life. First and most obvious were the space and separateness of the field. Other centers of local culture in the rural South—the home, the church, the plantation, and the town—gathered men and boys into large groups with established and fairly rigid customs. Southern hunts, with the rare exceptions of communal fox and deer hunts, consisted of solitary hunters or groups of no more than three or four. A number of diaries provide evidence of the popularity of solo hunting. Daniel R. Hundley, a Mooresville, Alabama, author and planter, went hunting for deer, duck, quail, or rabbit on twenty-five separate days in the first three months of 1861; only twice did he mention hunting companions, and even on those occasions he hunted with only one other person. With the single exception of a four-day camp hunt for deer, Clive Metcalfe, a young Mississippi planter, hunted with no more than two or three friends on his thirty-four bear, deer, bird, and raccoon hunts between August and December of 1888. Joshua Moore, a lawyer in

Franklin County, Alabama, went squirrel and bird hunting eight times with no more than one companion in the winter of 1860–61; and Monroe County, Mississippi, planter James Gordon hunted twenty-one times in 1873, never with more than two companions.[5]

Louis B. Wright recalled that for most Southerners even a fox hunt was a fairly small event. "In South Carolina in my youth this was not a fancy sport conjured up by pictures of Englishmen in red coats charging over hedges." Instead, it typically consisted of two or three men and boys chasing a few hounds through the fields. Southerners hunting small game and birds usually hunted alone. They stalked wild turkeys in silent solitude, often waiting hours for a single shot, and hunting quail and doves required dogs but no human company. Boys usually hunted squirrels by themselves and often formed small groups to run rabbits. Opossums and raccoons were the prey of a few farm boys or of a plantation boy following an older black farmhand. Whatever their quarry, hunters in the field were set apart from the normal cultural circles of Southern society.[6]

Just as hunts were distant in space from other pastimes, they were also separate in time. Adults often began their hunts well before dawn so the men could go to work after several hours of sport. Alabama planter and businessman Thomas D. Samford rose as early as 2:30 A.M. for predawn dove shoots. North Carolina lawyer and fox-hunting enthusiast David Schenck surely expected little sympathy when he complained of a hunt that "went hard with me, as we had a hard chase, and I got up at 2 o'clock, and when I returned at 8 o'clock I had to go immediately to work." Opossum and raccoon hunts were usually nighttime affairs, quite often lasting until dawn. Turkey hunts typically began at about 5:00 A.M., and fox hunts could begin at any time but, once started, could last through the night or even through two nights.[7] The Christmas holidays provided a special time for hunting, and Southern men and boys usually took a few days from the round of social activities to indulge. On Christmas Day in Columbia, Mississippi, in 1890, "nearly every man went out hunting, and we understand that birds, rabbits, and squirrels fell in abundance." A Greenville, South Carolina, farmer went hunting for rabbits or squirrels in the week after Christmas every year from 1865 to 1893, although he practically never hunted at any other time of the year. An Alabama man, disappointed by his Christmas activities, wrote, "We had a nice diner I tell you but I wood have enjoyed a good old rabbit or squirrel hunt."[8]

The most important characteristic separating the hunt from the rest of Southern cultural life was that it was almost exclusively a male activity. The few references to women joining men in the hunting field— a Georgia deer hunt for food after the Civil War, some elite horseback quail hunts in the Natchez region, and occasional opossum hunts— scarcely deserve mention.[9] Southerners always identified hunting with men only. A Mississippi farmer's son wrote that "traditionally the men on my father's side of the house loved the great outdoors. They have, from time immemorial, fished, hunted, and trapped." Around Salisbury, North Carolina, a woman recalled, "the men of the farms . . . hunted as they found opportunity." Near Fayetteville, Tennessee, "on Christmas eve men and boys went to the woods and shot gray squirrels, cottontail rabbits, or possums." And, in the 1860s, a Louisiana planter's daughter who caught a glimpse of a deer hunt stated, "The chase is certainly exciting sport. No wonder men like it so."[10]

Learning to hunt was an important step toward a boy's entrance into the male community. Raised more by his mother than by his father, a boy relished the male freedom of the field. Edward McIlhenny recalled the time his father and older brothers brought home some wild turkeys they had killed. "This made me long for the time when I would be old enough to hunt this bird." Each new hunting accomplishment was a step toward manhood, and the first step was getting a weapon. Three-year-old Joe Scott, Jr., of Cookeville, Tennessee, asked Santa Claus in 1914, "Please bring me a shotgun so that I may go bird hunting with papa. I have a little dog. . . . I think he will be large enough to set birds before long." Then came the first kill. Planter Archibald Rutledge, who killed his first deer at age nine, started his sons out even earlier. "As each of my boys reached the age of six I gave him a single-shot .22 rifle, and began to let him go afield with me. . . . It was a great day for each youngster when he shot his first English sparrow with a .22 shot shell." North Carolinian Basil D. Barr, after seventy-eight years, still remembered his first hunt in 1904. "The rabbit jumped up in the air (I can still see this), and went down kicking. . . . I had my prize, my hunting career had started." Even gaining permission to change ammunition from birdshot to the more powerful buckshot was one of the last symbols of a boy's acceptance as a man.[11]

Women seldom constituted part of the hunting picture, even as spectators. Daniel Hundley's detailed descriptions of the various forms of hunting in the 1850s contained not a single reference to women.[12] The many women's reminiscences from this period occasionally mention men's hunting but provide no descriptions. Women and girls knew that men were in the fields but seem to have had little interest in what occurred there. On rare occasions they protested that hunting often took men away from them. In North Carolina, Ida May Beard complained that her new husband "cared only for hunting, fishing and making a collection of different kinds of minerals. This occupation often caused him to be minus his meals for days at a time, and also gave me a great deal of uneasiness. Each time he failed to make his appearance at the usual hour I would think someone had killed him." A Georgia woman who usually allowed her son to hunt during the day complained when he wanted to spend the night "thrashing birds out of trees. . . . I do not think boys ought never begin the habit of spending evenings out from here."[13] The field obviously served its purpose well as a male quarter, giving men and boys a respite from the constraints of female-centered evangelical family life.

Even when they were away from their women and apart from society generally, Southern hunters had company they valued highly. Hunters since the time of Odysseus have revered their dogs and horses, but Southern men seem to have found their animals particularly suited to close companionship. A writer in 1901 speculated that the "close association of the three most noble forms of life—man, horse and dog—accounts largely for that peculiar fascination which the fox chase has ever had for the youths of the South." David Schenck felt this association so strongly that he even wondered in his diary about the state of his animals' souls: "Surely these animals the horse and the hound did not bring the curse of death upon themselves—they were once immortal, and shall they miss the happiness of eternity for no error of their own—God sent his 'son to suffer for man.'—shall they not be saved when no suffering is necessary for them, they not having sinned. I hope so." Others attributed more mundane human characteristics to their dogs and horses. An Abbeville, South Carolina, sheriff stated, "My life story would be very incomplete if I did not say something about the best friends man ever had; namely dogs," and he wrote sincerely of one hound that understood conversations. Another South Carolinian remembered pushing Archie, an old horse with a bad leg, too hard in an effort to keep pace with some other horses: "I was put to it. I hated to turn back and I didn't want to disgrace Archie. I knew Archie was awfully sensitive about it and would never get over the disgrace, should he fall. I was in a box for a while, so I had to concoct an excuse. . . . I stopped Archie, who was awfully grateful. You see, Archie had associated so much with his owners that he easily communicated with them."[14]

Though many could not afford horses, virtually all Southern rural families in the late nineteenth and early twentieth centuries owned dogs. Planters could afford large hunting packs and some owned and bred pedigreed dogs.[15] As a South Carolinian observed in 1921, "No plantation really looks natural unless there are some deer-hounds loafing on the premises." All classes took pride in their hounds and formed attachments to them. Backwoodsmen from Arkansas to the Carolinas used dogs to hunt everything from bear to wildcat, and the universally popular sport of bird hunting required a set of bird dogs. Even the poorest white families kept hounds. Poor white men in North Carolina, according to a Northern traveler in 1866, "live most of the time in the woods, and generally keep one or two dogs and own a cheap rifle." Seventy years later, James Agee described an Alabama sharecropper's animal as "a fair rabbit dog when he puts his mind to it, but good for nothing else; he is kept because dogs are a habit."[16]

Why, beyond their productive function, had dogs become such a habit? Possibly they served men and boys as companions outside the conventions of evangelical culture. No standards for upright behavior governed humans' treatment of animals; horses and, to a greater extent, dogs gave loyalty and friendship without expecting self-control or respect in return. As a young North Carolinian wrote of a hound he received for his tenth birthday in 1881, "For seven years, and until I left the plantation, she was to be my daily companion and playmate—the most admiring and slavish friend I ever had."[17] Southern males uncomfortable with the restraints of respectable behavior in family life and in popular recreations could appreciate a little slavish affection.

The relationships between some whites and blacks in the field held something of the same appeal. Many upper-class whites enjoyed having blacks serve as guides and assistants in the field. These whites attributed to blacks an animal-like nature that gave them special powers in the wild. Planters' hunting methods often put blacks and dogs in the same position of finding animals and driving them into view while the whites waited for a chance to shoot. Archibald Rutledge made clear the distinction between the whites on horseback and the blacks closer to nature in recalling a party that consisted of "five of us hunters, each mounted, three negro drivers, all walking, and eleven dogs." During a North Carolina coon hunt, white spectators applauded the combined tenacity of Amos, a black guide, and Jumbo, a dog, who worked together in a hollow log. "Presently [Amos] leans far in, and then pulls and tugs for dear life. He has hold of Jumbo, and Jumbo has hold of the 'coon. Both the holds are good, and out comes the coon."[18] And just as they liked to have animals serve them, whites often enjoyed

Rabbit hunters in Chatham County, North Carolina, 1901. The white men hold the rifles, the black man holds the animals. (Courtesy of the North Carolina Collection, University of North Carolina, Chapel Hill)

what they perceived to be the servility of black hunting companions. A South Carolina hunter's recollection of his childhood black companion evoked sharp class distinctions. "His allegiance to me was that of liegeman to lord, and I was more resplendent in his eyes than I was in another's."[19]

The structure of the hunt placed it outside the normal boundaries of evangelical culture. In the fields, alone or in small groups, hunters could enjoy themselves free of the rules and constraints of most other cultural institutions. The timing of expeditions—sometimes on holidays, often at night or in the early morning—reinforced this impression of hunting as a special activity. Finally, the absence of women meant that men and boys could enjoy themselves without worrying about violating female-centered notions of propriety. Hunting, unlike most other male recreations, was a thoroughly respectable activity that had the full approval of churchmen, wives, and mothers, but it was also an outlet for the self-assertiveness and self-indulgence that had long constituted an important feature of Southern male culture.

It was this self-indulgence and self-assertiveness that Southern white males found so appealing. Hunting promised excitement, freedom, and an opportunity for the unrestrained exercise of will that characterized male values. Men frequently recalled special hunts—usually those involving particular feats of marksmanship or cunning—as being among the most exciting and memorable moments of their lives. They reveled in killing large quantities of game of many kinds, often indulging in binges of slaughter more typically associated with the frontier period. Despite nominal lip service to a sportsman's ethos that frowned on mass kills, most Southern men and boys saw little reason to limit their targets or to give their prey a sporting chance. Given the special atmosphere of the hunt, few Southerners wished to allow anything to interfere with the excitement of the moment. And, as in most male sports, alcohol was a contributor to the sense of reckless freedom.[20]

Aubrey Lee Brooks, a North Carolinian born in 1871, fondly remembered his grandfather, whose strict moral attitudes allowed only one form of leisure. "His diversion, when not preaching the gospel, was hunting. He had a passion for it, which I inherited. In those days wild turkeys were abundant, and he told me that during his lifetime he had shot more than a thousand." Brooks described how his grandfather flushed a drove of turkeys: "He would race his horse near the flush while I held on for dear life. He would become so absorbed and excited that when he dismounted from the horse to build a blind to shoot from, he forgot all about me, and his long leg as he swung it from the saddle would swipe me and the sheepskin to the ground." South Carolina farmer Alfred Lee Taylor could become equally excited about turkey hunting. On one occasion, having baited an area in front of a blind, he thrilled to the sight of three turkeys at close range. He "turned loose with both Barrels and how I got out of the Blind I will never be able to tell. by the time I was out you could hardly tell there ever was a turkey Blind there. of all the jumping and pitching they would jump up to 10 feet all of them at the same time it was hard to tell what did take place. after I had conquered and all got quiet there lay Sixty pounds of turkey gobler meet." Taylor's response to his feat of slaying three at one blow was typical. "If there ever was a human being at the highest pitch of excitement and gratitude after the victory won I was one."[21]

A successful turkey kill may have been particularly exciting because of its difficulty, but all forms of hunting provided a charge of sheer excitement. C. Waldo Cox recalled that for his father, a planter in central North Carolina, "fox-hunting seemed to be a sort of 'involuntary response.' " Wiley C. Hamrick felt the same way, suggesting "that man hasn't got the proper amount of red blood in his veins whose heart doesn't beat a bit brisker and whose pulse doesn't thump quicker when he hears that unapproached concert pitch of a full pack of hounds opening up on a fox's trail." Daniel Hundley wrote of the "wild excitement and general abandon of the long fox chase," and E. Walker Duvall recalled that riding behind an uncle on a fox hunt was "one of the most exciting times possible."[22]

Other forms of hunting required more patience but also paid off in bursts of excitement. Sportsman Archibald Rutledge could "never get quite used to an old stag's tearing open a thicket ahead of me, making a Whitehead torpedo look like a piker. I always get a major thrill out of an encounter with an old buck." In Lenoir County, North Carolina, one could find "occasionally a deer to thrill the heart of the hunter." Even a hunter who tried to take things in stride could not wholly contain his excitement. A young woman in Louisiana stated that her brother, after killing his first deer in 1862, "puts on a very unchalant air, he has however admitted that he gave himself three cheers, out there in the woods where no one could hear him." The quieter sport of squirrel hunting could evoke a similar reaction. A Mississippi farmer's son recalled that "the sight of squirrel quietly running down a limb or vine within gunshot range quickens the pulse and breathing of a boy to a feverish pitch. Trembling hands raise the gun and eager eyes peep down the barrel until Mr. Squirrel is in sight."[23]

Actual physical danger could cause pulses to quicken and hands to tremble on many hunts. Triumphing over potential harm only added to the thrill of the pursuit. Ida May Beard felt that nothing gave her husband "more pleasure than to relate to me how near he came to losing his life while out hunting." On one deer hunt, Daniel Hundley "came near being killed by a fall from my horse. Fell between her legs, and it is almost a miracle that I escaped with only a few bruises." Winchester Jenkins's turkey hunt grew considerably more exciting when the game hunter himself became game for alligators in a Mississippi swamp. The most anarchic moments seem to have occurred during hunts for opossums and raccoons, animals that sometimes fight back when cornered. A newspaper reported that Jackson York of Cedar Falls, North Carolina, was training his dogs one night when a "'possum jumped down from a tree, nabbing his largest pup by the neck, and of course Jackson would have risked his life to save his pup's life. So he tried to take the 'possum off the pup, and was badly bitten through one of his fingers and has been off the job ever since."[24]

Raccoon-hunting stories show Southern hunters' fascination with such bedlam. Novelist Thomas Dixon recalled an incident during an 1870s hunt with a white tenant farmer named Hose and a dog named Boney. When the dog backed away from some raccoons cornered in a tree trunk,

> the act of retreat cut the huntsman's pride. He refused to believe his veteran warrior would retreat under fire. He knelt, taking Boney in his arms and moved into the dug out urging him to battle. The dog felt the hunt in his master's den and tried to grip a coon's back. He drew out with a gash in his nose marked with blood. . . . Hose urged him on in low angry tones. . . . "Go after him, old Boy! You won't take a thing like that from a coon. He cut the blood from your nose. Go after him! Eat 'em alive!"

As the animals finally converged in fur-flying combat, Dixon stated, "I have never heard a human being yell with such maniac, joyous power as Hose. For five minutes he stood over first one growling group and then over the other."[25]

Another hunt in North Carolina placed man, raccoon, and dog in the same creek. "Yancey was treading water, the coon was struggling to stay on Yancey's head—the only thing afloat—and all seven dogs were trying to get the coon off Yancey's head. Every time this happened, the dogs, coon and Yancey all went under." Alexander Hunter remembered a similar incident in southeastern Virginia when his group stumbled upon four raccoons:

> What a scene of action! Men, dogs, and animals in one complex, complicated, entangled struggle and shout and uproar, and furious rough and tumble, spill and pelt! It was a whirlwind of scuffing, jumping, hitting, stamping, kicking on the part of the men, and bites, snaps, clawing, spitting, and tearing on the animals' part. . . .
>
> It was a sight I never expect to see again; those half-starved dogs had tasted blood and it maddened them; they hung onto their foes, tooth and nail. As for the coons, they fought savagely, as they always do, and left to themselves they would have torn the dogs' faces to pieces; but the clubs of the men disabled them one by one, and they died game, and were defiant to the end.

Such scenes, in which the hunters derived excitement from the beastly nature of their animals, demonstrated the animal-like qualities of men that evangelicals wished to stifle.[26]

The conclusion to Alexander Hunter's story introduces the next feature of Southerners' love for hunting. "The butchery was over," he stated, "and men and dogs alike sank to the ground utterly exhausted."[27] Butchery, slaughter, excess, and often trickery characterized a large number of hunting methods. Southerners desired not simply a successful hunt but the excitement of a mass kill. A hunter's use of the word "butchery" implied no condemnation of his fellow hunters; only a few sportsmen held to any kind of moral ideal that precluded bagging as much game as they could in any manner possible. This delight in destructiveness represented the height of the hunt's function as an escape from evangelical culture. The wild excitement of a binge kill epitomized the ability of the hunt to work as an outlet for the untrammeled will of Southern men.

A recognition of the destructive bent in Southern hunting reveals the weakness of those interpretations that depict sportsmanship and fairness as part of a gentry code of honor. In *Violence and Culture in the Antebellum South*, Dickson D. Bruce concludes, from an examination of a few published hunting narratives, that white Southerners valued moderation and self-discipline in their hunting. Killing large quantities, he writes, "was contrary to that 'spice of chivalry' that every sportsman should have." Bruce asserts that most Southerners respected the animals they hunted, never wishing to kill something without allowing it a fair chance.[28]

To be sure, some hunters in the postbellum South did exhibit a sense of fair play. Archibald Rutledge, for example, described the common practice of shooting scores of rabbits that had fled to an upland area during a flood and stated, "I never could see wherein lay the sport." After discovering the reason that he was able to shoot a particular bird with surprising ease, he "felt as if some apology ought to be made to some one for shooting a blind turkey." In 1875 Georgia hunter George T. Nichols defined a sportsman as one who "never takes a mean one even of birds, giving them that chance they should have! but allowing them to take wing, before he fires—never shooting into a poor huddled flock of birds, on the ground, and then bragging of his success in the field." Concerns about the possibility of some animals' extinction appeared early in the twentieth century and with them heightened notions about fair play. Edward McIlhenny, in his 1914 volume, *The Wild Turkey and Its Hunting*, mentioned that he knew of "many nefarious tricks by which turkeys could be easily secured, but I shall not tell of any method of capturing turkeys, but those I consider sportsman-like."[29]

Despite the feelings of a few professional sportsmen and sports-writers, however, the prevailing sentiment undoubtedly favored butch-ery over sportsmanship. Newspaper accounts, which are probably more indicative of popular attitudes than sporting publications, told of binge kills without a hint of moral uneasiness. Diary entries conveyed no moral qualms over large kills gained by what some might consider questionable methods. And in reminiscences of their childhoods, very few Southerners—upper-class or otherwise—admitted in hindsight that such actions might have been considered disreputable. Even the three hunters mentioned above who spoke up for fair play saw the kill as more important than the hunt. Rutledge stated, "I confess that in the matter of hunting I do not care so much about moral victories. I like to have something tangible to show for my time and efforts." Nichols declared, "Give me one whose pride it is to kill, but to kill mercifully." And there is something of gloating in McIlhenny's opinion that "I have killed as many old gobblers with patriarchal beards as any man in the world."[30]

A survey of the methods employed in hunting demonstrates the thrill Southern white men and boys found in the self-indulgence of binge killing and ambush. No doubt these methods originated from need, but most had, by the time covered in this study, become sports. For exam-ple, many coastal hunters practiced fire-lighting, placing a light with a reflector in a boat to bewilder ducks and geese, which they could then shoot with ease. The spirit behind such a practice, the province of "adventurous young men who wish for some unusual excitement," also characterized an Arkansas quail hunter in the 1870s. "The way to hunt quail on the roost, so he said, was to put brimstone torches on the ends of cane poles and hold the torches under the roosting birds. The quail would soon be overcome with the fumes and fall into sacks which members of the hunting party were to hold open under the perches." In 1861 Daniel Hundley and his son "had rare sport to-day hare-hunting. We set fire to several broom-sedge fields and shot the poor fellows as they rushed out to escape the flames." As late as 1914 in Siler City, North Carolina, "some boys near town placed large seins around brush piles in a new-ground and then proceeded to run the rabbits out and captured them by the wholesale. Brush pile after brush pile was visited in this way, until 'toting' the game was a burden." R. B. L. Leonard recalled another method used during a snowfall in the 1890s. "It was hard to top and old rabbits couldn't get out, if you could find them you could get them. They could not go, only by making a tunnel. Me and my brothers got Dad to go with a horse and loaded her down with rabbits."[31]

Other methods made normally difficult sports much easier. Spreading bait to attract wild turkeys or doves seems to have been fairly common. Alfred Taylor gained his greatest thrill from shooting turkeys that were feeding in a baited area, and John Quincy Wolf had no criticism of an Arkansas neighbor who shot a turkey caught in a trap that had been placed in a baited field. Robert E. Hale, an Alabama farmer's son, recalled an incident in the 1870s in which "Uncle Frank baited some turkeys and took me with him one morning. We got in behind some bushes, and as the turkeys came to the corn and all put their heads down to begin eating, he shot and killed all six at one shot." Before an antibaiting law was passed in early twentieth-century Alabama, "hunters in great numbers would repair by day-break to the baited field, and the rapid discharge of firearms could be likened unto the raging of a mighty battle. As many as 6000 doves have been bagged in one field in Alabama in a single morning."[32]

Deer-hunting methods also revealed some Southerners' desire to do whatever was necessary to force their prey into their sights. The son of a south Georgia farmer recalled fire-hunting for deer in the 1870s. "If not aroused too soon from sleep in the early night, by someone carrying bright light, the bucks would not run, but would stand with head thrown up and stare at the light until the hunter came in range. It was this peculiarity that made fire-hunting popular." The planter practice of "driving" deer—in which the hunter took a stand at a strategic point in the forest and waited while assistants chased a deer into view—apparently had no counterpart in other parts of North America, and some Southerners felt a need to apologize to Northern hunters for their unorthodox practice of chasing deer with dogs.[33]

The desire to take as many animals as possible by whatever means necessary also characterized some fishing practices. Seining a stream for tremendous hauls was popular both for profit and for sport. The local news correspondent in Lanesboro, North Carolina, reported in 1881, "We had some very fine fishing in Lanes Creek this week. Last Tuesday we caught with seine five hundred. Some very fine ones yesterday. Friday we caught two hundred." C. Waldo Cox described the practice and his father's enjoyment of it:

He threw everything he had into it, just like fighting fire. And don't get the idea he ever sat for five minutes with a fishing rod in

his hands. He never "induced" either fish or wild game: he
"forced" them! . . .

Seining in Panther Creek was ideal; it was not too wide for a
twenty-foot seine to reach from bank to bank. Two good, strong
men held the seine poles down and against either bank, at the
lower end of a "hole," while three or four of us would jump in a
hundred feet up and come down, each with a hoe, simply tearing
up the creek bed. Just as we reached the lower end of the hole, the
seine was raised, and sometimes two dozen fish were caught with
one haul.

Other Carolinians used different methods. In Kinston, "The Kennedy
brothers, Alf, William and Jesse went on a fishing excursion at Kennedy's upper mill one day last week and caught with hook and line 453
perch and chubs. That night the three men, with Messrs. Haskitt and
Waller, took a canoe, and placing a torch in the head allowed 175 jacks
to jump in and be captured." A reporter from Peachland noted that
"some of the sportsmen from here went to Brown Creek last Friday
with a dip net and report a thousand perch." Heavy rains in Mississippi
in 1853 "raised the waters and the fish has come up the Ditches in the
Plantations, still we have caught 500 lbs a day. . . . We shut up the
Ditches, and Ketch them when we please." With no hint of criticism, a
Hazlehurst, Mississippi, editor wrote in 1875, "Some of our pleasure
seekers have adopted a new way of catching fish. They throw torpedoes
in the water, and the concussion from the explosion kills the fish, when
they immediately rise to the surface." This widespread demolition of
the South's resources seemed selfish, improvident, or unsportsmanlike
only to a tiny, if growing, number. For most hunters and fishermen,
such self-indulgence was the reason for sport.[34]

Newspaper reports indicate the respectability of bagging game in
large numbers. Editors and newspaper correspondents took pride in the
abilities of local hunters and often made special note of extraordinary
hunting feats. A weekly paper in Georgia boasted that "McDuffie
county, as in everything else, excells in successful hunters. Mr. R. R.
Reeves, who lives near Brier creek . . . has, during the past season, killed
twenty-seven foxes and seven wild cats. Now, then, who can beat that?"
In Nash County, North Carolina, "Burwell Cooper went gunning the
other day and killed sixty-five partridges. We call this pretty good work
for one day." Near Fishing Creek, North Carolina, "there have been
several turkeys killed around here lately. James Augustus Davis heads

A duck hunter displays his kill at Dean Hall in Berkeley County, South Carolina, ca. 1900. (Courtesy of the South Caroliniana Library, University of South Carolina, Columbia)

the list. He has killed six. Hurrah! for Jimmie Gus." A competitive rabbit hunt in Randolph County, Georgia, pitted boys from town against rural youths. "The town boys were defeated, but one hundred and eighty-four rabbits were killed." Even the *Alabama Baptist* got into the act, reporting that "a party of Selma merchants went on a camp hunt on the Tombigbee and killed 12 deer; another body went into Wilcox and killed 21." Special shooting feats also drew the notice of proud editors. In Springfield, Arkansas, "Bill Crane killed two large bucks at one Saturday morning," and a fourteen-year-old in Macon, Mississippi, "killed four gobblers at one shot, and they averaged nineteen pounds apiece."[35]

This fascination with counting the kill reflected the joy Southerners felt not merely in hunting but in triumphing over their quarry. A good hunt was one in which a large number of animals died; a bad hunt was the opposite. Clive Metcalfe put it simply when he noted one day in 1888: "Did bad hunting. Killed nothing." A month later he exulted,

"Went bird hunting and killed more birds than I ever killed in my life at one time." A Louisianian informed a friend that "the boys are having fine sport bird hunting now. Frank P. and Howard killed 34 yesterday." Many others wrote in the same vein. One day in 1885, George Howard "walked to Stokes Iveys & killed 20 birds"; he later complained of "poor success we found plenty birds & only killed 3." Shepard Perkins noted in 1888, "Lamar and I went shooting birds. Killed 8 partridges 14 doves and 1 woodcock." Archibald McKinley similarly recorded in 1871, "The boys went out this evening and killed twenty-four night hawks," and on another date he lamented, "We only killed fourteen birds." In 1873, Georgian Samuel Cook noted after a partridge hunt, "Dog being untrained killed only four," and David Schenck could state with precision in 1871, "We bagged 41 birds the other day."[36]

One merchant in Rapides Parish, Louisiana, made detailed records of his hunting successes. George W. Bennett went hunting fifty-three times between September 1883 and March 1884. His total bag of 518 animals included:

367 partridges	10 rabbits
64 quail	5 hawks
36 squirrels	4 robins
15 doves	2 larks
12 ducks	2 yellowhammers
1 woodcock	

The frequency with which Bennett hunted may have somewhat lessened his desire to bag incredible numbers of game at one time, but his records still show single days when he killed twenty-two squirrels, as many as twenty-four partridges, and twenty-seven quail.[37]

The most revealing feature of Bennett's records is simply his infatuation with counting his game. Why did the numbers have such significance unless each new kill represented a new victory? If hunting functioned as an outlet for masculine excitement and self-assertiveness, then we can read the concern with killing in quantities as a reflection of the hunters' desire to savor this opportunity of getting exactly what they wanted. One could almost say that Southern hunters wallowed in their abundance of game, indulging themselves by killing whatever animals they could find.

The question of whether the joy in binge killing was a distinctively Southern trait is beyond the scope of this chapter. But the conservation movement originated outside the South, and the writings of one prominent Northern hunter may point to the uniqueness of Southern attitudes. This hunter, writing in the 1880s and 1890s, called for game laws and game refuges to protect animals from injudicious hunters. Holding that "a hunter should not be a game butcher," he deplored as unsportsmanlike any practices that gave hunters an advantage over their prey. He suggested hunting not with a rifle but with a camera, believing that "the results in the long run give much greater satisfaction." These were the words of the symbol of American masculinity, Theodore Roosevelt.[38]

Neither Southern sportsmen nor Southern evangelicals considered popular forms of hunting behavior morally unacceptable. In the nineteenth century, few were even slightly uncomfortable with the idea of a reckless enjoyment of the chase, the kill, and the slaughter. Thus Southern men's tastes for combat and confrontation could express themselves in reputable forms, even if they were part of a larger complex of masculine attitudes that clashed with evangelical notions of harmony and self-denial. One reason women did not object to the way hunting behavior violated the norms of home life was that they saw it so infrequently. Hunters rarely pursued animals in view of the home, the church, or any social gatherings that might attract women. Perhaps, also, the hunt was acceptable because it was enjoyed infrequently, at special times and on special days. Other male sports hit closer to home and attracted much more criticism. To understand how other male recreations could raise serious moral opposition, we must turn to social life in the Southern town.

2

The Town: Main Street

How much treating, how much youthful
spreeing, how much sodden, determined
soaking went on in the sordid bar-rooms
that lined Main Street, or below the
courthouse, it was not for a girl to know.
On the few occasions when we must pass
these places, we would quicken our steps
as we neared them.
—Hope Summerell Chamberlain

IN today's culture, dominated by urban-based popular media
and endless possibilities for recreation, the notion of small-town culture
in the nineteenth century may seem almost self-contradictory. Small
towns in the South, perhaps even more than those in the rest of the
nation, encourage images of lifeless men sitting outside the courthouse
or country store, their greatest challenge finding their next whittling
sticks, their most strenuous movement wiping the sweat from their
brows, their greatest satisfaction the taste of a good plug of tobacco.
Contrary to this impression, the main streets of postbellum Southern
towns offered the most important range of cultural activities available
outside the home and church. Countless rural Southerners saw the
town as the liveliest place they knew. Jimmy Carter, born in 1924 just
outside the south Georgia town he made famous, spoke for many others
when he recalled, "During my childhood I never considered myself part
of the Plains society, but always thought of myself as a visitor when I
entered that 'metropolitan community.' "[1] A trip into town, even a
town as small as Plains, could be an exciting experience.

Recreation in the public areas of towns took one of two primary forms. The first, professional entertainment, did not begin to bring the excitement of the outside world to town and rural residents on a steady basis until the early twentieth century. The other, more important form consisted of a number of unorganized pastimes that men enjoyed on the main streets of the small towns. Recent urban historians have demonstrated the importance of areas they call male quarters in late-nineteenth-century cities. In these cities, a few blocks normally provided the settings for exclusively male professions, services, and recreations. The cultural tone of the men's quarter differed sharply from the home-centered morality of most of American culture. Few women had reason to go into such areas on business and few wished to go there for pleasure.[2]

At certain times the main streets of Southern small towns became men's quarters. On many Saturdays, on court days, and during the Christmas season, men filled the streets, sometimes combining recreation with court or commercial business, sometimes simply enjoying themselves. The line of grocery stores, saloons, blacksmith shops, livery stables, and the like, all leading up to the courthouse, were primarily for males at all times, but on certain days they teemed with men, and women knew enough to stay away. The men's quarters in the towns, like those in the cities, provided opportunities for behavior that contrasted dramatically with the norms of evangelical culture. The masculine aggressiveness of numerous fights, confrontations, and contests, the self-indulgence of the barroom, the easy profanity, and the presence of blacks enjoying themselves all marked the main street as a special place for men outside the moral boundaries of the home and church.

The public space of most towns was inhabited by a male element that was usually fairly small. Permanent residents living in or near the towns could spend much of their time pursuing that most leisurely of all leisure activities—especially in warm weather. A Georgia editor noted in April 1878 that "street loafing has become more common, since the pleasant weather has set in." Traveling journalists almost always noted the number of Southern men who appeared to do nothing but sit in chairs or on benches all day. One wrote that in Cricksboro, Georgia, near the turn of the century, "every store was supplied with several chairs, and these were seldom without occupants in good weather. The favorite position was just outside the door, where, sociably and comfortably, the loiterers could observe whatever was going on."[3]

Men linger in front of R. L. Worth's grocery store on West Main Street, Franklin, North Carolina, ca. 1890. (Courtesy of the North Carolina Collection, University of North Carolina, Chapel Hill)

Inactivity, in a society where the gospel of work had never gained full acceptance, was no sin in itself. White Southerners had never felt their religion demanded constant toil. Nevertheless, loafing in town had a number of morally questionable connotations. Many of the places where loafers gathered became the sites for roughness, competitiveness, and a pleasure taken in small personal confrontations that could not be found within the home. A western North Carolina man wrote that every community had a special storefront, blacksmith shop, or crossroads where "the young men and older boys would gather on Sunday afternoons generally and engage in feats of strength, horse shoe-pitching, etc. until sundown. Joking and laughing; also playing tricks, showing off their horses and taking part in foot-races were common practices." In Clay County, Alabama, in the 1890s, a small mill served as "a convenient place for idle men and boys to meet and match their skill at marbles or croquet, or simply sit and loaf. Here the male gossip of the community was exchanged and much smutty talk indulged in." A Pendergrass, Georgia, Methodist born in 1900 recalled, "Father never allowed us to sit around the stores and hear smutty talk." The combination of profanity and male competition—sometimes enjoyed on Sunday—marked these loafing points as sites for masculine self-assertiveness and, often, masculine forms of sinfulness.[4]

Loafing in the streets took place throughout much of the year. But most rural Southerners in the middle and late nineteenth century came to town infrequently. Some men came on Saturdays, others only during court weeks, and others during the Christmas season; but whenever they came, they enjoyed recreations of a sort they could not find in the home or in the church. The image of the Southern white man as a hell-raiser owes much to rural men's behavior on their infrequent trips to the county seat. North Georgian Walter McElreath recalled that, in the early 1870s, men in his rural neighborhood made a trip on horseback to Marietta twice a year to sell their crops and buy supplies. Drunkenness, he recalled, was infrequent in his isolated rural area, but few men went all the way to Marietta without indulging in this important element of small-town life. "There were eleven saloons in Marietta, and a jug of whiskey was one of the usual purchases." Rural men carried their feeling of license on the road as they returned home from town. Before they reached home, "the people in the caravan were in a state of hilarious or belligerent intoxication. They cursed and yelled, often in profane and obscene terms, so much that the women of the families who lived on the road were in constant fear."[5]

Women and children generally stayed off main street during the times of the roughest and most boisterous male recreations. On days when men flooded the streets, small-town women stayed within the quiet of the home. A Hampton, South Carolina, man clearly showed the division of recreations along gender lines when, on Christmas Day, 1869, he took his son to a show he deemed too unruly for his daughters. "The Show was here, and Nella and Marie went down to go to it; but there was so much drunkenness, that I did not deem it a proper place: so they came back much disappointed. I also came back, but afterward Willie and I went down to it." Novelist Evelyn Scott, born in 1893 and raised in Clarksville, Tennessee, found the rural farmers who came to town only on court days intriguing on those rare occasions when she was lucky enough to see them. "They fascinated me, yet, tantalizingly, it was on these very court days that we children were, almost invariably, forbidden the street." Hope Chamberlain recalled that, in the 1870s, her mother "tried to hold me away from the small-town life around me." In her hometown of Salisbury, North Carolina, "ladies and children never went to shop on Main Street on a Saturday. . . . How much treating, how much youthful spreeing, how much sodden, determined soaking went on in the sordid bar-rooms that lined Main Street, or below the courthouse, it was not for a girl to know. On the few occasions when we must pass these places, we would quicken our steps as we neared them." A former resident remembered that in Germantown, Tennessee, in the 1870s, "drunkenness was so common that it was never considered safe for a lady to go down on the streets on Saturday." Alberta Ratcliffe Craig had difficulty describing court days in the 1880s in Wentworth, North Carolina: "As ladies did not go to court in those old formal times, I knew very little what went on." A Tennessean agreed that no woman went to town on such days, writing, "She would have been scandalized if she did."[6]

Evangelical fears of the threat that town life posed to family religion are clearly expressed in a memorable scene from William Faulkner's *Light in August*. A farmer named McEachern takes his stepson, Joe Christmas, into town one morning, expecting to return home immediately without encountering an area where "the whole air of the place was masculine, transient." When he is delayed, the solemn Presbyterian takes his stepson to a seedy diner where he eats quickly, attempting with Christian resignation to ignore the men around him. McEachern ominously warns Joe to avoid such company. "There are places in this world where a man may go but a boy, a youth of your age, may not." The proper place for such a youth is in the home, far from the temptations and degradation of the male areas of town. And indeed, Christmas finds the allure of the diner so compelling that he eventually flees the constraints of home to pursue the excitement he associates with small-town life.[7]

Saturday was the primary day for leisure activities on main street. Employers usually gave workers at least a half-day off on Saturday, and farmers, except during peak work seasons, went to town on that day to do business and to enjoy themselves. On most days town life was lazy and quiet, but, as a travel writer in Georgia noted, "Saturday is . . . an exception. That is market day, and the public ways and hitching places are then crowded with mules and horses." Men who spent part of the day buying and selling usually had extra money to spend on themselves afterward, and the extent of drunkenness on Saturdays could be remarkable. In Newnan, Georgia, in 1889, "John Barleycorn held his usual Saturday's levee." Even after Prohibition outlawed drinking establishments, Saturday remained a day for enjoying alcohol, and men crowded the towns to receive packages of whiskey that had been carried in on the trains.[8]

An even greater event than Saturday was court week. The circuit judge came to the local courthouse for four or five days every month or two. In a litigious culture, such an event brought men streaming into the towns. Petty and substantial differences of all kinds attracted some men, possibilities for buying and selling commodities attracted others, and some men simply came to enjoy themselves at a major event. The sheer size of the crowds charged court week with a special excitement. South Georgian J. L. Herring recalled that, in the 1870s, the towns could hardly hold everyone who wished to attend. "Every house within two miles of the courthouse was a boarding-house, limited only by its capacity to spread mattresses in every room." Herring estimated that only about a third of this crowd had court business, the rest coming to attend to other affairs and pursue pleasure.[9]

The great mix of people and the prospect of a wide range of experiences gave court week a novel flavor that contrasted dramatically with the quiet routine of home life. A colorful variety of odd and disreputable characters crowded the main streets, many of them peddling goods and entertainment at the same time. According to a Grove Hill, Alabama, resident in 1893, "Court is in session this week, and a pedler, or rather auctioneer is holding forth in front of the Post Office, selling three papers of pins for a nickle &c. He is a great attraction of these people." Another Alabamian in 1873 "attended Court, at night went to see a slight of hand performance, also Prof. Fay's performance of making the violin play about the room in the dark— Think the whole a humbug." Lawyer Aubrey Lee Brooks described a scene in Roxboro, North Carolina, in the 1890s: "During the intermission of court, gayety and entertainment were provided by patent medicine vendors who had a cure for everything. . . . On another section of the square was a stand where ginger cakes and cider were sold. Some distance removed, on vacant lots, the horse traders gathered to swap their plugs."[10]

Horse trading added to the crowded and exciting confusion of court week. In Clarksville, Tennessee, "there was a smell about court days— manure, sweat, watermelons, niggers, horses, mules and tobacco!" Anyone wishing to trade brought his animals to main street, knowing he could find a number of potential buyers. During one court week in Jefferson, Georgia, in 1876, "the 'swapping brigade' was out in full force on Tuesday and Wednesday—and the 'horse-flesh' of all sizes, colors and descriptions was on exhibit on the parade ground." Some horses and mules passed from neighbor to neighbor as men tried continually to make the best deals. Horse trading had a long history as a male recreation in the South. It was clearly a sport, played out before an

Farmers in Wilkes County, Georgia, invade the Washington town square, ca. 1890. (Courtesy of the Hargrett Rare Book and Manuscript Library, University of Georgia, Athens)

animated and interested crowd. Honor was gained in making a good deal, shame in making a bad one. William Faulkner's Ab Snopes sought revenge for his public humiliation at the hands of Pat Stamper, a slick trader new to the region, in just such a horse trade. "Ab wasn't trying to beat Pat bad. He just wanted to recover that eight dollars worth of honor and pride of Yoknapatawpha County horse-trading, doing it not for profit but for honor." Trading offered men an opportunity to exhibit the bravado that usually characterized male recreation. A Georgian writing in the 1930s remembered a man from fifty years earlier who, "about half tight, said to a group engaged in the national sport of horse-swapping: 'Let me look at the horse, gentlemen. I'm the best judge of a horse in Ware county.'" Chance and competition were recurring elements in male recreation, and horse trading allowed for both. "Horse traders," a North Carolina native recalled, "were thought of as great gamblers."[11]

Accompanying all of the festivities was drinking—clearly the most popular recreation during court week. Men filled the drinking establishments while court was in session. No doubt the tension of the court proceedings and the nervousness accompanying business deals contributed to the amount of alcohol consumed, but it seems clear that rural Southern men enjoyed drinking whenever they came to town. Newspapers routinely rated the local population's court-week drinking behavior. The *Morehouse Clarion* in Louisiana reported in 1880, "This has been a good week for drinking whiskey, or at least there has been an ocean of it swallowed in this town. Court week, you see." A Columbia, Mississippi, editor predicted that "the young whiskey dealers will have some fun when the next grand jury meets." Evangelicals found the extent of drunkenness during court week particularly offensive. On a visit to Ashland, Tennessee, Betty A. Gleaves was appalled to see men who "were so drunk they fell off their horses oh! so distressing." A Methodist minister recorded that on a court day in Snow Hill, North Carolina, "a large number of persons were in town. Many were drunk. What beasts! What degradation!"[12]

Southern men saw the Christmas season as another excellent opportunity for drunkenness. An Arkansas store announced "a new arrival of Christmas goods—Whiskey." As a slack month in the agricultural year, December was a season when spirits of many kinds ran high. It was a time for parties in homes but also a time for men to drink heavily in the towns. A north Georgian raised in the 1880s recalled, "For the menfolks, whiskey played a large part in the celebration of the Christmas holidays. . . . They imbibed from a stone-crock jug while lounging near the dusty hardware or pungent horse collars in the back of a store. They were even served jiggers at the town blacksmith shop." On Christmas Day in 1876, a northern Mississippi man "went up to town & found a great many country men drunk. Spent the day keeping them from hurting each other." Small-town newspapers made yearly evaluations of main-street behavior during the holiday season. In Dahlonega, Georgia, "some of the boys became too intimate with John Barleycorn Christmas day and wound up the day's festivities by a first class fight." Some Southern men started their holiday drinking early. Another Georgia newspaper reported in mid-December 1885, "Some of the boys ordered their Christmas jugs too soon, they will be empty before the occasion."[13]

The Christmas season was the occasion for one other popular form of masculine recreation. "Oh, boys! didn't we have fun on Christmas day? Fiz!pop!!bang!!!" Boys learned early to be loud and competitive during the holiday season, drawing attention to their presence by firing guns and, more often, by setting off fireworks. As early as the 14th of December in Scottsboro, Alabama, the local paper noted in 1882, "the boys have commenced shooting their Christmas guns." According to another account, young men in Greenville, Mississippi, celebrated Christmas Eve in 1885 with "an incessant uproar of fire crackers and tin horns all day long, and continued at night with doubled fury, augmented by general drunkenness and sky rockets." On Christmas Day, the "uproar increased twofold, having lasted all night long." Southern males saw Christmas activities, as they did practically every recreation, as an opportunity for competition. Marion Blackman, who was raised in early twentieth-century Louisiana, recalled that on the Christmas Eves of his youth, "keen competition developed among a couple of my young neighbors and me to see whose fireworks could produce not the most arresting visual display but the most noise."[14]

This was a far from pious way to celebrate the holiday. Men in non-Christian cultures had for centuries marked late December with a flurry of activities featuring drunkenness, loud noises, and other boisterous recreations that dated from ancient celebrations of the change of seasons.[15] More important for Southerners was the idea that shooting off firecrackers on Christmas Day was surely a boyhood version of—and preparation for—shooting pistols. Men took great pleasure in shooting; the wanton firing of pistols carried a strong air of sinfulness, suggesting a quick temper, an overbearing aggressiveness, and a lack of self-control. Moreover, fireworks violated the evangelical belief in the virtues of peace and quiet. Some evangelicals considered it a religious duty to avoid making noise on Sundays, and many associated quietude with reverence. Thus the making of loud noises on a religious holiday was a way of expressing a lack of reverence for Christmas without openly rejecting its religious meaning. Perhaps the boys were reacting against a sentiment expressed by a Georgia Methodist minister who enjoyed the quiet piety of a group gathered around a church Christmas tree, noting, "how plesent good children are."[16] Southern males typically demanded excitement, and their behavior went far beyond being pleasant.

In the towns, men found their thrills in a number of competitive, physical contests and exhibitions. Like shooting off fireworks, these contests were loud, colorful, decidedly masculine, and usually suspenseful. Most involved some form of gambling, and most were associated with drinking and drunkenness.

The traditional Southern belief in the necessity of being armed, combined with the hunter's joy in skillful marksmanship and the general male zest for competition, made shooting contests enormously popular. Some of these meets were elite affairs limited to members of shooting clubs, which were perhaps modeled on English organizations. These clubs multiplied so extensively that by the early twentieth century a wealthy North Carolina marksman could belong to seventy-four. Such organizations laid claim to a high style of Southern aristocracy. In 1885 the North Carolina town of Garner planned "to celebrate Christmas on a grand style. The principal amusement will be a grand shooting match given by the 'Garner Shooting Club,' in which they will invite all their friends in Johnston and other counties to take part."[17]

A more democratic and much more popular event was the turkey shoot, an autumn competition still popular in many rural areas. Prizes were offered, but the sport's real allure lay in the opportunity for marksmen to display their abilities in a public setting. The emphasis was on competition. In one account, several boys in Kinston, North Carolina, " 'cleaned out' the Woodington boys at the shooting match on Saturday. They came home loaded with turkeys." Daniel Hundley described the event in his portrait of the recreations of late antebellum yeomen: "A live turkey is securely fastened to a stake at the distance of one hundred paces, and you pay five or ten cents for the privilege of each shot; if you hit the fowl in the head the carcass is yours, but any other hit is considered foul, and so passes for nothing." In the 1870s, shooting events in the northern Georgia town of Freemansville offered a variety of livestock.

> A chicken was tied to a stake at a distance of about one hundred
> and fifty yards, and each of the contestants gave ten cents a shot
> at it with a long rifle, the first man to hit the chicken to have
> it. . . . Next a turkey was tied to the stake at a shorter distance,
> the rules in the turkey contest being that it must be hit in the
> head. Then there was a contest for a cow.

The latter contest, happily, involved shooting at targets and compiling a score.[18]

The turkey shoot illustrates how a recreation could imply a rejection of the everyday behavior expected in home life. Shooting at livestock was an escape from and even a representative destruction of the daily responsibilities of farming. The farmer-marksman tried to kill a common farm animal, not in the typical workmanlike manner of a barnyard butchering, but in a dramatic contest played out before his neighbors. Tiring of cluck-clucks here, there, and everywhere, Old McDonald went to town and tried to shoot a chicken in the head. An element of risk charged the entire event with excitement, as shot after shot had the possibility of hitting the target and making the farmer-marksman a hero among his peers. Although the turkey shoot could be a boon to the farm, putting food on the table, it did not reward steady habits and thoughtful labor. Instead, it celebrated immediate physical achievement, providing a thrill in the sudden excitement, the cheers of the crowd, and the defeat of adversaries.

The drinking that accompanied turkey shoots also marked the events as masculine pastimes that contradicted the quiet virtues of the home. In Freemansville, "those who did not shoot kept up their spirits by frequent visits to a little brown jug from which drinks were retailed in a tin cup."[19] Such high spirits no doubt added to the exhilaration of the shoot, with cheers or groans greeting each hit or miss, making the marksman a hero or a failure in the eyes of a whiskey-soaked crowd.

Evangelicals found the gambling at these shooting matches particularly objectionable. The shooting and the competition themselves were apparently acceptable, but church members who gambled on the outcomes faced expulsion from the church. In 1877 a Baptist church in Rutledge, Tennessee, considered the question, "Is it right for a church to let her members engage in shooting matches or any other game of Chance?" After discussion, the congregation decided that participation in such events warranted church discipline only "where their is any thing at stak such as Gambling." Other churches charged members with "shooting for money" and "gambling at shooting for prizes." An unfortunate Baptist in Georgia faced charges for supplying the chickens used for one such event.[20]

Other disreputable amusements reveal the enjoyment of a rough masculinity that involved doing violence to animals. Robert Winston recalled a battle between dogs and a bear in a small hall in Windsor, North Carolina, in the 1870s: "The dogs, yelping and screaming with pain, as bruin slapped them helter-skelter against the rough walls and posts—the bear, snarling, snapping and delivering telling blows, but never complaining. After an hour of breathless sport the bloody dogs would limp away, all fight gone out of them." As did many male recreations, bearbaiting offered an opportunity for gambling, with the bear's owner wagering that his animal could beat any dogs in town. A southern Mississippian born in the 1870s recalled another sport involving animal combat. "The Kentucky Derby seems like a side show compared with an old-fashioned bull fight. . . . It was a rattle of horns, a push and shove with first one, then the other, gaining ground. Like a prize fight, it was something of an endurance contest, with each one trying desperately to win." Bearbaiting and bullfighting, sports with long histories in the Anglo-American world, revealed above all a delight in staged forms of chaos. Observers identified with the combatants, often betting on them, and then enjoyed watching a good fight.[21]

The streets of small towns echoed with the sound of profanity. Swearing was clearly a male domain; over 95 percent of church members charged with using profanity were male.[22] Women who were isolated from such language in the home might encounter a barrage of profanity on the street. A Concord, North Carolina, resident complained, "I have never known any place where boys behave so badly. It is really dangerous for a lady to appear on our streets without having her ears saluted by some vulgar sayings, or cursing." A Georgia editor complained of the same problem: "One cannot go on the streets anywhere without having his ears offended with the vilest words, and reverence shocked by the most profane use of sacred names." The Christmas season was a prime time for swearing, as it was for other masculine recreations. In Scottsboro, Alabama, in December 1882, "some of the men were under the influence of liquor, were boisterous and used profane language in the presence of ladies who happened to be out shopping. . . . Should men be allowed to cut up in such a manner simply because it is Christmas time?" Church records show that profanity very often accompanied drunkenness, suggesting that a trip to town was a prime opportunity to enjoy both forms of masculine freedom.[23]

Swearing was a consciously antifemale, antireligious pastime. We can assume that much Southern profanity, then as now, consisted of remarks that mocked the holiness of God and the purity of women, thus flouting both of evangelicalism's moral authorities. Swearing was part of a boy's passage to manhood; boys and young men proved themselves worthy in each other's eyes by the virulence of their language. In an essay on the subject of profanity, a devout Methodist schoolboy in Louisiana wrote, "There is nothing more disgusting than to hear a crowd of young boys curssing, but they seem to look with contempt on one that does not join them. It appears that they think they will never be men if they do not use profane language." Swearing provided yet another arena for competition and male honor. One man wrote of the male residents of Harrisonburg, Louisiana: "The man that can curse

the largest and fight the most he is the greatest man among them."
Southerners typically contrasted the crudeness of male profanity with
the purity of women. Evangelist Sam Jones recalled that even in his
sinful early days, "I never was low down enough to curse before a
preacher, or a woman, even when I was drinking."[24]

Profanity erupted with particular fervency in fits of anger. In swearing, men dropped all pretense to the self-control so valued in the evangelical home. At a Baptist church disciplinary hearing, an Alabama man
"stated that in a passion he had been tempted to use profane language
was sorry for it." A North Carolinian used "the Word dam you to a
collar man in a passion," and a South Carolina man admitted that he
"got into a violent passion with one of the neighbors and used unlawful
language."[25]

Despite the popularity of swearing, shooting, and animal fighting, it
is clear that drinking and drunkenness were the most popular recreations in Southern towns. Men drank while enjoying other recreations
or drank as their sole recreation, drank at large gatherings or in small
groups. But few drank in the home. W. J. Rorabaugh has shown that
Americans dramatically changed their drinking practices in the early
nineteenth century by giving up moderate daily drinking at home but
enjoying drunken sprees on public occasions.[26] Drinking had an almost
irresistible hold on some men on their trips away from home. The
father of a Mecklenburg County, Virginia, resident never drank at
home and promised not to drink away from it, "but as soon as he got
out with some of the fellows at the country store he would get drunk."
Even opponents of Prohibition believed in the virtues of separating the
drinking establishment from the home. A man in northern Louisiana
held that liquor, illegal or legal, would always be available, so it was
better enjoyed in saloons and not in homes. Under Prohibition, he
predicted, "men who now seldom ever keep as much as a pint of
whiskey at their homes and who never get drunk except when they
come to town, would buy it by the gallon and lie at home drunk weeks
at a time."[27]

Women occasionally objected to their husbands' and sons' passions
for the saloon. A Fairfield, South Carolina, woman wrote to her other
children that one son "has been in Columbia some weeks, got into a
drunken row, was knocked in the head with a weight, & has been laid
up ever since He spent 8 bales of cotton drinking, gambling." Louisiana
businessman E. J. Larkin angered his wife by spending most of his spare
time in Vicksburg, Mississippi, barrooms. He recorded that he "went to

Floyds store and played cards and the Madam got angry." Another time he "played cards at Floyds. Home late and had a little row with the madam." An Arkansas woman whose husband was fond of drinking seemed pleased and a bit surprised when he "did not go out in town after supper to night he stayed at home with me."[28]

The general store was the most important of the various drinking sites on main street. Unhindered by the zoning restrictions of the twentieth century, many establishments sold liquor by the drink as part of a larger business. The storefronts where men spent so much time were often the entrances to groceries, which frequently sold more liquor than anything else. In Gaston County, North Carolina, in the 1880s, "Carroll's 'grocery,' as everybody knew, was Carroll's groggery. Nobody stopped . . . for a gallon of kerosene oil, or a half gallon of molasses." Most stores counted liquor as part of their inventory and encouraged men to drink on the premises. In Quincy, Florida, "There is any quantity of whiskey drank, and not a bar room in the place. It is sold though in most every store—some way." A Blakely, Georgia, native wrote of the 1870s: "All the general stores in the days of my earliest recollection sold liquor under the head of groceries. The whiskey barrel, with its quart and pint measures, and with jugs on a near-by shelf, stood beside the syrup and vinegar barrels at the rear of the store or in a shed room."[29]

The fact that alcohol was available in such stores helped mark the town as a male domain. Drinking was not confined to a well-defined and restricted area. Many drinking establishments were located in areas most accessible to the public. For example, its proprietors advertised that Buckley and McNabb's Saloon was open from daylight until nine o'clock at night beside the post office and across from the courthouse in Raymond, Mississippi. Austin's Groceries, advertising "hats and caps, liquors, hardware," was located on Main Street in Van Buren, Arkansas, directly across from the public well.[30] Thus when anyone—woman, child, or evangelical male—wished to buy food or medicine, mail a letter, or do court business, he or she often had to brave the presence of drunken men. The grocery that did not sell alcohol was considered a refuge for the respectable. An establishment in Bastrop, Louisiana, advertised itself as "the only family grocery in town separate from a barroom. The most fastidious lady can call in and see no whiskey."[31] With such rare exceptions, store after store on main street served as the sites for male recreation.

Besides drinking, men at groceries and saloons engaged in various

Male conviviality: a toast in Mt. Pleasant, Tennessee, ca. 1900. (Courtesy of the Looking Back at Tennessee Photography Project, Tennessee State Library and Archives, Nashville)

rivalries. The camaraderie of the barroom always contained a strong element of personal conflict. E. J. Larkin often recorded that he "went to Saloon and played cards for an hour" or "played a game of whiskey Poker at Watters saloon." Larkin clearly enjoyed gambling, once emphasizing "I WON." In 1871 a young man in Arkansas likewise bragged that he had "played various games of Poker & with various success, but some ahead I am proud to say I only play for amusement & excitement and never unless considerably intoxicated. I have acquired considerable skill and am considered no 'soft swap.' " Other saloon sports were contests of skill and chance. Larkin welcomed the opening of a bowling alley at one of his favorite watering holes, and a lawyer who frequented the barrooms of Griffin, Georgia, recorded that he "drank four bottles beer yesterday. 2 games billards. 6 games pool. So!So!rara!" Southern men always placed great importance on achieving status through competition among their peers. Alcohol, as Edward Ayers has suggested, stimulated ever-present competitive urges to new heights.[32]

Fueled by alcohol, the rivalry that accompanied almost all male recreations easily turned to violence; points of honor, long-standing grudges, and petty disagreements could spark fiercely aggressive combat. Fights often erupted quickly over a matter of a few words. A resident of Bertie County, North Carolina, recalled that, in the postbellum period, "I would watch the combatants, half an acre of them, swearing and tearing each other's clothes, and all about the most trifle incident." E. J. Larkin's diary portrayed the drinking establishment as a setting for the typically masculine combination of drink, profanity, and violence: "Sam Sparrow and T. P. Coats had a little row. Sam pulled his pistol and cursed him in Watter's Saloon." Newspaper accounts of such events could be gruesome, showing that men took their drunken conflicts seriously. One 1875 report described a fight between two men with an old disagreement in a Madison County, Georgia, grocery:

> The old difficulty was brought up, and the two commenced fighting in the bar-room, when the two were ordered out by Thurman [the grocery's owner]. After going out of doors, Matthews, a friend of Hopkins, came to his assistance, Thurman came out as a peacemaker, became involved in the difficulty, was knocked down, and his head literally flailed to pieces.

In an eastern Tennessee saloon in 1881, "one word brought on others, and Will was being heartily cursed by Don when he seized a china dish and beer mug and hurled them at Don, causing the blood to flow. Will ran out doors and Don after him. Don fired his pistol twice, hitting Will twice, who fell dead."[33]

Fighting was at one end of the spectrum of male recreations. Men went to drinking establishments to enjoy the camaraderie of fellow drinkers, the taste of good liquor or the effects of bad, competition at cards and billiards, and escape from the propriety demanded by evangelical culture. But they knew that a fight could break out, if not at any minute, then at least very easily. The pursuit of pleasure went hand in hand with the tension that stemmed from the constant need for men to prove themselves to one another. Shooting at turkeys and chickens, watching animals fight, trading horses, playing cards and billiards, and fighting all involved competition in front of interested spectators. Personal conflict could be fun, or something close to fun, and the barroom was the best place for it.

The element of conflict that accompanied most main-street recreations, making them exciting for some and threatening for others, was sometimes particularly intense in the postbellum years as the races mixed in new ways. On the streets of many towns, white men passed their time in close proximity to black men and sometimes together with them. A devout Baptist, discussing the "heathen" in his area, wrote a friend in 1880 that in Collinsburg, Louisiana, "a Saturday hardly ever comes but the negroes and white men too will go to the stores and drink and gambol and then they will all have a general fight." A young woman was frightened by the mixing of several groups on the streets of Tuscaloosa, Alabama: "Our town for several weeks has been literally filled with—White men, Irishmen, Chinamen, and 'Colored gentlemen' all mixed up together—drunk, quarreling and fighting." On Christmas Day 1872, a wealthy North Carolinian gloomily recorded, "There is nothing unusual marking this from usual Christmas holidays; Negroes and 'Lewd fellows of the baser sort' surround the grog shops and engage in occasional fisticuffs, and continued profanity." A visitor to Wadesboro, North Carolina, complained that "all about the corners were crowds of drunken people—a mixture of both races."[34]

Other white Southerners were distressed simply by the growing numbers of blacks enjoying themselves on or near main street. Town life was, for many whites in the postbellum period, more threatening than it had been before emancipation. In the antebellum years, whites had always complained that blacks lounged around town too much, but their complaints intensified into fears after emancipation, when the irritation caused by unsubservient slaves gave way to concerns about the general moral decline of blacks. Rural whites viewed these groups of blacks, who seemingly had nothing to do and were unsupervised by whites, as one of the most menacing features of a trip to town. A Mississippi editor complained in 1867, "The streets of our village are now continually thronged with idle negroes. The older ones occupy the door-steps, the goods boxes, the curb-stones, etc., while the younger ones occupy the pavements with games of marbles." In November 1865, writer Bill Arp complained, "Why the whole of Africy has come to town, women and children, and babies and baboons and all." The roughest amusements enjoyed by white men in the towns had increasingly visible counterparts among black men. Saturday and holiday sprees of drunkenness quickly became a black as well as a white pastime. In Hazlehurst, Mississippi, "several nigs took too much of the ardent and freely used profane language on our streets during the holidays." A newspaper editor complained that Crawford, Georgia, "was filled every Saturday evening with country negroes, who spend their time wrestling, quarrelling and cursing around the streets."[35]

The Southern main street was the place men went to enjoy themselves, often as sinfully as possible. Main street—on Saturday, on court day, in the Christmas season—seethed with all the vices prohibited in the home. The competitiveness, the drunkenness, the possibility of violence, and the indiscriminate mixing of all sorts of men put emotions on edge. Home and church stood for harmony, but to experience main street was to experience a disharmony that most men found exciting.

Scholars in recent years have portrayed the nineteenth-century home as an all-important refuge that existed apart from other, more impersonal institutions. The home, according to this literature, was an escape from whatever features of life the historian happens to be studying— the office, the industrial workplace, the city, the institution of slavery. The home was warm; the outside world was cold.[36] But if the home had gained such moral significance, it stands to reason that certain features of male culture developed as a reaction against and an escape from the home. This tension charged white Southern culture with emotion as a rough male culture and a self-controlled evangelical ideal acted against each other, the strength of each contributing to the extreme nature of the other. If some men were extremely sinful on Saturday, some evangelicals were extremely virtuous on Sunday; and if some evangelicals pushed harder for self-control and virtue at home, some men sinned with added fervor on their trips into town.

3

The Town: Professional Entertainment

One of our ministers said the other
day that he intended to tell the Lord
of all the Methodists and Baptists
who attended the circus this week;
whereupon one of our beautiful young
ladies remarked—"Well, he certainly
will have a big job."
—*Warren Record*, 22 October 1897

OCCASIONAL sprees on main street constituted the most popular form of recreation in the public areas of nineteenth-century towns. Sin originated within the local area, not outside it. Throughout the century, professional entertainment played little part in the lives of rural Southerners. Few issues of small-town newspapers contained references to any recreations other than informal parties, visits, and church and school gatherings. Many nonurban Southerners rarely saw or heard anything that originated outside their immediate surroundings. The constant barrage of professional entertainment that we see today did not begin to penetrate the rural South until the turn of the century. Historians have discussed a "leisure revolution" that took place in the final decades of the nineteenth century as the growth of cities and large-scale industries created new markets for professional entertainment.[1] In the rural South, this revolution was delayed; it entered the region only with the development of new media in the early twentieth century.

Despite their relative isolation from the outside world, rural Southerners did witness and perhaps enjoy or condemn an occasional circus

56

or traveling show. By far the most discussed and popular form of professional entertainment in the nineteenth century—and one of the most popular in the twentieth—was the circus. The animals and the clowns, the tightrope walkers and specialty acts, the calliopes and brass bands, all coming only once a year to some towns and much less frequently to others, could stir Southerners to rare heights of giddy excitement. A circus transformed the villages Southerners knew so well into places of mystery. Children and adults fled the calm of everyday home life and indulged momentarily in the sights, sounds, and experiences of an entirely different world. The circus offered a colorfully novel counterpoint to the quiet self-control of evangelical morality. A North Carolina native recalled an incident that allowed the entire community to laugh at excessive piety. A clown approached a "solemn-faced, Baptist deacon, quite conscience-smitten at being caught at a circus, and took him by his long white beard. 'You have stolen my mare,' he sternly called out. 'Give her here or I'll pull her out!' And as the clown tugged away at the deacon's horsetail whiskers the good-natured crowd fairly roared."[2] This description of a crowd roaring at one of the town's most religious citizens suggests that the circus allowed people to escape for a few hours the moral standards that ruled their daily lives. Just as they sometimes ridiculed those who were normally respected, circuses occasionally pretended to exalt those who usually faced scorn. Huckleberry Finn was amazed by an Arkansas circus in which a man pretending to be a belligerent drunkard turned out to be a talented professional rider who received the applause of the crowd.[3]

The recollections of nineteenth-century Southerners show how important, and how outlandish, many considered the circus. As one recalled, "One of the most exciting things that ever reached the world of my childhood and almost depopulated it for a season was the news that John Robinson's show was coming to Hickory Station." A hard-working young man wrote that the circus was one of very few breaks from his routine on the farm. "We did not have many holidays, but we always went to our county seat, Shelby, North Carolina, on the Fourth of July and on circus day in October or November, when Barnum and Bailey's show came to town." Another North Carolinian recalled the circuses of her youth thus: "That was a day! From early childhood the circus parade gave us a feeling of gay exotic abandon." Southerners had few opportunities for exotic abandon; most who did not indulge in the masculine recreations of main street had few experiences that differed sharply from everyday life. Adults as well as children could be overwhelmed by the anticipation of a coming circus. Colorful posters, described by a Mississippian as "mammoth in size," announced to all the grandeur of the coming events, and many Southerners obviously felt that the circus was indeed the greatest show on earth. A Midway, Georgia, woman told a relative that the publicity had practically forced her to take her children to the performance. "When the children saw the bills stuck up about town they were almost crazy to go. and we had to take them." In southern Georgia, a man wrote of a coming event "which generally runs we citizens of Albany nearly mad. Albany is a great place on Circus day I assure you."[4]

Circus companies advertised themselves as having everything fascinating that anyone could want, and more. A company coming to Rowan, North Carolina, in 1909, for example, claimed that it was bringing five hundred horses, countless wild animals, one hundred acrobats and gymnasts, fifty aerialists and fifty clowns, and numerous other novelties. Other troupes offered balloon ascensions, military drill teams, cyclists, jugglers, and all sorts of death-defying acts. The emphasis was on quantity, on giving circus-goers as many exotic and unbelievable experiences as they could fit into one day. As an Alabama woman happily observed of her children's reactions to their first circus in 1867, "everything wore the charm of novelty to them."[5]

What did Southerners find so exciting about the circus? First was the crowd. Southerners of all races and classes went to the events, mixing there as they did in few other places. As one Georgian noted in 1875, "All colors sizes & ages are hurrying to Robinson's Circus." Indeed, the buoyant democracy of it all, for that one day every year or several years, seems to have added to its charm. A North Carolinian raised in the 1870s reminisced that "every person not bed-ridden, white or black, whether in Bertie or an adjoining county, had journeyed to Windsor to see his first sure-enough circus. And a jolly, hilarious crowd it was." A Clarke County, Georgia, man raised in the 1880s wrote, "There is something about a crowd at a sporting event or circus which appeals to me strongly—the free and easy, informal, democratic air that sweeps away all social barriers and makes everyone the same." In a culture divided sharply by race, class, and gender, an event that put everyone on an equal footing could lift emotions to rare heights and provide a nervous release from conventional behavior.[6]

Of the many exhibits in a circus, the animals always received the most attention. Southerners of all ages were fascinated by the world's oddest living curiosities; they often seemed to have noticed nothing but the menagerie. A Georgian noted in 1869, "Ames' circus & menagerie exhibited in Milledgeville to-day. Sallie delighted at the sight of the animals." A Tennessean wrote of another circus that a bear and a tiger "were all that were worth seeing." P. E. Roberts of eastern Texas could not stop talking about the animals at an 1873 event, noting, "ten Drumaderies followed by a cage of two large Lions and a leperd with their master siting in the center of them and then came the Elephant and other closed cages. . . . I saw many strange animals among the rest was a Baboon and an ostrage and a zebra." Writers of autobiographies likewise remembered the animals above all else. An Alabamian recalled the "parade of elephants and camels with their bespangled riders, prancing horses beautifully caparisoned, giraffes, zebras, lions, tigers, and a rhinoceros, all in red and gold cages, and an old hippopotamus lolling in his bath."[7]

Southerners were not alone in finding wild animals remarkable. Europeans had enjoyed watching exotic creatures for several centuries.[8] Like many rural dwellers, white Southerners had a close relationship with the animal world, a relationship that might have contributed to their particular fascination with unusual animals. Practically all Southern farm families owned hogs, mules, and chickens, and many also kept cows and horses; young men considered their hunting dogs to be close friends. Circus beasts were close enough to such animals to invite comparison but different enough that Southerners found them astonishing. More important than this was the presence of a race many whites felt had animal-like characteristics. White evangelicals were especially concerned with stifling the animal within man because they often identified black behavior with the animal world. The question of what was human and what was animal had real significance for people who felt a need to be something better than black.

Many of the animals exhibited at circuses had special, almost human abilities. Southerners noticed that some seemed able to transcend the boundaries between man and beast. P. E. Roberts noted that the circus he attended "had seven dogs that understood the english language well enough to do any thing their master told them to do. he made them walk on their feet like a man and then on their front feet and do many other things strang." Their understanding of English and the ability to walk on two legs made the dogs seem intelligent and nearly human. Many Southerners were particularly fascinated by performing elephants and educated seals; in Hartwell, Georgia, in 1877, for example, "Bolivar the trained elephant brought down the house." A circus in Tennessee capitalized on both animal intelligence and Confederate hero-worship by displaying horses and mules named Beauregard and Stonewall Jackson.[9]

The confusion about what was human and what was animal operated in both directions, because circusgoers, particularly in the twentieth century, were often treated to displays of men and women with beastlike features. In Chester, South Carolina, in 1915, "The side shows did an immense business. There was our old friend the wild man and all the freaks and curiosities and monstrosities garnered from the four corners of the earth." By exhibiting these strange characters next to seemingly semihuman animals, the circus raised an emotionally troubling but compelling issue: the question of just what makes an individual human. One circusgoer saw the animal and human oddities as part of the same phenomenon, later recalling "elephants, lions, tigers and zebras, fat women, two-headed babies and rollicking clowns."[10]

Other animals were frightening rather than semihuman, and here the peculiarities of Southern culture contributed more clearly to the allure of the circus. The restrained potential for violence obviously held a deep fascination for many male circusgoers who adhered to the confrontational ethos of the region. Southerners were intrigued by "fierce animals stalking back and forth in their cages." Georgian Clarence Hosch recalled his disappointment when the wild and savage beasts promised in advertisements turned out to be tame and lifeless: "Three animal cages appeared in the arena. The first contained two mangy-looking lions. In the second were several sleepy baboons. The last cage in line was full of monkeys. Twice the three cages were driven around the ring. Then they disappeared. The 'ferocious animal act' was over!" Hosch wanted to see real ferocity, as did a Georgia newspaperman who went to the menagerie first, then to the show, and finally back to the animals for "another squint at the animals, which increased in size from the fawn deer to the leopard, the tiger, the lion, the camel, the crocodile, and finally the huge elephant that killed his keeper in North Carolina." It is significant that of the seven animals named, four were potential killers and one had actually killed.[11]

Always ready for violence, Southerners obviously found exciting the possibility that the wild animals might escape. In 1868, circus promoters in Athens, Tennessee, played on this combination of fear and excitement, advertising that it would let "a Royal Tiger Loose on the Streets, untrammeled save by the watchful eye of his vigilant trainer." A Mississippian in 1857 was intrigued by the "inveterate hatred" a circus lion

The circus entering Highlands, North Carolina, 1923. (Courtesy of the North Carolina Collection, University of North Carolina, Chapel Hill)

showed for her trainer. When the keeper "called her by name—she immediately sprang up and endeavored to get out of the cage in the most ferocious manner." An 1870s incident in Windsor, North Carolina, demonstrated Southerners' quick response to what they mistook for animal violence. A gunfight between a ticket seller and some patrons outside the circus startled the lions and tigers, who began to roar and pace menacingly in their cages. "The alarmed and mystified crowd rushed for the streets, as the cry went up, 'The wild animals have broken loose!' " A number of men brandished pistols, and others ran home for their shotguns. Historian Pete Daniel describes an even more dramatic incident at a 1916 Tennessee circus, in which an elephant got out of control and smashed her trainer to the ground, then threw his lifeless body into the crowd. Male spectators, armed for any contingency, returned fire. Unsuccessful, they demanded vengeance, and after a decision by city officials, a large crowd watched as Mary the elephant was hanged from a nearby railroad crane. Violence was never far removed from any Southern male recreation; the chance of physical harm and the possibility of using firearms charged any proceedings with a powerful excitement.[12]

White Southerners had a special reason for their fascination with potential animal violence. Winthrop Jordan has shown that Englishmen and, later, white Southerners had long attributed a number of animal characteristics to blacks.[13] Since the 1600s they had worried about the possibility that slaves and then former slaves might turn suddenly to violence. The circus may have allowed them to raise that frightening issue and deal with it in the reassuring form of recreation. They could ease some of their fears and tensions by watching trainers control the restless, potentially violent animals. And if a wild animal got out of control, it could always be lynched.

The other important element of the circus consisted of the human performers: clowns, jugglers, tumblers, acrobats, and the like. These men and women showed Southerners—as they showed all circusgoers— the limitations of most people's daily lives and allowed them to question for a moment some of life's basic characteristics. Robert Isherwood writes of such events in eighteenth-century Paris, "These exhibitions at times seemed to reach beyond the physically possible. They were daring, occasionally death-defying, suggesting something miraculous." In circus performances, everyday physical laws that determine what persons can and cannot do were suspended, and simply being human became more mysterious, more colorful, and more dramatic. Young Southerners seemed to have found the stunts particularly fascinating, sometimes trying to replicate them when they returned home.[14]

One of the acts aroused far more attention than the others. Southern women rarely performed in public, and those that did usually performed only in moral dramas or in concerts to raise church funds. The circuses, however, featured scantily clad women performing stunts, often on horseback. A Virginia man clearly recalled "beautiful ladies in spangled tights." Clarence Hosch, however, was disappointed when the "beautiful maidens" advertised on circus posters "turned out to be one lone, short, fat woman in her thirties, who stood on the back of a tired-looking white horse as he ambled around the circle." Other women performers proved much more satisfying to the men and much more shocking to the women. Riding horses in one western North Carolina show were "gaudily dressed, or undressed, women who kicked up their padded legs to the scandal of the pious, orthodox portion of the crowd." Even more shocking was a turn-of-the-century trapeze artist in Mississippi who was "dressed in tights to the horror of the good ladies of the community. They even claimed that some of the men slipped around to the back of the show to see her put on a special performance. This was a special subject of conversation where women met for many months thereafter." Thus even if both sexes enjoyed the circus, the men had special reason to be excited, and, as usual, they found a special place within the circus separate from the women of the community.[15]

At first glance, the circus would seem a perfect candidate to be branded as sinful. In many ways, circus acts raised the heartbeat of all who attended, challenging Southerners' everyday notions about reality and about right and wrong. The races and the sexes all mixed in the crowd, the trained animals raised questions about the nature of humanity, the wild animals threatened violence, and the human tricks questioned the limits of most people's abilities. The scantily clad women performers only enhanced an already acute enjoyment of experiences far removed from the quiet propriety of the evangelical home and church. The great rush of amusements presented one after another was dizzying and exciting rather than morally uplifting. P. T. Barnum claimed that his animal shows could teach children natural history lessons described in the Bible, but no evidence suggests that circusgoers took those lessons seriously.[16]

Despite compelling reasons for evangelicals to shun the circus, they remained decidedly ambivalent about the virtue of the shows. To be sure, some evangelicals did condemn the circus. Georgia Methodist minister Lovick Pierce placed the circus on a list of "carnal entertainments" along with the dress ball, the common dance, the masquerade party, the skating rink, the opera, and the theater. Two other ministers also included it on lists of sinful amusements, along with dancing, horse racing, and card playing, and one young woman felt she was "reforming rapidly, as I did not go to either the German or circus." Occasionally, laypersons expressed disillusionment with the event and its popularity. William James Samford, the former governor of Alabama and a devout Methodist, complained in 1899 when two of his sons went to a show, "It is a pity that more questions are not susceptible of mathematical demonstration—It is a hard problem to give satisfactory reasons to a child, or to the worldly minded, why it is wrong to go to a circus." A young Methodist woman in Georgia complained that the circus distracted everyone in her town from more spiritual matters. "I care very little about such things. I seek a beautiful home above the skies far more brilliant & delightful than any thing on earth & which will give not momentary pleasure but exquisite joy."[17]

Such dissenters were in the minority. Almost all Southerners went to the circus whenever they could, even if it meant braving occasional criticism by their ministers. A North Carolina newspaper reported in 1897, "One of our ministers said the other day that he intended to tell the Lord of all the Methodists and Baptists who attended the circus this week; whereupon one of our beautiful young ladies remarked—'Well, he certainly will have a big job.' "[18] Many deeply religious Southerners loved the circus and apparently felt no guilt about attending. I have uncovered two Presbyterian ministers who attended the events, one of them taking his children, neither of whom felt a need to justify his actions. A Georgia man, in a letter to his future wife, moved easily from discussing a circus to a religious topic: "We are going to have a circus here next Friday; if you come at that time we will go over to 'see the animals.' I have just finished reading the book of Esther, preparing to teach a class in Sunday school tomorrow."[19] The clearest evidence that the circus was widely attended lies in the nature of the people who wrote about attending them. Some of the best descriptions of circuses appear in books that also give useful descriptions of church attendance and revival meetings.[20]

Morally questionable but not completely unacceptable, the circus was one form of titillating and mildly sinful entertainment accepted and attended by almost all rural Southerners. Newspapers constantly assessed the relative moral tone of particular circuses. A Fayetteville, Tennessee, editor wrote that Dan Castillo's Circus had a reputation for being "first class in every respect, and entirely free of the slightest objectionable features, so that ladies and little children have crowded his canvass, and on no occasion has the most fastidious taste been offended." Forepaugh and Sells Brothers' Circus was "conspicuous for good management, unobjectionable entertainment and wholesome fun." Such frequent defenses of any entertainment's moral virtues were sure signs that its genre was morally questionable. Indeed, one newspaper correspondent in Penfield, Georgia, did attempt an honest assessment. "Well! we went to the Circus and we saw everybody there. We saw much that was wonderful, some things that were objectionable—of such character as to offend eyes and ears polite. We don't think the Circus a good school of morals." Not a good school of morals, but everyone went anyway.[21]

The example of the circus helps illustrate the place of professional entertainment in the nineteenth-century rural South. The circus came to town so infrequently that it did not raise the same opposition as did sins committed daily or weekly or monthly. It stunned people's sensibilities and allowed them a release from conventional habits and manners, but only once a year at most, and never often enough to become a regular and predictable part of people's lives. Its moral status was dubious, but no one tried to make it illegal. Few ministers bothered to preach sermons against it, and congregations did not discipline their members for attending.

Other touring attractions drew mixed responses from Southern moralists. Traveling dramatic and musical companies usually had dubious reputations. The proprietors of America's most famous fictional touring show represent the shadiest side of these characters. In Mark Twain's *Adventures of Huckleberry Finn*, the Duke and the Dauphin advertise themselves as Shakespearian actors in a great tradition, but they clearly appeal to men's baser interests. Their great drawing card for the Royal Nonesuch is an advertisement claiming that their show is for men only. " 'There,' " says the Duke, " 'if that line don't fetch them, I dont know Arkansaw!' " Twain's story was not wholly fiction. In 1878, a newspaper reported that "a first-class humbug, in the shape of a pretended variety show made its appearance in [Washington, Arkansas] last Friday evening. It was slimly attended. . . . Neighboring towns should give the Parlor Minstrels the go-by, and a shove out of town."[22]

The suspicious character of the performers and the emphasis on a prurient appeal to male interests caused many Southerners to view touring shows as an affront to the purity of women, and many therefore completely shunned dramas and vaudeville acts. Josephus Daniels's Methodist mother considered the theater "worldly" and therefore ungodly, and many ministers condemned it with harsh language. Other Southerners attended such shows occasionally, but only at the expense of painful feelings of guilt. One young Kentucky man had his conversion experience and joined the church while suffering from guilt over seeing a touring group's performance of "Cinderella" in 1905. A young woman in Tennessee acted against her better instincts in going to the theater in 1872. "The music was good & the acting splendid but I felt the whole time that I was not in the right place & have since vowed that I will never attend another theatre." Only dramas that taught a clear moral lesson were completely respectable. *Ten Nights in a Barroom*, a sentimental religious drama showing how alcohol could ruin a family, was a popular play that eventually became a popular movie.[23]

With such rare exceptions, most touring shows carried a strong taint of disreputability. Medicine show vendors were always shady characters, using any line and appealing to any weakness to sell their products and interspersing their sales pitches with vaudeville or dramatic entertainment of morally questionable value. Other shows offended evangelical sensibilities more directly. In a northern Louisiana town in 1911, for example, a theatrical group called the Yama Yama Girls "created a sensation by the display of stunning harem skirts on our streets by day, and a like display of other extremities at night."[24]

Despite the limited popularity of such shows, morally questionable professional entertainment did not begin to dominate the culture of Southern small towns until the turn of the century. Until then they were, much like the circus, minor irritants that did not threaten the nature of Southern culture with permanent change. As long as outside entertainment penetrated the rural South infrequently, evangelicals were not particularly concerned about the corrupting influences of mass culture. A little sinfulness here and there was permissible, as long as all evidence of it was gone by the next day. The real evil was within, first within the individual soul, but more concretely within the roughness of male culture. In the nineteenth century, rural and small-town evangelicals worried far more about traditional forms of male sinfulness—frequent drinking, fighting, swearing, and shooting—than they did about the harm done by out-of-town professional entertainment.

4

The Plantation

His manners altogether proud, haughty,
even aristocratic-like, as if borrowed
from ancient knights or kings; polite,
graceful, beautiful, ever ready to dispute
with those who trespass on his rights,
and lords it over his less caparisoned
mates with a nobility unsurpassed by all
other fowls. . . . Woe is it for fowls of
low degree who undertake, when evenly
matched, to dispute with him.
—*Grit and Steel*, February 1905

IT was not easy to be a Southern gentleman in the late nineteenth century. The loss of the Civil War, the economic insecurities of the postwar period, the difficulties in securing dependable labor, and the class divisiveness of the Populist movement all worked to threaten the genial self-image of the South's self-styled aristocrats. Whether or not antebellum plantation society had ever reached the level of genteel elegance conceived by its mythmakers, postbellum Southern elites certainly felt that circumstances denied them the high-styled grandeur of their region's past.[1]

A major contributor to this feeling of lost glory was the increasingly important role evangelical religion played in all aspects of Southern culture. Viola Goode Liddell, an Alabamian born into a plantation family in the 1890s, clearly revealed the tensions between the two cultures in recalling the conflicting legacies of her grandfathers. One was a gentleman of the old school, with passions for racing horses, fighting cocks, and gambling on both; the other, a deeply committed evangelical, eschewed all such pleasures as overly reckless and self-indulgent. Liddell and her family, Presbyterians with some nonevangelical passions for the good life, suffered under such a dual legacy. "Little did those ancestors realize what crosscurrents they were implanting in our natures by being such vivid contrasts themselves, and little did they know that they handed down to each of us a ready-made battleground where intense internal conflicts, both mental and emotional, eternally rage."[2]

Of course, it was possible to be both wealthy and evangelical; a number of the evangelicals whose pious diaries and letters are quoted in other chapters of this book were wealthier than ordinary Southerners. But many wealthy Southerners had always been uncomfortable with a strict and introspective moral code. Evangelicalism demanded constant attention to the details of personal behavior, and wealth tempted individuals with endless possibilities for sinfulness. Many of the wealthy rejected evangelicalism altogether, adhering instead to a flamboyant cultural style they associated with the Southern past. Rhys Isaac's study of early eighteenth-century Virginia reveals a culture based on the English model in which recreation, as everything else, took place under the leadership of the gentry. The colonial gentry not only delighted in tapping kegs, racing horses, playing cards, and fighting cocks, they also enjoyed hosting such events for local middle- and lower-class whites.[3] Other recreations were for the gentry only, identifying participants as members of the wealthy and wellborn classes. Whether or not the lower orders were present, most gentry recreations consisted of large groups pursuing lively forms of enjoyment. Even if only a small minority of nineteenth-century Southerners believed in the virtues of gentry leadership in a rigid class hierarchy, the image of the genial, high-styled, fun-loving planter persisted. Some clung to the traditions of their own upper-class ancestors, and many with more questionable pedigrees liked to picture themselves as planters of the old school.

The religious perspective of Southern elites had once commanded great respect. One of Isaac's most important contributions is his portrait of how the seating patterns, liturgy, and leadership of Anglican churches in colonial Virginia reflected and supported a hierarchical culture.[4] But as evangelicalism developed in the South during the eighteenth century and flourished during the nineteenth, Anglicans and their Episcopalian successors became a minority that grew increasingly alienated from the mainstream of Southern culture. Reserved and unemotional in their expressions of religion, Episcopalians could be shocked by evangelical forms of worship. Virginian Martha Byrd Porter recalled her mother's dramatic introduction to evangelical church services. On her first visit to a Methodist church, "a gentleman sitting directly behind her 'threw a fit' and fell forward on Mother's head, all but banging her brains out. She believes until this day it was meant to be a lesson to her, and has never again strayed from the Episcopal fold." Tennessee writer Evelyn Scott, a "somewhat 'scamped' Episcopalian," was horrified by the weepy public confessions of some evangelical acquaintances. "The whole performance smacked of 'commonness'— something as abhorrent to a good Episcopalian as fastidious manners to a Baptist or Campbellite."[5]

Even more than their demeanor in church, elites' recreations separated them from the evangelical majority. Although the Episcopal church did not openly sanction such activities as horse racing and cockfighting, Episcopalians were conspicuous violators of the strict moral code of most religious Southerners. Presbyterian Hope Chamberlain recalled that in her North Carolina town, most churches "were the licensed forbidders of almost anything too thrilling and interesting. . . . A far more frankly and worldly view of things permissible was held by the Episcopalians, and this view was aided and abetted by freedom-seekers from other flocks." Clarence Poe wrote that most of the religious groups he observed during his childhood took strong stands against dancing, card playing, drinking, and swearing, but the Episcopal church's "greater tolerance sometimes attracted people to it but more often excited the condemnation of other denominations." Episcopalians were merely the most obvious targets for evangelical condemnations of all fun-loving wealthy Southerners. Wealth, for many, carried a strong air of license and self-indulgence. A devout Methodist man in Louisiana sneered at "the vicious, the profane . . . pleasure seeking elite of society," and a Georgia woman complained in 1882: "The 'first Circle' of Americus has lifted itself up to a dangerous heighth & 'High Life' as they call it is about the highest I have ever seen."[6]

A number of plantation pastimes violated evangelical notions of morality in ways unrelated to Southern men's tastes for aggressiveness and conquest. Large plantation dances, for example, offended evangelical sensibilities with their all-night pursuit of pleasure, their often ostentatious displays of luxury, and especially their open acceptance of physical closeness between the sexes. But some planter activities celebrated the rough aspects of manhood as fully as the main-street brawl.

The forms through which plantation men expressed their aggressive impulses were more controlled than the behavior of most Southern men, but they could be violent nonetheless. Steven Stowe has detailed the elaborate series of formal exchanges that preceded antebellum duels, but, he says, "no matter how much the specific rules seem to bury violence under a mass of restrictions and requirements, the chance for violent death was real."[7] Along with their violation of evangelicals' moral standards for class behavior, the wealthy also violated standards involving gender. Gentlemen thus faced condemnation for self-indulgence both in luxury and in masculinity. Two such indulgences were the ring-and-lance tournament and the cockfight.

The ring-and-lance tournament was by far the most colorful of elite recreations. The closest Southerners ever came to the days of Sir Walter Scott was this tournament, in which gallant young men rode for the honor of their ladies. This was a recreation for the upper classes, or for those who wished to identify with the upper classes. Knighthood itself, after all, was an upper-class prerogative, and tournaments had, since the eleventh century, celebrated the warlike and aristocratic ideals of chivalry. Maurice Keen's description of the early medieval tournament applies easily to postbellum Southern events: "The tournament was an exercise for the elite, and simply to appear there, armed and mounted . . . , was in itself a demonstration of a man's right to mingle in an elite society, of his own social identity."[8] Dressing as knights, taking knightly names, and riding the best horses dramatized this right in particularly self-conscious ways.

The details of the ring-and-lance tournament were simple. Metal rings two inches in diameter were hung about seven feet from the ground on ten-foot poles. The poles were placed at thirty-five-yard intervals along a straight or semicircular track measuring between 125 and 200 yards. Within a certain time limit, usually between nine and fifteen seconds, each knight rode his horse at full speed down the course, attempting to hook the rings with a seven-foot wooden lance. The winner was the knight who hooked the most rings in a specified number of rides—usually three, four, or five. Knights sometimes broke ties by trying to hook smaller rings.[9]

Newspaper reports sometimes discussed tournaments in such a jocular fashion that one might easily get the impression that they were nothing more than elaborate farces with little serious content. Perhaps some members of the community found them merely amusing, but it is clear that postbellum tournaments had deep significance for those who participated. Winning and losing were consequential matters, and the medieval and Confederate trappings only added to the importance of the event. In Allen Tate's 1938 novel *The Fathers*, a tournament set in 1858 is portrayed as desperately earnest. Competitors take pride in approaching the rings with perfect form and lifting them smoothly without scraping the hook. Impressed with the talents displayed, the novel's narrator comes to understand why young men practice constantly for the events. Contestants are so eager for victory that a panel's judgment to break a tie elicits a scuffle and a challenge to a duel. Scattered evidence suggests that these fictional characters were true to life. Katharine Obear recalled that Winnsboro's young men took the events seriously, practicing every afternoon, and a journalist in the 1890s wrote that "successful tourney riding is a matter of highly developed equestrian skill, matured after much practice and many failures." Honor was always a serious business, and at least one Southerner referred to the tournament field as "the field of honor." Just as a good run brought honor, a bad run could produce the shame all Southern men dreaded. Georgian Gertrude Thomas noted that a competitor who dropped out after a poor first pass at the rings "alleged as an excuse the lameness of his horse but I expect he disliked to run the gauntlet of so many eyes."[10]

The tournament's emphasis on fighting ability corresponded with the competitive drama of most male recreations. Riders were young men, most of them single and some in their mid-teens. At that age, Southern men were at their most competitive, feeling a special compulsion to prove themselves in a public setting by defeating worthy rivals. The emphasis on speed provided the touch of danger that enlivened almost all male sports. Any confrontation, from hunting to fighting to cock-fighting, involved a possibility of bloodshed. In trying to run the gauntlet at top speeds, knights in the postbellum South, like those in medieval Europe, faced a real threat of injury. Virginian Myrta Lockett Avary recalled that the tournament "had the spice of peril to make it attractive, if 'danger's self is lure alone.' " Gertrude Thomas worried about her son's participation after she heard of an Atlanta rider who broke his neck when his horse ran away with him. Adding to the drama of a large event in Charleston was a rider who "missed all the rings and at the last gallows got cut under the right eye, with the piece of iron to which a ring was suspended."[11]

Men from the plantations enjoyed competitions that made clear their rank in society. Young Southerners dubbed themselves with names that recalled the days of knighthood and allowed the participants to become whomever they wished to be. They could temporarily suspend the knowledge that they were the sons of struggling planters in a region reeling from military defeat. They could forget that their culture was slowly but certainly turning its back on high-styled elegance and good breeding. The tournament offered young Southern men the opportunity to be Willard of Ivanhoe, Kenneth of Scotland, Richard the Lion-hearted, Knight of Despair, Knight of the Golden Circle, Knight of Lee, Knight of the Lost Cause, Knight of the Golden Cross, Chevalier de Bayard, Knight of the Black Plume, Don Quixote, Edgar of Ravens-wood, or Henry of Navarre.[12] No doubt many of them had an imprecise notion of the origins of these names. Young men who grew up in the 1860s had other things on their minds than the works of Walter Scott and his fellow romantics. They simply chose names that indicated their desire to return to a time when it was fashionable to respect both history and wealth. Some became knights of their own towns or counties, thereby suggesting that their local area also had a long and noble heritage, and others took the names of their own plantations.[13]

Surely few things could have looked more out of place in the late nineteenth century than these imitation knights, dressed in imitation armor and cavorting on decorated horses. A competitor's appearance was extremely important, eliciting praise or criticism but always drawing notice. Dressing in medieval garb marked the knights as being wealthy as well as supposedly noble. The lower classes could not afford the finery available to the wealthy, and most no doubt would have considered such spending frivolous. Most observers, though, were fascinated by the knights' attire. Winnsboro, South Carolina, resident Katharine Theus Obear wrote of the clothes worn in an 1868 event: "Sherman had not carried off all of the velvets, satins and plumes stored away in the old trunks in the garrets for the apparel of the knights was gorgeous to behold." A Virginian recalled that "many of the knights wore imitation armour with plumes in their helmets. Some of the horses had coverings of supposed silk, but really only imitation." Gertrude Thomas carefully described her son's attire in 1870: "His costume consisted of a black velvet jacket & short pants the latter finished with a fall of lace a wide Honiton collar a black felt hat & the white plume of Navarre, fastened by two silver stars. A bright colored cravat with a very handsome sash of Lille Clantons completed his costume."[14]

Turner Thomas's final accessory indicates the element of nostalgia Southerners enjoyed in the tournaments. He dressed, "not forgetting his spurs which were formed of a portion of the band around the first shot which fired at Fort Sumter." The tournaments help to show just how quickly elite Southerners had mythologized the Confederacy. In 1868, wealthy Tennesseans held a tournament to raise funds to decorate the graves of the Confederate dead. By 1870 the Civil War years, like the medieval period, had come to represent a time of lost glory. Myrta Lockett Avary described an 1866 event that glorified the men in gray as it glorified the earliest days of chivalry: "Some wore plumed hats that had covered their heads in real cavalry charges, and more than one warrior's waist was girt with the red silk sash that had belted him when he rode as Fitz Lee's captain." A fighter, but always a captain; every element of the tournaments was designed to remind participants that they were among the upper ranks.[15]

These captains tried to remember only the best features of their past. The tournament no longer served its ancient purpose of preparing knights for war. Instead, it celebrated war in ways that let Southerners forget their recent military defeat. Describing the knights, Avary wrote that "a number were in full Confederate uniform, carrying their gray jackets as jauntily as if no battle had ever been lost to them."[16] The Confederacy had lost the war for many reasons, but Southern men did not think that a lack of fighting ability was one of them. They were still fighters, and good ones, and tournaments allowed them to take pride in their individual martial talents. The extraordinary complexity of modern warfare had made such traditional male virtues as physical ability, skillful horsemanship, and sheer courage less important in the conduct of battles. But a tournament winner could glory in those very abilities, proving himself worthy of the accolades superior fighters had enjoyed for centuries.

Most male competitions in the South had no place for women, even as spectators. The participation of women, however, was essential to the tournaments and helped mark them as a plantation sport. Young women watched as men ran the gauntlet for the glory of their lady fair. The winning knight crowned his queen with a laurel of flowers, and the king, queen, and their court received the accolades of the crowd. Young women tried not to show it, but they cared deeply about being chosen queen. A journalist laughed at the obvious excitement of "scores of possible fair queens and maids of honor, who in vain attempt to hide a flutter of coy anticipation and possible triumph under a thin cloak of assumed indifference." In Pendleton, South Carolina, a young woman of the Calhoun family seemed proud to record in October 1865, "two sent their lances for me to trim, & rode for me." Mary Alves Long recalled that one young man "sent me word that if Donna Brown didn't come and if he won the tournament, he would crown me queen. It was what Mr. Roosevelt would have called an 'iffy' proposition; nevertheless, it gave me hope."[17]

In this plantation recreation, women were Ladies, respected for their beauty and elegance rather than for their moral purity. They were not future mothers, preparing for the quiet piety of the home; they were queens, involved in the world outside the home and respected by it. Gertrude Thomas's diary illustrates the characteristics of a proper tournament queen. Her son wanted to ride for one of the young girls of the neighborhood, but Thomas knew that "the public would expect the queen to be a young lady in society." Together they chose a young woman who was both "very handsome" and a distant relative, wishing to honor their own family if possible.[18] Social class, beauty, and bloodline, then, identified young women as being worthy of the ideals of the tournament.

Many observers described the crowning of the queen as the tournament's most impressive moment. Newspaper reports occasionally concentrated on the queen and her court rather than on the tournament itself. Spectators excitedly debated about whom the winning knight would choose—a question that indirectly asked who was most worthy in a contest of beauty and bloodline. Mary Alves Long recalled that one Randolph County, North Carolina, winner, "with the crown for the queen, a gay little affair of flowers and ribbons, on the tip of his lance— rode up and down the lists inspecting the maidens in search for a queen, everybody wondering who the lucky girl would be." A North Carolinian who witnessed a wartime event in Virginia had little to say about the tournament itself but went into detail about the crowning of the queen. The winner,

> placing a beautiful wreath of flowers on his lance rode three times around the ring on a most elegant horse, prancing with conscious pride, dismounted and dropping on one knee besought the honor of crowning Miss Fields from our State queen of beauty & of his heart. Permission was gracious given & well worthy was she the honor conferred in that vast throng of beauty, with cheeks blending together the rose & lilly, lips like twin cherries and as graceful as the tapering boughs of the willow.[19]

With so many young men and women gathered from miles around, the night following a tournament provided a perfect opportunity for a plantation ball. In fact, many Southerners spoke as though the ball was an essential part of the tournament, writing of a "tournament and a big ball at night" in eastern Texas or of "a Tournament which comes off next Wednesday with a grand ball at Garris Johnson's at night" in Alabama. The tournament winner sometimes crowned his queen at these balls, and the couple was often afforded the royal privilege of the first dance.[20]

The tournament may seem innocent enough, involving no violent combat, no drunkenness, and little real disrespect for the virtue of women. The crowning of the queen placed women outside the boundaries endorsed by evangelicals, but it did not openly flout evangelical morality. Churches did not discipline members for participating in tournaments, ministers did not preach against the events, and at least two North Carolina preachers prepared texts for addresses to the knights.[21] I have found evidence of only one minister who complained about the events, and he did so more because they were frivolous than because they violated important elements of evangelical morality. In 1866 Presbyterian minister Drury Lacy complained of

> the miserable & expensive farces of Tournaments that were practiced for a while, & are yet, in some places, I believe. If I had not witnessed the vagaries of poor human nature so long, I might be surprised at the disposition of people to indulge in all sorts of fooleries at such a time & in such Circumstances. For us, at the South, to indulge in such things now—when we are poor & down trodden & ground under a strong military despotism, looks like a sett of maniacks dancing in their chains.[22]

Although evangelicals did not consider running the gauntlet sinful, they condemned other events that often accompanied the tournaments. Sponsors occasionally held tournaments at race tracks and scheduled horse races before or after the festivities. Gertrude Thomas expressed annoyance at her Methodist minister, who enjoyed the tournament and then "left when the race began but I saw the Catholic minister looking on with much interest and why not? . . . If people go to such places they had as well see it out—the sin would have been in betting on not in witnessing the horse race." The grand balls that typically followed the tournaments capped off the events with a touch of high-styled elegance that evangelicals scorned. Thomas complained of the self-conscious

and unnecessarily strict piety of those who "went to witness the coronation and left soon after as if some great crime was to be enacted when
the dancing began." The morally questionable nature of the tournament's climax brought an end to the events in at least one area. J. B. Ivey
wrote that, in the 1870s, tournaments in western North Carolina were
quite popular until the sponsors in one town followed the competition
with a dance. "This shocked the whole community as nothing of this
sort had ever before happened at Denver. This was the first and last
tournament ever held at Denver of which I know." Both the plantation
ball and the horse race were traditional gentry recreations; the former
allowed an impure contact between the sexes that the evangelicals
feared, and the latter displayed the excessive masculinity that evangelicals rejected. For the tournaments to be associated with either marked
them as morally questionable.[23]

The ring-and-lance tournament was a recreation that separated the
elite from the majority of Southerners. A few of the common folk saw a
tournament now and then, but the events were primarily parties for the
rich. Other traditional gentry recreations reflected attitudes about cultural hierarchy in a different way by including the common folk but
placing them in a decidedly subservient position. Backward-looking
planters sometimes sponsored recreations for an entire community,
recalling the days when an area's cultural life centered around the great
estates of the wealthiest members of the gentry.

The cockfight reveals with particular clarity the tensions between
cultural leadership and evangelical notions of proper behavior. It was a
traditional Southern recreation, enjoyed both on the great plantations
and in the barns of small farmers. We tend to think of the sport as the
province of the extreme poor, and probably most cockfighters were
poor farmers. But cockfights on the plantations expressed Southern
elites' notions of cultural hierarchy. Plantation cockfighters thought of
themselves as gentry sportsmen. Worried that many people considered
all cockfighters to be uncivilized rabble, one man advised his fellow
elites to "have one aim, one single thought and purpose; to reclaim the
cause with honor; to bring it back to the old days . . . when every pit,
no matter where located, was patronized by real, dear old-fashioned
gentlemen."[24]

The issue of hierarchy in sport is best discussed in Clifford Geertz's
1972 article on Balinese cockfighting. Geertz portrays the sport as a
way for the Balinese to express in dramatic fashion their stake in a

rigidly hierarchical society. The village elites owned the best birds and sponsored enormously popular fights for the entire community. Geertz's most intriguing argument concerns the significance of the Balinese fascination with gambling. The Balinese placed bets on cocks owned by elite members of their group, so that the cockfight became "a simulation of the social matrix, the involved system of crosscutting, overlapping, highly corporate groups—villages, kin groups, irrigation societies, temple congregations, 'castes'—in which its devotees live." And, more than merely rooting for their own group, the Balinese bet more than they could afford on the fights. Geertz uses Jeremy Bentham's concept of deep play to suggest that placing bets that could be financially devastating worked as a way for the Balinese to bring to the surface the central features of their culture. The "art form" of the cockfight had its highest significance not in reinforcing status discriminations but in displaying them in emotionally heated fashion. A final point Geertz makes is the identification of a winning cock with an aggressive manhood. Although the Balinese eschewed behavior that might seem animal-like and thus less than human, they let their birds do their fighting for them.[25]

Cockfighting in the South shared many features with the Balinese sport, but Southern cockfighters could never feel as comfortable about the practice as the Balinese. As in Bali, the fight was a decidedly masculine, aggressive pastime. Southern men judged cocks by how ferociously they kept up the battle. Just as important in both Bali and the American South was the social hierarchy expressed in the fights. Self-styled gentlemen owned and identified with the best birds and, more important, sponsored most of the larger cockfights. Gambling did not have the emotional significance it did in Bali, but Southerners at all income levels bet more than they could afford, revealing a degree of popular participation in the elite-sponsored events. Despite their talk about refinements that earned them respect throughout society, however, elite Southerners were never sure of their position at the top of the cultural hierarchy. Did their lower-class countrymen respect them or resent them? No such uncertainty afflicted the Balinese. Javanese officials, driven by a desire to modernize their nation, had outlawed the practice in Bali, but within the local community it had no moral critics. By contrast, cockfighters in the South had to contend with strong moral condemnation. Opposition came largely from ministers and women—people whose moral authority cockfighters generally respected, even if they did not always accept it. Whereas Balinese cockfighters were violating an externally imposed law, Southern cockfighters were violating their region's widely accepted moral code. Wealthy cockfighters had to struggle to balance their pride in the cultural hierarchy reflected in their sport and their joy in masculine recreation against the challenge of evangelical opposition.

The words of Southern cockfighters reveal the combative values they admired in their birds. Repeatedly they described the fowls with destructive metaphors such as "buzsaw," "a circular saw," "a good cutter," and "a cyclone." They spoke of their respect for a cock's gameness—a concept that implied a strength of character more important than mere fighting ability. A South Carolina breeder sent an enthusiast some birds, stating, "I believe all to be genuinely game. . . . And not one has run away." A Georgia sportsman asked if a particular breed were "dead game rapid fighters." A Quincy, Florida, man stated that although some particular cocks were unattractive, "they are game fellows though, no matter about their plumage." A Kentucky breeder bragged that his Grey Tormentors "are desperately game and cannot be counted out as long as they are able to move their beaks."[26]

Conditioning expert George Means of Concord, North Carolina, offered a definition: "What is gameness? It is the power of will to stand punishment, and even death. The game fowl has this characteristic to an extent unequaled by any other living creature." R. A. McIntyre, another sporting writer, similarly characterized gameness as "that quality of spirit which sustains a fighting cock no matter how badly he may be punished."[27]

The South's most prominent cockfighting magazine, *Grit and Steel*, from Gaffney, South Carolina, published countless reports praising birds' ability to keep fighting after suffering serious injury. An Edgefield, South Carolina, sportsman was effusive in his praise of a particular bird: "My cock lost an eye the first pitting and the other one the second pitting, and he fought over two hours blind and made a draw. . . . Over 100 pittings were made and it had to be drawn. They were the gamest pair of cocks I ever saw, but my blind cock won the loudest praise, because he would not suffer to be out-classed by being counted out. I could have wept over this noble hero." A Virginian similarly admired a bird that "made one of the gamest fights I ever saw. He was cut down on neck and coupled. . . . I handled him and he got up and won out at the surprise of all at the pit side. I never saw a gamer cock in my life."[28]

A bird that ran from a fight—hacked, in the vernacular—was not

Men of all classes and both races participate in a cockfight in eastern North Carolina. From a drawing in *Harper's New Monthly*, 1857. (Courtesy of the North Carolina Collection, University of North Carolina, Chapel Hill)

merely a loser but a dishonored coward. South Carolina's A. Burnett Rhett wrote that one cock was "a good fighter but he ran away disgracefully" and another "run like a buzzard." Losers received their share of praise if they were game. One Honea Path, South Carolina, breeder even suggested that defeat was acceptable by advertising, "Every cock guaranteed to win his fight or die game," and a Tennessee fight promoter promised that "those that are defeated, will go down to their defeat trying, and to their death unconscious and without backing an inch." A Collettsville, North Carolina, fight left a cock "dead but not dishonored."[29]

The emphasis on courage and tenacity in the face of possible death mirrored the martial attitudes of the Confederate army. Grady McWhiney and Perry D. Jamieson have argued that the prevalent Confederate strategy, the direct assault, was mounted in almost every battle, often in the face of greater numbers and superior weaponry. Of course, the popularity of cockfighting in the postbellum South need not be associated directly with the Civil War, except insofar as the war may have perpetuated and intensified Southerners' respect for battle. But Southerners clearly made the connection between military attack and cockfighting. George Means stated of the fighting cock that "in the centuries long gone by he was the ideal of courage to the leaders of men and many a warrior." A Barnwell, South Carolina, sportsman agreed, saying, "The great Confederate cavalryman, General Nathan Bedford Forrest, formulated a maxim of war that 'fifteen minutes of bulge on the enemy is worth a week of tactics,' and Napoleon nor Hannibal nor Caesar ever said anything truer. The fast, strong cock, that fights at the body of the other cock gets the 'bulge' and eventually that gives him the victory." Another South Carolinian noted that some cocks "are the heros of many battles like Stonewall Jackson, and Robert E. Lee." A Georgian stated that "we love to see an exhibition of bravery far greater than anything we are capable of ourselves," and a Virginia man praised the cock's "courage in necessity, promptitude in battle."[30]

Did non-Southern cocks fight in ways significantly different than the full-scale assaults of Southern birds? Southerners were proud to say that they did. The cockfighting journals often discussed the different styles of fights in the North and South. Southern cockfighters placed longer gaffs—sharp, knifelike weapons—on their birds' heels than their Northern counterparts used. Longer gaffs enabled birds to make deeper cuts, hence spilling more blood and bringing on speedier deaths. Using shorter gaffs resulted in longer, more calculated fights with less dramatic action. Supposedly, a Northern cock required more skill, whereas a Southern cock required more power and speed. In 1902, an Arkansas man described the regional differences in style: "The cockers of the South like a fast furious fight that ends quickly and furnishes the greatest amount of sensation in the least time. On the other hand Northern fanciers like a steady going cock, that plays a waiting game, and one that does not rush and mix it furiously at the go off."[31]

Southern cockfighters, then, wanted to see the feathers fly. The central experience of the Southern fight was the enjoyment of violent combat. This was a pleasure that cut across class lines; the reckless spirit that enjoyed a game attack was not limited to the planter class. Periodicals liked to claim that cockfighting was a democratic sport, but the largest fights featuring the most combative birds were typically held at pits run by wealthier Southerners. A large event, called a main, consisted of a number of fights—usually anywhere from seven to twenty-one—between the birds of two prominent enthusiasts. On these occasions the Southern economic elites sponsored the rough amusements of the entire male culture, as they had done since the Virginia culture of Rhys Isaac's description. A Gaffney, South Carolina, cockfighter promised in 1899 that if he could find an opponent for a main, "he will erect a regular cock pit on his plantation for the occasion and he will make it as pleasant for the boys as possible." Mains were gentry-sponsored social events that few cockfighters of modest means could match. Lacking both the complete array of fighting cocks needed for a main and the facilities necessary for a large spectator event, poor and middling cockfighters staged single fights known as hack fights after the mains had been completed.[32]

It is not easy to determine the extent of gambling on Southern cockfights, but it is clear that the element of chance was one of the sport's greatest attractions. A Eufaula, Alabama, man invited a friend to a fight, saying, "I think you can have some fun and plenty of betting." The proprietors of a main sometimes bet large—even fantastic—amounts, wagering specific sums on each fight and a larger amount for the total score. Much rarer was the Alabama man who "will fight to the tune of Ten Thousand anytimes" or the antebellum sportsmen who, according to a former slave, "bet their money, their horses, their plantations, their negro servants, the clothings on their backs." More typical at mains were stakes between fifty and two hundred dollars, and winners of hack fights earned much less. A Mississippian asked a breeder to send a cock "that is quick to kill as I will fight a friend's cock Xmas for 10.00," and many such events were fought for twenty or twenty-five dollars. The betting at Southern matches, as in Geertz's Bali, was as heated among the spectators as it was among the owners of the birds. At a fight in western North Carolina, "anything was bet from a handful of chestnuts to a plantation." In Caradine, Mississippi, "we boys always bet all we have on a cock fight," and, after an Orangeburg, South Carolina, event, "all went home well pleased, but some of course out of pocket chink." Betting does not seem to have been the end-all of the sport as it was in Bali; nor, apparently, did it mirror specific lines of family or class ties. However, by allowing lower-class Southerners to participate, but in a subordinate way, in events sponsored by wealthier sportsmen, gambling showcased the gentleman's position at the top of a cultural hierarchy.[33]

Because they owned the best birds and were able to indulge in the often arcane training procedures necessary to develop the best fighters, wealthier Southerners had a decided advantage in the sport. They could afford to buy the best stock, to breed from the best bloodlines, and to prepare their cocks to be healthier and stronger than could cock enthusiasts of more modest means. Cocks fought at the more prestigious mains were typically the finest birds; hack fights featured birds of more ordinary parentage and less costly care.

The first concern was breeding. Bertram Wyatt-Brown has described antebellum Southerners' constant desire to identify with male ancestors and thereby to prove the power of blood.[34] So too did many postbellum cockfighting enthusiasts see in breeding an importance beyond the obvious fact that better birds descended from better parents. In 1905 a Virginian described the best-bred game fowl using the language of nobility: "His manners altogether proud, haughty, even aristocratic-like, as if borrowed from ancient knights or kings; polite, graceful, beautiful, ever ready to dispute with those who trespass on his rights, and lords it over his less caparisoned mates with a nobility unsurpassed by all other fowls. . . . Woe is it for fowls of low degree who undertake, when evenly matched, to dispute with him." *Grit and Steel* editor Edwin de Camp advised proper care of the cocks, "if you would not see an individual now and then go back upon his lineage." George Means was equally adamant that some cocks were better than others because of their blood. Discussing gameness, he stated that "each game fowl descended from blue-blooded ancestors has received his characteristic of his inheritance."[35] Many cockfighters attempted to combine the best features of different breeds through crossbreeding. The interest in breeding was overwhelming, filling pages of the cockfighting journals with long descriptions of particular strains. The very different prices for different breeds, ranging from a dollar or two up to twenty-five dollars, reveal that only the wealthiest sportsmen could afford the finest birds.[36]

Enthusiasts felt that, although most well-bred birds were naturally game enough for ordinary fights, proper conditioning was necessary for fighting the best opponents. The most important step in developing gameness was walking a cock. This involved allowing a young cock, aged six to twelve months, to walk free among a number of hens in order to give him the feeling that he could have anything he wanted. Wealthier cockfighters had an advantage in walking as well as in breeding the birds. Many Southerners of ordinary means could not afford to keep a large area free of male fowls and had to keep their young fighting cocks in coops. In *The Art of Walking Cocks*, Ewing A. Walker condemned the latter practice as a poor second choice, used only because of economic necessity: "Some men are so situated that they must depend, at least in part, upon coop walks, but no man can, with logic, maintain that a coop is as advantageous as a free-range or farm-walk."[37] Some wealthy cockfighters liked to walk their birds at the homes of small farmers who had a few hens, showing their belief that nonwealthy Southerners should have some small role in the sports of the wealthy. For example, Means wrote that a young cock should be left to walk with those "who work the soil for their daily bread and who, although they are not owners of real estate, are steady workers, honest and saving." For a small fee, such farmers would allow a cock to walk with their hens. Walker was more than a little condescending in his advice about how the owners of cocks, on returning to retrieve their newly walked birds, should speak to these small farmers: "When you lift a cock in splendid flesh and plumage glossy and brilliant, praise the man who walked him. It costs you nothing and touches the pride and pleases him who owns the walk."[38]

Postbellum cockfighters who thought their own blood was as blue as that of their birds brushed off evangelical criticisms of their sport as being directed only at lower-class cockfighters. In fact, most Southerners saw all forms of the sport as part of a series of rollicking masculine activities that evangelicals considered sinful. Both rich and poor "cockers" bore the stigma of an array of disreputable associations. In 1860 Daniel Hundley described the God-fearing middle-class Southerner as one who "keeps away from race-courses, cock-pits, groggeries, brothels, and the like; makes no bets; plays no cards." A Baptist preacher in Anniston, Alabama, condemned "the beer garden, the base ball, the low theatre, the dog fight and cock fight and the ring for the pugilist and brute." Some denunciations of cockfighting singled out the participation of the wealthy. In 1899 a Georgia Baptist minister saw the sport as one of many pleasures of the self-indulgent sons of wealthy Southerners. "I know healthy young men who 'dude' around our streets all the week, spin yarns, fight cocks, 'root' for base-ballers, play cards and read novels, and think nothing of going to their old fathers Saturday nights and demanding 'spending change.'" In eastern Tennessee in 1905, one report claimed that "some of the better citizens of that section of the county, including younger boys of prominent well-to-do families, have become involved to the great sorrow and distress of their parents. Preachers have spoken out against the sin from their pulpits."[39]

What gave cockfighting its unsavory reputation? One obvious answer is the threat it posed to the moral purity of the home. The cockpit was a thoroughly male institution outside the pale of the softening influences evangelicals associated with women. One Southern defender of cockfighting warned that "where there is one man upholding it there are a dozen opposed to it (to say nothing of the ladies!)." Some women complained harshly of their husbands' passion for the sport. The grand-mother of Viola Liddell "unceasingly and vehemently opposed the cru-elty and bloodshed that a cock fight necessitated." North Carolinian Ida May Beard likewise complained that her husband "did a great many things I did not approve of, one thing especially, and that was fighting game chickens on the Holy Sabbath day."[40]

Certain features of the cockfights offered particular threats to a peaceful home life. One, obviously, was the high degree of gambling. Spectators who bet more than they could afford were sometimes betting money that could have been spent on the household. Another was the tendency for some events to drag on for hours. A 1902 South Carolina main that lasted until 4:00 A.M. could not have helped the family lives of its participants.[41] The widespread use of profanity at the fights likewise marked the events as sinful. Describing what he called the Southern Bully, Daniel Hundley wondered "how he manages to survive the constant damnings he is ever heaping upon every hair of his head, and every bone of his body; verily, it surpasses belief! Oh! to see him at a chicken-fight—when there are gamecocks in the pit, and the bets range from one to five dollars! We tell you, Sir, it is sublime—the swearing and profanity he can give utterance to—perfectly sublime, so wholly is it beyond the conception of less depraved and more scrupu-lous minds!" Finally, drunkenness often accompanied the events. As a cocking enthusiast in Rockingham, North Carolina, reported, "Can't say we had a very orderly crowd, for there was liquor in it, and too much for a cock fight." The wife and family who waited for a cock-fighting father to come staggering home at a late hour, probably drunk and possibly penniless, had concrete reasons for their aversion to the sport.[42]

Beyond such practical concerns, cockfighting violated the entire tone of evangelical culture. A scene of wild-eyed, half-crazed, shouting men watching two angry cocks slicing at each other's throats, pecking at each other's eyes, and battling to a possibly bloody death violated the quietly self-controlled official morality of the evangelical South. If many men enjoyed the sport out of love for the aggressiveness of battle, evangelicals condemned it out of disdain for the same experience. The clash between the frenzied intensity of the fights and the well-ordered propriety of the religious set showed nowhere more clearly than in an incident reported in memorable detail by the *Mobile Daily Register* in 1873:

Reverend Mr. Pinkney, of Slawsom, bought a game rooster from a Danbury dealer Saturday. Mr. Pinkney informs us he was not aware the fowl was of the game species. . . . [On Sunday morning he] saw his new rooster and a rooster belonging to the widow Rathburn squaring off in the street for a fight. Surprised and pained by this display, he immediately started out to repel the disturbance, but he was too late. When he got there half a dozen young ruffians with cigars in their mouths and evil in their eyes had surrounded the birds which were already in the affray. . . . When the boys saw him they shouted out, "Hurry up, baldy (Mr. Pinkney is a little bald) or you'll miss the fun." Mr. Pinkney was inexpressibly shocked. It was Sunday morning; the houses of two of his deacons and several of his prominent members were in sight, and here were those roosters carrying on and a parcel of wicked and profane boys standing around and shouting their approval and noisily betting on the result. . . . Just as he attempted to catch his rooster a rough looking individual, with his pants in his boots, and a cap with a drawn-down fore-piece, came, and taking in the scene at a glance, sided with the other rooster. "Fair play," shouted the new comer for the benefit of the crowd, and "Don't step on the birds, old codger," for the particular benefit of Mr. Pinkney, who, crazed beyond reason, was jumping about, swinging his arms and muttering incoherent things, to the great danger of stepping on the combatants. "Good for old Pinkney's rooster," screamed the boys in delight, as that fowl knocked a handful of feathers from his opponent's neck. "The parson knows how to do it," said a one-eyed man gleefully. Mr. Pinkney could have swooned. . . . "My friends," protested the unfortunate minister in a voice of agony, "I cannot, I cannot." "I'll back you sir," said an enthusiastic man with a fish pole. The clergyman groaned. . . . Mr. Pinkney clutched it [the widow's bird] dropping on his knees as he did so. At the same time the rough man, by a dextrous move, caught the clergyman's bird, and also dropped on his knees opposite. Just then Mr. Pinkney looked up, and there saw two of his deacons and several of his members staring upon the scene, which brought blood to his face, and with a groan of intense pain the unhappy man dropped Mrs. Rathburn's fowl and darted into the house.

After an investigation, the congregation declined to accept Reverend Pinkney's resignation.[43]

This sort of incident, clearly, was not the sport of gentlemen, and wealthy cockfighters rejected such scenes as being beneath their dignity. Elites preferred forms of masculine amusement that were more refined, more civilized, and less anarchic. They always claimed that evangelicals, if they understood the difference between elite and common cockfighting, would have no criticism of the upper-class sport. During the late nineteenth century, when elites felt their influence threatened in many ways, some upper-class cockfighters mounted what could almost be considered a reform movement, proposing to take control of the sport and thus to restore it to a respectability they felt it had lost.

The worst fault in Southern cockfighting, as the elites saw it, was dishonest gambling practices. Many cockfighters rigged matches, misrepresented the values of particular birds, or unfairly doctored birds prior to a fight. Cockers who considered themselves gentlemen repeatedly tried to distance themselves from shifty potential opponents. One man wrote in 1869 that "the cockfighters about Selma generally are of the lowest grade. But Dr. J. T. Gee himself is as much a gentleman as a cocker can be. No low bred unfairness in him at all." George Means advised, "If a man you believe to be a gentleman is willing to make a main with you, accept, but never engage in the sport with a questionable character, or a known crook. You may be able to defeat him, and get his money, but the chances of damage to your own character and of undesirable publicity is not worth it." Another Southerner stated in 1904 that the sport had once been the province of gentlemen, but doctored birds had brought about its downfall: "Honor fled when gamblers entered the arena with their 'lightning duffers,' taking chances for a quick cut down." As late as the 1930s, a Northern journalist found that genteel Southerners felt their form of the sport differed dramatically from lower-class cockfighting. Ushered to a lower-class event in North Carolina by a self-styled gentleman named Sam, this journalist wrote that the participants "were interested solely in the gambling phase of the event, and the tricks they could perform. To hear Sam, it would be a dirty, nauseous travesty on cockfighting and should be stamped out. When I suggested to him that every time he fought a main he was violating the same laws, he said there was a distinction."[44]

Elite sportsmen felt certain that the scheming of the rabble was responsible for the cockpit's bad name. Edwin de Camp asserted in 1904, "All game chicken people are not liars, thugs and thieves. No, not by a good deal. But there is no denying the fact that that element in the sport has had much to do with bringing it into disrepute among those who imagine that every cocker is a reprobate because there is a reprobate element in it." Eleven years later he repeated, "Many think that cocking has been prohibited in nearly all the states because of the cruelty of the sport . . . but the truth is, the lawlessness and cheap trickery of men engaged in the sport brought about the adverse reaction of the great free-thinking public." R. A. McIntyre agreed, noting that "pitters of low instinct and given to dirty methods lose the confidence of all their acquaintances, and degrade the sport."[45]

Why did dishonest gambling techniques so threaten the tradition of gentlemanly cockfighting? Certainly it was not due to an upper-class aversion to gambling. Believing that "the instinct to sport is born in a man," de Camp advised, "if you must yield to that instinct endeavor to be an honest gambler."[46] Rigging matches and doctoring birds, though, were forms of gambling that threatened the dominance wealthy cockfighters had long held over the sport. The best birds attracted the crowds to cockpits at the plantations, where lower-class spectators bet on cocks owned by the planters. But if underhanded tricks allowed a seedier element to control the sport, the fights would lose their character as genteel settings for masculine aggressiveness. Without gentry leadership, the sport seemed abandoned to displays of the anarchic recklessness of the lower classes. Masculinity the gentlemen admired, but they feared a masculinity that lacked the ennobling influences of the elites.

The other feature of the sport that gentlemen found unsavory was drunkenness. Of course upper-class Southern men drank, and sometimes drank to excess, but gentlemen cockfighters believed that overindulgence had contributed to the sport's bad name. At least one cockfighting writer, Louisiana's Sol McCall, toured the South in the early 1900s giving lectures on temperance. Another writer linked alcohol to other male activities, advising sportsmen, "Unless you have some special desire to ruin the game, never fight on Sunday or carry a bottle or gun with you." Yet another was frustrated by the constant criticism of cockfighters' moral character. "This is the outcome of allowing a few loud-mouthed, whiskey-soaked individuals to make themselves too conspicuous in and about the pit. . . . Let us 'cut out' the rowdy and raise the limit of the respectable."[47]

The solution to this degradation—a degradation the South's self-styled gentlemen felt was growing more pronounced—was obvious. The low element "must be condemned and suppressed if the genteel class of cockers expect to raise this amusement to the plane of bird hunting and the chase." De Camp wrote, "The ignorant, low bred species could not in reality tell what a gentleman is. . . . Cut their acquaintance, sportsmen, and fight cocks decently with gentlemen." Some hoped that persuasion could perhaps improve the tone of the sport. De Camp seems almost to have surprised himself with a sermon against the sport's dishonorable element:

> Viciousness is a consequence of environment—association—and if the vicious will associate with the gentler element it will inevitably yield to that element. Therefore the gentlemen of the fraternity can do much to elevate the pastime. We have yet to see the man who would not yield to the gentle influence if he possessed the least trait of manhood. Preaching morals! Are we! Yes, for while we believe a gentleman can engage in cock fighting we see no reason why all cock fighters should not be gentlemen.[48]

To the planters, then, morals meant civility and an acceptance of hierarchy, but they certainly did not mean a rejection of the traditions of Southern masculinity.

5

The Farm

Sometimes the stronger man on the end
of the lifting stick could pull the one
down who was on the other end. To be
pulled down in such a fashion was an
embarrassment, and considered as a
reflection on a man's muscle power.
—J. Harold Stephens

HISTORIANS of American popular culture have shown little
interest in harvest celebrations. The elaborate, animated ceremonies
that reveal so much about the culture of premodern peoples seem on the
surface to have had few counterparts among Americans. Were Americans not rational and scientific in their view of nature? Protestant and
hence unceremonial in their recreations? Capitalistic and unsentimental
in their treatment of the land? However, Americans have long taken a
special pleasure in the harvest, and the different forms of Southerners'
celebrations reveal important changes in the nature of rural life.

Spokesmen for Southern white farmers in the postbellum period
routinely paid tribute to the harvest. In October 1901 the editor of the
Southern Cultivator wrote, "We have toiled through the sweat and the
dust of the long summer days, now we are cheered by the rewards of our
toil. We rejoice once again to see fulfilled the blessed promise—That
while the world remaineth, seed time and harvest shall remain." Another editor agreed that the harvest held special pleasures for Southern
farmers. "We have always liked the fall work on the farm. Planting
cotton or hoeing it never suited us half so well as drawing the fleecy
locks from the open bolls. Hoeing corn or plowing it was never so

89

pleasant as harvesting the sweet-smelling fodder and the big, yellow pumpkins." Farmers themselves occasionally expressed the same sentiment. A farmer and Presbyterian minister wrote in November 1866 that he had "finished gathering my corn crop 268 bushels God be thanked for his goodness in so supplying."[1]

Studying the ways in which farm families celebrated such occasions can provide particularly fruitful insights into local culture because they highlighted the roles different groups played in the productive process. In Southern white farm families, work roles mirrored men's and women's clearly defined cultural roles. On the farm, men's physical self-assertiveness took the form of pride, not in the dry tedium of daily agricultural tasks, but in successful farming—in wresting a living from the soil. Male harvest recreations emphasized the physical, the masculine, and often the combative. Women's harvest recreations—cooking and quilting—mirrored their roles in caring for the family and generally celebrated the evangelical values of domestic harmony.

Anthropologists usually deal with community rituals in one of two ways. The first method of interpretation sees the components of popular rituals as outgrowths of features prevalent in the community's society and culture. These ceremonies are pictures people create about their society or, in Clifford Geertz's words, "a story they tell about themselves." Attitudes and relationships are dramatized and heightened in what may at first appear to be only meaningless diversions.[2] The other interpretation deals with rituals that seem to defy the logic of a culture's attitudes and relationships. Many anthropological studies have dealt with rites of inversion, in which conventional roles are substantially changed and the repressed becomes manifest. In early modern Europe, for example, outlandish carnival festivities represented "the world turned upside down." Such inversions often support the existing social system and cultural relationships by allowing tensions and suppressed desires full reign for a short time.[3] The two methods of interpretation, which do not necessarily conflict, ask questions we can use in trying to understand the meaning harvest celebrations had for rural Southerners. Nineteenth-century harvest celebrations mirrored the conventional division between masculine and evangelical values, but they also allowed a moment of release from evangelical constraints.

Work sharings were events in which, as one Southerner recalled, "work was turned into play." Reminiscences and contemporary newspaper accounts recall the excitement white farm families throughout the South found in corn shuckings, cotton pickings, fodder pullings, log rollings, hog killings, and the accompanying quiltings and cooking. A Crawford, Georgia, editor heard that "a rousing corn-shucking came off recently at the farm of James Escoe." In 1876 the *Greensboro Herald* in North Carolina announced that "the gay season has fairly opened—surprise parties, candy jerkings, quiltings, corn shuckings and shin-digs are all the go." Ten years later, a Louisiana woman wrote, "Cary has had his log rolling he finished in one day and a frollick at night." Work sharings could even provide the occasion for traditional events; a corn shucking in Tennessee in 1888 preceded a New Year's Eve party. A striking number of twentieth-century Southerners discussed such recreations in their childhood reminiscences. Agriculture expert Clarence Poe recalled that work sharings provided "opportunities to express a neighborliness that was not merely a duty but to a great degree a joy." South Georgian J. L. Herring said that the events "relieved the monotony and loneliness of country life; brought the people closer together and facilitated work, for they gave to the task a zip and enthusiasm lacking even with the most illustrious when alone." Tennessean Lila May Pamplin recalled that a log rolling "was got up to have fun," and Arkansas native John Quincy Wolf stated that in all such events, "the claims of neighborliness were strong, and the pleasures of a community get-together were genuine." North Carolinian Alberta Ratcliffe Craig also recalled that "like corn shuckings and the ice harvest, the slaughtering of hogs was a community occasion, for men, women, and children," and Mississippi's Elijah L. Shettles agreed that "our chief amusement was had at neighborhood gatherings, such as house raisings, log rollings, quiltings, and road workings."[4]

The work sharings mirrored the division, evident in most of white Southern culture, between male combativeness and female domesticity. The events began with a clear separation of the sexes, with the men enjoying contests and feats of strength. Most men's events turned seemingly dull tasks into competitions. At corn shuckings in Tennessee in the 1880s, men and boys "talked, told jokes, and held contests to see who could shuck the corn fastest." Wiley C. Hamrick, a Cleveland County, North Carolina, resident, recalled of the 1860s: "Prior to the starting of the shucking, the pile, small or large, was divided by running a fence rail through the middle. Then two captains selected the shuckers for the race. After teams had been selected, every one settled down to shuck in good earnest, each side vieing to beat the other." Although men, women, and children all worked in community cotton pickings, only the young men seem to have turned the job into a contest. In southern

Georgia, "there were always two boys with some reputation as swift pickers to start a race." The difficult nineteenth-century practice of fodder pulling (stripping leaves off corn plants still in the field) was an entirely male responsibility and also sparked contests between young men. At Georgia fodder pullings,

> races were run between group after group to see who could out strip the other in a round of 2 or 4 rows or even up to 8 rows (endurance tests), betting was heavy and high, quickness and aptness were pitted against strength and endurance. The field was finished and all were washed and combed well before high noon. The long porches and walkway were filled with men and boys talking in high glee about why so and so won and the good reason why the other guy lost and just wait until next time and see who won.[5]

These feats of physical ability were a few of the many forms of competitive toughness among nineteenth-century Southern men. The corn-shucking or cotton-picking or fodder-pulling contest represented a convergence of two of the central features of male culture. The first was the idea that a man's job was to gain a living from the soil. The yearly corn shucking celebrated the successful accomplishment of that responsibility. The second was Southern men's constant need to prove their mettle, not merely to their peers but to themselves. Turning group work into a race reflected the men's desire to assert their wills over nature as well as over each other. Simply accomplishing their work responsibilities was not sufficiently rewarding; they felt a need to do their work as dramatically as possible, flexing their muscles in a community setting.

Accompanying many male activities was the usual stimulant to aggressive behavior—alcohol. Competition, in the barn as on main street, intensified ever-present urges to fight and win. A South Carolinian recalled that "if the farmer giving the shuckin' was a bit devilish, he would have a demijohn of 'One X Corn' hidden out back of the barn, to the utter disgust of the ladies. Most of the men did not drink. But those that did soon got merry, and occasionally one wanted to start a fight." The significance of alcohol in the corn shucking is demonstrated in a work chant quoted by Frank L. Owsley:

> Give me a dram, sir, Give me a dram;
> Round up the corn, boys, Round up the corn.

Owsley writes that the chant became more spirited as the shuckers lived out its lyrics.[6]

Other forms of group work likewise allowed men to express their self-assertiveness and their mastery over nature. Clearing ground and rolling logs were strenuous group activities that emphasized masculine strength and the ability to conquer nature. Wiley Hamrick described the common practice of clearing forest land: "The choppers and rail-splitters would assemble and in this way acres of forest timbers on one farm would be felled and cleared in one day. . . . This kind of work was what is termed a real 'man's job,' and the strongest men of the community were pressed into service. They displayed extraordinary feats of strength and prowess." Tennessean J. Harold Stephens recalled that these occasions contained numerous possibilities for competitions that resulted in either conquest or shame. When two men were lifting a particularly large log, "sometimes the stronger man on the end of the lifting stick could pull the one down who was on the other end. To be pulled down in such a fashion was an embarrassment, and considered as a reflection on a man's muscle power."[7]

Another arena for physical achievement in group work was the winter hog killing. In this, as in rolling logs and clearing ground, men showed their power over nature, this time in a dramatically gory process. The faint-hearted cringed at the sights and sounds of the hog killing, and parents often shielded children, especially girls, from the bloodiest moments. North Carolinian Belinda Jelliffe recalled her horrified reaction to the custom: "Oh! The shrill frightened squeals they made! A sound accusing, asking for help, full of consummate awareness of annihilation! The completely unbearable fact that every pig was a member of the family." The significant feature of such activities is that they were group recreations—as one recalled, "a sort of holiday"—as well as group work. Killing a hog was not merely a hot, ugly responsibility but a tough, manly act performed in public.[8]

While the men raced through contests and performed feats of strength and toughness, women generally stayed in the home quilting and cooking. Both were cooperative group activities and both reflected the domestic values of Southern female life, which lacked the competition and bravado of the male work sharings. Many Southerners recalled both activities as the female counterparts of the male corn shuckings and log rollings. Hamrick stated that "the same day the forest was being felled the women of the neighborhood would hold a quilting party in the same home. These gatherings were just as appealing and congenial to the opposite sex as the heavier work was for the men." A Louisianian planning a log rolling in 1883 wrote, "We are going to ask about forty hands to it and about that many quilters." Ruth McBroom likewise recalled that "sometimes people having a corn shucking would have a quilting on the same day," and Alabamian Mitchell Garrett stated that on arriving at corn shuckings, "the womenfolk repaired to the house to help with the preparation of the supper or to take their places around the quilting frame; for of course there was also a quilting bee." In rural Arkansas, "at both log rollings and house-raisings the women would be preparing dinner for the whole company, talking women's talk all the while." The difference between the masculine pleasure in competition and muscle power and the female involvement in "women's talk" and quiet domestic arts reveals the way work-sharing recreations celebrated the divisions in white Southern culture.[9]

The domesticity of women's recreations certainly characterized the popular quilting. Women sewing quilts did not compete or show their strength as did the men in their activities, nor did they taunt each other or feel a need to prove their abilities. Quilting was a cooperative enterprise requiring considerable discipline, thus reflecting the peace and harmony evangelicals valued in their family lives. Seated around quilting frames prepared in advance, the women created lasting items that would be used by a family for decades. Several Southerners recalled quiltings as events filled with constant friendly chatter; in the 1940s one stated that a quilting held in her childhood "was equal to a bridge luncheon of today." The quilts themselves often symbolized both family unity and Christianity and, sometimes, the connections between the two. Pieces of clothing that belonged to different members of a family were woven into many of the quilts, thus tying images of family members together into a single unit. The names of some of the quilt patterns, such as Grandmother's Flower Garden and Grandmother's Pride, reflected a desire to keep family memories alive for generations. The popular Wedding Ring and Double Wedding Ring patterns celebrated those symbols of a lasting marriage. Many other quilts drew their names and patterns from Christian sources. At least one quilt in Tennessee was stitched together by Bible verses. More commonly, women worked together to sew the Star of Bethlehem, the Star of the East, the Tree of Life, the Tree of Paradise, the Rose of Sharon, and the Crown of Thorns.[10]

Women's other activity at work sharings was cooking. Southerners recalled the meals accompanying these events in such detail that the feasts obviously were important as more than just the nourishment necessary for hard work. Cooking was a hot and difficult task, but at the work sharings women worked together to prepare the meals and enjoyed the pleasure their efforts brought to the crowd. Willard Bond clearly recalled the menus at past southern Mississippi work sharings: "baked sweet potatoes, corn pone (with finger prints on it), big pans of chicken pie, egg custard, turnip greens, backbone and rice, home-made cake, huckleberry pie, etc., and coffee."[11] Such a spread confirms that these feasts were celebrations of domesticity, with the women working most of the day to prepare a memorable meal for the families gathered at the events.

Although work-sharing recreations primarily displayed the standard white Southern values of masculinity and domesticity, they could also provide something of a release from those values. Conventional standards of proper behavior were suspended in the communally accepted mating rituals that occurred as part of some work sharings. These rituals did not involve the wild explosions of some inversion rituals or the dramatic role reversals of others. However, in the evangelical South, these courting rites represented a substantial change from conventional courtship, which typically took place in the home, the church, or the school. In the home, the young met under the eyes of watchful parents. In the church, adults could also oversee the young. And in schools, faculty members did their best to prevent their students' inclinations, in an Alabama teacher's phrase, "to give us some trouble along a line that is quite natural to the human family, that of the opposite sexes trying in every way to establish and maintain communications."[12]

The first of the harvest courtship rituals occurred at the end of a quilting, which usually climaxed with the game of "shaking the cat." According to an Arkansas native, "each girl would take hold of the quilt—at corners, sides or ends, to accommodate everyone present— and began shaking it for dear life. Someone would pitch a cat into the center of the quilt, there was great glee in seeing which girl it ran closest to—that girl would certainly get married first." The practice seems to have been common throughout the South, with some local variations. In northern Mississippi, only four young women at each quilting had the privilege of shaking the cat, and in southern Georgia young women and men shook the cat as couples.[13]

In the second ritual, women and girls joined the men near the end of a corn shucking for a game involving a red ear of corn. As C. Waldo Cox recalled, "the appearance of the girls had quite an effect on the entire operation," because all knew that any young man who found a rare red ear of corn gained the right to kiss a young woman, hopefully the young woman of his choice. The method by which the choice was made apparently varied slightly. Lila May Pamplin recalled that the lucky youth "had the privilege of kissing the prettiest unmarried woman present," whereas a South Carolinian stated that "the fellow who found one could kiss the lady of his choice." Cox described a somewhat more complicated process in which a young man supposedly could kiss a young woman when he found the red ear, but despite the fact that "it was an old and long established custom—and mutually accepted, too— . . . quite often he found to his dismay that, though he had a right, he didn't get the privilege—and what a scuffle." According to Cox, considerable planning went into the process of seat selection, with some men bringing special stools or chairs in hopes of luring particular young women to their sides; party leaders could also make the process fairly elaborate:

> To make certain the plan would be the greatest success, a seating committee distributed the girls the whole length of the corn pile, and even *re*distributed them every thirty minutes, for some *over-industrious* young blades had been discovered storing up a few extra red ears, one every ten minutes, in front of the girl next to him. And the committee took special pains to place "a confirmed old maid" alongside a "weather-beaten old bachelor"—just to see what would happen.[14]

The public kissing could become downright giddy. "The women dodged or hid their faces, and as the men came toward them everyone laughed and talked, and advised the women what to do so the men couldn't kiss them, and the men what to do to get the kisses. Finally all the chosen women were properly kissed on the cheek."[15]

The widespread interest in who kissed whom showed the very public nature of this mild and respectable form of mating ritual at the corn shuckings. Similarly, all of the women who participated in a quilting either watched or joined in the shaking of the cat. We can better understand the meanings these rituals held for Southern farm families by seeing them together. First, a group of women engaged in a ceremony that used a cat to indicate which of the younger women would be the next to marry. Then all hurried down to the corn shucking for one of the few—if not the only—public displays of premarital physical contact, displays in which the entire group participated.

Why a cat? Why would a cat be a particularly telling object to indicate forthcoming marriage? Robert Darnton has shown that cats signified many things to eighteenth-century Frenchmen, from witch-craft to cuckoldry to bourgeois acquisitiveness.[16] As far as we know, cats did not hold such a fascinating range of meanings for postbellum Southerners. However, some young Southerners explicitly made the connection between cats and unmarried women. Approaching her nine-teenth birthday and somewhat concerned that she was still unmarried, Jennie Samuel of Tuscaloosa, Alabama, worried, "I'm getting to be such an old maid that I actually touched a cat the other day. And I was never known to do such a thing before; for of all the things in the world, I think a cat the last."[17] This curious statement seems to suggest an identification of older, unmarried women with cats, perhaps only be-cause older women liked to keep cats as pets. A young man in Louisiana made a different connection between cats and the sexuality of young women, saying that an old girlfriend "gave her pussy" to her new husband.[18] For the young woman, the cat was a symbol of unmarried old women; for the young man, the cat symbolized something the new bride had lost. For both, though, cats indicated virginity and, we can speculate, latent sexuality. Thus a cat that ran toward a certain young woman in a group of quilters was pointing out the virgin and allowing all the women to enjoy the fact that she might soon lose her virginity.

Perhaps as important as these two Southerners' references to cats is the nature of cats in general and their place in the Southern household. First, cats were, more than any other animals, associated with the home and with women. While dogs and horses often accompanied men on sporting excursions far from the home, cats spent most of their time in or near the house and, simply for that reason, symbolized a closeness to women rather than men. The mating practices of cats may be relevant as well. Unlike other animals around the house—dogs, horses, cows—cats did not normally mate in public view. Their mating was a secret affair, hidden except for an occasional howl in the night. This seeming shyness or even disinterest in mating should be interpreted in relation to the air of haughty self-control and self-assurance that almost everyone sees in cats. Cats, simply because of their bearing and facial expres-sions, seem to know more than we do. To toss a cat into any chaotic situation—such as a quilt being shaken by a roomful of laughing women—was to enjoy watching a loss of composure. Pamplin recalled that the shaken cat was "astonished" and "bewildered."[19] That such a loss of composure should indicate a forthcoming wedding, and that the entire ceremony should precede a giddy kissing custom, suggests that shaking the cat was an acceptable public acknowledgment of the emotional intensity and, quite possibly, the pleasure of youthful sexual experience.

The young women who anxiously shook the cat and the young men who searched madly for red ears of corn were enjoying liberties not usually allowed in the evangelical South. The young may have constantly desired, in the Alabama teacher's phrase, "to establish and maintain communication" with the opposite sex, but very rarely did the entire community allow them to express their desires in such physical ways.

The meaning of such festivities becomes clear when we consider them in light of other harvest celebrations. The harvest is a time of special importance for all agricultural societies. After successfully gathering a crop, agricultural societies can put aside their worries about survival for at least a short time, and their practical concerns become secondary to the pursuit of more immediate pleasures. Crop celebrations often allow a release from the norms of daily behavior, particularly in relationships between the sexes. Harvest celebrations throughout the world support folklorist Roger D. Abrahams's claim that "in our agrarian past, there was a common-sense connection made between the fruitfulness of the earth and human sexuality." At traditional Harvest Home festivals in England, young men and women enjoyed a number of sexual freedoms unusual at other times, teasing each other and engaging in special dances. Revealing the symbolic ties between youthful women and the harvest, members of farm families often constructed a corn dolly, a female figure made of corn or ivy. In Nigeria, the Yakö culture celebrates the harvest season with an elaborate series of rituals including a priest's prayer:

> Today we will eat new yams.
> When a man lies with a woman let her conceive and bear a live child.

Women in some societies in Borneo rub a combination of soot and rice on their bodies, and men giddily chase them. "For a short space of time a certain license prevails among the young people; and irregularities, even on the part of married people, which would be gravely reprobated at all other times, are looked upon very much less seriously." Trobriand Islanders celebrate the yam harvest with a period during which older men and women use "beauty magic" to restore sexual potency and attractiveness. The period of celebration closes with a large dance in which ritualized sexual advances can lead to sexual encounters and often to marriage.[20]

It might be an overstatement to characterize the Southern customs as fertility rituals in the tradition of other, more dramatic harvest celebrations. White Southern farm families did not overtly make the connection between sexual potency and the fertility of the soil; a kiss on the cheek cannot be considered a tribute to the regenerative power of the soil. Nevertheless, the end of an important part of the work year gave Southerners a sense of release from conventional roles and everyday responsibilities. Many of the more important work sharings—corn shuckings and hog killings in particular—occurred in December, the traditional month for recreation in the rural South. Thus, even if Southerners did not make a direct link between the harvest and sexuality, they saw the end of a work season as part of a celebration that allowed the young to take liberties that were unusual and exciting by the standards of Southern evangelical culture. Although the rituals were not really inversion processes as some anthropologists define them, they nonetheless represented a substantial release from prevailing cultural conventions.

The harvest celebrations were a release from evangelical norms, not a sin against them. In an age when personal behavior received close moral scrutiny, no one accused the crop celebrations of immorality. The sexually charged excitement of the cat shakings and the red ear of corn provoked no sermons, no church disciplinary proceedings—as far as records indicate, no moral condemnations of any kind. The same recollections that contain much discussion of religious practices and religious morality give no suggestions that anyone worried that the harvest events might be a bit sinful.

Harvest celebrations vividly illustrate the balance that allowed masculine and evangelical culture to exist side by side. On most social occasions, either evangelical or masculine attitudes were clearly prevalent. Rarely did the institutions of male culture impinge on the daily lives of most evangelicals. Only on such a special occasion as the harvest was it acceptable for the sexes to come together in a way that violated evangelical morals. The fact that the harvest celebrations allowed a release from everyday morality suggests not that Southern evangelicalism was weak or hypocritical but that the culture in which it operated had developed ways to balance its conflicting forces.

Part II
Evangelical Culture

6

The Home

Papa read in his Bible every night. He
usually read the Old Testament. The
New Testament was too meek for him.
Papa was a fighter.
—Sallie B. Comer Lathrop

OFTEN the most mundane activities are the most important.
The most meaningful demonstrations of evangelical Southerners' religious attitudes took place every day or every week, within the home,
usually in the privacy of the family. Despite the importance assigned to
it by historians, the home is still a fairly mysterious place. We know
more about the ideal goals of parenting than we do about what actually
took place within the home. Some feminist historians have taken pains
to find those rare women who professed their discontent with home
life, but we should be sure to examine the activities through which the
great majority of women showed their faith in the virtues of their roles
as wives and mothers. Other historians have described the sense of self-
worth women gained from their home lives without describing exactly
which activities they found so valuable. What religious practices did
families pursue in the home? What nonreligious activities reinforced
their notions of the home as the seat of morality? And what activities
within the home were considered morally unacceptable?

Evangelicals worked hard not to allow into their homes any recreations that seemed to contain masculine forms of excitement or that
threatened the idealized purity of women. Evangelicals did not consider
their homes as places without amusement or recreation; the home did
not represent the denial of all pleasure. However, a degree of serious

piety touched all features of cultural life in the home, making most amusements suspect if not always disreputable. The evangelical home was a sacred institution, standing as a place without sin in contrast to the world outside the home and church. Evangelicals expressed their belief in the religion of the home with four broad qualities—prayer, quiet, harmony, and self-control. All were observed more by women than by men, although men certainly had a part in evangelical life. And all four characteristics identified the home as a counterpoint to and rejection of the aggressive, self-indulgent pleasure seeking of male recreation.

Prayer. In 1863, a home in Mississippi became a church on a Sunday when no local church held services. "There being no service in Bovina, Pa read it at home. Mrs. Wilkinson and daughter and Molly Eggleston came and it seemed really like public worship."[1] The best proof of evangelicals' feeling that the home should have some characteristics of the church can be found in the family customs of group prayer and Bible reading. It is impossible to determine how many Southern families worshiped together in the home, although the numbers were probably far fewer than preachers and church leaders wished. A small South Carolina Presbyterian church reported in 1915 that "about half of our families observe family worship."[2] Nevertheless, religious gatherings in the home enjoyed considerable popularity despite the typical male discomfort with displays of religious sentimentality.

Caroline Coleman, a Presbyterian in western South Carolina, may have overstated the pervasiveness of family Bible reading in generalizing that "in the rural homes in the little Scotch-Irish communities where we grew up, the big Family Bible was the center around which family life revolved." But there is no reason to question her recollection of her own family's evening ritual. "Fresh lightwood knots would be thrown on the fire and the father or grandfather would pick up the Book. Then with the soft firelight flickering on youthful faces in the family circle, he would read slowly and with feeling a chosen passage from the word." Sue Ellen McDowall, the daughter of an Arkansas planter, recalled the family prayers of her 1880s childhood: "This service was a very lovely ritual, participated in by all the household, and to which we were called by my mother ringing a bell for us, to assemble in her room at seven A.M. and nine P.M. daily." A South Carolina Presbyterian minister held that such activities were vital elements of the Christian life: "Family worship is essential to the well-being, if not the very existence, of the family church. . . . The word of God is to be read and expounded as need may require. God is to be addressed in prayer, giving thanks for mercies received, and supplicating his favor and blessing."[3] Bible reading, like all cultural activities, could divide along the lines of gender, as some men found certain sections too mild for their tastes. Alabamian Sallie Lathrop wrote that "Mother was never too tired to teach us the Bible. Papa read in his Bible every night. He usually read the Old Testament. The New Testament was too meek for him. Papa was a fighter."[4]

The evangelical South was a culture dedicated to the importance of prayer, and one of the most important forms of prayer was a family event. In these events the man usually took his place as the head of the family. North Carolina planter David Schenck wrote in his diary in 1880, "According to my usual habit I called my family around the family altar last night and with a melting heart, earnestly and tenderly prayed to my Heavenly father to preserve and bless them all." A young Georgian wrote similarly in 1879, "After dressing my self I went to the breakfast room and there met my dear mother and other relatives around the family altar in prayer." Not all family prayers took place at meals. The son of a Georgia farmer recalled that "one of the first memories of my father was of his prayers with the family at the close of the day as we sat about the open fire in what we called 'their room'— the bedroom of my father and mother. It was in that room we gathered in family worship."[5]

The belief in the power of family prayer was strong enough to inspire intense anxieties in evangelicals whose families neglected the practice. H. C. Morrison, a devout young Kentuckian who became a Methodist minister, recalled that, after his religious conversion at age thirteen, "the fact that we did not have united prayer in the family was the cause of great grief to me. I thought and prayed much about it in secret. I was impressed that I should take up the cross, read the Scriptures and pray aloud with the family . . . every night before retiring." That his family accepted his initiative suggests that the custom of family prayer was well known and respected, if not universally practiced. In a year-ending prayer in 1856, Tennessean Jane Jones worried about her family's neglect of the custom: "I also pray that my dear husband may have strength given him and be enabled to engage in family worship."[6]

Other forms of prayer also show the importance Southerners placed in the activity. Small prayer groups that met in private homes seem to have been fairly common. According to a Methodist journal published in McMinnville, Tennessee: "It is the practice of pious persons, who are striving to be conformed to the divine image, to have private weekly meetings for the purpose of enjoying religious conversation." Georgian Evelyn Jackson wrote of such an event in 1885 without suggesting it was unusual. "Father led prayer meetings and I raised the tunes and Mrs. Hammond talked and Joe Jarrell and Will Reaves prayed and we had a good meeting." Group prayer was for some an evangelical alternative to less acceptable recreations. A Baptist preacher in Osyka, Mississippi, wrote that in the early 1870s his congregation organized a "Young People's Bible Study Circle of a social character, meeting at the homes weekly in rotation. This kept our young members busy, and away from the worldly entertainments that sought in every way to draw them away and into sin."[7]

Quiet. The commitment of Southern evangelicals to an ethic of self-control showed most clearly in their observance of a very quiet Sabbath day. Sunday was the day of "preparation for that rest which remaineth for the people of God." Preparing for heaven meant devoting Sundays to church attendance and, perhaps as important, to quiet religious activities at home. Evangelicals took precautions to avoid work and, especially, any levity or secular excitement. In 1909, a Presbyterian minister in North Carolina expressed the ideal of Sabbath piety when he said that people who rode horses on Sunday "appear to enjoy life even if they desecrate the Lord's day by recreation." The quiet of the day marked it as more sacred than weekdays. A northern Mississippi planter often enjoyed "a quiet Sabbath day." A Louisiana woman commented in a letter in 1892, "How quietly the day has passed, but you know—Sunday is always a quiet day in our home." Some went to extremes to preserve the quiet of the day. A Georgia minister recalled that his grandmother made children walk on their toes "for fear of making the slightest noise."[8]

It was on Sundays that young Southerners first learned the lessons of evangelical self-denial. Clothing reflected not only respect for the church and for the day but also a stifling of freedom and the necessity to act like adults. Girls had to wear their heaviest, most confining clothing. As Caroline Coleman recalled in her autobiography, *Five Petticoats on Sunday*, "Come Sabbath morning and time to dress for going to the meeting house, we would don our quota of stiffly starched petticoats no matter how warm the weather." Boys suffered through corresponding experiences. When he dressed for church on Sunday, Mark Twain's Tom

Sawyer "was fully as uncomfortable as he looked; for there was a restraint about whole clothes and cleanliness that galled him." Louis B. Wright concluded a discussion of his childhood Sabbaths with the recollection that "the worst trials were the Sunday garb we had to wear and the tiresome sermons we had to sit through. In summer we ran around barefoot on weekdays, but on Sunday we had to pull on laboriously shined shoes and to wear a white shirt and necktie." Another South Carolinian dreaded childhood church attendance partly because "they always made us wear shoes. In the summer they burned my feet something awful in that seam that formed when I crammed my feet, that had otherwise been bare and free, into those Sunday shoes that were always getting too small."[9]

Children's normal amusements were prohibited; Sunday was the day for evangelical parents to teach their children to limit their pleasures. Already constrained by tight shoes and hot petticoats, children faced parental frowns at almost every turn. Wright recalled, "We were not supposed to go fishing, to play ball, or to engage in the usual activities characteristic of weekdays." Another Southerner said her mother "made a sharp distinction between 'Sunday' songs and 'everyday' songs. Croquet and other 'everyday' games were nowhere in evidence." A daughter of North Carolina Presbyterians noted, "Sometimes our parents took us for a walk in the woods, but we were allowed no noisy games and no visiting." An Alabamian recalled that she could not play with her dog, and a Tennessean remembered that he "could walk around some, but was never allowed to whistle, to knock on the fence or to throw a stone at a bird." Caroline Coleman and North Carolina native Mary Alves Long shared the strikingly similar memory that "you might sit on the swing, but only if you kept perfectly still." "Should we begin to joggle the swing we were certain to hear the reproof: 'My child, this is the Lord's Day.' " Parents even put temptations out of reach. "Our toys were put away, no games of any kind being allowed."[10]

Sunday afternoons, Coleman recalled, "were long. We were required to learn Scripture verses, the Catechism and hymns." With everyday amusements prohibited, parents tried on this day to make the home resemble a church. Long remembered it as "a day for getting ahead on Bible reading, and Mother several times a day would assemble us in a semicircle, calling on us to read in turn." Evangelicalism's stark and painful side showed most clearly on Sundays, when the demand for propriety often produced either guilt or rebellion. A young Kentuckian showed the pain Sunday ethics could provoke: "I would have great fear lest I should die in my sleep and awake in torment. Especially was this the case if in any way I violated the Sabbath day. Sometimes a party of neighbor boys would come by on Sabbath afternoons and allure me away to the woods for a ramble. . . . In the excitement I would forget, but when the boys would separate for home, I would hurry to the house, trembling with fear. Everything seemed to accuse and condemn me." In a memorable scene from William Faulkner's *Light in August*, the orphan Joe Christmas refuses his stepfather's stern and repeated orders to learn his catechism. Twenty years later he remembers, "On this day I became a man."[11]

For many evangelical adults, Sunday was a day of quiet contemplation. The most pious spent the day in religious pursuits at home. Anna Green, a young woman in Georgia in the 1860s, recorded her efforts to use Sunday as a day for religious purification: "Sundays, Thank God for the day! I can return undisturbed to my religion, and note the progress I am making as a child of God." On a Saturday night she felt she "ought to try to drive from my mind worldly thoughts and imaginings and prepare a frame of mind for the holy services of the Sabbath." Georgian Evelyn Jackson called a Sunday in March 1903 "quite a fine day for meditation, prayer and reading and I think I'll enjoy those blessings much needed." James Hervey Greenlee faithfully recorded his Sabbath meditations for over three decades. Frequent diary entries read, "The holy sabbath day Oh Lord prepare us to keep it as becometh the sacredness of the day, by reading meditation and prayer. May we feel the influence of the holy spirit drawing us nearer and nearer to thee."[12]

As Greenlee's diary suggests, reading religious literature was a popular Sunday activity. At least one denominational journal—the Methodists' aptly named *The Home Monthly*—published special sections for Sunday reading in the home. A Jackson, Tennessee, woman took such reading very seriously, recording on one Sunday: "I have spent the day in reading Sunday School books, and my bible, and prayed 8 times in secret." Rain kept a Georgia woman home on a Sunday in 1868, but "I read 'Child of Jesus' aloud for Mollie, Bobbie and Horace." In 1865 a Louisianian "spent the day alone, read the 'Book of Esther' and several other stories of the Old Testament," and a Georgian recorded, "There was no preaching at the Methodist church last Sunday. I read one of Mr. Spurgeons sermons upon the folly and inconsistency of christians."[13]

Adults examined their own Sunday behavior as closely as they supervised their children's amusements. They often censured themselves for activities that contained a degree of levity or self-indulgence unbefitting the day. A planter and Methodist from Alabama wrote in his diary that a Sunday "was unprofitably spent not as it should have been, reading religious books or periodicals, the bible &c but in luxurying around. I will not do it again I dont think." Georgian Elizabeth Harris fretted on a Sunday night in 1867 that "we have *not* remembered the day. but spent it in idle and worldly conversation." A young man from rural Mississippi realized that he was not fulfilling his Sunday responsibilities after he had moved to Memphis: "To-day like most of my Sundays passed in reading a book, smoking a pipe and loafing around generally. Hardly up to the standard from a religious point of view." Men rarely went hunting on the Sabbath and faced serious criticism when they did. It almost seems that some Southerners looked for reasons to feel guilt. A young woman in Mississippi wrote in her diary in 1908, "We made 'fudge' again Sunday morning and that has been worrying me ever since."[14]

One might argue that a commitment to a Sunday of quiet contemplation and personal propriety betrayed an insecurity in the religious convictions of its adherents. By this argument, the strict Sunday observances involved a concern for the forms rather than for the spirit of religion. After all, if evangelicals were truly pious, God-fearing, and home-loving, why should they need a special day to remind them of their deepest beliefs? Did not Protestants reject the idea that certain days were more sacred than others? For some, no doubt, a pious Sunday followed an impious Saturday night. As minister Numa Reid reminded his listeners, "A people may professedly reverence His Sabbath, and commit abominable wickedness on other days."[15]

It is clear, however, that the observance of a sinless Sunday at home and at church was, for most, a deeply pious activity that was part of a generally pious life. It served both as a weekly day of purity and a weekly reinforcement of evangelical values. Men's diary entries for Sundays differed sharply from their entries for weekdays, showing that Sunday was a day set apart for home and church. Those two institutions—the centers of evangelical life—held a power on Sunday that they held on no other day. Georgia Presbyterian minister James Stacy considered this combination of family and religion vital to a full understanding of the benefits of the day. Nothing, he felt, was "so well suited to the wants of the family, as this weekly reunion. It gives an opportunity for quiet social communion and intercourse which no other day can so well afford. It furnishes a time for parental instruction and training, and also spiritual improvement and heavenly communion, which no other can give. The Sabbath and the family are but the necessary complements of each other." Southerners who strayed outside the boundaries of home and church on this day did so at the risk of strong feelings of guilt. Young Mississippian Clive Metcalfe recorded, "Sally went to church to day. What I ought to have done my-self. . . . Spent the day at the Store with the boys."[16] Spending time with the boys always had a few disreputable connotations—swearing, drinking, perhaps gambling. But on Sundays, Southerners' deepest feelings about proper behavior came to the surface, evoking feelings of guilt in some, in others inspiring deeper feelings of the virtues of the religious life.

Harmony. The most popular Sunday activity aside from church attendance reflects once again the importance with which Southerners regarded the home. The lives of most rural and small-town Southern families were centered in their homes; when they craved some variety, they visited someone else's home. Family visiting was an enormously popular Sunday recreation. Many routinely followed a trip to church with a visit to the home of friends or relatives. Because going to church often required a lengthy trip, staying to eat with local acquaintances was a logical form of recreation.

More than just a time to eat and rest before the trip home, the Sunday visit was a part—for some an almost inseparable part—of the Sabbath experience. In fact, one Louisiana Baptist even hoped that the joys of a Sunday family dinner might compensate for a less than satisfying sermon: "I am sorry that you did not enjoy yourself at church last Sunday. however the dinner you had at Uncle Hugh's made up for all." In the 1890s in central Tennessee, "after church those who lived near were expected to invite those from a distance home with them to a bit of luncheon." Ruth McBroom, born in 1904 and raised in a small community in North Carolina, recalled a schedule of visits that depended on which of four churches her family attended. On the first Sunday of the month the family went to a church near the home of an aunt and uncle, "and we usually went home with them for dinner and to spend the afternoon. . . . On the second Sunday, Little River would have the service. Usually some friends or relatives would come home with us for dinner. . . . The third Sunday church service was at Berry's Grove (Missionary Baptist), and fourth Sunday service was at New Bethel Methodist Church. Usually we went home with someone for dinner and to spend the afternoon after these services."[17]

Many Southerners expected to pay visits or to receive visitors on practically every Sunday. In Madison County, Tennessee, a young woman recorded her activities on one Sunday in 1897. "This afternoon Terry Dozier, Albert Robins, Arthur Roberts and Jessie Groom came over. Late in th Aft. Tip, Terry and Arthur went to Vinson, and Albert and I rode over to see Annie Hudson." North Carolinian William Wallace White noted that on a Sunday in 1907 his household had "quite a lot of company. Misses Annie Sue and Sallie Harris with Wallace from Henderson. Wallace and John Cawthorn. C. M. wife and children. Mrs. Watkins and Miss Emma Hope and Lucy Edwards. Dr Perkins Miss Nettie Seymour." All of the Whites' visitors were traveling to or from church, as was a northern Mississippi man in 1876: "Went with Ginne to church on horseback to Munroe Mr Savage preached. Dined at Mr Camerons. Met Frierson and Wert. Came back by Uncle Daggett's to see Hattie. Ed Miller there."[18]

A visit spent discussing friends and relatives, telling stories, and eating was an unexciting, quiet recreation in the morally pure institution of the home. On these Sunday family visits, men and women congregated in different areas. While the women stayed inside, according to a minister speaking on the subject, the men could "take your pipes and go out on the porch and discuss your business, your farming interests, and your interests of every kind."[19] But the sexes came together for the much-discussed centerpiece of the visit—the Sunday dinner.[20]

Men were thus an important part of Sunday visiting, and many of them participated in the religious idealization of the home on that day almost as fully as women. But on most days visiting in the home was an exclusively female activity. Weekday visiting was clearly the most popular available recreation for rural and small-town women. This was a practice for women of all social classes, with the visits between wealthy Southerners differing from most others only in being longer and sometimes more formal. Carroll Smith-Rosenberg has argued that in the nineteenth century visiting was an essential part of female circles of affection. Joan Cashin has shown, for antebellum Southern plantation women, that visiting among relatives showed women's softer, affectionate natures in contrast to men's friendships that were based on more commercial concerns. Smith-Rosenberg even describes visiting as one of three institutions composing a clearly defined women's sphere, along with the family and the church. Women visited their friends and relatives to help one another with common household responsibilities and with particular problems such as sickness and childbirth, or they visited simply to enjoy the company.[21]

Women practically always enjoyed this recreation in the home, the accepted seat of moral purity where opportunities for sinfulness—particularly overt, aggressive sinfulness—were few. Rural and small-town life in the South was not as isolated as it might seem. Rural women who rarely went to town and small-town women who shunned most town recreations as morally unacceptable nevertheless enjoyed a variety of cultural experiences by visiting in the homes of their friends.[22] They saw different though familiar faces and discussed different though familiar subjects. Women knew what to expect at each other's homes, but visiting was one activity that helped make their lives more interesting and more satisfying.

Countless Southerners spoke of the popularity of visiting. A farmer's daughter born in rural Clinton County, Tennessee, in 1894 recalled that "a lot of visiting was done among close friends. Once or twice a year they would spend the day with each other, and all the news was talked over." During the early postbellum period in rural Arkansas, "folks went to see one another when they wanted to, never out of politeness, and were as likely to drop in at dinner time as at any other hour of the day." Caroline Coleman recalled of her childhood household, "All through the year we expected to have company occasionally, but along in July the visiting really got underway and it lasted unabated until September. . . . Friends simply took turns spending days, and you knew about when the Blanks' visit was due."[23]

The diary of an Arkansas woman, relating her everyday activities, provides detailed evidence about visiting among women. In 1890 Nannie Stillwell Jackson was the thirty-five-year-old wife of a poor farmer in rural Desha County in south-eastern Arkansas. Her diary reveals an extraordinary amount of visiting among women, who traveled usually by foot and occasionally on horseback. The most complete series of entries records her activities during the final months of one of her pregnancies. In a sixty-four-day period, she received visitors on forty-eight days and visited other people's homes on thirty-three days. These visits were almost exclusively among women. On a few occasions, usually on Sundays, her husband accompanied her to the home of their nearest neighbor, but on only seven days did she mention men visiting in her home, and several of those visits were paid by one of her daughter's suitors.[24]

Jackson visited among a circle of about twelve women. All helped each other with their housework, and Jackson and her closest neighbor and best friend, Fannie Morgan, helped each other almost daily. Typical entries referred to sewing together, cooking together, and giving or receiving food. The other practical reason for a visit was to help out or to sit with a sick friend. The number of Jackson's visitors increased in the final days of her pregnancy from a norm of one or two to four or five a day. Her first entry after having her baby reads, "Have been in bed a week; have had a heap of company this week."[25]

Along with these practical reasons, Jackson and her friends also visited simply to chat. Proof that Jackson considered visiting a special, albeit everyday, activity was her habit of changing clothes before a visit, even one to Fannie Morgan. Jackson so enjoyed her friends' company that she complained, despite thirty-three visits in two months, that her pregnancy rendered her life somewhat dull. "I have not been any where only where I could walk since I came home from Mrs Coopwoods the first day of May."[26]

The diaries of most women reveal similar patterns of visiting. A southern Louisianian wrote in 1874 that she "went visiting last week I went some where every day from Sunday mourning untill Saturday night." A woman in northern Louisiana realized that a day without a visitor was a rarity. Mary Elizabeth Rives noted in 1868, "I scarcely know how to write without saying 'company here.'" The schedule of a Handsboro, Mississippi, woman in 1890 showed that she had a visitor almost every day.

Mar. 25. Sue Seaman called this evening, also cousin Lou.
Mar. 26. Mrs. Glen called with Dona Liddle this evening, she is a lovely woman. Mother enjoyed her visit very much.
Mar. 27. Emma Seaman and cousin Lou called this evening.
Mar. 28. Mamie Henderson came up from Pass Christian this evening. We are all glad to have her with us.

Some women who lived in remote rural areas had to make the rounds of their acquaintances on infrequent trips to town. Elizabeth Harris, who lived on a plantation a good distance from Sparta, Georgia, made a day of it. "Started about ½ past 6 to town. . . . I went first to see Mrs Burt— found her better, and she met me at the door. stayed there nearly an hour. then went on up town met Emma Pratt. came in to meet her mother. saw them at the little wagon in front of Littles store as they went home. met Sallie at the store on her way down to Richards. went to cousin Juda Ann's and stayed till after dinner . . . left about 3, came to M's and stopped a little while."[27]

What were the topics of discussion on these visits? All evidence suggests that women typically discussed the mundane features of run-

Women visiting on the porch in Maury County, Tennessee, ca. 1900. The man in the picture is decidedly in the background. (Courtesy of the Looking Back at Tennessee Photography Project, Tennessee State Library and Archives, Nashville)

ning a household. Mattie Cole Stanfield, the daughter of a small farmer in Alabama, once sneaked into her house to hear the conversation of a group of women visiting her mother. The talk "was mostly of children's dresses, of the price of coffee and sugar, and eggs at ten cents a dozen."[28] Also suggesting the probable domestic nature of these conversations was the frequency with which household tasks were combined with visiting. The daughter of a farmer and blacksmith in Leicester, North Carolina, remembered female visiting as a very practical activity: "When neighbors came to visit, they brought their own needle and thimble, and they quilted while they visited." In 1863 a young North Carolina woman noted that "Aunt Lucy and Sarah Shaffner called this afternoon, Sara staid to supper, and we spent the evening sewing, crocheting, &c." In 1907 another Carolinian wrote that a minister's wife "had a 'button hole' party yesterday evening and got a lot of work out of the Ladies who enjoyed the evening." A Georgia woman answered her husband's question, "What have I been doing since you left? Well, Friday after you were gone Mother and I helped sis Sallie on her dress and finished it by night."[29]

If Stanfield's statement that women typically gathered to discuss household affairs is accurate, it may suggest a corrective to historians who have seen female friendships as a veiled protest against the mythology of the home-bound woman. A number of historians, portraying closeness between women as an alternative sphere outside the confining responsibilities of wifehood and motherhood, have endowed the concept of sisterhood with connotations of a latent feminism.[30] Certainly some evidence from the late nineteenth-century South seems to support this argument. Stanfield's recollection that, when women visited, they always sent their children outside suggests that mothers saw visiting as a break from maternal responsibilities. Nannie Jackson's frequent visits to her best friend's house so annoyed her new husband that he "got mad at me for going there 3 times this evening said I went to talk about him. . . . I just talk to Fannie & tell her my troubles because it helps me to bear it better when she knows about it."[31]

Despite this suggestive evidence, however, it seems clear that most women could be satisfied wives and mothers and still enjoy the activity of visiting. If, when women congregated in each other's homes, they talked about their homes, their families, and their households, surely they were expressing something other than a lack of fulfillment. No doubt visiting was not as free from conflict as many women liked to imagine. Opportunities for argument were many, and gossip was surely a common pastime. But women kept their personal conflicts under the surface. In contrast to the competitiveness of the male world, women required in their recreations no clear winner and loser. Such a requirement would have meant renouncing the calm values of domestic life. Visiting was a part of home-centered culture, not an escape from it. A Monroe, Louisiana, woman with a new baby saw visiting as a chance not to avoid motherhood but to glory in it. "Yesterday was a day to make visits, so you know how the day was spent—one round of admiration for my baby she was beautiful indeed."[32]

Particularly illustrative is a well-known form of useful recreation pursued by women during the Civil War years. Sewing circles became popular during the war, in part because they gathered women to do work for "our boys" and in part because they allowed the cultivation of female friendships during a trying time. A Clinton, Louisiana, plantation woman recalled that during the "agonizing, silent seasons the women drew nearer together, and kept busy scraping lint for the hospitals and converting every woolen dress and every carpet left in the house into shirts and bedding for our boys at the front." A group of women in DeSoto Parish, Louisiana, decided that, as the soldiers of the Confederacy had "recently furnished us with a signal instance of their willingness and ability to defend our homes, we propose to organize a . . . sewing society." The sewing circle provides the best example of a domestic recreation. In these groups, women enjoyed themselves in the quiet of their homes while making something useful for husbands and sons at the front. Sewing circles, like other forms of female visiting, showed women enjoying the fact that they were wives and mothers.[33]

Self-control. Only one feature of female visiting drew the criticism of evangelical moralists. Many women, particularly wealthy women, liked to play cards, sometimes for small stakes. Mississippian Mary Susan Kerr, for example, was a frequent churchgoer but nevertheless noted in 1892, "Oh! how gay we are getting! Mrs Klein's Whist party was charming. . . . Last night about 8 o'clock Mr. Rand came and was my partner in a game of Whist against Mr. Jones and Minna, and we beat them quite as badly—We are very dissapated."[34]

A number of evangelicals felt that card playing was indeed dissipation and that female card playing was particularly disgraceful. Clarence Poe recalled that, in postbellum North Carolina, "In some churches card-playing was almost a cardinal sin, and I still remember some flinching of my own conscience when I had to sell a pack of cards in my uncle's store." In the 1860s, "when one joined the church he was expected to give up all such things as cards." Viola Goode Liddell, a wealthy Alabamian who enjoyed flouting evangelical standards, took an almost twisted pleasure in card games: "To indulge in these amusements at ordinary times was bad enough, but when camp meetings were in progress or revivals were sweeping the countryside . . . such pleasures were vehemently denounced as sinful and diabolically wicked."[35]

In an emotional condemnation of all gambling practices, a Methodist minister in Nashville lamented in 1903 that "the seeds of gambling are sown indiscriminately in the home. There is no harm, so far as principle goes between an elegant lady playing cards in an elegant parlor for a cut-glass vase and the ebony-player casting dice for a dime in the back alley."[36] This was strong language to apply to women. After all, women, in Southern thought, represented the height of purity, whereas men generally represented sinners lacking self-control, and blacks—those "ebony-players"—represented the depths of savagery.

The reminiscences of a North Carolinian provide a clue as to why evangelicals considered whist and euchre so sinful. Presbyterian Hope Summerell Chamberlain, born in Salisbury in the 1870s, recalled that as a teenager she and her friends were allowed to play only with a kind of cards that were not from the conventional four-suit deck. "We used to play on the porch of afternoons openly and unchallenged, although cards such as are used in games of chance were forbidden." It was the association with gambling—with the elements of risk and chance—that made card playing in the home so reprehensible. If card games contained no hint of gambling, they were acceptable, though perhaps not thoroughly respectable. A Methodist minister in Georgia complained of playing cards only because he believed it promoted gambling. "Card playing is almost invariably associated with gambling. Without check, the one invariably leads to the other." In 1904, Mississippi Baptist church members included "euchre-playing for prizes" in a long list of activities that they considered sinful, and in 1869 a Tennessee Baptist who was called before the church to answer gambling charges suggested that it was betting, and not merely playing cards, that evangelicals considered particularly unacceptable. He "acknowledged that he played cards for amusement or Pas time for which he is sorry and ashamed but did not bet or hazzard any thing in said game."[37]

Even a Tennessee editor who defended female card players against the criticisms of a Methodist minister made a distinction between simply playing cards and playing for prizes. In one of the very rare occasions in which a local newspaper criticized a minister, the *Giles County Record* defended "a modest and harmless little band of women known as the 'Pulaski Whist Club.' " It is composed of some of the purest and best women of Pulaski and Giles County. Such being the case, it is needless to say that no gambling, or semblance of gambling is indulged in by the ladies."[38] If Pulaski's women had been gambling, apparently, the minister would have had grounds for criticism. In the editor's view, however, the minister overstepped his authority in criticizing a game that did not include an element of risk and the hope of profit.

Gambling generates an excitement that comes from putting oneself on the line by identifying with the element of chance. The amateur gambler takes joy in the hope of getting something for nothing and in the thrill of beating the odds. The gambler becomes as one with the dice, the cards, the racehorse, or the fighting cock and suffers or rejoices as a result of factors largely out of his or her hands. In the evangelical view, home activities ideally represented the antithesis of the experience of gambling. The home represented a constant, a place without chance or risk, a place where permanent values and moral development held worldly excitements in check. Gambling, whether done by women in the home or by men in saloons and at cockfights, violated this belief in the virtues of the quiet harmony of the home.

The home was also the setting for yet another form of visiting that evangelicals feared might lead to sinful excesses. Young men often visited young women in their homes, either during large parties or on less organized calls. Of course, young people met at some social functions outside the home, but the home was probably the most popular setting for courtship. One North Carolinian who was a teenager at the turn of the century recalled, "One never thought of having a date except on one's own porch or in one's own parlor. There seemed to be no need for additional entertainment."[39]

Courting under parental supervision was part of evangelical life. Parents hoped that their children would learn the self-control that would eventually make them responsible evangelical parents themselves. These parents believed—or at least hoped—that they had some degree of supervision over their daughters' callers. In 1910 a Virginia magazine writer advised taking a strong line, insisting that "the mother should choose the company for her daughter." William James Samford, a lawyer, planter, and former governor of Alabama, described a party at his home attended by "one invited, whom Susie knew I did not wish here—(I think she did)—I pray God that I have no Pharaseism in me . . . but a father should be allowed to have some say who should visit his daughters." At young people's parties in Lawrence County, Tennessee, around the turn of the century, "the fathers and mothers of this bunch watched over us with eagle eyes and pretty well kept us in the straight and narrow way deriving their enjoyment from ours." Parents never gained the control over their teenaged children that they wanted, but they felt that youthful recreations could not go far astray under their care.[40]

Evangelical parents always worried that a social gathering might include the sin of dancing. Some even spoke as though dancing could break out unexpectedly against their wishes; the price of dance-free homes was eternal vigilance. Georgia Baptist Henrietta Smith could not withstand the pressure of her houseguests in 1897: "Quite a crowd came. They clamored for a dance but I refused. Finally they persisted in dancing one cotillion which I did not approve but had to submit."[41] Church members had to answer charges before their congregations when dancing took place at their homes, even if they themselves had not indulged in the excitement. Some were excluded from the church simply for hosting dances.[42] One man tried to defend himself by arguing that a gathering at his home "was not intended to be a dancing party, but that the young people met there turned it into a dance."[43]

What features of dancing did evangelicals find so troubling? The dance carried a host of disreputable associations, many of which struck at the heart of evangelical notions of home life. First, dancing was simply too much fun. It showed an open desire for pleasure and violated the quiet and serious introspection evangelicals dem·ded of themselves. Methodist minister V. V. Anderson argued that the activity "banishes serious reflection, promotes levity, folly and useless conversation." Second, dancing promoted—or represented—sexual promiscuity. A minister in Georgia worried that "the close relations into which the sexes are thrown are such as to inflame the animal passions to a very high degree," and Alabama farmer Charles Lewis was concerned that dancing "tolerates a freedom between the sexes both immodest and often resulting perniciously." Third, many forms of the dance were associated with luxury and self-indulgence. Evangelicals had long feared any activities that were part of the flamboyant high style of the plantation elite. In 1876 Louisiana Baptist Nancy Willard wrote that dancing parties showed the degree to which dancers aspired to a luxurious lifestyle: "When I was A child they were not allowed to ware A ruffle on their garments much less go to a dancing party."[44]

Finally, dancing was often accompanied by drunkenness among the men, an event particularly discomforting because women were present. J. Thomas Moore recalled that in the 1890s in rural central Tennessee, "church people opposed dancing and parents would not allow their daughters to attend them. So dances in the neighborhood during my early boyhood were rowdy affairs and not participated in by the best class of young ladies. These were drunken brawls lasting sometimes two or three days and nights at a time. Often ending up by fights and blood shed among the young men." At square dances in rural North Carolina in the early twentieth century, "there were no refreshments; but of course some of the men had their whiskey, and sometimes they would drink too much and have a disagreement." A visitor to Harrisonburg, Louisiana, found that young women had reason to be shocked by men's behavior at dances. "I was at a dance friday night and saw some very nice girls and some prety ones but the men as a general thing are very rough they all get drunk and swere."[45]

Some young evangelicals found ways to enjoy dancelike activities that they did not call dancing. Too many people, especially young people, danced for evangelicals to avoid the activity completely. Clifton Johnson, a travel author who toured the rural Deep South around the turn of the century, found that dancing was popular at parties "if girls enough were present who did not belong to the church. But most of the young women joined the church by the time they were fifteen or sixteen, and after that they would not indulge in so doubtful an amusement." These young women shunned dancing but enjoyed such games as Stealing Partners, Twistification, and Fancy Four, which involved moving while music played. One participant in Cricksboro, Georgia, assured Johnson, "Of co'se these games ain't regular dancing. That wouldn't be allowd at most houses. They're Christian dancing." A native of Rockingham County, North Carolina, born in the 1870s, recalled the same effort to find acceptable substitutes for disreputable amusements, writing that "a 'sociable' was a party without dancing. This latter being so heartily condemned by the elders, games were substituted that required just as much jumping about, if less skill. The music consisted of hand-clapping and singing as they played 'Steal Partners,' 'Husco Ladies Turn,' and other motion games." A Baptist from northern Georgia recalled that his acquaintances did not violate church rules by dancing, "but we played 'Tucker' and 'Twistification.' The former was simply the old fashioned square dance under another name, and the latter a somewhat modified version of the Virginia Reel." Thus, although evangelicals found dancing so objectionable that it was among the most common reasons for church disciplinary action, some found acceptable ways to enjoy activities that closely resembled dancing without the sexual suggestiveness that accompanied some dances and the drunkenness that accompanied others.[46]

But what about music in the home? Secular singing always posed a moral issue. North Carolina Methodist Elizabeth Hawks recalled that, in the 1860s, church members "were not expected to sing anything but hymns. If you happened to hum a popular air, or sing 'Sweet Barbara Allen' or 'Lord Erin's Daughter' someone would say, 'I thought you were a member of the church.' " Tennessean Betty A. Gleaves wrote that "Uncle Wash came that evening and stayed till this morning. he is more worldly than I ever saw him—singing Bright Alferetta and Rosalie the

Prairie Flower."[47] Numerous evangelicals liked to gather in homes to sing hymns. A young woman in Mississippi noted in 1886, "Mr. Patterson is down on another visit. he called last night and we sang hymns until I was hoarse." Another Mississippian wrote to her daughter that on "Sunday, in the evening, whilst we were still sitting around the fire, Jennie commenced playing and singing her evening Hyms." A North Carolina woman told her minister husband in 1867, "Mr. Rankin and Willie are here tonight, we have been singing and talking on religious subjects."[48]

The important point here is that Southern evangelicals felt a constant need to evaluate their behavior. Did a particular activity allow too much sexual freedom? Did it allow too much masculine aggressiveness? Was it too frivolous, too exciting, too giddy? Did it involve drunkenness or suggest an acceptance of luxury? Above all, did it involve a loss of the self-control evangelicals valued so highly? Playing card games but not gambling, singing religious but not secular songs, moving rhythmically but not dancing, all these things bespeak efforts not to violate the boundaries of moral propriety. Evangelical Southerners enjoyed themselves in their homes only within a carefully circumscribed range of activities. If all home activities were not overtly religious in the manner of family altar services, they at least did not involve levity or highly charged excitement. Even childhood amusements—surely the least self-conscious of all forms of recreation—could contain a religious element. A native of rural eastern Tennessee recalled that, in her childhood, "in the fall when the leaves came down, we piled them up and played at baptizing each other."[49] It was in the home that evangelicals faced their primary concerns about personal morality. Despite evangelicals' constant concerns about purifying their own behavior, the South did not see its first serious efforts to enforce a standard of personal morality through legislation until the late nineteenth century. Until then, the virtue of the home and the church was, for most evangelicals, virtue enough.

7

The Church

Crying in the pulpit, crying in the pulpit!
A man ought to be a man even if he does
wear a cloth.
—Louis B. Wright

LIKE the home, the church was a sacred institution in the South. In theory, Protestants did not divide the world into sacred and nonsacred spheres, believing instead that every Christian was a priest and that the entire world was his or her parish. In theory, Protestants communed with God in their daily lives, either through their own understanding of the Bible or through experience with the Holy Spirit, and therefore needed no special rituals to secure or strengthen their faith. In practice, though, Protestants depended primarily on the Sunday service to preserve and reinforce their religious sentiments. It was in the church that people felt closest to God. It was there they heard the sermons that explained the Bible and upheld the evangelical ideal of moral behavior. People acted differently in church, paying a respect to ministers whose strict notions of proper conduct they might or might not have fully accepted in their everyday lives. With a few important exceptions, Southern evangelicals refrained from anything that might resemble sinfulness while they were on the church grounds. The church's own recreational activities were usually designed to have a morally edifying purpose untainted by any hint of sinful self-indulgence.

In 1870 a woman in Alabama wrote to her niece about the significance of a relative's decision to join the church: "Oh I have such good news. We had a letter from Aunt Martha Towers of Jefferson Texas last week telling us that Brother John had joined the Baptist church & had been baptized. I felt to rejoice in the glory of 'His' love & make my vows anew, to love & serve the Lord. John was wild & reckless, & away from home, & friends. To think that he has been regenerated & is truly a christian is one of the happiest thoughts of my life." Joining a church was an important public announcement of an individual's desire to assume the demands and embrace the joys of evangelical life. Church membership was extremely important both to the individual and to all of his or her acquaintances. The information that someone had joined a church was always newsworthy. A. N. Ogden, a young man in Mississippi, reported to his family that his brother Dunbar "has joined the church and I hope and pray that he will always feel as he does now."[1]

This major decision contained important ramifications for future behavior. When Dunbar Ogden told his aunt about joining a church, he added, "I hope you approve of the step I have taken, for I certainly am trying and will continue to try to be a better boy." A young woman in Georgia wrote to a suitor that she was happy he had taken the step even though she had not. "Although I am without the fold, I am glad to see a friend enter. One can have no better testimonial of character than to have it said of him he is a consistent member of the church." A young Louisiana woman wrote to a friend that all her friends had become members, "but I could not feel like I was good enough to join."[2] The frequency of such remarks shows the tremendous importance Southerners placed in church membership. The language of the remarks—"good enough to join," "be a better boy," "no better testimonial of character"—shows that belonging to a church implied a clear commitment to a code of moral behavior. As Elizabeth Hawks recalled of the 1860s, "when one joined the Methodist church he was expected to give up all such things as cards, dancing, theatres, in fact all so called worldly amusements."[3]

Church bodies made clear that membership separated their congregations from the behavior of the larger world. Many churches examined potential members before admitting them. Though it was intended mainly to determine whether a potential member had experienced genuine faith, the process could also weed out those who showed no signs of forsaking a sinful lifestyle. A North Carolinian who presented himself as a candidate for baptism in 1866, for example, "was rejected for the reason, that he has been typsy." Members faced similar scrutiny even after joining the church. The covenant of the Sawyers Creek Baptist Church in Belcross, North Carolina, written in 1872, held that church members should "watch over one another, and in brotherly love pray for each other, and if necessary and in the most tender and affectionate manner reprove each other," according to New Testament instructions. The Brushy Creek Baptist Church near Greenville, South Carolina, formed a covenant in 1868 promising: "We will Exercise Christian Care and watchfulness over each other, and faithfully warn, rebuke, and admonish each other as the case may require . . . that we will seek Divine aid to enable us so to walk, circumspectly and watchfully in the world, denying Ungodliness and every worldly lust."[4] Of course, not every church member lived up to this goal. One Baptist, who often described the sinfulness of her northern Louisiana town, wrote, "It looks strange to me why any one would want to be a church member and still walk in the sinful ways of this Wicked World."[5] Nevertheless, everyone expected church members to behave better than nonmembers.

It was Sunday sermons that inspired Southerners to live up to evangelical ideals. Southern churchgoers took their sermons seriously. They frequently spoke about a sermon's subject, their response to a preacher's ideas and presentation, and the effects the sermon had on their lives outside the church. Georgia Methodist Anna Green, for example, relied heavily for emotional support on sermons she heard during the 1860s. On a Sunday in 1861 she "heard an excellent sermon from Mr. Pierce. He preached about religion affording peace and happiness. The sermon affected me very much." Five years later she repeated the theme. "Mr. Pledger preached a touching sermon, and I felt better than I have in a long time."[6]

The most reassuring Protestant ritual was the simple activity of attending church and hearing the sermon. When denied the opportunity because of health, family responsibilities, or bad weather, many evangelicals lost the sense of peace and happiness Green described, becoming restless or uncertain of the depth and intensity of their religious feelings. One North Carolinian who was in poor health complained, "I greatly feel the lack of not being able to meet with the dear Saints as often as I desire," and a Georgia woman wrote in February 1863, "I have almost become a Heathen, if never hearing preaching makes one. I have been to ch but twice, since the 18th of Sept." Georgian Henrietta Smith described the problem clearly. "I havent been to church in over a month, and the consequence is I am feeling slightly demoralized. I think it is necessary in order to keep ones religion to attend the house of God regularly." Clive Metcalfe, who spent most of his time hunting and running his plantation, worried that his often lonely existence isolated him from the civilizing influences of church attendance. He recorded in 1889 that he "went to church this morning for the first time, I am ashamed to say, in a year. Living in the country one almost becomes a heathen." Temptations to sin were many, and seemingly only the inspiration of frequent sermons could keep evangelicals in line. Southerners' concerns about missing sermons were not due to worries about the ultimate state of their souls; they did not think that church attendance alone would save their souls or that failing to attend meant damnation. Instead, they worried about their personal conduct and the depth of their religious feelings.[7]

Only emotionally stirring sermons could stimulate the commitments of many evangelicals to proper behavior. Southern preachers have long been famous for their fiery and passionate sermons. Baptist leader John Broadus listed the tactics he found common among Southern ministers:

> Among the commonest are a fluttering of the hands, which with some persons becomes a marked habit; a shoving motion, which is appropriate to express abhorrence, or any repulsion, but not otherwise; and a sort of boxing movement. Some work the arm up and down, like a pump handle, and others flap the fore-arm only, like a penguin's wings. . . . It is a common fault to bring down the hand with a slap on the thigh, a movement necessarily ungraceful, or to slap the hands frequently together, which is very rarely appropriate; and some preachers have quite a time of banging the Bible.

A Grover, South Carolina, native, born in 1909, recalled that the preacher at the Baptist church of his childhood used several of these methods: "He could YELL. 'Seemed like sometimes the winders was gonna fall out a' the church. He made col' chills run over me with that thunderin' preachin' he did, yellin' 'n' hollerin', 'n' jumpin' up an' down, poundin', poundin' his fist on the pulpit."[8]

More important than the preachers' methods were the ways their listeners participated in the services. Neither the preaching nor the responses in a church service approached the intensity of those in revival meetings; as we will see, the zeal for conversions gave these services a special fervency. But even the typical Sunday service contained a degree of solemn emotionalism. Mississippi Baptist minister Sereno Taylor considered a service successful when "even the little children wept. . . . Few dry eyes only in the house." A North Carolinian feared for the state of religion in his town when no one cried at the church service: "I heard a good sermon preached to day heare in Kinston—but I didnt see one teare shed. it seems like we are all be come very hard harted."[9]

In general, softheartedness had no place in the masculine world; crying involved the renunciation of masculine selfishness and sinfulness that was central to evangelicalism. Even more frequently than they cried, apparently, church congregations shouted agreement with the minister. At a Methodist church that Charles Dudley Warner visited in Abingdon, Virginia, "at times the able preacher roared so that articulate sounds were lost in the general effect. It was precisely these passages of cataracts of sound and hard breathing which excited the liveliest responses—'Yes, Lord,' and 'Glory to God.' " An observer who disapproved of this practice provided another description. English visitor Mary Allan-Olney wrote that, during a long prayer at the Methodist service she visited, "an old man, near the pulpit, began to groan in the most dismal manner, ejaculating 'Lord!' 'Amen!' 'O-o-h Lord' at intervals, which one would have thought would distract the preacher dreadfully."[10]

How often did rural Southerners attend church? At first glance it might seem that this much-discussed activity occurred infrequently. Small-town and rural churches typically had pastors for only one or at most two days a month. Small congregations could not afford to pay full-time ministers, and, even if they had been able, the number of ministers would not have satisfied the demand. A number of Southerners did indeed attend church only once a month. Ministers typically served three or four churches, preaching in each every four weeks. Many churchgoers, particularly those who lived in the least-populated areas, could not reach any church but their own. An autobiographer from Lake Como, Mississippi, entitled one chapter of his reminiscences "Church Once a Month." A North Carolinian wrote that, in her 1860s childhood in Warren County, "we had preaching at the little country church once a month, and not always on Sunday, it would be when the circuit rider could get there, sometimes on Sunday, or Friday or Wednesday." Even as late as the 1920s, rural sociologists were struck by the number of churches that had preaching only once a month.[11]

Evangelicals, however, found ways to compensate for the infrequency of the services. For example, the members of churches that did not meet every week apparently wanted, and definitely received, sermons that were considerably longer than those preached in urban churches. The lengths varied, but the average sermon in nonurban evangelical churches seems to have lasted close to an hour. John Broadus wrote that a typical sermon in churches that held two services each Sunday should average between thirty and forty-five minutes. But "in the country, where people ride or walk some distance, and have but one service a day, it may be much longer than in town." A Baptist raised in the 1880s stated that sermons in his rural Virginia church averaged about an hour. "Back in those days people did not go as often as now, but they stayed longer." A North Carolina evangelical recalled hearing "a preacher exhort for two or three hours on the awful fate of the sinner, portraying minutely the horrors of a burning hell." Tennessee native Paul Welch remembered the Methodist minister he had to tolerate in his impatient youth as "one of these long winded Parsons[.] from Eleven AM to 1:30 or Two O'Clock was every sundays sermon, and I had to sit through it still as a Cat after a mouse." North Carolinian Fannie A. Tilley showed she had more patience when she wrote of a favorite pastor, "I felt like I could sit and listen to him 3 hours longer and not get tired."[12]

Besides having long services, once-a-month churches tried to extend the time spent in church by having as many services as possible. Many met on Saturday night for a business session, then for a Sunday morning sermon, and perhaps again for another sermon on Sunday night. Church attendance slacked off somewhat in the winter, when transportation was difficult and buildings were cold,[13] but many churches "had extra preaching in August. On Sunday, some churches held three services—morning, afternoon and evening. . . . The really devout attended all three meetings." During summer services at a Presbyterian church in rural Rowan County, North Carolina, "some of the congregation who had come in ten or twelve miles to church did not expect to be fobbed off with but one skimpy discourse; so it was the custom to preach a second sermon after dinner."[14]

Their desire to attend as many services as possible made ordinary Southern churchgoers largely indifferent to denominational differences. In the space of one year, for example, a Clinton, Louisiana, man went to the Methodist church fourteen times, the Baptist church twelve times, the Presbyterian church five times, and the Episcopal church once. Like many Southerners, he wanted to hear preaching and was not very particular about where he found it. On a Sunday in 1876 he recorded, "After going to the Baptist and Presbyterian Churches and finding no service, went to Methodists and listened to a sermon from Rev. Mr. McLauren." Countless rural Southerners habitually rotated their church attendance. A North Carolinian raised in the 1870s wrote that, "there being no Presbyterian Church in the neighborhood, Mother took us by turns to the once-a-month services of the Methodists, Baptists, and Lutherans at their churches." A Grover, South Carolina, native recalled that, by the early twentieth century, multidenominational attendance had become systematized: "For years Grover had two churches. They had the First Presbyterian and the First Babtis'. An' neither one of 'em had a full-time minister. They'd have a preachin' service every other Sunday. They worked out their Sundays so the Babtis' congregation could go to the Presbyterian Church for preachin' on Sundays that they didn't have it. An' the same way with the Presbyterians. . . . They worked together an' got along just fine."[15]

One denomination, though, did not satisfy the emotional needs of evangelicals. Since the eighteenth century, Southern evangelicals had found first Anglican and then Episcopal services too formal and too ritualistic for their tastes. After Methodist Anna Green attended an Episcopal service in Milledgeville, Georgia, she complained that she "could not listen to the sermon, the preachers manner was a little monotonous, then I always find it difficult to follow a written discourse." A Baptist raised in rural South Carolina was very uncomfortable with an Episcopal service in Columbia. "I found it hard to feel a becoming solemnity while they were going thro' their High Church bowings and c. . . . I concluded to consider the source, however." A Southern Baptist professor wrote that the Episcopal church could never find popularity in the United States because "the common people weary of its stiffness and formality. The elevation and uniformity of its ownership would make wide popularity impossible." Upcountry South Carolina native Ben Robertson bore out the professor's words, recalling, "We were opposed to Episcopal ritual, to vested choirs, to stained glass windows."[16]

The ease with which Southern evangelicals moved among churches of different denominations suggests more than the obvious fact that rural churchgoers wanted to attend as many services as possible. Methodists, Baptists, Presbyterians, and many members of smaller denominations saw in each other far more similarities than differences. Even if Presbyterians tended to be wary of the emotionalism of the other denominations, they all shared the same moral beliefs. This common ground helped make the moral attitudes of Southern evangelicalism the accepted morality of the region. Even if many Southerners often deviated from that moral code, virtually everyone had the same ideas about what was right and wrong. Under those standards, it was certainly possible to be a sinner but almost impossible to reject evangelical standards altogether.

William Faulkner's character Joe Christmas shows how church life reflected the primary moral division among white Southerners: "On the Saturday afternoons during and after adolescence he and the other four or five boys hunted and fished. He saw girls only at church, on Sunday. They were associated with Sunday and with church." The place women had in the church showed their role as guardians of virtue. Evangelist Sam Jones linked women and religion in arguing that men who indulged in vices went "farther and farther away from purity, the influence of a mother's prayers and the restraining and helpful ordinances of the church."[17]

More women than men were church members and more attended church.[18] Observers often worried about the churches' inability to attract men. Sam Jones complained that "the altars of our church are pitiably devoid of young men," and Quincy, Florida, minister Charles E. Dowman despaired, "There has scarce been a religious young man here in years." An editor in Elm City, North Carolina, felt the problem was more that "there are but few married men who attend services at any of the churches."[19] Few congregations had the ratio of a tiny Baptist church in Coffeeville, Mississippi, whose membership in the 1870s consisted of twelve women and one man.[20] However, a survey of evangelical church rolls in the postbellum period shows that women constituted a healthy majority of church members. Records for twenty-seven evangelical churches reveal that between 1868 and 1906 women constituted about 62 percent of the churches' members.[21]

Women took part in church activities more than men. A native of Chapel Hill, North Carolina, recalled that in her church, "as is often the case, the day-by-day business of church work was left to the ladies." A business session was scheduled on Saturday at a Baptist church in South Carolina, but "from the absence of the male members there was no meeting." Sunday school teaching was almost entirely a female enterprise, and at least one church feared that, as a result, Sunday school was reaching only female students. The superintendent of the Sunday school in a small Methodist church in Newberry County, South Carolina, felt that the church should make a greater effort to appeal to young men and boys: "I know women are more religious than men naturally. . . . It is right and proper for them to be in charge of the

Members of the Church of Christ in Celina, Tennessee, ca. 1900. By my count,
the picture shows 60 women, 39 men, 2 children of indeterminate sex, and a
dog. (Courtesy of the Looking Back at Tennessee Photography Project, Tennessee
State Library and Archives, Nashville)

school but we are neglecting one of the most important elements of our
congregation . . . the boys of today. Where are they?"[22]

Church seating patterns served as a visible reflection of the religious
division between the sexes. Evangelical churches typically had separate
seating areas for men and women, sometimes with a mixed section for
young people. Numerous descriptions of postbellum churches show
that the seating division was an ironclad custom. One man insisted that
his church's seating arrangement "was strictly adhered to, and I don't
remember ever seeing a person out of place," and another recalled that
"if a man or woman got on the wrong side of the house, that person was
looked upon with suspicion." A Baptist in rural Virginia wrote, "Of
course now and then one would see a man and woman sitting together.
We always knew that they were from Richmond or Lynchburg, or some
other city where folks did not know any better."[23] Practices varied
slightly from church to church. Some buildings had separate doors as
well as separate sections for men and women.[24] Others had a single
central aisle with the men's seats on one side and the women's on the

Wallerville Baptist Church, New Albany, Mississippi. The two front doors repre-
sented the segregation of the sexes in the churches. (Courtesy of the E. C.
Dargan Research Library, The Sunday School Board of the Southern Baptist
Convention, Nashville)

other.[25] In some churches, a more complicated arrangement provided
large male and female sections but also allowed men who so wished to
sit with their wives and children; in others, young men and women were
allowed to sit together at the front of the church.[26]

Moving from the women's section to the men's was part of a boy's
transition to manhood. As a South Carolinian born in the 1890s recalled, "when we boys got about ten, we started sitting with the men,
and felt big." Girls, of course, made no such move. Except perhaps for a
few years in the mixed pews, females spent their entire church lives in
the same section. But boys gained some small freedom from female
constraints on behavior by moving to the men's side. For at least one
Georgia boy, being forced to sit on the female side after having made
the move was one of the traumatic moments of his childhood. G. L.
Vaughn had angered his mother by slipping out of the men's section and
harassing some mules in the churchyard. "Mamma went out and got

me by the eight year old hand, hauled me in through the back door, and sat me on the floor by the chair. And that on the women's side of the house. I had deep humiliation, but not the kind that the preacher told the people to have."[27]

One gets the impression that the male section could be considerably less restrictive than the female section. In 1852, Maria Dyer of northern Alabama explained her preacher's irritation with his congregation. "The male members are noted for their regular naps, and after sleeping during the sermon, come kneel and pray as though they heard it all." Other male activities were even more noticeable. At a Methodist church in rural Virginia, "the women sat on the left and the men on the right, and the right-hand benches were well garnished with spittoons." At a Lutheran church in Spring Hill, South Carolina, "most of the men sat with their group on the left tier, with those addicts who just had to keep their tobacco sitting at the windows, where they could spit." In one rural North Carolina church in the 1870s, "men and boys sat in the galleries by prerogative, and with them associated themselves the hounds which always made part of the congregation."[28] Of course, spitting tobacco and lounging with hounds were not always considered irreverent activities, but in this context they showed that men carried a masculine swagger into the female-oriented institution of the church. For many, spitting tobacco carried disreputable associations. In 1874, a young man from east Texas described spitting, smoking, and drinking as the threesome that made him "the most disapated man you ever saw." A newspaper editor in Hartwell, Georgia, in 1881 agreed, condemning "so-called Christians who go to God's house and spit tobacco juice over the floor so that a decent man can not kneel for prayer. . . . Do these filthy fellows think they would be admitted into Heaven with their pockets full of tobacco, and be allowed to squirt the filthy fluid over the pearly gates and golden streets?"[29]

Some boys, even while in church, openly flouted their rejection of evangelical behavior. The minister of a Methodist church in Camden, South Carolina, complained in 1883 about "certain boys who congregated at the door of the church and by smoking, loud talking and mischievous tricks annoy the congregations. At one time during our meeting a cat with a string tied to its tail and a tuft of paper at the end was put in. At another time a chicken was caught and put in the door." Making a mockery of the services was no doubt unusual, but such behavior shows the hostility of many males toward the demeanor expected of them during church services. From an early age, Southern males wanted a freedom and an excitement that the stern-faced church-goers rejected. It is not surprising that some young people annoyed their elders at church, but it is noteworthy that girls apparently did not talk during services or participate in church pranks. An editor in Conyers, Georgia, condemned "the young gentlemen, and boys who are in the habit of disturbing religious services, by talking and laughing and other disorderly conduct." In Bastrop, Louisiana, in 1881, the editor complained about boys who "talk, and snigger, and wriggle, and twitter while the preacher looks upon them with pitying contempt." The scene outside the churches could turn ugly when young men saw churchgoers as open targets for derision. An editor in southern Mississippi wrote harshly that "the heathen are not all in China. This fact was forcibly demonstrated last Saturday night after preaching when the heathenish hoodlums began shooting their pistols." Such actions were outright harassment, not mere disrespect.[30]

Most men, however, tried to find ways to balance evangelical beliefs with some less upright sentiments. The men's section of the church was always the last to be seated. A Pontotoc County, Mississippi, native suggested that the men from his childhood Baptist church waited as long as possible before trudging into the building at the last moment. "It was customary for a man to accompany his wife or sweetheart to the door, help her up the steps, then turn away and assemble with the other men under the shade of a nearby tree until the preacher began to sing the opening hymn." James M. Eleazar recalled some men who waited even longer. Women and children went into the church immediately for Sunday school, but "the men never went in for that. That is, none except Cousin Tom, the superintendant. . . . The rest of the men congregated under a large oak outside, sat on its roots that had been exposed by erosion, and just whittled and passed the news of the day. When Sunday School was over, Cousin Tom called for the men to come in. But none ever moved until the first hymn was almost finished. Then one or two would start, and the others followed." A Methodist from Algood, Tennessee, even remembered that "a large number of young men who attended church never went inside the church," instead waiting outside to accompany the young women home.[31]

By missing Sunday school, coming in late, sitting in their own section, and spitting tobacco during the sermon, men were indicating that they were not fully comfortable with church life and evangelical sentiment. The aggressiveness and toughness of male culture clashed with the softness and humility of evangelicalism strongly enough that many men had to find ways to stand their ground against full acceptance of all facets of church life. Nevertheless, most men considered the church sacred and believed in the virtues of evangelical Protestantism even while their inclinations warred against some of the church's demands.

Much evidence suggests that men could accept the righteousness of their culture's prevailing religious attitudes without accepting fully the accompanying standards for behavior. In 1884, a Georgia man spoke for many when he recorded as part of a yearly meditation on the state of his life: "I feel religious disposed, but lack much of being a devotee." Louis B. Wright recalled that his grandfather in Donalds, South Carolina, was extremely annoyed by the sentimentality of his Methodist minister but still considered himself a religious man: "He did not frequent church any more than decorum required but he went at proper intervals and saw that I tagged along too. I soon learned that one reason for his spasmodic attendance was his loathing for the preacher, who was accustomed to work himself up into a weeping spell over the sinfulness of man. 'Crying in the pulpit, crying in the pulpit! A man ought to be a man even if he does wear a cloth.' "[32]

Southerners often wrote that their fathers respected religion, but not enough to be faithful in church attendance. The father of comedienne Minnie Pearl, a Tennessee Methodist, was reluctant to accompany his family to church: "It's funny that Mama didn't put more pressure on him to go to church, since it was such an important part of her life. . . . His theory about going to church was that he could communicate with God just as well at home." A Methodist minister raised in Kentucky recalled that although his father "was not a Christian yet he was in sympathy with our mother and did nothing to discourage her in the religious life and made every possible arrangement for her and the children to attend Sunday School and church." A northern Louisiana newspaper reported in 1881, "A Sunday-school boy was asked by the superintendent, the other day, if his father was a Christian. 'Yes, sir,' he replied, 'but he does not work at it much.' "[33]

Evangelicals showed the relationship between gender and morals most clearly in disciplining members for improper conduct. Church members' choices of which activities merited Godly discipline expressed the evangelical connection between home life and the church as well as the tendency to consider men far more sinful than women. According to the disciplinary records of ninety-seven white evangelical churches in the rural South between 1866 and 1915, men were charged

Table 7.1
Disciplinary Charges for 97 Evangelical Churches, 1866–1915

	Males	Females	Total
Drunkenness	1,038 (99.5%)	5	1,043
Drinking	58 (100 %)	0	58
Selling or making liquor	62 (96.9%)	2	64
All drinking charges	1,158 (99.4%)	7	1,165
Profanity	552 (96.8%)	18	570
Fighting	110 (95.6%)	5	115
Gambling	68 (100 %)	0	68
Dancing	312 (57.4%)	232	544
All recreational offenses	2,200 (89.4%)	262	2,462
Sexual and family offenses	108 (40.4%)	159	267
Miscellaneous moral offenses	39 (75 %)	13	52
Unspecified moral offenses	526 (79.7%)	134	660
All moral offenses	2,873 (83.5%)	568	3,441

Sources: See note 34.

with moral offenses five times more frequently than women.[34] Almost all of these offenders in some manner violated the sacred nature of the home or the quiet self-control expected of home life. Almost 70 percent of the specified charges involved the sins of masculine aggressiveness—drunkenness, profanity, fighting, or gambling. If we concentrate only on recreations and rule out charges dealing with fornication, bastardy, adultery, the abandonment of spouses and children, family cruelty, separation, and improper divorce, it becomes clear that churches considered the sinfulness of public recreations to be almost exclusively male. Almost all of the church members charged with drinking and drunkenness, swearing, fighting, and gambling were male. Only on charges of dancing did women hold their own, and even for that sin more men were accused than women.[35]

One might argue that these statistics reflected differences not in men's and women's behavior but in the methods churches used to enforce their moral standards. It was, after all, men who made the charges and, being men, were thus in a better position to observe the unacceptable behavior of other men. Surely women sinned more often than the disciplinary records indicate. But male activities were more public and, usually, more dramatic. They made it fun to be a man in the South, and congregations felt compelled to take strong stands against them.

Some of the most intriguing disciplinary cases involved fighting, because congregations who made such charges were facing a long legacy of Southern honor. Frequently, church members who were accused of fighting also faced charges of drunkenness and profanity, suggesting that many of the fights accompanied the recreational drinking of Saturday afternoons on main street. Churches always demanded apologies for such activities. According to tradition, however, a Southern man, when crossed, was supposed to fight. A number of men argued that circumstances had made it necessary for them to fight, and congregations typically accepted their explanations. A Baptist in Darlington County, South Carolina, "reported him Self for fighting he Stated that he tried to avoid it but he was followed up & struck he further Stated that he was Sorrow that he was forced into it but if it was to occur again in the same way he would act in the same way." He received the church's forgiveness, as did a Mississippi man who told his church that he "unavoidably got into difficulty & a fight & that he was sorry that it had occurred." The latter's language suggests that he wished the incident had not occurred but was not really sorry for his actions. A South Carolina church also accepted the explanation of a member charged with fighting and swearing. He apologized for the latter, but "he could not say he is sorry for having struck Bro. Dodson as he felt he did it in self defense." Given the tension between evangelical culture and the traditions of male culture, fighting was occasionally justifiable, but men still had to defend themselves for it, making it clear that they fought not from malice or for enjoyment but in self-defense.[36]

Just as church life expressed the supposed moral superiority of women over men, so too did it express whites' feelings of superiority over blacks. In the years following emancipation, traditional lines separating the races were blurred. Whites saw blacks pursuing many new activities and, just as important, no longer saw them confined to certain places. It is well known that white planters felt postwar blacks were lapsing quickly into a sad combination of indolence and immorality. It may be less well known that middle- and lower-class whites were also troubled by the moral aspects of racial questions. Many whites felt that postwar poverty and indebtedness put them in a position of dependence and degradation they had usually felt was reserved for blacks. As their fears of living like blacks grew, Southern whites also grew more concerned with moral issues of long standing. More than ever before, they endorsed a view in which blacks represented a savagery that white evangelicals hoped to overcome in their own hearts and lives.

Almost immediately after emancipation, many freed slaves left the antebellum churches of which they had been members, some to form or join local black churches and others to leave the area or join no churches at all. We should not make the mistake of believing that antebellum whites and blacks who attended the same churches in any way participated in a religious communion of equals. Slaves sat in special areas of the churches and often heard special sermons on the religious duties of obedience. Nevertheless, slaves had worshiped in the same churches as whites, and, as long as they did, churchgoing was a mutual activity for both races. But by 1870, most blacks had left the white evangelical churches, and those who remained constituted tiny minorities.[37]

One effect of this black movement out of the white churches was to remove blacks from any contact with whites in a sacred setting. In the postbellum period, most blacks and whites saw each other only outside the sacred and quasi-sacred areas of church and home. As white churches became exclusively or almost exclusively white, black culture came to seem even more alien than it had in the antebellum years. The intensification, in the postbellum period, of white fears of blacks' seemingly animalistic, savage natures surely owed something to the separation of white and black churchgoers. White evangelicals viewed the world outside the home and church as increasingly sinful and threatening, and they felt that blacks constituted an important part of that threat.

Professional entertainment was another outside influence that threatened the purity of church life, and the churches offered respectable forms of recreation as an alternative. More than a place for worship, the church was the most reliable place for many evangelicals to enjoy the company of friends and relatives. We have already seen that churchgoers frequently went early and stayed late simply to enjoy each other's company. The setting gave an air of respectability to most activities that took place on the church grounds. From simple conversations to courting to church fund-raising events, evangelicals could enjoy themselves in a morally acceptable atmosphere. But this atmosphere made some people scrutinize church recreations particularly closely. Much as evangelicals were always wary of home recreations that might violate the home's quasi-religious purity, they likewise worried that some amusements could violate the church's religious purposes.

Perhaps the most important church recreation was also the most unexceptional. The church was the only place many people saw each other, and thus, like the home, it was a primary setting for visiting. S. G. Thigpen described his church in Mississippi in the 1890s as "the only place where people met regularly and visited with each other. Almost everyone would arrive at the church early in order to talk to the neighbors. If the church service was over by 12:30 we would be lucky to get started home by 1:30 as everyone wanted to talk to everyone else and hear the news." Churchgoers frequently mentioned seeing particular acquaintances at church. A Tennessee woman "went to the church met a heap of old friends." In 1876 one Louisianian "went to Sunday school this morning. I saw Bee and Day at the gaite, they were both well." Another "saw Calvina at sunday school she said aunt Bly was not very well." A Mississippian recorded in her diary that she "saw Mrs Gregory at church, had a long talk."[38]

Such conversations apparently concerned mundane, everyday subjects. Some churchgoers discussed absent friends and relatives, and others tended to speak of more practical concerns. Thigpen remembered that while no one would do business at church, "many a horse trade got started at church by some man remarking that he had a nice saddle or plow horse that he did not need." At the Presbyterian church that North Carolinian Mary Alves Long attended, "men swapped news and jokes while their wives exchanged confidences, recipes, or patterns, and saw with their own eyes the latest style in hats or dresses." Cleveland, North Carolina, native Robert Lee Durham recalled the church service as "a community convention, a disseminator of crop reports, a neighborhood news-stand, and a service station of scandal."[39]

Durham also characterized the church as a "rendezvous of romance." This social feature of churchgoing was the most discussed, both by contemporaries and by later autobiographers recalling their halcyon days. For some young Southerners, a trip to church was not complete unless it involved some sort of date. A wealthy young Alabamian had Sunday dates for weeks in advance: "Once a 'new' man asked me when I could go with him to church on Sunday night. I said, 'Eleven weeks from tonight.' " On one night in 1905 a churchgoing young woman in east Tennessee recorded that "this is the first Sunday night I haven't had engagement in a long time."[40]

The parents of young churchgoers, and many of the young people themselves, saw courting at church as an important part of evangelical life. As Mary Long asked, "If marriages are really made in heaven, at what better place to begin than a church?"[41] Meeting under the approving eyes of parents, ministers, and other adults in and around the church building, young men and women would, in theory and often in fact, form the basis for a Christian relationship. Marriage in church would sanctify these relationships, and the couples would go on to live as Christian husbands and wives and, eventually, as Christian parents. In church buildings that had special sections for the young and unmarried, a young man who sat beside a young woman at church was making a very public statement, symbolizing the joining of religion and romance. At least one Tennessee church tried to preserve only a token separation between the sexes: "A narrow piece of lumber down the middle of this row of long seats divided it into two sections. The young folks sat here—the men on the right side of the center, and the girls on the left. Sometimes a brave young man and his girl friend would sit side by side on either side of the dividing plank, and would even share the same song book." Novelist Thomas Dixon, writing of a Baptist church that had no courting section, recalled that his move at age fourteen into the women's section took great courage. "My appearance with a girl on the ladies' side of the church would be a public announcement of myself as a candidate for matrimony. Only boys who were sparking girls were allowed to sit on the ladies side. . . . It was a tremendous thing I'd done on a foolish dare."[42]

For some young Southerners, this opportunity to enjoy the company of a young man or young woman clearly had little or no religious meaning. Some went to church largely or only because young people of the opposite sex were there. The diary entries of one young Arkansas man show his passions for gambling and drunkenness but no apparent religious inclinations. Yet he frequently recorded, "Dan Brannin Sam Pryor and myself carried young ladies to church I carried Joanna Pryor—Dan Sallie P, Sam—Mary Massie." Clive Metcalfe wrote that he "went to church. Long and hot ride but enjoyed myself Went riding with Virginia. I some times think I would like her very much." A college student in Louisiana did at least notice the sermon: "I went to church to night and heard Mr AG Miller preach and had a very pleasant time, and made a mash on a pretty little blond." But a real-life Rhett Butler in North Carolina in 1890 carried no pious notions home from a church service. Writing of a girlfriend, he told a friend, "I gave her a little talking Last night as she went on from church. I talked to her about her soul salvation. she said she believed that she had religion. I told her that she did not have no more religion than my 'ass.' I screwed her before she got home that night, and dont you forget, it was good to me."[43]

For most young churchgoers, however, combining courtship and religion posed no contradiction. The trips to and from church were among the few private times young couples were allowed and thus were very important in bringing a couple together in a religious atmosphere. Adna M. Doyle, a devout North Carolinian, wrote that in 1915 she "fell in love with a wonderful man. . . . We belonged to the same church. We had much in fun together. We would walk to the church and most of our courting was going to prayer meetings on Wednesday nights." Georgian Anna Green described how she got to know her fiancé: "Regularly he would walk from church Sabbath afternoon with me and take tea and spend the evening." Doyle and Green took churchgoing seriously and listened to sermons as part of their Christian commitments; for them, getting to know one's future spouse on the way to or from church was part of living as a Christian youth. Green's son, Thomas Cook, expressed this theme with particular clarity in an 1894 letter to his future wife: "Last evening was the first Sunday evening for many a day that we did not attend church together. The source of pleasure those Sunday night engagements have been to me could not be expressed in words, and perhaps a spiritual benefit that could be lasting."[44]

Dramatizing the connections between church sociability and the domesticity it celebrated were summertime dinners on the church grounds. Between the two services, women served large, memorable dinners for the entire congregation. All churchgoers, even the young men who stayed outside the church during the sermon, met for this meal under the approving eye of the church mothers. These dinners united the church and motherhood in a celebration of domesticity that cast a glow of religious respectability over ordinary activities. Young men and women found in this environment a particularly good opportunity to enjoy each other's company. A native of rural Tennessee recalled, with perhaps too much nostalgia, that "during the noon hour the gathering was, indeed, of a wholesome nature, and many of the teenage boys and girls looked 'cross-eyed' at each other for the first time and later got up the courage to smile at each other." A North Carolinian recalled of the 1870s, "Sports on Sunday being then unheard of, young men would ride miles to attend church, looking forward, of course, to meeting the pretty girls afterward at the 'spring,' or picnic dinner spread on a white cloth."[45]

Another popular recreation—the Sunday school picnic—had several forms, most of which combined religious worship or moral instruction with secular but respectable recreation. Most picnics were for children. At least once each summer, female Sunday school teachers took their students for a day of supposedly constructive play in the country. The children typically spent the earlier part of the day singing religious songs and making religious speeches, and at many of the larger events, local celebrities followed up with moral lectures. A Georgia man wrote that a typical lineup included "a talk by the superintendent, preacher or guest speaker, a song or two, a prayer," all of which supposedly prepared the children to be active churchgoers. After these moral exercises, the children were allowed a degree of freedom they could rarely enjoy in such large numbers. A cynical North Carolinian recalled of one such picnic in the 1880s, "We older girls were needed because there were so many children wild as colts. There was no organized play; they just cavorted when let loose in the country. They terrified the little birds and beasts and made them think it was an incursion of the bloody Huns." But, as in many religious recreations, the entire crowd eventually gathered around the civilizing agent of a huge meal. Even if the children's free play violated the moral lessons of the religious songs, mothers retained ultimate control through their responsibility for the centerpiece of the day—the picnic.[46]

An especially popular recreation for young people was the all-day sing. Small groups met at church or in private homes to sing hymns for two or three hours on selected Sundays, and once a year each church hosted a large event for young people from throughout the area. A travel writer described the events in Cricksboro, Georgia. On most Sundays, according to his account, thirty or forty young people gathered at the church to sing for about two hours, and the larger once-a-year event—"perhaps the greatest pleasure of the year"—drew young singers from a radius of ten to twelve miles. "They came on foot, on saddle-horses, and in all sorts of vehicles, and they brought feed for the horses and lunches for themselves, and each who owned a copy of 'The Old Christian Harmony' brought that to sing from. Not half the people could get into the church, and the surplus lingered about outside and visited."[47]

In 1891 a young Mississippian wrote to his family asking for money because "there is to be a church entertainment at the Methodist church next Saturday night and of course we want a good deal of money." Such entertainments turned contributing to the church from a duty into an amusement. Along with church meals, the most prevalent form of fund-raising entertainment was the moral drama. These tableaux, typically produced by the young women of a particular church, raised money while—it was hoped—teaching a moral lesson. The secular stage usually bore the stigma of immorality, but church plays had no hint of indecency. In Franklinton, North Carolina, in 1890, the local newspaper reported that "the young people are preparing an amateur theatrical for the purpose to aid the moving of the Baptist church. They intend to give the 'Old Homestead,' one of the greatest plays now on the boards." At a Methodist church in Oxford, Georgia, in the late 1860s, "during the Christmas season the young people would sometimes present an entertainment at the church. My mother used to recall especially a play based upon the life of Queen Esther."[48]

These various church amusements may seem innocent enough, but preachers often warned that too many church social functions violated the sacred nature of the church. Some events introduced the element of chance and competition into the church building, and others violated the idealized distance between young men and women. Events that too closely resembled secular entertainment drew frequent criticism. A Disciples of Christ minister in early 1920s Virginia had to tell his new congregation that raffling a quilt to raise funds was an unacceptable activity for churchgoers. In 1904, Tennessee Methodist minister George R. Stuart preached against a host of church amusements:

> I have known church societies to take the gates of a base ball
> park, the receipts of the game to apply to the church building. I
> have known a church to raffle a silk quilt to procure funds for the
> Master's use. I have known the church to solicit the kiss from her
> maidens' lips to augment the treasury of the church. I have
> known the church to defraud the public by so-called oyster soup,
> ice cream and other articles offered for sale, which were but
> abominable cheats and frauds. Let us down with all this business.

A Baptist minister in southern Mississippi in 1889 fully addressed the question of church recreations. Rejecting the extreme position that all social entertainments were by nature evil, T. S. Powell spoke glowingly of the need to accommodate "the large body of young people who find pleasure in society as well as in the service of religion." However, Powell rejected simple parties at the church and all entertainments that raised money, arguing that these events fostered materialism, gave an incorrect impression of worship, and were "also favorable to levity and revelry."[49]

Powell thus rejected anything that introduced into the church an element of risk or the unstructured mixing of the sexes. He suggested that churches could hold sociables, Sunday school picnics, and literary entertainments, all of which were events with adult supervision and an element of moral instruction. Protestants in previous centuries had attacked Catholic saints' days and other festivities that took the form of flamboyant, exciting, gregarious parties. The concern over whether a box supper might violate their culture's notions of propriety only shows how closely Southern evangelicals evaluated all of their actions.

The church provided its members with a social world of recreation in a sacred or almost-sacred setting. From birth to death, evangelical Southerners looked to church life to provide both religious reinforcement and religiously acceptable social entertainment. Many nineteenth-century rural Southerners, particularly Southern women, had few contacts with any cultural institutions outside the home except the church. Numerous diaries describe practically nothing but home activities and church attendance. The church offered a wider variety of experiences than the home, but all those experiences took place under the leadership and scrutiny of preachers and women—the evangelical South's accepted moral authorities. Sunday sermons confirmed the minister's place as the ultimate authority on moral questions. Laymen did not always conform exactly to ministers' ideals, but they did view sermons as a means of strengthening their religious feelings and reinforcing their moral commitments. Although women could not serve as church officials, they nonetheless asserted their civilizing, religious influence over Southern male culture through their place in church seating patterns, their leadership of Sunday schools, and their roles in church recreations. The cultural world outside the home and church was judged by the standards of these two institutions, but only in the home and the church did evangelical values have the accepted upper hand.

8

The Revival Meeting

As the week moved on a boy would
finally pick himself up from the back
benches and stumble up the aisle, and I,
looking back at his fellows, could see
their heads duck and bodies fidgeting:
their turn had come and they knew it.
—Katharine DuPre Lumpkin

REVIVAL meetings were festivals that celebrated the church-centered, home-centered values of evangelical culture. Usually held once a year, they brought together almost every white person in a local area and united them, at least for a few days, in respect for an ideal of upright behavior. For the revival season, the evangelicals held a clear edge in the ever-present tension between evangelical self-control and the aggressiveness of the masculine world. As popular recreations, the meetings mirrored the values of home life and worked against the recreations condemned by evangelicals. As religious events, the meetings made public the commitment of Southern whites to evangelical Protestantism. The public conversion experiences, the mourning at the altar, the emotionalism among church members, and the new commitments to upright behavior were all ways of binding community members to the same attitudes and beliefs. Even people whose wayward behavior placed them outside the Christian community came to the meetings, thereby showing their belief in the truths of the prevailing religion. Revival meetings, some large and noisy, others small and fairly tame, were powerful events that helped maintain the strength of evangelicalism.

144

Revival meetings took three principal forms. The most prominent was the protracted meeting held in a church, during which a visiting minister served for the duration of the revival. Larger and becoming more popular in the twentieth century was the denominational or multidenominational revival meeting held in the towns. Local church leaders often hired a traveling evangelist to hold such meetings in a large tent or public building. The most famous form of revival, the camp meeting, was a community's largest religious gathering, often employing two or even three ministers. Held either outside a church or at a campground established for that purpose, a camp meeting attracted substantial crowds from throughout the area. Though the large camp meeting declined in popularity in the early twentieth century, local meetings continued as a lively and important cultural institution.

Churches almost always scheduled their meetings for the late summer or fall. Newspapers typically began reporting meetings in late July and continued through October. Although one observer suggested that meetings were scheduled "at the height of the summer heat, possibly because at this season the emotional nature of individuals is more readily attuned to religious fervor," most agreed that the timing coincided with "lay-by time," a free period before cotton and corn harvesting.[1]

Since the meetings were held at the same time each year, people could build up considerable enthusiasm and anxiety in anticipation of the events. Church and tent meetings usually lasted about a week, but they might run only three days, or, again, they might gather strength and continue for weeks. Preachers frequently stayed longer than they had planned at a successful meeting; in Georgia one of the longest meetings lasted nine weeks.[2] Camp meetings usually lasted closer to two weeks but could also continue indefinitely.

In one sense the revival meetings were parties—indeed, the largest parties many rural Southerners ever attended. According to participants, the meetings practically emptied the towns and countryside. Businesses closed during the hours of morning sessions, and many closed early for the day so that everyone who wished could attend the night sessions. Members of different denominations felt free to attend any meetings they could reach in a revival season, and the different evangelical churches worked together to ensure that their meetings would follow one another. Even many Episcopalians attended, some in North Carolina participating in a Methodist choir.[3] Packing the meetings even more than members from other churches were many nominal church members and nonmembers. The sinners whom the evangelicals wished to reform typically came to church only for the revivals. A woman from Cowpens, South Carolina, remembered that the three main groups at meetings were "the warm-hearted Christians, the backsliders, and the class who were in those days called 'the lost.' Everybody went to church, the church being the social center, with nowhere else to go and nothing at home to keep one there."[4] The size of the meetings, of course, varied from small church meetings to huge town meetings, but it is safe to say that revival meetings were the largest regularly scheduled events most of the participants attended. One North Carolinian wrote in describing the size of the events, "one would think that Ringling Brothers Circus was in town, not so, just protracted meeting," and a Louisianian wrote in 1881 that "there has been so many protracted meetings and of course everybody went."[5]

The secular festivities at the meetings reflected the home-centered nature of respectable Southern white evangelical life. Revival participants showed a reverence for home life most clearly in the dwellings they constructed at camp meetings. The crude tents of earlier frontier meetings did not satisfy the standards of these Southern evangelicals; by the late nineteenth century they required small temporary wooden homes. Each family had its own miniature home, and each of these huts contained an open fire for cooking. A native of Burke County, North Carolina, recalled that by the 1870s the camp meeting setting "had progressed from the camping stage to selecting some central point and building rude plank huts, still called tents." A Disciples of Christ campground near Okolona, Arkansas, in the 1880s first consisted of a variety of temporary dwellings, from canvas tents to covered wagons to plank buildings, but soon progressed to small permanent cottages. By the turn of the century these cottages were in many areas the accepted camp-meeting dwellings. Campers at the Arkansas campground surrounded themselves with all the features of home, "bringing along their cows for their milk supply and live chickens in coops as well as cured hams, canned vegetables and other foods needed during the ten-day periods. Pine and oak saplings were used to build pens in which to keep varmints." By building surrogate homes in a circle around the church or pulpit, camp-meeting participants created a central setting for the worship services and, more important, a symbol of the union of church life and home life that the meetings celebrated.[6]

The main social event of each meeting was the dinner on the grounds, a huge celebration of the virtues of domestic life. Women cooked their

Dinner on the ground at a protracted meeting at the Alamance Presbyterian Church near Greensboro, North Carolina, ca. 1913. (Courtesy of the North Carolina Collection, University of North Carolina, Chapel Hill)

finest dishes in enormous quantities and even competed informally to see who could prepare the best meals. In South Carolina, one witness remembered, "housewives baked and cooked and fried, and piled the tables under the trees high with lordly food—ham and fried chicken, cakes and pie, hidden among mountains of light bread and beaten biscuit." A minister's son, showing that a revival participant could enjoy the festivities without feeling any accompanying stirrings of the soul, recalled a meeting in his youth: "I was in no hurry to get excited over religion. I would take my time, eat fried chickens and watermelons and think it over." Some evangelicals referred to daylong or two-day meetings as "basket-meetings," confirming the importance of such picnics during the time one Disciples of Christ minister designated "fried chicken season."[7]

Far more than ordinary church services, meetings provided a respectable and popular setting for courting. Young people's letters glowed with language suggesting that they saw the meetings as the social events of the year; the youthful question of who was taking whom to a meeting carried considerable importance. A young woman in Oxford, North Carolina, wrote of a meeting in 1873: "Mr. Peace calls to see if Lillie and I have escorts, nearly every night, and as there are so very few young gentlemen in town, he sometimes has the unspeakable pleasure of escorting us both." Another young North Carolinian wrote to her sister, "I am sorry there isn't a camp-meeting in Eliazar; I am thinking you will not have the pleasure of seeing J.S.M." A Louisiana man wrote to his future wife in 1860, "I am so happy to hear that you will be up at next Camp Meeting. I shall count the days and even the hours." A woman from Greenville, South Carolina, enjoyed her recollections of the social side of the meetings. "The couples drove in buggies along the country roads to church. Moonlight shining through the trees, the rhythmic beat of the horses' feet keeping time to slow moving wheels, made buggy driving to the Protracted meeting one of the long remembered pleasures of the good old summer time."[8]

Despite their popularity as social events, the revival meetings had far greater significance as religious institutions. Good times, gossip, and huge meals gave way to more solemn business as the meetings progressed. Revival meetings meant different things to three very different groups of participants. For some, particularly the young, meetings provided opportunities to undergo conversion experiences and join the church. Long-devoted church members welcomed the opportunity to renew their Christian commitment. Finally, and least obviously, the meetings allowed many of the so-called sinners of a community to show their acceptance of evangelical Christianity even while their actions belied that acceptance. A revival sermon by Georgia Methodist preacher J. W. Quillian discussed the three levels of experience at the meetings: "The toiling Christian strengthened, encouraged. His hope is brightened, and fruit increased. The indifferent and backslidden, with withering leaf and dying hope, bloated fruit is revivified. The sinner whose heart is hard is softened and good seed falls in good ground and springs up to eternal life."[9] These three levels of participation—initiation for new Christians, rededication for longtime Christians, and hope for the salvation of the wayward—reveal the meaning of the meetings as yearly festivals celebrating evangelical beliefs and morality.

To achieve the goals of initiation, rededication, and salvation, each town's evangelical community made solemn preparations for its meetings. In the weeks before the great events, preachers gave special sermons, churches held special prayer meetings, and smaller groups formed to pray for the meetings' success. Newspapers advertised forthcoming meetings and expressed their high hopes for a renewal of religious feeling and a successful harvest of conversions. A Methodist minister in Florida told his congregation to "keep the family altar crowned with prayer for the progress of the work of the revival. Pray for those members of the household who most needed the influence of the revival. Pray for neighbors and friends." A North Carolinian wrote her brother of her preparations, "Two or three of us agreed when the meeting was first appointed to observe every friday before as days of fasting and abstinence, and special prayer for the outpouring of the Holy Spirit." Prior to a large multidenominational meeting in Salisbury, North Carolina, in the 1880s, "there were public prayer meetings, and cottage prayer meetings. Choirs were organized. Pious old maids— people not usually considered of any importance—went around with that expression of joyful exaltation which means the knowing of some blessed secret. Dr. Rumple [the Presbyterian minister] ceased expounding doctrines and began to talk about conduct."[10]

The power of family religion influenced preparations for a revival as it did all aspects of evangelicalism. Parents began teaching their children early to prepare for the events both with prayer and by a denial of pleasure. A child in North Carolina wrote of her birthday, "I had thought I would have a party but the meeting was going so I couldn't so I decided to have a girl's prayer meeting at our house."[11] Parents knew that they played an important role in the success or failure of the meetings. They usually took a son or daughter aside and suggested, sometimes subtly, that he or she consider making the decision to accept the offer of conversion. Before one meeting in Georgia in 1882, Methodist Gertrude Thomas privately told her son "that I would like for him to go to the altar and be 'prayed for' and 'Julian,' said I 'my dear if you would like to unite with the church do not hesitate to do so. Your father nor I will object but will rejoice." Julian Thomas heeded his parent's advice, as did ten-year-old Thomas Dixon when his father made a similar suggestion. The elder Dixon, a Baptist minister, "had become greatly anxious during the last few months for my conversion and baptism into the fellowship of one of his churches." Not until J. B. Ivey was fourteen did his father give him the same advice: "He thought it was about time I was making a profession and joining. I had not thought of it but at the next meeting I went up as a penitent."[12]

Such encouragement was all part of the public nature of religious conversion at revival meetings. Preachers and devout church members used various methods to prompt decisions from nonmembers. T. Elbert Clemmons, a North Carolinian born in the early twentieth century, wrote that mothers often took an active role not only in preparations for the meetings but also during the meetings themselves: "Sometimes they would be asked to go over and speak to their children and urge them to come forward. Good-looking girls would go down the aisles and beg individuals who were known to be lost to turn to a new life before it was too late." W. Clark Medford wrote of a similar custom: "This good preacher and his 'amen corner' members would arise at the song and altar call—and look toward the rear of the church where, indeed, most of the so called 'sinners' made their seats. Then the preacher would call out—as the singing roared to the rafters—for all the Christians to come and help pray for these precious unsaved ones." A well-known sinner in Wilcox County, Alabama, finally made the trip to the Presbyterian altar to the tune of "Oh, Why Not Tonight?": "Whether it was the cue or not, I do not know, but all the worthy sisters and brethren began to file out and descend upon poor Uncle Dave. At first he looked like a lamb before the slaughter . . . as the crowd hovered about him and one began to pray and another to say, 'Amen, Brother.' " A Kentucky Methodist recalled that, at an early age, "immediately after my conversion I took an active part in revival work, going in to the audience to seek souls, instructing penitents to the altar." Members of the evangelical community had a deep interest in enlarging their number during the course of a meeting; not obtaining a substantial number of conversions was their failure as well as a failure for the Christian cause.[13]

Ministers crafted their revival sermons hoping to produce the emotional stress and guilt that would stimulate a desire for conversion. They contrasted in vivid colors the glories of Christian life and afterlife with the ugliness of sin and the horrors of hell. Whereas Sunday sermons typically concentrated on explaining biblical passages, meeting sermons went directly to the point. As Methodist minister William H. Moore said, "The object of these meetings is to promote a revival of religion. It will be well to keep the object definitely before us. A marksman shoots at a particular bird." At Baptist meetings in rural Mississippi, "the preaching was earnest and evangelistic. The appeal was to the heart, in expectation of immediate response."[14] Many meetings were worked by two ministers, one an honored visitor whom few of the revival participants had seen before. One preacher would give a sermon lasting about an hour, and the other would follow with an exhortation, an emotional appeal for conversion that usually lasted about fifteen minutes but could continue much longer.[15]

The climax of the meeting came when the exhorter called penitents to the altar. The Methodists used a special mourners' bench while the

Baptists, Presbyterians, and other denominations generally left an empty space at the front of the church or campground, but all reserved a special place for those who wished publicly to proclaim their acceptance of evangelical beliefs. The Christian churches were an exception; their adherents believed that designating a special bench for mourning seemed to place on God the onus of beginning the process of salvation. Some churches positioned their mourners' bench at a right angle to the other pews so the congregation could get a better view of the penitents' distress.[16]

Going to the altar was a great step; it showed that an individual was willing to humble himself or herself before the local evangelicals. Gertrude Thomas rejoiced when her husband finally expressed a desire to become a Christian "by going up to the altar 'to be prayed for,' thus showing that he wished a change of heart." In Chapel Hill, North Carolina, in 1864, a Baptist minister reported with pleasure that a "meeting [was] increasing in interest. Some 20 or 25 asking prayers." Arthur G. Powell described the events at a meeting in northern Georgia: "After an impassioned sermon, there would be thronged around the altar rail dozens who were weeping and praying, some silently, some aloud, seeking the death of the old man and the birth of the new man, while those who had professed the attainment of the new life stood around singing psalms of praise and crying 'Glory to God!'" The mourners' bench or special altar is perhaps the best symbol of the church-centered evangelical culture of most Southern communities. Before an approving crowd, penitents at the bench admitted their vile natures and behaviors, asked God's grace in converting them, and, at the same time, asked to be accepted by the evangelical community.[17]

Many penitents made the trip to the altar with deep trepidation, fearing the step even as they recognized its importance. To many young men, especially, the trip seemed to tie them to a strict and confining moral code. One minister in Virginia "confronted a young man in the congregation on the importance of seeking religion and his only answer was, 'I am not done sowing my wild oats yet.'" Katharine DuPre Lumpkin eloquently described the tensions inherent in the response to the altar call in upcountry Georgia:

Who would be the first one? Each night there would be a first one. It seemed hard to lead the way. . . . A young girl would go up, her face flushed, her eyes shining; the preacher would take her hand and say, "God bless you, daughter," and kneel down at the front bench. Another would somehow get the courage. It seemed so plainly an act of courage, even though they were all ready for conversion, being of the right age. As the week moved on a boy would finally pick himself up from the back benches and stumble up the aisle, and I, looking back at his fellows, could see their heads duck and bodies fidgeting: their turn had come and they knew it. Some came, but some were a disappointment, as everyone said after revival. Well, maybe another year.

Lumpkin's distinction between the girls with shining eyes and the boys with ducked heads shows how difficult it was for young men to humble themselves by publicly accepting the attitudes of evangelical culture. These men knew they should make the trip—many felt it was inevitable—but they still found it difficult to leave behind the pleasures of male culture. An Alabama woman confirmed this distinction in discussing her children's decisions to join the Baptist church at a revival meeting. "Ruth wanted to join right away but Joel seemed a little undecided. . . . A boy has so many temptations." A Methodist minister in Quincy, Florida, was particularly troubled by the male resistance at meetings. "My heart has been much drawn out for our young men, but though they have been serious and thoughtful hitherto they have been unmoved."[18]

What did the trip to the altar mean? Most penitents went to the altar looking for something that they might or might not receive. Seekers of salvation wanted to know that their worries were over, that they had crossed the gulf between the lost and the saved. Thus many who mourned at the bench did not get the assurance they wanted, especially not on their first trip. Typical was a Methodist's note about a meeting in Virginia. "Much seriousness. Six penitents at the altar; one converted." Some humbled themselves by asking the congregation's prayers many times before finally becoming convinced of their salvation. South Carolinian Bertha Smith told of her troubles between the ages of eleven and fifteen. When she went to her grandmother's church, she "would just have to go to the Altar. Occasionally we went to other nearby country churches for their summer meetings, and I could not but make my distress known. I went forward so much at my home church that I was afraid people would think that I was just going for the fun of it. I could have assured them that it certainly was not fun. Sometimes I would almost hold to the bench to keep from going forward but then I went home feeling worse than when I went; and when I did go, it did no good! Oh, the wretched girl I was!"[19]

Paul Etheridge likewise began going to the altar at age eleven and continued for several years, stating that he "frequently went forward as an earnest penitent to be prayed for. When a protracted meeting would come to an end without my having found relief, I would be fearful that I would not live to attend another protracted meeting." Methodist minister Thomas S. Hubert summarized that the altar service "helps to that self-renunciation without which there is no true repentance. *It is a going from.* It breaks the continuity of influences that are upon the sinner. *It is a going to.* It brings the sinner within reach of other influences, favorable to repentance and faith."[20]

Initiation rituals often hold as much meaning for the larger groups as they do for the individual being initiated. Most people go about their daily tasks without giving serious thought to the question of what, if anything, gives ultimate value to their lives. But members of an in-group are reminded of their deepest, often unexpressed values when an initiate wishes to join their group. Beyond their importance for the unconverted, altar experiences were community events in which church members helped and cajoled the unconverted toward the altar and then observed as the penitents wrestled with and hopefully resolved their spiritual crises. Church members loved the penance and conversion rituals; they found few things more satisfying than seeing someone, whether a young child or a well-known community reprobate, come into the evangelical fold. As one deeply pious Tennessee woman recorded in her diary in 1878, "I talked to the mourners and I felt the love of God in my soul." The relatives of a Methodist in eastern Tennessee "spoke first of this one and then the other who had 'come through' and what a change it would make in the community as many of them were bad boys." Revival meetings, by making the conversion experience a public one, reminded longtime Christians of the meaning and power of their own religious commitments.[21]

Large public baptisms, held at the end of the revival season, showed the importance in which the community held conversions gained at the meetings. North Carolinian C. Waldo Cox described the solemnity of an 1890s baptizing, which took place at a convenient body of water,

> where the spectators might sit on the circular banks and see and hear perfectly. The crowd was immense, and the banks for two hundred yards were full of people; hundreds came early, for it was the crowning ceremony for all the neighborhood churches taking part in the six-week religious effort.
> . . . There were sixty-seven in all, and it took about twenty min-

utes, for it was done slowly and with great dignity. Nobody made a misstep or a fumble in any way. And not another voice was heard, nor a whisper, as the crowd sat spellbound through the entire ceremony.

A Clinton, Louisiana, man recorded an 1876 event at which the crowds were too large to view the relatively small number of baptisms. "About 3 O.clock the people in large numbers assembled at Pretty Creek about one mile from the town to witness the baptizing of six individuals who have recently joined the Baptist Church. . . . The crowd was so great around the small space of ground where the ceremony took place that many were unable to see the parties when immersed in the water." And in 1921 1,500 people in the Greersville, Tennessee, area gathered to watch 40 people baptized in two churches. For most evangelicals, the traditional Christian rite of initiation had become a major spectator event; new converts were pledging union not merely with God and a specific church but with a locality's entire evangelical community.[22]

After the revival season closed with the public baptism, evangelicals had only to count the results. Churchgoers had a terrific interest in the specific numbers of mourners, converts, and new church members. All were concerned with rating the meeting's success and, if possible, savoring the meeting's glory. As a Baptist minister in Mississippi wrote, with a hint of criticism, "The number who join is made the standard of success. Let some one mention a protracted meeting. The first question is, 'Did you have a good meeting?' The second, 'How many joined'; or, 'how many did you get?'" A young Methodist minister in Tennessee spoke for many who pined for concrete results: "I had six penitents last night. I want fifty, but I know it can't be done in a day or a week." A Virginia man wrote hopefully, "The church seemed much revived. Upwards of twenty have been baptized." A multidenominational meeting in Columbus, Mississippi, in 1886 yielded "many accessions to all the churches. About 90 to the M.E. Church, 40 to the Baptist and some to the other churches."[23]

Newspapers frequently published conversion statistics for local churches. The newspaper in Clinton, North Carolina, characterized a Methodist meeting as "a great success from every standpoint of view. There were eighty-six additions to the church." Another paper noted that, at a Presbyterian meeting in Fort Mill, South Carolina, "a good work has been done. Thirty-three names were added to the church roll." Yet another rhapsodized, "Think of 175 people being converted

A river baptism in the mountains of North Carolina, ca. 1910. (Courtesy of the North Carolina Collection, University of North Carolina, Chapel Hill)

in one night! And yet that is what occurred at the Methodist Episcopal tent revival at Siler City last Sunday night." Such references, usually in smaller numbers, appeared throughout the autumn of the year, showing the tremendous interest Southern evangelicals took in increasing their number. A failed meeting was one that garnered only a small number of conversions; many recorded sentiments were similar to those of a Louisianian who complained that "only three joined the church."[24]

Longtime evangelicals thus took joy and pride in seeing their community unite around their beliefs and behavioral standards. But revival meetings did not simply celebrate Southern evangelicals' vision of a Christian life through the communal experiences of the altar call and the public baptism. They also strengthened their commitment to that life. The intense moralizing of the meeting sermons stimulated self-examination in longtime professing Christians as well as in young people and outsiders. For many, the meetings' ability to revive dormant faith was just as important as their ability to produce conversions. A man in Washington, Georgia, equated the two in writing of a coming meeting, "We hope and pray it may be the means of reviving all the church members and the conversion of many sinners in this community." Indeed, when a meeting failed to produce the desired number of conversions, evangelicals consoled themselves with the hope that the sermons and the emotionalism might have strengthened the faith of church members. For example, a Tennessee man noted in 1909, "A protracted Series closed tonight with no additions but we feel that much error and prejudice has been removed and many have learned the way more perfectly." A young Georgia woman similarly described an 1878 meeting. "Only one addition to the Church but I think the church is revived, which is a great blessing." A Christian church minister even preached to a Kentucky congregation in which "the brethren expected no additions, but wanted a meeting for the encouragement of the faithful few."[25]

Many evangelicals described the revival meeting's revivifying function as a simple increase in religious interest. Mississippi Baptist preacher T. S. Powell held that the goal of the meetings "should be a nearer approach to God by all who name his name, a fuller consciousness of the divine presence of the Holy Spirit, pardoning, refreshing, comforting, and strengthening, for the duties devolving upon every follower of Christ." A meeting in North Carolina had this effect on Mary Bethell in 1860: "I have felt since the campmeeting at Carmel that my faith is strengthened I enjoy more religion than I ever did before." By evoking such feelings, the meetings helped restore religion to its proper place in evangelicals' daily lives, giving them new determination to purify their private lives and to become more devoted family members.[26]

Other church members were confronted more dramatically with public sins condemned by preachers at the meetings. Ministers aimed the "heavenly hatchet thrown in the main tent" at churchgoers and longtime public sinners alike. By inspiring or prodding backslidden or moderately committed church members to renounce wayward behavior, preachers used the meetings to stimulate new worries about public sinfulness. Thus these religious festivals often lost their happy, buoyant character and became times of serious self-examination. Sermons were often very specific in the activities they condemned. At a multidenominational meeting in Louisburg, North Carolina, the evangelist was "especially severe on church members who fail to walk circumspectly.

Church members who drink liquor get a severe blow." A Georgia Methodist wrote that, at early twentieth-century meetings, "there was a vigorous denunciation of personal sins, such as card-playing, dancing, theatre-going, mixed swimming [boys and girls], and the like."[27]

Many meetings were successful in reforming a community's behavior, at least for a time. A local correspondent in Wrencoe, Tennessee, reported that during a meeting in 1898, "everybody has quit dancing, and have got to be very sanctimonious, and some of them wear very long faces." Katharine DuPre Lumpkin and her friends also found dancing the object of scorn at a Georgia meeting. They had formed a youthful dancing group at odds with local standards, but at an August meeting, "the preacher aflame at our arrogant wickedness, began his denunciation of our stiff-necked ways, our straying on the downward path, our risking of our precious souls to eternal damnation. . . . Then it began. First one, then the other of our erstwhile companions with the hymn and invitation began to go down that fated aisle, tearful and contrite." Hope Summerell Chamberlain wrote more skeptically of a long series of meetings in her town in the 1880s: "The 'great revival' put the churches of Salisbury in command of the town for a time, making it as decent outwardly as small towns ever are."[28]

One preacher used particularly dramatic methods to inspire renunciation of specific sins. This minister at a large protracted meeting in Greenwood, Mississippi, in 1906 scheduled one night as a "Renunciation Meeting," to which worshipers came prepared to cast off their favorite sin. Some women, for example, renounced their tastes for luxury by throwing their jewels on the altar. In the biblical tradition of smashing idols, one man brought forward a bottle of whiskey, and the minister gave him a hammer with which he dramatically destroyed it. One young boy went to the altar with a deck of "sin cards," which the minister had him burn in front of the congregation. Southerners attempting to find a middle ground between their evangelical sentiments and less proper inclinations heard themselves roundly condemned. Meetings thus worked to keep wayward church members in line either by shaming them into public confession or by at least reminding them of their errors.[29]

Outbursts of emotion often testified to church members' need for religious rededication. Most popular among the lower-class denominations, emotional exercises were a prominent part of many revival meetings; among evangelicals, only the Presbyterians were usually too sedate to take part. These exercises could take many forms, but all helped express and renew religious feeling. Stimulated either by guilt over sins condemned in the sermons, by the emotions of potential converts mourning at the altar, or by the joy of affirming a Christian commitment, the emotional outbursts show the effect the revival meetings had even on devoted church members.

Most of the emotion was intensely solemn and seemingly out of character for such typically controlled evangelicals. Emotional exercises usually centered around shouting. One young North Carolina woman wrote to her sister, who was attending a series of meetings, "I expect when you come home will have to hollow at you, you will be nearly deaf from hearing so much shouting." An Arkansas Methodist recalled that "shouting was free, like salvation, at protracted meetings, and a good many Christians took part in this exercise. Sometimes there would be fifteen or twenty shouting at the same time." At a memorable meeting in Georgia, "One night at the end of the service, somebody began to shout; and in a little while one or two others began to shout; the evangelist stood on a bench and waved his arms dramatically, and he began to shout. In a little while men and women were falling over each other, turning over benches, and everybody shouting at once. It was a regular pandemonium."[30]

A colorful diary entry by a detached observer in western Tennessee shows that a successful harvest of converts could spark particularly heated emotions. While some church members talked to mourners at the altar, "others would be shouting and yelling and pounding the mourners on the back, as if they expected to beat religion into the penitents whether they desired it or not. Occasionally one would 'come through,' then look out for an extra amount of shouting whooping and laughing, more especially was this the case with the women for when one of their friends 'came through' the women could not hold themselves still: They would jump up and down, throw their arms wildly about, laugh and cry by turns." East Tennessean Dora Williams agreed that the typical gender divisions in Southern life showed in the shouting: "When people shouted they were so happy they felt like expressing it in some way. . . . For the most part it was women who shouted, but occasionally a man would shout."[31]

We should see religious emotionalism in the late nineteenth and early twentieth centuries not as a part of other forms of Southern emotionalism but as simple reinforcement of evangelical values. Many past historians, focusing particularly on the frontier period, have described revival-meeting enthusiasm as part of Southerners' tough, hearty, emotional natures. W. J. Cash, for example, claimed that the white Southerner required "a faith as simple and emotional as himself."[32] The solemnity of the exercises, however, and the social ideal upheld at the meetings indicate that shouting represented the very opposite of the assertive self-indulgence of male culture. Suggesting that emotionalism, rather than functioning as a release from domestic constraints, actually expressed the seriousness of Southern evangelical commitment to those virtues are Hope Summerell Chamberlain's description of her town's revival as "intense, earnest" and Plautus Lipsey's recollection that "in the church their faces were serious and tense, their singing was fervent and whispered prayers could be heard all around."[33] According to evangelical belief, women were not expected to express extremes of emotion; they should be constantly warm but never hot. Here, in the revival, was reason for heat. Women rarely saw concrete, immediate achievements quite so dramatic as the view of converts at the altar, and they responded with rare displays of emotion.

Literature's most famous young Southerner helps shed light on another level of revival participation. Mark Twain's Huckleberry Finn shows his belief in the validity of the prevailing standard of conduct he is violating when he decides to accept the consequences of helping Jim escape from slavery. He does not claim that his behavior is morally proper and that he will therefore suffer no consequences because of it; instead he decides, "all right, then, I'll go to hell."[34] In making that decision, Huck shows that even those people who act against the prevailing mores can nevertheless believe those mores to be morally correct. In this instance, he is not a rebel defining new moralities, but a tragic figure, accepting the dominant morality even as his own inclinations rail against it. Many white Southerners—particularly Southern males—were in a similar, if less dramatic, position. Their inclinations toward drunkenness or fighting or dancing or loose living of any kind barred them from full participation in the evangelical community, but they nevertheless believed the quieter, more self-controlled evangelical life to be morally proper. Unlike the fictional Huck, however, most Southerners refused to accept hell as a just punishment for their wayward inclinations. They needed a way to show some loyalty to Christian culture in order to soothe their fears of their immorality and its possible consequences for the next life.

The revival meetings served this purpose well. Many flagrant sinners came to the meetings year after year, confessed their sins, promised to try to do better, and then returned to their old habits. As with traditional Catholic penance and pilgrimage ceremonies, in which participation in a symbolic religious ritual could secure a penitent's salvation, the practice of mourning and professing conversion served to bind to the Christian community many who lived what were, by prevailing standards, wayward lives. For these outsiders, the protracted meetings served the function of a Christian pilgrimage—religious renewal through a trip to a special sacred place. We should not think that the only people who felt a need for religious renewal were those with upright, morally acceptable lifestyles; many of the pilgrims in Geoffrey Chaucer's *The Canterbury Tales*, like many mourners at Southern revival meetings, sinned frequently and openly. Far from rejecting the dominant morality of their time as being inapplicable to their own lives, both Chaucer's pilgrims and the South's outsiders tried to purge themselves of the consequences of these sins through public rituals confirming their Christian beliefs.[35]

One might think that people who rejected evangelicalism would have stayed far away from revival meetings. But on the outskirts of the camps or lingering outside the churches were the outsiders—men and boys lured by the crowds and the excitement but uncomfortable with the religious sentiments expressed and the introspection demanded at the meetings. John Andrew Rice recalled that, at the lowcountry South Carolina meetings of his childhood, "when the going got hot and I felt Hell closing in on me I sought the cool woods, where the talk, and action, was of a different kind. Somewhere in the bushes there was a furtive dispenser of corn liquor, which unregenerate sinners drank, and staggered under the blow. Here was sin indeed, for anyone to see." A newspaper report complained that, at an 1873 Methodist camp meeting in Walterboro, South Carolina, "rowdyism and bacchanalian revelry was carried on to the disquiet of the meeting." At meetings in Auburn, Georgia, according to an observer, "there were always some men and boys who had no intention of going inside the church. They stood outside around wagons, buggies, and cars talking and enjoying themselves. As they swapped stories, arguments sometimes developed, and these arguments could lead to fights." In 1854, at Balls Creek Campground in North Carolina, two boys rolled a hornet's nest to the altar "just as some of the good sisters started shouting." No doubt the mood was more somber twenty-seven years later when the campground experienced its first murder.[36]

Sometimes these outsiders included unsavory characters who so shocked the revival participants with their drunkenness or fighting that meeting planners formed special disciplinary programs. In 1876 the editor of a Georgia weekly was "delighted with the plan adopted by those in authority for the preservation of order during the meeting. The Trial Justice of the District organized his court on the ground—a police force was deputized who had full powers to make arrests, and had it been necessary, disturbers of the peace could have been arrested, tried, and punished without delay." The outsiders at that particular meeting stayed quiet enough that no arrests were made, but in Denver, North Carolina, "the rowdies began making trouble at the camp meetings. They would congregate in the woods at night, their favorite amusement being to throw rocks over the tents and let them fall on the wooden roof of the arbor." Denver's evangelicals formed a special force to combat such disruptive behavior.[37]

Many outsiders went to the meetings just to mock the devout, but some were drawn into the proceedings. Unfortunately, we have no accounts from Southern outsiders telling what it meant to them to participate. Religious sources show that so-called conversions made at the meetings often had little influence on the converts' lives but that committed evangelicals remained hopeful that the apparent conversions would have lasting effects. In 1883 an Alabama Baptist wrote that it was troubling to see those people, some of them nominal church members, "who were the most enthusiastic and prominent and conspicuous in other places and other ways that give no evidence of Christian life. Some of them are sometimes seen in grogshops, drinking with the drunken, or reeling under the influence of some intoxicant, with words and acts degrading to any man, and much more to a man professing godliness. . . . I am objecting to this going back on our profession, this great contrast in so short a time, this falling away." A North Carolina woman wrote in the same vein in 1886, "I hope the peoples goodness will not close with the meeting," and another family member wrote six years later that "all are agreed that the meeting was a grand success if Mr. Krider, one of the converts, is lastingly converted." An Alabama man in 1873 was hopeful about a "glorious revival of religion. Several conversions some of them promise to do well." A less pious local correspondent in Arkansas also doubted whether some conversions were genuine: "The season for protracted meetings has passed. . . . What would the preachers do for material to work on if nobody didn't backslide through the winter?"[38]

Katharine DuPre Lumpkin's autobiography provides the best description of how meetings worked as penance rituals for outsiders. She recalled that "drunkenness was talked about almost boldly, everyone knowing who were the heavy drinkers and who at each annual revival might come up to the mourner's bench once again to vow again to forsake their old past." Louis B. Wright wrote that, in revivals in his western South Carolina hometown, "the town drunk always got up, asked for the prayers of the congregation, and pledged himself to a new life—which usually lasted two or three weeks." Lumpkin described the yearly ritual of a particular mourner, the father of three children conceived out of wedlock. "Once again he was true to his past. Once again the devil and hell and the fiery pit became too much for him; again he repented and went up to the mourner's bench." The mother of this man's children, who stood morally outside the evangelical community as much as any white person in the region, likewise came to the meetings each year but never answered the prayers of church members by mourning at the altar. Although "Miss Sarah" never participated in the singing, praying, or mourning, she must have seen the meetings, her only church attendance of the year, as a way to keep in touch with Christian ideals.[39]

Revivals could inspire momentary commitments in questionable evangelicals of all ages. Mark Twain's Tom Sawyer, always torn between disdain for propriety and awe of religious respectability, is troubled to find his once wayward friends responding to a revival by studying the Bible, taking tracts to the poor, and quoting scriptures. Tom "crept home to bed realizing that he alone of all the town was lost, forever and forever," fearing that a sudden thunderstorm signifies the loss of his soul. Soon, however, he forgets his worries about reforming and is happy to find Joe Harper and Huck Finn enjoying a stolen melon.[40]

We can call the South an evangelical culture only if we realize that people who rarely attended church and who lived far outside the evangelicals' moral code nevertheless found ways to express their belief in the virtues of the dominant religion. Revival meetings provided many white Southerners with the best way to express this belief. For some outsiders, torn between the enjoyment of nonevangelical pleasures and a combination of faith in Christian virtue and fear of damnation, the meetings worked as a release for tension, allowing them to blow off steam in self-effacing fury at the mourners' bench. No doubt most of these mourners sincerely intended to adopt a new lifestyle after the meetings, and all at least saw their revival experiences as important religious events that kept alive the hope of salvation. For other Southern outsiders such as Miss Sarah, the meetings were a time to show they were Christians, if Christians of a special sort.

Committed evangelicals viewed the meetings in a different way. Churchgoers who lived upright lives could tolerate those with objectionable lifestyles because they could always hope that those sinners might, at the next revival meeting, turn their lives around. Partly because of this hope, white Southern culture in the nineteenth century rarely included face-to-face conflict between its saints and its sinners. Despite evangelicals' disdain for nonevangelical behavior, they rarely made frontal attacks on local centers of vice as long as they could hope that sinners might find religion at the coming meeting. The knowledge that almost everyone in the community was a Christian of some sort worked against complete despair over the impure state of society.

Historians have often pictured revival meetings as pleasant social occasions that showed the neighborliness and local character of rural America.[41] In one sense this picture is accurate; the meetings were happy times for experiencing good friends and good food. For example, in 1866 an Alabama man characterized a meeting as "a pleasant week of religious intercourse for the Christians of the neighborhood."[42] However, serious business took place at the meetings, as committed evangelicals, novice evangelicals, and nominal evangelicals all participated in solemn, sometimes painful religious exercises. How can we explain this apparent tension between the meetings' emotionally strenuous side and their easy-going, pleasant side? The only acceptable social recreations were those that met the standards of church and family. The picnics, visiting, and courting in a family setting were the most acceptable secular recreations for evangelicals. Church members welcomed those whose sins violated evangelical standards in hopes that those sinners would finally be converted and change their lives. When those outsiders became disruptive, the evangelicals might bring in a special police force to keep them in line. The emotionalism of the meetings—the mourning at the altar, the churchwide expressions of feeling—was an excitement of a special kind. Unlike the self-indulgent excitement of many consciously masculine recreations, the excitement of revival meetings involved denial of self and renunciation of nonevangelical pleasures in the name of God.

The meetings thus became festivals in celebration of evangelical sentiment. Devoted churchgoers renewed their commitment and enjoyed welcoming new converts into the churches and into a Christian lifestyle.

Nonchurch members and members with weak moral commitments used the meetings to affirm their belief in the essential truths of evangelical Protestantism, even if their behavior often belied that belief. Evangelical religion was never as pervasive in all areas of Southern life as its most devout proponents desired. During the annual revival meeting season, however, evangelicalism reigned.

Part III
Change and Reform

9

Reform: Town, Field, and Fair

The State is only a home
on a larger scale.
—Sallie Colvin

SOUTHERNERS managed to balance the tensions between masculinity and evangelicalism fairly well during the antebellum period. The nature of Southern life enabled men to take both sides, embracing masculine competitiveness while still respecting evangelical self-control. The institutions of evangelical culture allowed men outlets from a normally strict moral code. Both men and women expected men to adhere more closely to evangelical values inside the home than outside it. The church allowed men to slink into the building at the last minute, to sit on their own side of the building, and to spit tobacco. The revival meeting allowed open sinners—most of them men—to make a periodic statement of repentance, even if they tended not to live up to their momentary commitments.

This cultural balance continued as long as rural culture remained relatively isolated. The moral tone of the rural home did not suffer when men drank, swore, and fought only on main street. Evangelical town residents could look the other way easily enough when sin-starved rural dwellers invaded their towns only on infrequent Saturdays and court days. Evangelicals knew where and when the most hot-blooded sinfulness took place in the towns, and it was easy enough simply to avoid the area. Masculine recreations could take place largely unchallenged as long as those who disapproved rarely had reason to see them. Many men sobered up before or during the trip home, leaving the roughness of main street behind them and thus posing no direct threat to the virtue of the family.

Evangelicals' relationship with the law reflected the balance that had long allowed the two cultural forces to exist side by side, if not at peace. Ministers in the antebellum South preached against numerous masculine recreations, but moralists did not appear particularly interested in passing laws to restrict the activities they considered sinful. They accepted the legality of many activities even while they used all their powers of persuasion and condemnation to convince individual sinners to give them up. Church bodies were slow to adopt concrete political stances, generally feeling that changes in behavior could only result from individual conversions. Scattered efforts to reform morals through legislation showed that Southerners were aware of the possibilities of such tactics, but few of them mounted serious, sustained efforts to restrict male recreations. Always uncomfortable with political action, antebellum ministers made only halting and limited efforts at reform. Anne Loveland has discussed "how alienated they were from the society in which they lived."[1] The necessity of compromise and the heated nature of political debate seemed to violate the purity of thought and action demanded by evangelicals. Into the early postbellum period, most seemed to have resigned themselves to the idea that sin had its place on main street just as virtue had its place in the home and church.

The town was the center of male culture, and the most important reforms attempted to purify life on main street. Once Southerners, both male and female, began to have more reasons to go to town and easier ways to get there, evangelicals increasingly felt a need to regulate main-street behavior. In *The Roots of Southern Populism*, Steven Hahn shows that the self-sufficiency of most small farms declined dramatically in the postbellum period. Increasing indebtedness, much of it necessitated by the difficulties of rebuilding after the war, brought a dramatic shift from the production of corn and hogs for home use to the production of cotton for a nonlocal market. As white farmers were drawn into the cash economy, they had more goods to sell and more supplies to buy. With their economic lives no longer restricted to the farm, they had reason to come to town far more frequently.[2]

As the necessity of producing for the market worked against the isolation of the rural areas, so too did the new possibilities for consumption. Historians are only beginning systematically to study the allure of consumer goods in nineteenth-century America, but it is clear that Southerners in the postbellum period were exposed to a tremendous variety of new products. The classic agents of American consumerism—the standardized newspaper and magazine advertisement and the mail-order catalog—were quickly changing Southern life. The postwar expansion of the railroads into rural counties connected urban suppliers to the rapidly growing number of general stores, exposing Southerners to a new range of goods and whetting their appetites for more products than most could afford.[3]

Improved possibilities for travel likewise hastened the decline of the isolation of rural culture. A comprehensive study of individual travel in the South remains to be written. We need to analyze more fully the significance of the isolation of families for whom a ten-mile trip in the 1870s "was an all day undertaking" and for whom a forty-five-mile round-trip took three days—and could last much longer when the creeks spilled over their banks.[4] It is clear, however, that better roads and new railroads, built for the first time to transport people as well as cotton, allowed a degree of mobility that many had never before enjoyed and opened to rural Southerners a panorama of potentially sinful experiences they had not previously encountered. Aside from the experience of travel itself, improved transportation made the towns much more accessible to once isolated rural dwellers. With the coming of better roads and the later popularity of the automobile, the town was no longer so distant from the rural home.

Just below the surface of any feature of Southern life lurked the issue of race. The presence of blacks on the streets, in the drinking establishments, and on the highways intensified whites' traditional association of blacks with a savagery offensive to evangelical norms. Increased access to the towns brought many whites of ordinary means into frequent contact with blacks for the first time. Emancipation led whites to examine many moral issues more closely, out of a new need to identify themselves as distinct from and superior to blacks. Activities long considered unclean, reckless, violent, and self-indulgent seemed even more so when they became linked with the freedmen.[5]

The shrinking distance between Southern towns and the countryside and the new presence of blacks on the streets made the towns increasingly threatening for numerous white Southerners. Evangelicals, both in the rural areas and in the towns, grew more troubled by the frequency of male sinfulness on main street. Religious spokesmen slowly began to mount a series of largely uncoordinated efforts to refine the roughness of male culture. One by one, new laws made crimes of activities long considered to be sins, thereby limiting the ways men

could enjoy themselves. The towns that had been largely a male preserve increasingly felt the influence of those who lived according to the
values of the home and church. In contrast to reform movements in the
Northeast, where new moral issues often concerned the rise of the city
and large-scale immigration, the South's moral reform efforts concentrated on main street. Prohibition, the most important effort to enforce
evangelical values in the South, received its support from the countryside rather than the cities.

The impulse to purify Southern culture found its most dramatic
outlet in the movement to prohibit the drinking of alcohol. Drinking
and drunkenness accompanied almost all male recreations; the campaign against it was an attempt to reform male culture itself. The
history of temperance and prohibition in the South reveals a gradual
decline of the cultural balance that had long allowed masculine aggressiveness and domestic evangelicalism to coexist. Moralists had spoken
and preached against drinking for decades before they tried to make it
illegal. Antebellum temperance societies, never as popular as they were
in some Northern areas, asked only that their members refrain from
drinking.[6] Efforts to pass prohibition laws in the 1850s were scattered
and poorly coordinated, and only a few counties banned the sale of
liquor. In the late 1870s and the 1880s, when more evangelicals began
to grow concerned about drunkenness and its effects, many accepted
compromise measures aimed at isolating drinking establishments rather
than abolishing them altogether. Only near the end of the nineteenth
century did most counties begin outlawing the sale of liquor, and only
in the early twentieth century did those efforts succeed at the state level.

A number of historians have discussed the important role of the
evangelical family in shaping the prohibition movement. The saloon
died out as the combined influence of home and church moved beyond
the former boundaries of those two institutions. In *Deliver Us from
Evil*, Norman H. Clark describes the ideology of the middle-class Protestant family as the central motivation behind prohibition. Clark has
made a good start toward identifying which features of alcohol seemed
to threaten the sanctity of the home. First, and most obviously, drunkenness squandered money that could be used to support the family,
wasted time that could be spent more profitably, and rendered the
drunkard unfit for either work or family life. Second, the saloon allowed forms of behavior that violated the peace and harmony expected
within the home. As Clark writes, "It was the *public* character of saloon
drunkenness—the foul-mouthed, blasphemous drunk, reeling and stag-

gering from saloon to street—that so deeply offended the sensibilities" of the religious set, even when it posed no practical threat to the family income.[7]

Historians who neglect this second objection to drunkenness miss much of the emotional force behind the prohibition movement. Too many sophisticated works deal with drinking and drunkenness only as ways in which people relieved psychic stress or expressed communal or ethnic loyalties. Certainly this was one of its purposes, but it is essential to remember that drinking, above all, was recreation, and that the movement to prohibit drinking was, in large part, a movement to abolish an important male recreation. Scholars in recent years have treated prohibitionists with a remarkable degree of sympathy, reacting against an older position that saw them as antimodern hayseeds trying to impose village values on an increasingly complex society. One after another, historians have argued that prohibition was a logical and, many suggest, laudable way to deal with specific social problems. Anne Firor Scott, Jean E. Friedman, Ruth Bordin, Barbara Leslie Epstein, and Anastatia Sims have portrayed the Woman's Christian Temperance Union (WCTU) as an agency of heroic feminism that allowed women to use political activism to break free from the shackles of domesticity. W. J. Rorabaugh does not praise the prohibitionists, but he sees their movement as a logical response to the pressures of high economic expectations and limited opportunities in nineteenth-century America. James Timberlake, Paul A. Carter, and K. Austin Kerr have portrayed prohibition in the early twentieth century as an important and worthwhile part of the Social Gospel movement.[8] No one, apparently, wants to see the prohibitionists as sour-faced neo-Puritans trying to make sure that no one had too good a time. They were more than that, to be sure, but sour-faced they were. It is essential to remember that prohibitionists managed to make illegal an enormously popular recreation with roots deep in the history of human civilization.

The clearest evidence that Southern moralists were concerned not merely with the practical consequences of drinking and drunkenness but also with drinking as a sinful recreation can be seen in their efforts to reform the nature of the saloon. In early compromise measures, antidrinking forces tried first to isolate drinking and then to regulate it before they attempted to abolish it completely. Four-mile and five-mile laws, which some counties passed in the early postbellum period, outlawed drinking establishments near schools, churches, and camp-meeting grounds. This early form of zoning legislation attempted to protect the balance that had long existed between masculine culture and the home and church. Under these laws, children did not have to see drinking establishments between their homes and schools, and churchgoers did not have to turn their heads as they passed saloons on Sunday mornings. Drinking could continue only out of sight of more respectable institutions.[9] Proponents of dispensary systems hoped to go one step further by eliminating the saloon and its attendant evils without eliminating drinking. Operated by state or county governments, dispensaries allowed no drinking in groups or on the premises and none of the saloon's accompanying activities such as gambling and billiards. Thus, the dispensary system was, above all, recreational reform, attempting to take the fun out of drinking. Evangelicals were never happy with the system, but it nonetheless stood as a symbol of their desire to tame main-street drinking behavior.[10]

Prohibitionists always associated drinking with a loss of self-control, a concern that was becoming ever stronger in the postbellum South. Just as many prohibitionists outside the region were concerned with the drinking behavior of the great numbers of recent non-Anglo-Saxon immigrants, white Southern prohibitionists were troubled and often frightened by the drinking behavior of blacks.[11] Antebellum laws had prevented the sale of alcohol to blacks, slave or free, but after the war black men enjoyed drinking in the towns as much as white men did. One of the many hostile and suspicious beliefs of Southern whites linked the freedmen with wanton alcoholism. An Arkansas editor, complaining that "every Saturday is a day for free fights," asked, "Is there no way to stop the boistrous profanity of drunken negroes here?" A Georgia prohibition writer argued in 1890, "The contrast between the race sober and the race free and addicted to liquors is very great. It reveals the mightiest evil that has come to them as a consequence of their emancipation." A Methodist minister in southern Georgia made the same complaint in 1899. "We talk of the negro problem, of the brutal crimes of the black men, and the mobs that disgrace our civilization, when every thoughtful man must know that the problem is intensified ten fold by the saloon and the jug. . . . Stop the sale of intoxicants in Georgia and every white woman will breathe more freely." The concerns went beyond drinking; many complained that blacks were involved in selling liquor illegally, poisoning the minds of young whites both with their company and their crime.[12]

Fears of drunkenness among blacks only contributed to the image of the drinking establishment as an arena for masculine sinfulness. Blacks, in the minds of white Southerners, signified closeness to the animal world, lack of self-control, and lack of civility—qualities that evangelicals also associated with the recreations of white men. Opponents of the saloons often used dramatic and vivid language that portrayed drinkers as near-animals controlled by their passions. One called alcohol "the ravager of the negro" because it "fed their animalism." Other whites worried that the same trait was exhibited by drinkers of their own race. Evangelicals felt that "the appetite for strong drink rages like an inward fire." Whiskey, they said, left a man "a worthless beastly non entity." Intemperance "inflames our baser passions and leads to ruin." The saloon served the combined forces of "avarice, appetite and lust." An instigator of a drunken brawl was "a very passionate and lusty man." Drinking establishments bred not only crime and violence but also "beastliness and shame."[13]

As this rhetoric suggests, prohibitionists often linked their cause to notions of sexual purity. Particularly revealing of their efforts to control the beast within men was a pledge the WCTU required of boys who joined an auxiliary organization in Georgia in 1888. The boys promised to treat women with respect, to refrain from profane language, to "avoid all conversation, reading, pictures and amusements which may put impure thoughts into my mind," and to preserve their bodies "in temperance, soberness and chastity." Saloon decor in particular drew the ire of antidrinking moralists. One pointed out "how 'the nude in art' had long been used to degrade the dignity of womanhood by saloon-keepers." A Methodist minister wrote of the same phenomenon in 1870, urging that a decent man should "turn away mortified because of the depravity of his own sex and the exposure of the female sex. Is there pleasure—can there be pleasure—to a son or brother as he looks on and sees his mother's and sister's sex exposed and placed in so many different and nude attitudes?"[14]

Some moralists spoke as though prohibition could produce an effective reformation of all features of Southern morality. Ending both the temptation and the opportunity to drink, they hoped, would raise the moral tone of all male culture. But others tried to smooth away the roughness of male recreations with various laws prohibiting activities long considered immoral. Counties, and then states, passed a series of laws that attempted to bring main street up to the evangelical standards of the home and the church.

These moralists went after swearing as well as drinking. During the postbellum years, almost all Southern states either passed some form of antiswearing law or refined antebellum laws. Virginia, Tennessee, and Mississippi had antiswearing laws before the 1850s, and the rest of the states followed suit between 1859 and 1909. The fact that several states passed laws designed to reinforce those already in existence and to expand the areas in which swearing was forbidden shows the influence of the new moralists. Into the early twentieth century, evangelicals were still trying to find new ways to control the excesses of Southern masculinity.

Some laws made all public swearing illegal, but many punished people only for swearing where women could overhear.[15] Like zoning laws that did not allow drinking establishments near churches or schools, these antiswearing measures did not outlaw masculine recreations but instead attempted to isolate them. Indeed, a Methodist minister in Georgia complained in 1907 that the laws allowed too much profanity. Laws, he said, prohibited many other sinful activities, "but no account is taken of this fearful sin, unless it happens to be committed in the presence of ladies." Alabama and Tennessee punished "any person who, by rude or indecent behavior, or by profane or obscene language, willfully disturbs the females at any public assembly, met for the purpose of instruction, amusement, or recreation." Other laws in Georgia and Alabama simply outlawed all swearing in the presence of females, and the goal of protecting women from the vulgarities of profanity surely guided other laws that prohibited swearing in or near homes.[16] Activities that were regulated or prohibited along with profanity show that the sentiment against swearing was part of a larger reaction against masculine recreation. Louisiana's antiswearing law also outlawed firing guns in public and racing horses on public streets, and laws in South Carolina and Alabama specifically associated profanity with drunkenness.[17]

Evangelicals were particularly concerned that the improved transportation and communication networks of the postwar period would expose the chaste to a degree of vulgarity they had never before encountered. As the world outside the home became more accessible to rural Southerners, moralists felt an intensified need to cleanse their society of its many impurities. Because improved roads and railroads brought women to town and into a larger world and thus threw them together with numerous profane individuals, new laws were passed to outlaw swearing on trains. Because the telephone added a degree of impersonality to communication between men and women, a 1913 law in North Carolina outlawed swearing at female telephone operators.[18]

Also facing new attacks in the late nineteenth century were the traditional connections between recreation and violence. Whereas antebellum laws had prohibited acts of personal violence, laws in the postbellum period made new efforts to refine the overall roughness of male culture. These new laws went beyond merely protecting citizens against injury, attempting as well to restrain passions and promote harmonious relations among individuals. Coupled with some of the antiprofanity laws were others forbidding the use of language that, according to a 1909 Arkansas law, "in its common acceptation is calculated to arouse the person about or to whom it is spoken or addressed, or to cause a breach of the peace or an assault."[19] Other activities related to personal violence also came under attack. For the first time, several states passed laws against carrying concealed weapons, and some outlawed the firing of guns near homes or on streets or highways.[20] In 1897 the Georgia legislature outlawed shooting on railroad pleasure excursions and at picnics.[21] Moralists were particularly concerned about the exposure of children to the roughness of male culture, so some states passed laws that forbade giving or selling guns to minors, and Tennessee even prohibited the distribution of toy guns.[22]

Blood sports first drew the attention of evangelical-minded lawmakers in the postbellum period. Between the 1870s and the 1890s, several states outlawed the increasingly popular sport of prizefighting.[23] But boxing was more a modern, urban phenomenon than a traditional sport of the small-town South. More important were laws prohibiting the fighting of animals. Between 1875 and 1881, every Southern state but one passed laws outlawing activities that inflicted unnecessary pain on animals, and Florida finally followed suit in 1901. Some of these laws specifically outlawed sports involving the fighting of bulls, bears, dogs, or cocks, while others more generally forbade the torturing or tormenting of animals.[24] The proponents of self-control gained new police powers, as the states granted members of authorized societies for the prevention of cruelty to animals the right to arrest animal abusers and turn them over to local authorities.[25]

As James Turner has suggested in his study of Anglo-American humanitarian sentiment, this heightened concern for animals was part of a broader desire for increased self-control that developed in the late nineteenth century. Taking joy in purposeless violence seemed to be a pleasure related to the animal kingdom and hence was unbefitting to the self-controlled evangelical. Identifying with animals, as those who enjoyed blood sports did implicitly by betting on and rooting for certain animals, seemed the height of uncontrolled savagery. Humanitarian sentiment in the South always had a strong religious element to it; proponents of self-control had no stronger ally than the churches. Women of the humane society in Shreveport, Louisiana, easily secured the cooperation of local ministers in proclaiming Humane Sunday, a day on which ministers mentioned cruelty prevention in their sermons and facilitated the distribution of anticruelty literature. Also linking humanitarian sentiment to Christian progress was a young South Carolinian who spoke at the unveiling of a new water fountain for animals. Bringing an end to cruelty, he said, was important "in its tendency to develop a Christian spirit, and a gentle nature in the human race; for there is no doubt, that cruelty in any form, manifests a hard heart and one that regards not the teachings of the Bible."[26]

Religious reformers were equally concerned about Sunday recreations that contradicted the values of home and church. Writing to support the restriction of Sunday train travel, a Presbyterian minister in Georgia spoke up for maintaining the tradition of the Sunday dinner. "Nothing," he said, was "so well suited to the wants of the family, as this weekly reunion. It gives an opportunity for quiet social communion and intercourse which no other day can so well afford."[27] Since the colonial period, laws had prohibited work and some forms of recreation on Sunday, but postwar Southerners felt a need for stronger legislation to ensure the quiet of the day. Not until the postbellum years did most states forbid the sale of alcohol on Sunday.[28] Several states prohibited the Sunday enjoyment of specific activities such as baseball, football, golf, tennis, and bowling, and some banned any activity that involved shooting guns, including target shooting.[29]

By the end of the century, men in Southern towns faced a host of restrictions on their ability to enjoy themselves with their traditional vigor. Their freedom from constraint on main street was quickly becoming a thing of the past, as men had to examine their drinking and sporting habits and even their language in response to new laws. The fierce combativeness through which men had proved themselves worthy in each other's eyes gradually succumbed to the dictates of evangelical self-control as fighting animals, fighting with words, shooting guns in public, and carrying weapons became illegal. Of course, the passage of state laws did not mean that all these restricted activities ceased. Only a detailed study of local laws, the methods and frequency of enforcement, and state and local judicial decisions could reveal the degree to which some activities continued and others declined. But the passage of such laws indicated a heightened sense of the need to reform the moral tone of the towns. The newspaper advertisements that in the nineteenth century had proclaimed the public acceptability of saloons could not be found in the twentieth. Masculine recreations could continue only under restrictions; men had to limit their pleasures and play by rules designed by moralists and legislators with evangelical values. They had to think before they fought, scheme before they bought whiskey, and look over their shoulders while they enjoyed themselves. Even if many still sinned in traditional ways, they were no longer *free* to do so. Men faced laws demanding that the towns be places without combat, without personal drama, without profanity, without drunkenness—in short, places very much like the ideal evangelical home.

During the late nineteenth century, the hunting field, like main street, lost its character as a setting for complete freedom from restraints. The campaign against certain aspects of hunting was not an overtly religious effort, but the evangelical goal of self-control provided the moral basis for hunting restrictions, as it did for prohibition and the other offensives against masculine recreation. Facing, for the first time, restrictions on when, how, and where he could hunt, the Southern hunter found it increasingly difficult to blast away as freely as he wished. Words of caution first joined and then replaced words of praise in local newspapers. As a Northern sportswriter noted of the typical Southern hunter in 1909, "Nowadays he seldom exhibits a photograph of himself in the midst of a ton of birds he has shot."[30]

The first challenge to the freedom of the hunt came in the form of postbellum changes in fencing practices. The antebellum practice of fencing in crops and allowing livestock to run freely on the open range allowed Southerners to hunt over tremendous areas and to claim any game they killed as legally their own. Although a few planters growled about the open range prior to the Civil War, none made serious efforts to enact mandatory fencing laws until after emancipation. The laws were part of the planters' larger effort to secure exclusive rights to their own properties and to restrict the movement of freedmen, but they also had the effect of frustrating hunters of both races in their pursuit of game. A landowner had only to post a no-trespassing notice in a public place or on his land to make hunting on his property illegal. Some antebellum Southerners had always considered it ungentlemanly to hunt on someone's land without asking permission, but laws passed in the postbellum years made first verbal and later written permission mandatory.[31]

Fencing laws in the 1860s were passed, according to historian

Charles L. Flynn, because of fears of what the freedmen might do, not from any desire to force drastic changes in traditional hunting practices. Few local authorities wanted to spend their days chasing roving hunters off marked land.[32] On the whole, fencing laws posed little threat to hunting practices until the early twentieth century, when game wardens working under new state agencies began more vigorous prosecution of trespassers. When these wardens—who were paid by the number of convictions they made—began cracking down on offenders, hunters for the first time had to be careful about trespassing. Around Wadesboro, North Carolina, in 1907, for example, "not only the law but landowners also are getting less lenient with hunters who find it quite difficult to take a very extensive hunt and not 'trespass.'"[33] Despite their sloppy enforcement in the nineteenth century, the laws increasingly restricted the freedom of hunters to indulge in the full thrill of the hunt unrestrained by human conventions.

A far more serious threat was the conservation movement that mounted slowly and crystallized in the shape of laws and state agencies designed to protect game from overly indulgent hunters. An Alabama man remembered that in the 1870s, "There were no game laws or reservations on hunting and the slaughter was terrific."[34] But local and state laws multiplied throughout the postbellum period, particularly in the 1880s and 1890s—establishing hunting seasons, setting bag limits, requiring hunting licenses, and outlawing certain hunting and fishing practices. Planters and nature lovers were concerned that binge hunting during animal mating seasons would lead to a depletion of resources and to the possible extinction of a number of species. Part of the drive for restrictions came from sportsmen who professed a new willingness to limit their kills and refine their hunting practices in order to safeguard the declining animal population, and part came from planters who wished to keep farm workers out of the forests and in the cotton fields.[35] But the moralistic rhetoric behind the new laws shows that the conservation movement represented more than a simple desire for social control.

In the conservation movement, hunters finally faced the limitations on behavior that evangelical culture demanded. Conservationists were offended by the excesses and the cunning and savagery of so-called game hogs. They valued balance in all forms of behavior and could only respect the hunter who confronted his prey face to face and limited his number of kills. Hunting reform, like laws against drinking, swearing, shooting, and animal fights, was part of an effort to instill self-control in those members of the population who lacked such a virtue. As James Turner has written, the urge to control the animal within man helped give rise to the animal protection movement. "Wildlife conservation itself taught the sportsman a valuable lesson in self-control and self-sacrifice."[36] One can hear the moralist who is shocked by the vulgarities of the untamed rabble in a 1908 report by the Alabama Department of Conservation:

> Wise and discreet individuals who feel no inclination to make as-saults on Nature's store-house should have their rights protected by the enactment of strong laws to restrain the hands of the wan-ton and reckless, whose vandalism would annihilate every visible thing of fin, fur or feather, to gratify their savage instincts. . . .
>
> The strongest tendency of game laws toward conserving the public weal is the effect they have of taking guns out of the hands of the shiftless roving class.

Four years later, another report from the same department condemned those who "masquerade as sportsmen who in reality are but rapacious slaughterers of wild life. These seek to satiate their desire to accomplish its destruction even with voraciousness of their savage progenitors."[37]

"Satiate," "desire," "voracious," "savage"—this is the language of evangelical moralists. Even if only a few considered themselves part of a religious crusade, hunting reformers interpreted the need for change from an evangelical perspective. Conservationists directed much of their most righteous language at black hunters. A game warden in Choctaw County, Alabama, for example, complained in 1914: "The darkeys in this community commenced to hunt opossums weeks ago. . . . We should be protected against these night marauders." Others complained of a "roving army of pot-hunters and negroes," of "the worthless negro strolling over the fields with guns," and of "negro boys and ignorant persons."[38] These blacks posed a practical threat to the economic interests of white landowners. But they also represented a threat to whites' conceptions of their own morality. White men had long walked a line between the enjoyment of unrestrained hunting and a desire to feel more civilized than blacks. In the postbellum years, white hunters found that balance harder to maintain. White men could not hunt with the wild self-indulgence of their forefathers because wildness and self-indulgence were, more than ever before, identified with blacks.

The hunt, perhaps the last respectable male outlet from Southern evangelical culture, had by the early twentieth century come under the scrutiny of those who demanded self-control and a balanced life. The setting in which men and boys could indulge in the fury of unrestrained pursuit and the gluttony of a binge kill had finally drawn the ire of evangelical moralists. Throughout the nineteenth century, few women or churchmen had even hinted at criticism of Southern males' hunting habits. But by 1910 a Baptist weekly stated that "conservation is another word for sunshine in the hearts of men and women. It signifies the holding of the good things of the earth in their proper places, and scattering rays of happiness wherever its principles are practiced."[39] Women's groups provided some of the funding for Audubon societies. And, surely symbolizing the conjunction of female and evangelical cultures, the South's first Audubon Society was formed in 1902 in the chapel of the North Carolina College for Women.[40]

The laws of North Carolina counties in 1906 illustrate the extent of the new hunting restrictions. Almost every county limited deer hunting to two or three winter months and hunting for quail, wild turkey, and most other game birds to three or four winter months. Fourteen counties set hunting seasons for woodcock, nine counties set seasons for snipe, and twelve set seasons for pheasant. Fourteen counties prohibited opossum hunting, and three others set three- or four-month opossum seasons. Fifteen counties prohibited squirrel hunting, and seven others set squirrel seasons. State law prohibited the hunting of non-game birds, and a number of counties required hunters to obtain written permission for hunting on land other than their own. Other states passed similar laws, set bag limits, and restricted hunting practices that had made killing game particularly easy. Laws in some areas prohibited killing more than one deer, two wild turkeys, or twenty-five game birds in one day, and county laws in most states prohibited night hunting, hunting with lights or fire, hunting with handguns, and killing young deer, does, and turkey hens. In the same spirit, new fishing laws prohibited the use of nets, seines, and dynamite.[41]

Like the fencing laws, hunting laws were only weakly enforced until the early twentieth century. In 1908, according to the newly formed Alabama Department of Conservation, county hunting statutes "were never respected and were openly and notoriously violated. The cause of persistent infractions of the local game laws was that there was no specially constituted service to enforce these statutes. No one felt called upon to prosecute his neighbor, and while all agreed that the game and fish should be protected, yet these were constantly violated by prominent persons." The Audubon Society of North Carolina likewise asserted that, before they began their work, "many magistrates found it difficult to believe that game laws were seriously intended to be enforced."[42] The proliferation of game wardens, hired by the state conservation agencies that formed throughout the South between 1900 and 1920, helped alleviate this problem. The state departments quickly began to record numerous arrests each year. North Carolina secured 108 convictions in 1907, South Carolina had 98 in 1908, Alabama had 472 in 1913–14, and Arkansas had 240 in 1917. By the late 1920s, North Carolina officials were securing over 1,000 convictions each year.[43] These numbers were hardly enough to fill the prisons with convicted doe hunters and seine fishermen. However, a hunter faced with a possible fine or short jail sentence had to think twice about bagging more than his limit, hunting out of season, or using hunting tricks.

Southern hunters recognized that they faced new limitations. Editors began to boast of the lawfulness of their local hunters rather than their abilities as marksmen. One reported that a party of Macon, Mississippi, quail hunters in 1914 "had good luck, but like all good citizens did not break the law by killing more than the law allows." By 1921 a Tennessee editor could ask his readers, "Won't you and every citizen of Martin feel the responsibility of protecting the squirrels in our park and throughout our town? Some boys are doing their best to kill them. What are you doing to prevent it?" The same editor, in a direct slap in the face to the traditions of Southern manhood, also suggested collecting nuts to help feed those squirrels. In the early 1930s, farmers in Arkansas told a sociologist that they allowed their dogs to chase foxes but did not try to kill them, explaining, "They's a law in Arkansas protectin' foxes, and if any one should get caught it would be onfortunate for ever who owned the dawgs." In 1907 Thomas Samford had bragged that he and a partner had killed ninety-seven doves; two years and a new state law later, he stated of a dove hunt, "I killed 25, the limit the law permits, and had to quit shooting." This irritating necessity to quit shooting ran directly and painfully against the joy the hunt had long provided—the joy of unrestrained self-indulgence.[44]

Of course, the new restrictions did not ruin the sport of hunting. Southern men and boys continued to enjoy the hunt, in large part due to the conservation laws that protected game from extinction. Men and boys could still find excitement outside the normal bounds of cultural life, and they could still experience the passion of the kill. However, the laws were part of a larger effort to organize society around the goals of self-control and moral propriety, and the more they restricted hunting practices, the less Southerners could enjoy the wild freedom of the field.

"The State," according to a speaker at a Louisiana county fair in 1907, "is only a home on a larger scale."[45] With the growing importance of agricultural fairs, the farm, like the town and the field, began to feel the effects of government reforms that upheld evangelical values. Along with their mission to bring modern scientific methods to rural farms, the fairs offered a model for each gender that celebrated domestic life and criticized the rough and physical nature of traditional male culture.

The harvest and work sharing celebrations once so meaningful to rural culture fell before the commercialization of agriculture and the technological innovations that accompanied it. With the decline of self-sufficient family farming came a new desire to mechanize most agricultural processes. The fodder pulling was the first to go when agricultural experts began telling farmers that fodder pulling harmed plants' growth. New machines introduced in the early twentieth century were able to grind corn stalks and ears into feed.[46] New technology likewise brought the downfall of the corn shucking when a machine that could pick corn and remove the husks was marketed in 1902.[47] The growth of the marketplace also worked against work sharings. The hog killing lost its significance as a cultural event simply because of the decline in ownership of hogs for consumption.[48] Log rollings became unnecessary as the South's lumber industry, which had long catered primarily to markets outside the region, had by the 1910s begun selling to average Southern farmers.[49]

We can also speculate that commercial farmers were probably less inclined than their predecessors to take part in group activities. Perhaps farmers who helped friends and neighbors feed their families were less willing to help them succeed in a cash economy. By the 1910s and 1920s, Southerners routinely recalled work sharings as part of an almost forgotten past. A South Carolinian born in the 1890s wrote that he "came in about when the old-time corn shuckings were going out." An Arkansas native recalled that "log-rollings and house-raisings, which had been a familiar part of frontier life for generations, were on the ebb" during his 1870s boyhood.[50]

The small fairs that became extremely popular in the first quarter of the twentieth century reflected the changing ways in which farmers celebrated the harvest and the end of the work year. Folklorist Roger D. Abrahams argues that the local fair is the clearest continuation of the harvest celebration in twentieth-century America. "Here each year the products and processes of farm work are cleaned up and transported to the fairground for purposes of display and competition. No occasion more fully projects images of increase and plenitude in their ideal forms. For here the animals, fruits, and vegetables are presented to us in cleaned-up and cooked-up form."[51] In Southern fairs the "images of plenitude" were transformed from images of the corn shucking or the fodder pulling into images of scientific agriculture and technological improvement, carried out under the approving eye of state departments of agriculture. State agricultural extension offices sponsored most of the new fairs, particularly the smallest ones, providing cash prizes and setting standards for judging exhibits. It may seem odd to view the local fair—typically seen as a classic institution of traditional rural America—as an agent of modernization and centralization.[52] However, by providing a setting in which rural Southerners celebrated their harvests in a self-consciously modern way, the fairs reflected the changing directions rural culture was taking in the twentieth century.

Both county and community fairs gained their popularity as the agents of modernity. Fairs grew quickly as state agencies sponsored attempts to educate farmers about new agricultural techniques. In 1873 the *Rural Carolinian* counted only twenty fairs in all of the Southern states, most of them fairly large, urban gatherings that had little effect on small-town life.[53] Comprehensive statistics do not exist for all Southern states, but figures for North Carolina show the striking growth of smaller events. According to an Agricultural Extension Service report, the state's total of 30 fairs in 1914 had increased to 251 just four years later.[54] Between the 1880s and the 1910s, each Southern state formed farmers' institutes in hopes of taking to the smallest towns the latest developments in scientific agriculture and, eventually, the latest in the household arts known as domestic sciences. State colleges and universities typically made modest beginnings by sending experts to speak to local agricultural societies, and by 1910 the legislatures in each state had placed the farmers' institutes under the auspices of the state departments of agriculture.[55]

Agricultural innovators had long wondered how to interest small farmers in scientific advances, but the rhetoric of modern agriculture began to penetrate rural life only with traveling speakers from the institute programs and with contests at the fairs. Contests at fairs were certainly nothing new, but the custom of having the state provide the prize money, set the standards, and train or even recruit the judges was novel to the South. Local boosters interested in modernizing their communities started fairs in the county seats and then in smaller communities with the help of institute speakers and prize money. Fair programs and local newspapers sang about the joys of progress that the events could bring to rural areas. A 1924 fair in Winterville, Georgia, resembled "a mirror reflecting the progress made in every line of activity in which this community engages." The purpose of a 1916 parish fair in Lafayette, Louisiana, was to "keep abreast with advanced agricultural methods that our community may take front rank, and cope with the revolutionizing influences and changing customs that are annually taking place."[56]

What did these notions of progress mean for the traditional tensions between masculinity and evangelicalism? What moral ideal did the fairs uphold? The experiences of people who attended local fairs in the twentieth century in some ways resembled those of Southerners who took part in nineteenth-century corn shuckings, cotton pickings, and quiltings. The division at the fairs between male and female contests continued the division at work sharings between male and female recreations. Like the work sharings, the fairs had specific locations reserved for men and women. The area for stock and crop contests became a male quarter much as the barns and fields had been at work sharings. The women's sections replicated the home, the center for most women's recreations. A small community fair in Gleason, Tennessee, in 1921 illustrated the rigid distinction between the recreational spheres of the sexes: "In the men's section a good corn exhibit was to be seen and a special display of corn exhibited by the Boys' Corn Club members which attracted much attention. . . . In the Ladies' Department everything was to be seen that make up the art and fruit exhibits seen at a fair. The nice needlework, canned fruits and vegetables were attractively arranged and of nice quality."[57]

Not present in the educational exhibits and contests of the fairs, however, was the sense of release that rural Southerners had enjoyed through the rituals of the red ear of corn and shaking the cat. The fairs celebrated the virtues of motherhood with their domestic science exhibits and contests for the best household articles, but they did not include swaggering masculine attitudes as the work sharings had. Whereas the work sharings had allowed men and boys to show off their strength and speed, agricultural contests at the fairs emphasized reason and technical skill. Mind rather than muscle became the central feature of these harvest celebrations. By diluting the toughness of male recreations, then, and by upholding women's domestic virtues, without allowing any form of release, the fairs' exhibits and contests represented a turn toward the moral goals of Southern evangelicals.

Women who visited the household exhibits encountered attempts to bring modernity to everyday home life. Spreading the gospel of domestic science became as much a crusade as spreading the good word of progressive agriculture. In a speech delivered at a fair in Opelousas, Louisiana, in 1898, Mrs. Stephen F. Read dwelt on the virtues of modernized motherhood: "The wife, having given careful study to the laws of hygiene, knows the urgent necessity of properly cooked food, and cheerfully acknowledges the culinary art to be the finest of the fine arts. . . . The educated farm wife fully understands the importance of sanitation in all its many ramifications of ventilation, cleanliness, pure water, sensible clothing, and so on through all the elements that make up comfort, contribute to health, and thus make happiness possible."[58]

By setting standards for even the most mundane household products, state agencies used the fair contests to promote a state-sponsored definition of progress. Fairs offered contests for women in hundreds of practical categories from sewing to cooking to canning. Some even touched on the smallest areas of housework, offering prizes for specimens of patching, for remade dresses and hats, or for the most ordinary foods such as biscuits and corn bread. Quilts, which had been such an important part of the traditional work-sharing rituals, became only one of many exhibits under the movement to make all things modern and improved, to make routine work easier, and to improve the health and cleanliness of the home. Extension agents developed detailed guidelines for judging all products, rating canned vegetables in seven categories and garments in eleven categories.[59]

Even baby contests were described in the language of progress. Fair planners urged mothers to enter only babies that had been raised according to modern ideas about hygiene and nutrition. The Chilton County Fair in Alabama offered a prize for "the nearest perfect, best developed and best nourished baby." In 1916 the Lafayette, Louisiana, fair committee extolled its Better Babies Contest as

a popular yet scientific movement to insure better babies and a better race. It consists of entering, examining and awarding prizes to children of five years or less on exactly the same basic principles that are applied to live stock shows. Mere beauty does not count. . . . The Better Babies Contest insures a better race of Americans, because it teaches parents how to improve the physical condition of children already born and to protect those yet unborn. It arouses interest in the conversation of child life and health and in all forms of child welfare. It forges a connecting link between parents and teachers, between the home and the scientific study of child life.

The fair promised, "If your baby is up to standard, he will win a prize. If he is not, you will be told how to make him a prize winner next year." Pediatricians were on hand to deliver on this promise.[60]

An increasingly popular feature of the fairs were competitions intended to prepare girls for modern homemaking. Girls entered contests of their own in many of the same sewing and cooking categories as their mothers, but their greatest interest was in the canning clubs that the extension services helped form in the 1910s. Members of these organizations, also known as tomato clubs, often prepared huge spreads of fruits and vegetables; girls in Spartanburg, South Carolina, canned several hundred jars of tomatoes apiece in 1911. In the spirit of progress that marked these events, many fairs offered canning-contest winners the prizes of a ten-day or thirty-day university course in domestic science.[61]

The men's contests and exhibits matched those of the women and girls in their goals of progress and modernity. Many of the technological changes that had brought about the decline of work sharings became objects for display and competition. For example, the Farm Implements and Agricultural Machinery Exhibit at a Washington, Georgia, fair included contests for the best cotton planter, corn sheller, corn mill, pea thresher, peanut picker, mowing machine, and feed cutter. The Talladega County Fair in Alabama awarded the winner of the contest for the best specimens of corn by grinding the corn in an innovative new device, and manufacturers of all new farm machines typically showed them at the fairs.[62]

The drive for modernity also transformed the more traditional contests, with extension agents developing elaborate categories for judging crops and livestock. Competition for prizes of several dollars required attention to very detailed agricultural techniques. The cattle contests drew especially great attention, as farmers attempted to breed and groom the finest specimens possible according to the standards of scien-

GASTON COUNTY FARM LIFE SCHOOL
SANITARY SANDWICHES AND COFFEE
5¢ EACH

At Gaston County Fair Oct '16

Modern domesticity: a booth for young women at the Gaston County Fair, North Carolina, 1916. (Courtesy of the North Carolina Collection, University of North Carolina, Chapel Hill)

tific agriculture. In North Carolina, stock raisers faced elaborate score-cards by which their stock was judged; the extension agents had to consider twenty-four features of beef cattle, twenty-two features of hogs, and thirty-seven features of draft horses.[63]

Boys' corn clubs and pig clubs resembled the girls' canning clubs in their use of the fairs to prepare the young for modern life. The clubs became enormously popular, partly because they had well-attended yearly shows at the fairs. Membership in Alabama's corn and pig clubs, for example, grew to 60,000 in only ten years, and the state began subsidizing the clubs in 1919. Soaring rhetoric accompanied the clubs' fair contests; extension agents and club members hoped that knowledge gained by the boys at the fairs would inspire their fathers to try new methods of raising crops and livestock. On occasion adherence to the extension agents' instructions could pay off immediately, as in

Henry County, Alabama, where a pig-club member won three hundred dollars in prizes at a fair in 1920. The contest winners, like their female counterparts, could also win short courses at the state colleges.[64]

The boys' clubs best reveal the ways the fairs represented a change in sentiment from the work sharings. Whereas young men had once raced through contests of physical prowess, at the fairs they learned the fundamental principles of agriculture in hopes of producing the most scientifically perfect product. A cartoon run in 1920 by an agricultural journal showed the new sentiments embodied by the boys' agricultural clubs. In an attempt to show the benefits of the corn and pig clubs, *Alabama Farm Facts* pictured five "Keys to Success." Four small keys were labeled "heart," "head," "health," and "hands," but the large key—the key that unlocked the door to success—was labeled "Balanced Life."[65] Southern males had never before wanted a balanced life; their pleasures had long been immediate and self-indulgent. The balanced life was the life of evangelical America, the life white Southern males had always found too quiet and civil for their aggressive temperaments. No longer did the fairs celebrate physical strength and immediate achievement. Replacing the races and bravado of nineteenth-century work sharings was an emphasis on the virtues of education and modern practical science. Agricultural newspapers in the 1910s and 1920s ran scores of stories in which boys told of their long, calculated efforts to raise prizewinning corn or a prizewinning pig. Some judges at the fairs evaluated not only specimens of the boys' work but also the step-by-step records each boy had kept.[66]

In contrast, the women's sections at the fairs upheld the virtues of motherhood as fully as had the quiltings and communal cooking that accompanied work sharings. Motivating the drive to modernize the home was a desire to free the woman from overwork so she could concentrate on the joys of being a wife and mother. As the women's editor of the *Progressive Farmer* stated of the need for specific household improvements: "Strength is a definite thing; if it is spent for lifting tubs it cannot go to the unborn child, nor to brain power, nor to the energy back of the inspiration that is imparted to children for higher things." Mrs. Stephen Read, lecturing on new methods of cooking and hygiene, noted that "the original meaning of the word woman was 'bread maker.' . . . A bread-maker, and thus a joy and health-giver! Surely no woman could covet a higher privilege than to build up the physical and inspire the spiritual."[67] These references to "higher things" and "the spiritual" revealed the religious impulse upheld in the educational portions of the fairs. It would be an overstatement to say that the fairs were extensions of the church, but the religious idealization of home life was almost as marked in the fair demonstrations as it was in revival meetings. The household contests were, in part, attempts to purify further the already pure institution of the home.

Southerners often identified the movement to refine traditional domestic virtues as distinctively Southern. In Mississippi, tomato-club girls sang of the virtues of modern domesticity to the tune of "Dixie." A North Carolina newspaper wrote in 1915, "All of us have talked much about Southern chivalry from time to time—some of us quite heatedly—but the best evidence of Southern chivalry may be found in that rural home provided with running water."[68] Certainly beliefs in the virtues of domesticity and this form of chivalry were not limited to the South, but the particular fervency with which such ideals were portrayed at Southern fairs seems unique to the region. The evolution of harvest festivals into celebrations of the virtues of modern motherhood and quietly thoughtful agriculture shows that the modern institution of the fair was strongly influenced by some of the attitudes of evangelical culture.

Undeniably, the contests and exhibits were responsible for bringing many, possibly most, fairgoers to the grounds. But many fairs also promised exciting entertainments that often differed sharply from the quietly domestic events in the agricultural and household booths. Whereas the attempts to modernize the farm and home were decidedly moralistic, the midway amusements included a suspiciously immoral form of modern culture. Some Southerners looked forward to the entertainment at the fairs as a pleasurable release from the long work year; for them, pure enjoyment was part of the celebration signifying the end of the harvest. As a North Carolina editor wrote of fair week in October 1926, "At this time farmfolks cut loose from farm duties and come to the Cabarrus Fair for real pleasure and profit. Mostly it is playtime for them after harvest." A larger fair in Alexander City, Alabama, promised excitement along with the promotion of improved agriculture, saying that "a little fun, now and then, is a good thing for all people." The program of another Alabama fair combined the two functions in screaming headlines: "Fun! Frolic! Education!" At least at the larger events, fairgoers enjoyed the first two attractions as much as the third.[69]

With their variety of unusual experiences, midway recreations enabled Southerners to suspend everyday reality. John Kasson has written that New York's Coney Island amusement parks offered turn-of-the-century urbanites a host of extraordinary physical sensations and exotic sights, "altering visitors' perceptions and transforming their consciousness, dispelling everyday concerns in the intense sensations of the present moment." The midway recreations at rural Southern fairs were, of course, far less spectacular than the wild roller coaster, water rides, exaggerated architecture, and top-of-the-line freak shows at Coney Island.[70] But rural Southerners with a daily agricultural routine found it far easier to suspend reality than did New Yorkers living in the midst of rapid industrial and technological change. The East Alabama Fair promised "Thrilling Free Shows or Free Acts. . . . Among the 10 Big Shows on the Midway, you may enjoy the Dog and Pony Shows, Goat Circus, of Educated Goats; the Motor Drome, 10-in-one-Circus, Plantation Shows, the great Ferris Wheel, the superb Merry-Go-Round; and the Jitney Swings." Most county fairs offered small midways, and many promised balloon ascensions, airplane exhibits, or tightrope acts. For example, the fair in Chester County, South Carolina, featured "Sensational Smithson, the man who has made them all ask for several years, 'how does he do it,' and the Stirewalt Family, five of the best acrobats before the American audiences."[71] All midway rides and shows mocked nature, either by placing the fairgoers in unusual physical situations—on Ferris wheels, for example—or by displaying the latest seemingly miraculous technological innovations, such as airplanes, or common animals with extraordinary abilities.

Most of the midways carried some taint of immorality. County fairs constantly promoted their midway amusements as clean and uplifting, but the very repetitiveness of their claims shows that they never quite succeeded in cleaning up the attractions. Too many midways offered games that involved gambling, and the sheer novelty and physical character of many amusements offended fairgoers who enjoyed the moral respectability of the agricultural and household exhibits. The 1904 Haywood County Fair in Georgia promised a midway with sideshows that were "not the kind that demoralizes, but clean, up-to-date amusements." Twelve years later, in Rutherford County, North Carolina, spokesmen promised, "This year every one may rest assured that the entertainment will be absolutely clean and high class." The East Alabama Fair advertised a midway that was "by far the best we have ever had, and composed of clean and decent men, women and children. No gambling, nothing indecent or suggestive permitted." Despite this optimism, however, concern about the midways was still evident in 1929, when the Association of Georgia Fairs stated hopefully that "the undesirable type of carnival is gradually being weeded out and the higher-class carnivals, with no gambling devices, and clean amusement features, are being brought into the state."[72] This constant concern among event planners betrayed their fear that the fairs, planned as educational events, actually encouraged novelties of very questionable virtue. The important feature of the midway amusements is that they represented a release from codes of everyday upright behavior, but unlike the rituals of the red corn ear and the cat shaking, they violated the evangelical moral standards of many Southerners. In the midway shows, a modern institution was bringing to the rural South the supposed decadence of the cities.

Many larger fairs also included a more traditional form of disreputable recreation. Horse races—not merely shows of the best animals but speed races with organized betting—grew in popularity as the larger fair associations built grandstands to attract substantial crowds. The East Alabama Fair, for example, trumpeted its "New Ten Thousand Dollar Race Track."[73] Many such races were large, organized affairs that resembled urban mass-spectator events rather than the small races of an earlier rural America. By organizing traditional events into large spectator affairs and by creating a setting for gambling, the fairs offered new opportunities for what was widely considered disreputable conduct. As popular evangelist Sam Jones complained in 1912, "So many of our towns have county and district fairs. What is the principal attraction? The races, of course. . . . Oh the gang that follows up the race course to bet on the races! Where will you find a more debauched, disreputable crowd?"[74]

Churches were quick to warn their members against the temptations of fairs. In 1889 a Mississippi church considered the question of whether its members could support "by their influence, money, or patronage Fair Associations that permit gambling Schemes, Horse racing & such like." Another Mississippi church accused a man of having been "drunken last year at the fair at Summit," and a Tennessee church member had to answer charges of gambling at a fair "on them wheels of fortune."[75]

The fairs provide some insight into the complicated changes that twentieth-century institutions brought to rural Southern culture. The work sharings of the nineteenth century both mirrored the traditional distinction between male and female culture and also allowed courtship customs that were thoroughly respectable releases from conventional notions of proper behavior. Having long roots in Southern culture, those customs bore no stain of immorality. Whereas these forms of release from evangelical standards were acceptable, however, the escape from evangelical sensibilities offered by midway amusements at the fairs always carried a strong hint of sinful self-indulgence. The *Progressive Farmer* cautioned fairgoers hopefully but unrealistically in 1911, "You wouldn't enjoy yourself at a fair where there were gambling machines, indecent shows and other things which you would not wish the children to learn about. . . . It is an insult to your wife and daughters for a fair management to place a lot of questionable amusements before you."[76] Southerners, particularly Southern men and boys, enjoyed themselves at such events, but they did so under the disapproving eye of the evangelical community.

Can we reconcile this change from a respectable to a disreputable release with the fact that the central experiences at the fairs were, for many, decidedly moralistic? In fact, some parts of the fairs celebrated a heightened form of evangelicalism through their goals of the improved homemaker and the quietly thoughtful farmer. The change in the meanings of harvest celebrations must be considered in light of the larger changes in rural Southern life. Until late in the nineteenth century, few organized urban institutions affected the daily lives of most Southern farmers. But the agents of change—the increasing significance of a national market and the decline of self-sufficient farming, improvements in technology and transportation, and the growth of important inland cities—brought Southerners in much more frequent contact with nonlocal cultural institutions. Better roads, the rural mail, and, eventually, such innovations as motion pictures and the radio brought rural Southerners into a larger cultural world.

As long as popular recreation retained its decidedly local character, Southern evangelicals could tolerate a substantial degree of deviation from conventional moral standards. The trip into town was a generally accepted form of male sinfulness, and church members were allowed to drink as long as they did not disgrace their families and church bodies by repeated public drunkenness. Hunters could blast away as freely as they wished. And the recreations that accompanied work sharings at important points of the crop year allowed young people opportunities to enjoy each other's company in a public setting outside the home and church.

The modern, urban-based institutions that began to penetrate the rural South in the late nineteenth century threatened the tenuous acceptance of certain forms of sinfulness, particularly male sinfulness. The checks that communities had posed on excessively undesirable behavior weakened as Southerners learned to enjoy new forms of recreation totally outside the influence of home and church. Thus, the late nineteenth and early twentieth centuries saw such developments as intensified attempts to purify the home through prohibition, new movements to restrain the animal within man through hunting restrictions and laws against sports that supposedly abused animals, and increased concerns about the sanctity of the Sabbath. State and local fairs exemplified both of the paths that Southern rural culture was taking under the influence of urban culture. The midway amusements offered new opportunities for excitement outside the boundaries of traditional morality, whereas the contests and exhibits represented attempts to persuade men to use their minds rather than their muscles. The fairs demonstrate that modern institutions brought to the rural South both new threats to the stability of evangelical culture and newly intensified efforts to purify and preserve the virtues of that culture.

10

Mass Culture and Southern Culture

Vote like you pray.
—*Alabama Baptist*

IN 1925 a Florida Baptist minister described the course of modern life in the South. "We have all been brought closer to each other by new methods of communication and ways of travel," he said. "This has been at once a great blessing and a great curse. While the things that are elevating are more easily reached by the masses, the things that are evil are more accessible also. Our relationships have become more complex and varied, and the problems of society have become more difficult."[1] Too often we think of twentieth-century America as becoming increasingly secular, as a powerful wave of mass culture has overwhelmed traditional religion with skeptical ideas and new opportunities for the pursuit of pleasure. Instead of seeing religious life as being displaced, however, we should see that the growing threat of mass culture has intensified the long-raging battle between the godly and the ungodly. The South's cultural balance, which had grown increasingly precarious in the late nineteenth century, began in the twentieth to tilt back and forth dramatically, as mass culture extended its influence throughout the population and evangelicals responded by trying to infuse all of Southern culture with their values.

Not until the twentieth century did professional entertainment based in urban centers outside the South begin to revolutionize everyday life. National fads of the 1890s, generally operating among the wealthy in the urban Northeast, expressed new desires for physically open and exciting forms of pleasure. The so-called strenuous life stressed youthful energy, athleticism, and a physically active womanhood. Theodore

Roosevelt helped introduce many Americans to the joys of vigorous sports. Amusement parks placed individuals in new and amusingly embarrassing physical positions. Enjoyment of the body also showed in new forms of popular music and dance. For the first time, white Americans embraced a black form of music, dancing to ragtime and to other unsentimental songs with up-tempo tunes. The "new woman" was perhaps the most vivid symbol of the invigoration of upper-class American culture. Many upper-class women began to reject traditional symbols of respectability, indulging in the new dances, the new games, and all that accompanied the new search for pleasure. It was the involvement of women in morally questionable pursuits that would stimulate the most antagonistic responses among evangelicals.[2]

It took years for urban fads to invade the South as new technology gradually revolutionized rural life. Oddly, perhaps, Southern moralists welcomed that technology until they began to see its revolutionary effects. In 1904 a Presbyterian minister in Clinton, South Carolina, recorded in his diary that he was "very much interested in the moving photographs. Really we have now the preservation of voice features and even the very actions, passing before us, of dead men. Ours is an age of wonder."[3] We tend to think of rural Americans as resisting most cultural changes, particularly changes brought by strangers from outside their area. However, most Southerners in the nineteenth century were not particularly concerned about the moral effects of the technological advances that would eventually alter their culture so dramatically. The phonograph, the motion picture, and their predecessors typically received warm welcomes from those who saw and heard them, providing interesting diversions and carrying few negative moral associations.

Technological innovations themselves often provided reasons for recreation. People wanted to see what was new and intriguing, and they went to see new machines much as they went to see the circus. Touring "professors" often exhibited—for a fee, of course—the machines that would eventually change everyone's lives. Descriptions of the new wonders typically mentioned the amazement with which audiences responded. In a Georgia town in 1878, "The phonograph was on exhibition two days and nights in Conyers. It talked, laughed, whistled, sang and played cornet solos, to the wonder and amusement of a number of our citizens." Their fascination was clearly as much with the phonograph as it was with the sounds it produced. Advertisements centered not on the music or other recorded novelties, but on the phonograph itself as "the greatest wonder of science." Southerners' earliest reactions to the telephone likewise focused on the wonders of the medium rather than the wonders to be heard through it. Mississippian S. G. Thigpen recalled his first encounter with a telephone at a circus early in the twentieth century. The circus barker invited listeners: "For only a dime you can talk over this wonderful, this fantastic, this out-of-the-world new invention and have an experience that you can in the years to come tell your grandchildren about." Thigpen paid ten cents to talk to the owner of the general store a quarter of a mile down the road and considered it money well spent.[4]

Revolutions in sight were sometimes even more exciting than revolutions in sound. Professional photographers made the circuit from town to town much as those hawking medicine and exhibiting phonographs did. Rural Southerners in their best clothes hurried their families into town to have their own faces reproduced for the first time.[5] More dramatic were Southerners' first encounters with motion pictures. Early moving pictures, played on primitive machines called kinetoscopes, attracted attention as much for the technology as for the pictures they presented. Indeed, the first encounter with that technology could be absolutely frightening, if an event in South Carolina was in any way typical. After a magic show and an exhibition of a phonograph, show-men stretched a sheet across the wall.

> Look! Here came the horsemen chasing Indians! Really! We
> were astounded. . . . The flicker from the machine, and up the
> track yonder the engine came, headed straight at us. . . . And it
> came fast. Faster than we liked. And when it got to us it seemed
> to burst right out of the picture at us! Women and children
> screamed! Men grabbed for their folks! Several jumped out of the
> windows. . . . There was a pandemonium for a moment until the
> lanterns were again lighted.[6]

Evangelicals had no reason to consider such experiences morally objectionable. They had no idea that mass professional entertainment would eventually dominate their culture and no conception of the nature of that entertainment. Indeed, many of the early forms of technologically sophisticated entertainment contained a religious element. Evangelicals hoped that mass culture was bringing more opportunities for religious expression to an area already very conscious of religion. Before the phonograph brought to the South the suggestiveness of Tin Pan Alley and the near-lewdness of race records, it played in Waynes-boro, Georgia, to benefit the local parsonage. Before the motion pictures brought stories of the fun-loving rich, they brought illustrations of biblical settings. Two of the more popular motion pictures of the early 1900s were *The Passion Play*, a portrayal of the life of Jesus, and *The Shadow of Nazareth*, which, one editor wrote, was "produced with due reverence for its sacred theme."[7] Some early advertisements claimed that motion pictures were moral and instructive. Just as circuses and many touring dramatic companies prepared their way into small towns with advance billing proclaiming their respectability, some theaters tried to portray themselves as institutions for the preservation of evangelical values. Owners of a new theater in Wadesboro, North Carolina, for example, assured the citizens in 1908 that "the pictures are decent and worth seeing," and the local editor predicted that the pictures would be well attended "so long as they are not immoral."[8]

The motion picture was the most revolutionary of the new media, creating the setting for entirely new recreations. As Lary May argues, the motion picture brought "the birth of mass culture."[9] By the 1920s churchmen considered it by far the most important means of entertainment. "It reaches more people every day than any other agency whatever, not excepting the daily paper."[10] The movies enabled many Southerners to pursue pleasure two or three or four nights a week, and the theaters scheduled Saturday afternoon matinees to appeal to the farmers on their weekly trips into the towns. For a nickel, Southerners could enjoy sights, music, and a cultural variety that few had experienced before.

The world created by the movies in many ways denied the distinctiveness of Southern culture. Even the physical environment of movie theaters denied Southerners one of their region's special characteristics. W. J. Cash has argued that part of the reason for the intensity of much of Southern culture was the look and feel of the region's climate and geography. The searing heat could make hot tempers even hotter. But the movies promised something new to the South, something that eventually changed Southern culture dramatically. In 1925, a theater in Forest City, North Carolina, installed an "Arctic Nu-Air cooling system," an early step in bringing an end to a vital part of Southern distinctiveness.[11] Cash also argues that the South was a land of "extravagant colors, of proliferating foliage and bloom, of flooding yellow sunlight, and, above all perhaps, of haze." But the early movies created a world without colors. As the intense physical world of the South gave way to a flickering light in a dark room, young Southerners grew up, as Eudora Welty wrote, with "a vast inner life going on in the movies."[12]

The most important change that the movies brought to the rural South was simply a shift in cultural leadership from the local area to a distant urban center. Young Southerners had traditionally learned how to become adults by emulating individuals they knew. Whether they learned the lessons of evangelical culture from their parents, their preachers, and perhaps their schoolteachers, or the lessons of masculine culture from storefront loafers and older boys, they learned by watching fellow Southerners with whom they had much in common. The leaders and the led shared the same accent, the same past, perhaps the same family, and, most important, the same notions about the range of possible ways to behave. The movies, however, brought brand new leaders whom young Southerners might choose to emulate.

Any optimism that the movies might promote evangelical morals was short-lived. Soon newspaper advertisements teemed with suggestions of sin, corruption, and intrigue. On consecutive nights in 1919, moviegoers in Cookeville, Tennessee, could watch *The Great Romance*, *The Parisian Tigresse*, *What Every Woman Wants*, *The Human Desire*, and *Miss Adventure*. In another Tennessee town in 1925, viewers could see *The Cobra*, featuring Rudolph Valentino as an Italian aristocrat "trying to fight down his weakness for women. The wife of his best friend falls in love with him." The next night they could watch *The Teaser*, in which "they took her fiance from her, so she smashed hearts right and left, ruthlessly, carelessly." Two nights after that, *The Way of a Girl* posed the question, "Has the modern girl too much freedom? This is the story of a society beauty who thought she didn't have enough." In the space of two weeks in 1921, residents of Gaffney, South Carolina, could watch Lionel Barrymore "employ a beautiful and innocent girl in a revenge plot—blacken her reputation and then marry her to his bitterest enemy for the sole purpose of ruining him—control a gang of crooks and blackmailers . . . and himself elude detection," and then watch Ethel Clayton suffer the leering advances of " 'Joy-hound' spenders, hunting night life where she danced." The allure of sexual license became so important in drawing customers that one advertisement depicted two movie-mad women discussing a film in which a newly married couple scandalized their neighborhood by "carrying on" with other people, the wife with an already married man and the husband with "a French woman here in town brazenly calling him her 'twin soul.' " One woman concluded, "You don't say? But the affair is so shocking, really, come, let's get tickets!"[13]

The movies were so shocking that countless Southerners bought tickets. Lary May argues that the first two decades of American movie-making represented a profound moral revolution. The earliest mass-produced movies, made in the first decade of this century and aimed at urban immigrants, often ridiculed or overturned reigning moral attitudes. With the exception of D. W. Griffith's moralizing epics, the movies struck at the heart of traditional evangelical values. Characters played by such actresses as Theda Bara openly enjoyed sexual promiscuity. Mack Sennett's bathing beauties titillated watchers in ways few professional entertainers had ever done with such regularity. Charlie Chaplin's characters ridiculed respectability and seriousness of all kinds. More than anyone else, Douglas Fairbanks and Mary Pickford embodied the new image of fun-loving vigor that all the new media were bringing to the South, with Fairbanks exemplifying the cult of youth by glorifying the body and physical achievement and Pickford portraying forceful and independent women.[14]

It quickly became apparent that the motion pictures posed a threat to evangelical values. Parents began to look closely at the movies their children attended. The son of a Methodist preacher recalled that, in the 1910s, his parents checked the newspapers for descriptions of coming attractions, forbidding his attendance at pictures featuring such stars as Mary Pickford, Charlie Chaplin, and Margarite Clarke but allowing him to see less objectionable pictures such as Westerns. Ministers began to use the motion picture as a prime example of the decadence of modern times. The movies, according to one, tended "to inflame the passions and leave an indelible blot upon the minds of the young." Another complained that the movies, with "utter disregard for the home," had "flooded the nation with a deluge of irreverence, immorality and crime." Evangelicals were particularly concerned that the movies glorified sexual immorality. One placed them in the same group of activities as "vulgar styles of dress (or undress), the shameless exposure of female nakedness, the lust-provoking dances." Another complained, "The picture show men know that their shows are utterly putrid, indecent, vulgar, saturated with sex."[15]

The movies were the most obvious representative of a whole array of modern amusements that evangelicals were beginning to find threatening. By the 1910s the phonograph had become commonplace. Listening to recorded music became a routine part of socializing. A wealthy Alabama man recorded in 1907, "After supper we had a 'phonograph concert' and played dominoes." For a young South Carolinian, a date with a local teacher consisted of "a pleasant evening complete with

Victrola recordings and sparkling conversation." Cash Bundren, a member of the isolated family William Faulkner creates in *As I Lay Dying*, is intrigued by the possibility of buying "one of them little graphophones" and ordering records through the mail. "I dont know if a little music aint about the nicest thing a fellow can have." Bill Joe Austin, a white jazz musician born in Smithfield, North Carolina, in 1911, first encountered recorded music through the influence of a black nurse. Austin began listening to her phonograph at age two, and as an older child he spent much of his spare time at her home listening to her collection of records. The phonograph thus brought about the connection between white and black culture long feared by white evangelicals. Through the medium of the phonograph, a small but increasing number of white Southerners were finding ragtime and the new jazz beat more exciting than traditional music, much of which had a strong religious element.[16]

A teenager in the early 1920s in the college town of Athens, Georgia, clearly revealed the phonograph's allure as a form of fashionable sinfulness. Maude Talmadge Wood passed the time in her home by dancing to recordings of such songs as "Limehouse Blues." The local record store became a popular spot in which the young passed their afternoons far from the morally pure institution of the home. Wood's circle of friends, referring to themselves with the less than pious name of "The Wild Cats," "would go to town in the afternoon and spend hours listening to records. Sometimes we would buy them if we liked them very much. Then we would ride around town, past the fraternity houses and wave at the boys."[17] Listening to recorded music, then, was part of the urbane and sophisticated nature of the new mass culture. Wood was a "new woman," enjoying a jazz beat, an exciting cultural life outside the home, and an active pursuit of pleasure with young men.

The pleasure of listening to stylish new music had become a nightly event by the early 1920s. Southerners typically noted the distance from which the radio transmissions had come when they discussed their early experience with radio. A South Carolina man heard his first radio at a corner drugstore: "I remember I heard band music, and it was coming from Philadelphia." In 1924 an Alabamian took pride in his own radio. "We can plainly hear music and addresses in various parts of the U.S. and in Cuba. We listen each night to Pittsburgh, New York, Washington, Chicago, St. Louis, Kansas City, Memphis, Dallas, Fort Worth, Louisville, and a number of other places." Of course, not all of this music was charged with black jazz rhythms and tainted by impure associations. But by bringing the outside world into the home, the radio brought much that was morally questionable.[18]

The home was becoming less isolated every day, and any recreation that could expose people to pleasures outside the family, night after night, drew the criticism of Southern moralists. One of the most vivid symbols of the hectic, all-consuming search for pleasure in early twentieth-century America was joyriding. Like the motion picture, the phonograph, and the radio, the automobile allowed young people to pursue experiences far outside the traditional boundaries of the home and church. Joyriding quickly became a popular pastime and a frequent topic of conversation. A wealthy young woman in Florida frequently wrote a boyfriend, "I went auto riding this afternoon it was fine," and she later sounded the popular theme of the automobile as a setting in which young men and women enjoyed each other's company: "Clifford Robertson and some more of the girls and boys are coming around to go auto riding."[19]

Early criticism focused on Sunday driving. The automobile allowed people to pursue pleasure on that day in particularly visible, nonreligious ways. Instead of just staying home, nonchurchgoers could motor past the houses of worship, thumbing their noses at the devout. By the early 1920s evangelicals considered joyriding on any day of the week a symbol of the youthful, fun-loving, sexually open nature of mass culture. One writer sadly discussed the frequency and "disastrous effects" of joyriding: "Girls from the best families participate in these adventures, the principal features of which are petting, using the contents of hip flasks and patronizing road houses." Baptist minister William McGlothlin advised an audience in 1921, "One needs but to drive out a few miles from any of our cities and towns in the early evening to get an idea of what the automobile means to the purity of the rising generation." In 1925 a Tennessee woman went into detail describing a scene that took place beside the road in front of her home. She saw a young woman who

> fell bodily on the young man, grabbed him around the neck in a vice-like grip and jammed her face into his Adams apple. In the course of ten or fifteen minutes she repeated the onslaught half a dozen times or more, with variations. Sometimes she would clutch him frantically and pull his head down on her chest and hold him close. Once she enveloped him in her embrace and batted her face into his jugular vein, another variation was butting

The "new woman" and her automobile in Mt. Pleasant, Tennessee, ca. 1925.
(Courtesy of the Looking Back at Tennessee Photography Project, Tennessee
State Library and Archives, Nashville)

her head into his breastbone while she gripped him in her arms.
Once she folded him to her bosom with one arm, and tousled and
rumpled his hair with her free hand.

The Tennessean's response was typical of evangelicals. "That set me
wondering what is the home-life of such young people. What propor-
tion of the petters and pettees comes from homes where the Bible is
studied and revered."[20]

The automobile and the new popular media brought worries of a
new kind to evangelicals who were always concerned about personal
morality. The so-called strenuous life of mass culture differed from the
Saturday afternoon main-street drunken brawl; the media brought new
forms of what many considered sinfulness to a culture already obsessed
with questions of sin and righteousness. All of the new media exposed
young people to experiences that conflicted dramatically with the values of the evangelical home, placing the purity of women—ever the
cornerstone of evangelical morality—under siege in new ways. The
motion picture showed brave heroines openly throwing off traditional
female responsibilities and openly pursuing pleasures of many kinds.

The new music had young men and women swaying to a beat that had no precedents in white Southern life. The automobile put young men and women together in an environment that could take couples where they were far from home and hidden from public view. These developments primarily affected young people, and evangelicals throughout the South responded by bemoaning the declining moral influence of parents and the home. In 1921 Baptist writer Victor I. Masters lamented the loss of the family's "joyful fellowship" to "the movie, the theatre, the club, the social function, the automobile ride, the endless pull of petty things that promise amusement. These things appeal mainly to the superficial and ephemeral, while they cheat the home of its opportunity to perform functions for the souls of children required of it by God." McGlothlin closed a long diatribe against the decadence of the early 1920s by imploring his listeners to remember that it was "the solemn duty of the home, of the parents, to conserve the morals of the race."[21]

How did twentieth-century evangelicals meet the challenge of conserving the morals of the race? A change in their strategy for controlling morally disreputable recreations highlights evangelicals' changing conceptions of their place in Southern life. In 1870, evangelical church members who sinned in public could remain in the church only if they faced their congregations, acknowledged their sins, and asked forgiveness. By 1915, church members very rarely had to endure such proceedings. By that time, however, laws passed with evangelical support had made many objectionable recreations illegal. Drinking, for example, had become an offense against the state rather than the church. As the use of church discipline to punish and correct supposedly immoral recreations declined, the popularity of legislation to prohibit such activities was on the rise. This dramatic change in strategy is particularly revealing of evangelicals' beliefs about the relationship of religion to the secular world. Church discipline had attempted to maintain the moral connections between the home and the church, regulating and softening the sinful excesses of male behavior. But by the early twentieth century, exponents of the values of home and church had become committed to the goal of enforcing those values in all segments of Southern life.

In theory, all church members in the 1800s had equally deep commitments to unblemished personal behavior, and the purpose of discipline was to help members live up to that standard. With rare exceptions, congregations wished not to expel erring members but to bring them under the authority and influence of the church. A Baptist manual on the subject, written in 1860 and reprinted in 1912, emphasized, "Corrective discipline, even in its highest censures, is an act of kindness to the offender, and designed not to injure but to reform." A Baptist congregation in Florida likewise emphasized the helpful, loving goal of church discipline, promising in its covenant "to watch over each other in brotherly love for the mutual good of each other with an eye single to the glory of God."[22]

The desired response to an accusation of sinful conduct was a public admission of guilt before the church body. Congregations wanted members to acknowledge their failings publicly, to ask forgiveness, and, often, to ask the congregation's help in living a better life. The desired response was also the most common response. Time after time members professed deep regret for their actions and promised to do better, in language that suggested the individual's dependence on the church body. A North Carolina Presbyterian, charged with drunkenness in 1874, "frankly acknowledged the charge, waived his right to trial, expressed the hope with tears of yet being enabled to overcome the sad habit, asked the prayers of the church in his behalf & finally left it with the session to dispose of his case as they thought best."[23] In accepting a congregation's admonition, the disciplined church member was affirming that he was one of the group. They were right, he was wrong, and he accepted their right and responsibility to help lead him to more Godly conduct. Always in theory, and sometimes in reality, church members were genuinely thankful for their congregations' efforts to keep them in line, hoping that together they could keep each other pure.

The central function of church discipline, then, was to separate the immoral from the moral. A Baptist manual quoted Paul's injunction in First Corinthians to "put away from among yourselves that wicked person."[24] In churches that used discipline frequently, it was difficult for members to sit on the fence, professing Christian virtues on Sunday morning after enjoying a less-than-pious Saturday night. Discipline did not separate the saved from the unsaved; evangelicals knew that God's ways were beyond their comprehension. Instead, the use of discipline marked church members as active adherents to an ideal of strictly moral behavior.

Southern congregations gave up church discipline in the postbellum period, gradually during the late 1800s and then more rapidly in the early 1900s. Tables 10.1, 10.2, 10.3, and 10.4 show that the number of churches disciplining their members and the number disciplining them frequently both decreased sharply in that period. The Baptists, with

Table 10.1
Disciplinary Proceedings in 37 Baptist and 7 Primitive Baptist Churches,
1866–1915

	1866–75	1876–85	1886–95	1896–1905	1906–15
Number of churches using discipline	44	43	39	35	31
Number of churches using discipline at least 5 times	32	24	24	14	11
Number of churches using discipline at least 10 times	17	16	15	9	6
Total charges	511	455	479	312	143

Sources: See note 26.

their insistence on a church of mature, converted believers, had long placed special emphasis on discipline, and each of the Baptist churches under consideration disciplined its members in the first decade after the Civil War.[25] But more than a quarter of these had dropped the practice entirely by the 1910s. Both the number of churches using discipline at least once a year and the total number of disciplinary charges declined almost threefold.[26] A smaller sample of Christian church minutes reveals the same general pattern.[27] In Presbyterian churches, where discipline had always been less common than in other denominations, it was virtually a thing of the past by 1910.[28] The period of the most dramatic decline, as table 10.4 shows, was between 1886 and 1915.

We can only speculate about the reasons for the dramatic decline in churches' use of discipline. I have discovered no explanations by church members as to why this once-popular practice faded away. In later years, those who called for a return to godly discipline seem to have had little hope of success. In 1910 a Baptist minister in Georgia asked his association, "When have you heard of a church vindicating her righteous claims by an effectual arraignment of her malicious or delinquent members? Church discipline, it seems, must be reckoned as a thing of the past."[29]

Two obvious but flawed explanations for the decline present themselves. It could be argued that by the early twentieth century churchgoers had learned to control their conduct, at least in public. This interpretation obviously will not suffice. Specific sins may come and go, but in evangelical belief, Sin is a constant. If congregations had retained

Table 10.2
Disciplinary Proceedings in 7 Christian Churches, 1866–1915

	1866–75	1876–85	1886–95	1896–1905	1906–15
Number of churches using discipline	7	6	6	2	3
Number of churches using discipline at least 5 times	3	2	3	2	0
Total charges	29	38	67	13	8

Sources: See note 27.

Table 10.3
Disciplinary Proceedings in 30 Presbyterian and 2 Cumberland Presbyterian Churches, 1866–1915

	1866–75	1876–85	1886–95	1896–1905	1906–15
Number of churches using discipline	22	20	13	10	4
Number of churches using discipline at least 5 times	10	4	1	2	0
Total charges	85	59	30	30	4

Sources: See note 28.

Table 10.4
Total Disciplinary Proceedings of 83 Churches, 1866–1915

	1866–75	1876–85	1886–95	1896–1905	1906–15
Number of churches using discipline	73	69	58	47	38
Number of churches using discipline at least 5 times	45	30	28	18	11
Total charges	625	552	576	355	155

Sources: See tables 10.1, 10.2, and 10.3.

their interest in ridding the church of unrepentant sinners, they unquestionably could have found activities worthy of discipline. On the other hand, one might argue that churchgoers had grown more worldly and no longer felt a need to judge each other's behavior. A public sin here or there was easier overlooked than exposed to the public condemnation of the church. Perhaps church members were beginning to see these minidramas as a bit tawdry. Perhaps, as church members became part of a larger world, their willingness to submit to the authorities of small local bodies diminished. A recent historian has attributed the decline of Southern Baptist discipline to the growth of a happy complacency that developed when "the churches made peace with the surrounding culture."[30] This interpretation neglects an important change in how Southerners enforced notions of proper behavior. The churches never made peace with their culture. Claiming that churches became soft on sin overlooks the vital significance of the rise of moral legislation. As churches were losing interest in disciplining the behavior of their members, they were trying to reform the behavior of all Southerners.

Discipline had helped maintain the balance between evangelical and nonevangelical culture. It clearly identified individuals as being part of or separate from their evangelical community. Those who ascribed to evangelical beliefs and the virtue of evangelical behavior, but who felt unable to live up to a strict moral standard, had to make a choice. Would they accept the moral governance of their churches, proclaim themselves one of the congregation, and promise to reform their behavior? Or would they refuse to apologize for their behavior, allow the church to exclude them, and accept their status as nonmembers? By using discipline, churches were attempting not to reform the world but to purify the church. Churches that frequently disciplined members were, in some ways, utopian institutions, keeping themselves separate from the corruption of the outside world. The pure institution—the church—kept itself pure and left the rest of the world to its hellish ways. Moral legislation, in contrast, showed that evangelicals were coming to terms with a larger world by trying to conquer it. No longer satisfied to separate themselves from the sinful excesses of nonevangelical behavior, they now tried to stamp out many sins altogether. By giving up church discipline, evangelicals were not giving in to the world but redefining their place in it. For people with such ambitious goals, discipline simply became irrelevant.

Evangelicals had used church discipline to try to tame the most public excesses of male culture. Drunken staggering, loud swearing, fighting on the streets—these were very public sins, and they received extraordinary attention from the churches. But laws that actually made drinking, swearing, and many forms of personal violence illegal were part of a new strategy to enforce evangelical morality. Whereas churches in the nineteenth century used discipline in an effort to help their members abstain from such activities, in the twentieth they increasingly turned to legislation that prohibited them altogether. These laws constituted a direct assault on many of the most important elements of male culture. At about the same time that new laws against drinking, public swearing, and recreational fighting were being passed, additional laws were outlawing other traditional masculine sports such as fighting, bearbaiting, and dogfighting and restricting many hunting and fishing practices. No longer content to protect the purity of the female-centered institutions of the home and the church, evangelicals now wished to extend their influence over all the institutions of male culture as well. The Southern male who had once raised his hell, laughing at churchgoers while perhaps fearing occasionally for the state of his soul, now faced laws prohibiting much of his pursuit of pleasure.

There was a tremendous difference between not wanting members of one's own church to get drunk and not wanting anyone to be able to buy alcohol. The former was the attitude of people in a small world who were trying to protect and preserve their world from harm. The latter was the attitude of people in a much larger world who were attempting to change the nature of that world. Greater threats to evangelical culture, particularly threats from outside the boundaries of the rural South, inspired intensified efforts to keep Southern life true to what had for generations been its semiofficial morality.

By the early twentieth century, rural Southerners, whether they liked it or not, had become part of a larger world. Farm life was less isolated from town life, and town life was less isolated from city life. The home and church no longer marked the parameters of most evangelicals' everyday experience. As new forms of professional entertainment exposed Southerners to a range of potentially sinful experiences, life became more exciting and more tempting, but also more threatening. Evangelical Southerners responded to these changes with a newly aggressive approach to reforming the sinners of the world. It was no longer good enough to have pure churches and pure individuals; evangelicals now wanted to rid their society of all of its impurities.

Concerns over the pervasiveness of new sins lent strength to efforts to reform the old ones. Throughout the 1910s and 1920s, evangelicals pushed for stronger enforcement of laws already in place, hoping to search out sinfulness wherever it occurred and bring an end to it. A group of Baptist ministers, eight years after Georgia had passed its 1907 prohibition law, recommended new ways to use the law to control immoral behavior. "First, know whether there is any liquor in your community, observe closely, and at the opportune time assist in every possible way the civil authorities to bring the alleged guilty party to justice." Ministers urged church members to vote only for local officials who would enforce the laws and even to examine the members of juries to ensure that those accused of making and selling whiskey received full punishment. Some, seeing that men were able to obtain liquor illegally, urged that drinking itself should be made a crime.[31]

Fresh from their success with prohibition, evangelicals in the 1910s and 1920s vowed "to eliminate everything detrimental to the welfare of the human family." Minister William McGlothlin, for example, suggested a novel way to combat the evils of the automobile, urging newspaper reporters to cruise popular parking spots and report whose cars they found there. Others looked to the law, and large numbers of evangelicals took up a challenge by the *Alabama Baptist* in 1920 to "vote like you pray." Closing laws in some states banned the sale of gasoline on Sundays, thereby answering the complaints of ministers who denounced "gasoline Christians." Other states closed the theaters on Sundays, effectively stifling another of the churches' major sources of competition. Politically minded evangelicals also showed an interest in regulating billiard parlors, carnivals, vaudeville shows, and dancing schools. Some tried to prohibit midway amusements at county fairs, hoping to clean up the disreputable side of those complex institutions. Some county school boards forbade dancing on school property in response to questions like that of a Methodist woman in Tennessee: "To which should the public school cater, the class who demand dancing in the class or the class who demand the teaching of the Bible in the school?"[32]

In the 1910s, evangelicals began wondering how they could control the threat posed by the movies. By the middle of that decade, religious groups were calling on local governments to regulate the content of movies. Considering how "to do its best to censor the films of the local picture shows," an interdenominational group of ministers in Salisbury, North Carolina, asked movie proprietors to change their Friday schedules to show only educational pictures for children. The following year, a similar group in Lincolnton, North Carolina, met with theater owners to make a "firm and kindly request that they endeavor to show pictures of moral worth." For some evangelicals, reforming the movies' content was not enough. Just as they had conquered alcohol, many felt that they could do away with the theater. "If it cannot be cleaned, then we should declare unending war on it till it is destroyed from the land as was the saloon." Arkansas minister L. P. Thomas was more blunt. "As to the movie it has no rightful place this side of hell."[33]

Of course, moral reform was far from being an exclusively Southern activity in the early twentieth century. The nationwide Progressive movement stemmed from some of the same impulses and contained many of the same goals as the various reform movements in the South. Indeed, in an exhaustive study of Southern Progressivism, Dewey Grantham has discovered few elements of reform that one could call distinctively Southern.[34] Many of the region's reformers had agendas other than the upholding of moral ideals. Some wished to advance middle-class business interests, making the towns stable places for commerce. Some reformers supported the efforts of plantation owners to keep blacks in the fields and out of trouble. Some supported the goals of modern professionals, who wanted to take systematic government and modern science to a rural South more comfortable with tradition. But virtually all reformers spoke in evangelical language. Southerners' answers to new social questions almost always incorporated evangelical notions of self-control, the moral significance of family life, and the fear of behavior associated with blacks. Whatever the evil, as J. Wayne Flynt has argued, religious morality was part of the remedy.[35]

Evangelicalism, so long a vital part of Southern private life, had by early in the twentieth century become central to the public life of the region. Ministers and religious leaders felt comfortable contributing to the discussion of countless public issues. Moralism was an important element of the nationwide Progressive movement, but nowhere was that element so strong as in the South.[36] Evil had long been a particularly dramatic foe, whether it took the form of the Saturday afternoon drunken white man, the self-indulgent wealthy man, or the seemingly bestial black man. But in the late nineteenth and early twentieth centuries all three evils became even more threatening with the growing accessibility of the towns and hence the saloons, the predominance of a mass culture that glorified the luxurious pursuit of pleasure, and the never-ending fear of blacks. Satan seemed to lurk at every window, and evangelicals, more than ever before, were determined to subdue him.

What of the recent South? The fighting, drinking, swearing Southern man is hardly a thing of the past, even if he is no longer the only enemy of today's evangelicals. But the old tension between sinfulness—often masculine sinfulness—and evangelical virtue remains a powerful part of Southern life. The region's musicians—the best spokespersons for many Southerners—alternate between sin and repentance both in their own lives and in their songs. Willie Nelson, for example, can begin a concert with the line, "Whiskey River, take my mind," and end it with "Amazing Grace." Elvis Presley, one of the more flamboyant sinners in American history, included gospel singers and evangelists in his entourage.

Have the South's evangelicals, faced with the combined forces of traditional masculinity and twentieth-century mass culture, backed away from their commitment to enforcing moral purity? It would be easy to argue that the region's interest in religion is on the decline. Southern writers of pious autobiographies almost invariably lament the loss of the purity of behavior and depth of belief that characterized their early days. The practices that once preserved the sanctity of the home—family prayer and the quiet Sunday—and the purity of the church—discipline for moral offenses—have declined dramatically since the late 1800s. Evangelical churches, which once tried to isolate themselves from all but the most strictly moral recreations, now participate in their own versions of a wide range of pastimes. Whereas evangelicals once shunned most forms of drama, they now have their own television and movie companies to compete with the secular cinema that many church people see as the enemy. Whereas churches once denounced all organized sports, they now sponsor softball and basketball teams that battle at least as ferociously as professionals. And most churches have come to a shaky truce with some masculine institutions such as the football game and the stock-car race. In many areas of the South, both of these events still begin with a prayer that asks for safety, fair play, and a brief consideration of matters more important than sport.[37]

But this partial accommodation is only one side—and not the most important side—of the relationship of Southern evangelicals with the larger world. One often hears that we live in a culture in which anything goes and the pursuit of pleasure has no limits. But countless laws restrict the pursuit of pleasure at every turn, and Southern evangelicals have been particularly interested in such laws. Today's nationwide crusade to purify American culture through Christian legislation speaks with a decidedly Southern accent. The region's evangelist-politicians unceasingly advocate new laws dealing with everything from prayer and Bible reading in school, to abortion, to pornography, to the content of popular songs and television programs, to the old standby, the sale of alcohol. The evangelical rallying cry has not changed since the nineteenth century. Spokesmen for these laws still claim to be the protectors of the home—a religious institution today as it was in the nineteenth century. The conflict between the evangelical culture of the home and church and the culture of largely masculine sinfulness is still with us, but it has become a very public conflict, and one evangelicals feel more hopeful than ever that they may finally be able to win.

Notes

Abbreviations Used in Notes

ALDAH   Alabama Department of Archives and History, Montgomery, Ala.
DCHS   Disciples of Christ Historical Society, Nashville, Tenn.
Duke   Perkins Library, Duke University, Durham, N.C.
Emory   Special Collections, Robert Woodruff Library, Emory University, Atlanta, Ga.
FSA   Florida State Archives, Tallahassee, Fla.
GDAH   Georgia Department of Archives and History, Atlanta, Ga.
GHS   Georgia Historical Society, Savannah, Ga.
LSU   Special Collections, Louisiana State University Library, Baton Rouge, La.
Montreat Historical Foundation of the Presbyterian and Reformed Churches, Montreat, N.C.
MSDAH   Mississippi Department of Archives and History, Jackson, Miss.
NCC   North Carolina Collection, University of North Carolina, Chapel Hill, N.C.
RBRL   Richard B. Russell Library, University of Georgia, Athens, Ga.
SBLA   Southern Baptist Library and Archives, Nashville, Tenn.
SCHS   South Carolina Historical Society, Charleston, S.C.
SHC   Southern Historical Collection, University of North Carolina, Chapel Hill, N.C.
TNSLA   Tennessee State Library and Archives, Nashville, Tenn.
Tulane   Special Collections, Howard-Tilton Memorial Library, Tulane University, New Orleans, La.
UAL   William Stanley Hoole Special Collections Library, University of Alabama, Tuscaloosa, Ala.
UGA   Special Collections Division, University of Georgia Library, Athens, Ga.
USC   South Caroliniana Library, University of South Carolina, Columbia, S.C.

Preface

1. Wilson, *Baptized in Blood*; Hill et al., *Religion and the Solid South*, 37.

Introduction

1. Cash, *Mind of the South*, 52. Although he is discussing poor white men, Cash states that this description applies to all white males in the South.

2. Breen, "Horses and Gentlemen," 243. For the best example of such a study by an anthropologist, see Geertz, "Deep Play."

3. See Norbeck, "African Rituals of Conflict," 1272; Gluckman, *Order and Rebellion*, 110–36; Turner, *Ritual Process*, 166–203.

4. Marriott, "Feast of Love," 212.

5. See Eliade, *Sacred and the Profane*.

6. On the sacralizing of the English and American home in the nineteenth century, see Douglas, *Feminization of American Culture*; Ryan, *Cradle of the Middle Class*; Welter, "Cult of True Womanhood"; Cott, *Bonds of Womanhood*; Davidoff and Hall, *Family Fortunes*; Calder, *Victorian Home*. For the arguments about the origins of that sentiment, see Macfarlane, *Marriage and Love in England*; Stone, *Family, Sex, and Marriage*; Greven, *Protestant Temperament*; Morgan, *Puritan Family*; Ozment, *When Fathers Ruled*; Demos, *A Little Commonwealth*; Schama, *Embarassment of Riches*.

7. Mathews, *Religion in the Old South*, 111–20; Friedman, *Enclosed Garden*.

8. Haygood, *Our Children*, 78; Annie Blount Diary, 6 May 1883, UGA; Stacy, *Day of Rest*, 272; English, *Family Religion*, 3; Donner, *Giving the Devil His Dues*, 24; Haygood, *Our Children*, 171–73. One might object that because the above and other published works were written by urban ministers, they did not represent the opinions of rural evangelicals. But virtually all those ministers spent the first part of their ministries in the rural South and developed their sermons there.

9. Rutherford, *Church Members' Guide for Baptist Churches*, 130; Quillian, *His Life and Sermons*, 147–48.

10. John Potts Brown Notebook, n.p., LSU; Harrod C. Anderson Diary, 190 (19 June 1888), Harrod C. Anderson Papers, LSU; Jane M. Jones Diaries, 31 Dec. 1856, TNSLA; Sally Randle Perry Diary, 28 Jan. 1868, ALDAH.

11. Jane M. Jones Diaries, 30 Jan. 1859, TNSLA; Henrietta Carroll Smith Diary, 21 Apr. 1898, GDAH; Nannie Haskins Williams Diary, 31 Oct. 1880, SHC.

12. Nannie Haskins Williams Diary, 21 Aug. 1869, SHC; Jacobs, *Diary*, 121–22 (2 Feb. 1865); Calvin Henderson Wiley to Mittie Wiley, near Greensboro, N.C., 13 Oct. 1865, Calvin Henderson Wiley Papers, SHC; Mittie Wiley to Calvin Henderson Wiley, Jonesboro, Tenn., 8 Mar. 1870, ibid.

13. *The Home Monthly*, Mar. 1870, 180–81; Rev. Joseph B. Stratton Diary, 346 (1 May 1875), LSU; Ann Hassell to Caroline House, Williamston, N.C., May 1896, Sylvester S. Hassell Papers, SHC; Helen L. Quartermain to John Jones, Walthourville, Ga., 26 Aug. 1877, Rev. John Jones Family Papers, UGA. Some historians have argued that white Protestants in the nineteenth century sentimentalized death, expecting heaven to be a continuation of life's most satisfying elements. See Ariès, *Western Attitudes toward Death*; Douglas, "Heaven Our Home"; Stannard, *Puritan Way of Death*; Friedman, *Enclosed Garden*, xiv. Others counter that nineteenth-century Americans had a gloomy obsession with the possibility of serious illness and the inevitability of death. See Oakes, *Ruling Race*, 110–17; Saum, "Death in the Popular Mind."

14. Bounds, *Heaven a Place*, 13; Dunbar H. Ogden to "Dearest Auntie," Home-

wood, La., 13 July 1895, Ogden Family Papers, Tulane; Anthony, *Life and Times*, 154; M. Alexander to John Jones, Augusta, Ga., 21 July 1879, Rev. John Jones Family Papers, UGA; Rebecca Sharp Clayton Diary, 1 Aug. 1878, TNSLA.

15. George M. Nolan to John Davis Gray, McDonough, Ga., 2 June 1879, Burge-Gray Family Papers, Emory; Jacobs, *Diary*, 214 (16 Mar. 1878).

16. Ryan, *Cradle of the Middle Class*; Welter, "Cult of True Womanhood"; Cott, *Bonds of Womanhood*; Van de Wetering, "Popular Concept of 'Home.' "

17. *Baptist Advance*, 9 June 1910, 16; Jones, *Revival Sermons*, 141; Lowber, *Devil in Modern Society*, 47.

18. Robert Toombs DuBose, sermon preached in Madison, Ga., 27 Aug. 1899, 15, DuBose Family Papers, UGA; Jones, *Sermons and Sayings*, 83.

19. Ella Gertrude (Clanton) Thomas Journal, 169 (29 Aug. 1870), Duke; Elizabeth Eloise Wilkes Diary, 1908, 7, Elizabeth Eloise Wilkes Papers, GHS.

20. Bounds, *Heaven a Place*, 93.

21. King, *Great South*, 372; Macrae, *Americans at Home*, 320. On fighting among individuals, see Gorn, " 'Gouge and Bite' "; Wyatt-Brown, *Southern Honor*; Bruce, *Violence and Culture*. On honor and southern politics, see Greenberg, *Masters and Statesmen*; Cooper, *South and the Politics of Slavery*. On honor and the military, see Franklin, *Militant South*; McWhiney and Jamieson, *Attack and Die*.

22. Ayers, *Vengeance and Justice*, 13; Gorn, " 'Gouge and Bite,' " 42.

23. Cash, *Mind of the South*, 55–60; Wyatt-Brown, *Southern Honor*.

24. R. H. Rivers, in Rivers and Morrison, *Arrows from Two Quivers*, 115–16.

25. Harrod C. Anderson Diary, 4 (27 Sept. 1887), Harrod C. Anderson Papers, LSU; Julia Gold to Pleasant Daniel Gold, Goldsboro, N.C., 26 Dec. 1865, Pleasant Daniel Gold Papers, SHC; Sereno Taylor Diary, 5 Mar. 1857, Sereno Taylor Papers, LSU.

26. See Breen, "Looking Out for Number One"; Kulikoff, *Tobacco and Slaves*, chap. 6; Sydnor, *American Revolutionaries*, chap. 4; Wyatt-Brown, *Southern Honor*.

27. Drew Gilpin Faust has shown that when Southern men faced the likelihood of death in the Civil War, they turned quickly to the evangelical elements in their culture (Faust, "Christian Soldiers"). On white Southern evangelicals' particularly strong commitments to righteousness in personal behavior, see Hill, *Southern Churches in Crisis*; Loveland, *Southern Evangelicals*; Spain, *At Ease in Zion*; Eighmy, *Churches in Cultural Captivity*.

28. For different explanations, see Wyatt-Brown, *Southern Honor*; Cash, *Mind of the South*; Ayers, *Vengeance and Justice*; McWhiney, *Cracker Culture*; McWhiney and Jamieson, *Attack and Die*; Franklin, *Militant South*; Moore, *Frontier Mind*; Cason, *Ninety Degrees in the Shade*.

29. Roosevelt, *Outdoor Pastimes*, 254. On professionals and masculine recreation, see Rotundo, "Body and Soul"; Filene, *Him/Her/Self*; Stearns, *Be a Man!*; Stearns, "Men, Boys, and Anger"; Mrozek, *Sport and American Mentality*. On reformers and male sports, see Boyer, *Urban Masses and Moral Order*; Cavallo, *Muscles and Morals*; Hardy, *How Boston Played*; Hantover, "Boy Scouts."

30. Quillian, *His Life and Sermons*, 149. For the best study of the origins of fears of blacks' bestial natures, see Jordan, *White over Black*.

Chapter 1

1. Robertson, *Red Hills and Cotton*, 186.
2. On game as a source of food, see Hahn, *Roots of Southern Populism*; Flynn, *White Land, Black Labor*; Singleton, "Utility of Leisure." On race relations, see Kirby, *Rural Worlds Lost*, 252. On the Virginia fox hunt, see Higginson and Chamberlain, *Hunts of the United States and Canada*; Street, *American Adventures*, 175–77. For conspicuous display in leisure, see Mrozek, *Sport and American Mentality*, 103–35.
3. Rutledge, "That Hunt at Jasper Hill," 897.
4. James Obelkovich describes the tensions between the English gentry and the churches, particularly in the matter of fox chases, which often invaded church grounds (*Religion and Rural Society*, 40–46). Also on hunting as a symbol of gentry culture, see Horn, *Changing Countryside*, 44–46; Ruffier, *Big Shots*. Horn and Ruffier describe the shooting of tremendous numbers of birds as arising out of an enhanced need to show gentry status in an economically difficult period.
5. Daniel R. A. C. Hundley Diary, 5 Jan.–31 Mar. 1861, SHC; Clive Metcalfe Diary, Aug.–Dec. 1888, SHC; Joshua Burns Moore Diary, 14 Dec. 1860–26 Jan. 1861, ALDAH; James Gordon Diary, 1873, Robert and James Gordon Diaries, MSDAH.
6. Wright, *Barefoot in Arcadia*, 45. Also on fox hunting, see Cox, *Hoot Owls*, 154; Long, *Son of Carolina*, 25; Whitney, "Fox-Hunting in the United States," 21. On turkey hunting, see Wolf, *Life in the Leatherwoods*, 46; Rutledge, *An American Hunter*, 83–87; Brooks, *Southern Lawyer*, 3; McIlhenny, *Wild Turkey*, 5–10; Jenkins, *Wild Life in Mississippi*, 16–25. On squirrel and rabbit hunting, see Roberts, *Some Oaks Grow Small*, 57–58; Leonard, *Some Personal Experiences*, 21; Long, *Son of Carolina*, 62; Hamm, *From the Hills of Carolina*, 29; Garrett, *Horse and Buggy Days*, 196–97. On opossum and raccoon hunting, see Robertson, *Red Hills and Cotton*, 186–88; Thomas Dixon, in Crowe, "Southern Horizons," 156–57; Plyler, *My Life as a Minister's Son*, 54; Isbell, *World of My Childhood*, 69–71.
7. Thomas Drake Samford Diary, 10 Feb. 1907, Samford Diaries, SHC; David Schenck Diary, 25 Aug. 1869, SHC; Mrs. Leonidas L. Polk Diary, 10–11 Oct. 1873, Gale and Polk Family Papers, SHC; Stockbridge, "Sacrilegious Possum," 166–70; Salley, *Happy Hunting Ground*, 10; Hamrick, *Life Values*, 69; Cox, *Hoot Owls*, 154–58.
8. *Pearl River News*, 2 Jan. 1890; Alfred Taylor Diary, 1865–93, SHC; Tobias Goodman to G. E. Goodman, 31 Dec. 1892, William S. Powell Collection, SHC. Also on Christmas, see Wolf, *Life in the Leatherwoods*, 83–84; McCravy, *Memories*, 365–67; Olds, "Christmas Morning in Carolina," 383–84; Fort, "Reminiscence," GDAH.
9. Leigh, *Ten Years on a Georgia Plantation*, 64, 118–19; Wilkinson, "Southern Sportswomen," 775–78; Drummond, *Hoot Owls and Orchids*, 76; Rosengarten, *Tombee*.
10. Roberts, *Some Oaks Grow Small*, 57; Chamberlain, "Fifty Years Ago," 50, NCC; Pamplin, *Scamps of Bucksnort*, 108; Holmes, *Brokenburn*, 63. See also Gohdes, *Hunting in the Old South*, xvi; Thigpen, *Ninety and One Years*, 47.

11. McIlhenny, *Wild Turkey*, 4; *Putnam County Herald*, 17 Dec. 1914; Rutledge, *Those Were the Days*, 30; Rutledge, *American Hunter*, 142; Barr, *Big Game Hunting*, v. On birdshot and buckshot, see Campbell, *Arkansas Lawyer*, 20.

12. Hundley, *Social Relations*.

13. Beard, *My Own Life*, 37; Anna Cook to Thomas F. Cook, Midway, Ga., 6 Dec. 1890, Green-Cook Papers, UGA.

14. Avirett, *The Old Plantation*, 183; David Schenck Diary, 25 Aug. 1869, SHC; McCravy, *Memories*, 360, 371; William Porcher DuBose Reminscences, 77, SHC. See also Julian Wilkes Reminiscences, 10–11, Wilkes Family Papers, GDAH.

15. See Nichols, "Notes on Dogs and Hunting," May 1875, Duke; William Harleston Huger to Thomas J. McKie, n.p., 18 Apr. 1890, William Harleston Huger Letters, USC.

16. Rutledge, *Plantation Game Trails*, 127; McGaffney, "Hunting Wildcats," 770–74; Douglas, "Quail Shooting in the South," 548; Butler, "Sportsman's Paradise"; Andrews, *South since the War*, 177; Agee and Evans, *Let Us Now Praise Famous Men*, 192.

17. Brooks, *Southern Lawyer*, 6.

18. Rutledge, "That Hunt at Jasper Hill," 896; Olds, "Christmas Morning in Carolina." On blacks as guides, see Rutledge, *Plantation Game Trails*, 36; Salley, *Happy Hunting Ground*, 3; Jones, "Turkey-Hunting in the Old Dominion," 751–52.

19. Babcock, *My Health Is Better in November*, 118.

20. On hunting and alcohol, see Anthony, *Fifty Years in the Ministry*, 130.

21. Brooks, *Southern Lawyer*, 3; Alfred Taylor Diary, 2:65, SHC.

22. Cox, *Hoot Owls*, 153; Hamrick, *Life Values*, 67; Hundley, *Social Relations*, 36; E. Walker Duvall, "Memories of E. Walker Duvall," 10, SHC.

23. Rutledge, *American Hunter*, 90; Isbell, *World of My Childhood*, 14; Mary Dickinson to "Lodo," Live Oak, La., 6 June 1862, Andrew Haynes Gay and Family Papers, LSU; Roberts, *Some Oaks Grow Small*, 58.

24. Beard, *My Own Life*, 37; Daniel R. A. C. Hundley Diary, 11 Jan. 1861, SHC; Jenkins, *Wild Life in Mississippi*, 35; *Asheboro Bulletin*, 21 Oct. 1914.

25. Thomas Dixon, in Crowe, "Southern Horizons," 156.

26. Cox, *Hoot Owls*, 171; Hunter, *Huntsman in the South*, 1:48–49.

27. Hunter, *Huntsman in the South*, 1:49.

28. Bruce, *Violence and Culture*, 197–98.

29. Rutledge, *Plantation Game Trails*, 32–33, 49; Nichols, "Notes on Dogs and Hunting," Jan. 1875, Duke; McIlhenny, *Wild Turkey*, 8.

30. Rutledge, "My Greatest Thrill," 19; Nichols, "Notes on Dogs and Hunting," Jan. 1875, Duke; McIlhenny, *Wild Turkey*, 7.

31. Audubon Society of North Carolina, Second Annual Report, 1904, 8–10; Wolf, *Life in the Leatherwoods*, 84; Daniel R. A. C. Hundley Diary, 30 Jan. 1861, SHC; *Siler City Grit*, 4 Mar. 1914; Leonard, *Some Personal Experiences*, 21. See also Jenkins, *Wild Life in Mississippi*, 116.

32. Alfred Taylor Diary, 2:65, SHC; Wolf, *Life in the Leatherwoods*, 81; Robert Eugene Hale Recollections, 7, Robert Eugene Hale Papers, ALDAH; Alabama Department of Conservation of Game, First Biennial Report, 1908, 10. See also McIlhenny, *Wild Turkey*, 17; Lanier, "On the Trail of the Wild Turkey," 882.

33. Herring, *Saturday Night Sketches*, 236; McGaffney, "How They Hunt Deer," 648–52; Rutledge, *Plantation Game Trails*, 89; Ralph, *Dixie*, 326–28; Salley, *Happy Hunting Ground*, ix.

34. *Anson Times*, 21 July 1881; Cox, *Hoot Owls*, 169–70; *Kinston Journal*, 31 July 1879; *Ansonian*, 28 Mar. 1907; Y. F. Griffin to Micajah Wilkinson, Washington County, Miss., 20 Mar. 1853, Micajah Wilkinson Papers, LSU; *Mississippi Democrat*, 28 July 1875. See also Garrett, *Horse and Buggy Days*, 201; Smith, *Boyhood Memories of Fauquier*, 66–68.

35. *McDuffie Weekly Journal*, 1 Mar. 1876; *Franklin Times*, 14 Feb. 1890; *Warren Record*, 17 Dec. 1897; *Atlanta Constitution*, 15 Mar. 1880; *Alabama Baptist*, 20 Dec. 1883; *Arkansas Traveler*, 20 Sept. 1877; *Macon Beacon*, 2 Apr. 1887.

36. Clive Metcalfe Diary, 14 Oct., 24 Nov. 1888, SHC; R. Hatch to Buckner Purvis, Buckner, La., 27 Dec. 1903, George C. Purvis and Family Papers, LSU; George W. Howard Diary, 20 Feb., 18 Dec. 1885, UGA; Shepard Ezekiel Perkins Diary, 16 Mar. 1888, GDAH; Archibald C. McKinley Journal, 14 Aug. 1871, 1 Feb. 1872, UGA; Samuel Cook Diary, 3 Feb. 1873, Green-Cook Papers, UGA; David Schenck Diary, 23 Jan. 1871, SHC.

37. George W. Bennett Record Book, no. 194, 1–3, George W. Bennett Account Books, LSU.

38. Roosevelt, *Wilderness Hunter*, 255; idem, *Outdoor Pastimes*, 188. See also *Wilderness Hunter*, 51, 52, 256; *Outdoor Pastimes*, 227–229; idem, *Hunting Trips*, 261, 273. On Northern naturalist sentiment among sportsmen, see Reiger, *American Sportsmen*; Altherr, "American Hunter-Naturalist," 7–22.

Chapter 2

1. Carter, *Why Not the Best?*, 19.

2. On the urban men's quarter, see Kingsdale, "Poor Man's Working Class Saloon"; Thomason, "Men's Quarter"; Wilentz, *Chants Democratic*, 53–54; Rosenzweig, *Eight Hours*, 53–64; Peiss, *Cheap Amusements*, 16–21; May, *Screening Out the Past*, 17–19. On male and female areas in smaller towns, see Roubin, "Male Space and Female Space."

3. *Conyers Examiner*, 27 Apr. 1878; Johnson, *Highways and Byways*, 76, 97. See also Ralph, *Dixie*, 126; Long, *Son of Carolina*, 27.

4. Medford, *Finis and Farewell*, 100; Garrett, *Horse and Buggy Days*, 19; Long, *My Long Life*, 29. See also Faulkner, *Intruder in the Dust*, 19. On a tradition of leisure, see Bertelson, *Lazy South*; C. Vann Woodward, "The Southern Ethic in a Puritan World," in *American Counterpoint*; McDonald and McWhiney, "South from Self-Sufficiency to Peonage"; Ownby, "Defeated Generation at Work."

5. McElreath, *Walter McElreath*, 44–45.

6. James Washington Moore Diaries, 25 Dec. 1869, USC; Scott, *Background in Tennessee*, 218; Chamberlain, *This Was Home*, 170, 209; Lipsey, "Memories," 26, TNSLA; Craig, "Old Wentworth Sketches," 201; Pamplin, *Scamps of Bucksnort*, 78.

7. Faulkner, *Light in August*, 162, 164.

8. Johnson, *Highways and Byways*, 79; *Newnan Herald and Advertiser*, 18 Oct. 1889. See also Long, *My Long Life*, 78.

9. Herring, *Saturday Night Sketches*, 138.

10. Sennie Lull to Cabot Lull, Grove Hill, Ala., 11 Nov. 1893, Cabot Lull Collection, UAL; Joshua Burns Moore Diary, 1 Apr. 1873, ALDAH; Brooks, *Southern Lawyer*, 22.

11. Scott, *Background in Tennessee*, 218; *Forest News*, 4 Mar. 1876; Faulkner, *The Hamlet*, 36; Anthony, *Fifty Years in the Ministry*, 98; Craig, "Old Wentworth Sketches," 196.

12. *Morehouse Clarion*, 25 Sept. 1880; *Pearl River News*, 5 Dec. 1889; Betty A. Gleaves Diary, 23 Feb. 1859, TNSLA; Washington S. Chaffin Journals, 21 Mar. 1871, Duke.

13. *Southwestern Press*, 24 Dec. 1880; Hosch, *Nevah Come Back*, 160; *Mountain Signal*, 2 Jan. 1880; *Sumner Free-Trader*, 17 Dec. 1885.

14. *Mississippi Democrat*, 5 Jan. 1875; *Scottsboro Citizen*, 14 Dec. 1882; Henry Waring Ball Diary, 24–25 Dec. 1885, SHC; Blackman, *Look Away!*, 63. See also Cumming, *Reminiscences*, 6–7; Powell, *I Can Go Home Again*, 68–69; Anthony, *Fifty Years in the Ministry*, 189. Suggesting that this was a practice unique—at least in the United States—to the South are Kane, *Southern Christmas Book*, 4; Myers, *Celebrations*, 317.

15. Auld, *Christmas Traditions*, 34–48; Miles, *Christmas in Ritual and Tradition*, 166; James, *Seasonal Feasts and Festivals*, 219–96.

16. James V. Morris Diaries, 25 Dec. 1877, Emory.

17. Unsigned biography of George Leonidas Lyon, George Leonidas Lyon Papers, Duke; *Clayton Bud*, 23 Dec. 1885.

18. *Kinston Journal*, 20 Dec. 1878; Hundley, *Social Relations*, 199; McElreath, *Walter McElreath*, 18. See also Winston, *It's a Far Cry*, 48.

19. McElreath, *Walter McElreath*, 18.

20. Buffalo Baptist Church Records, Dec. 1877, SBLA; Crocketts Creek Baptist Church Records, Sept. 1875, SBLA; Longfield Baptist Church Records, Mar. 1898, SBLA; Bethsaida Baptist Church Records, Dec. 1885, SBLA.

21. Winston, *It's a Far Cry*, 48; Bond, *I Had a Friend*, 11–12. See also Cox, *Hoot Owls*, 135. For historical works, see Malcolmson, *Popular Recreations*, 45–47; Greaves, *Society and Religion*, 444–46.

22. See chapter 7.

23. *Concord Register*, 19 Feb. 1876; *Forest News*, 9 Oct. 1875; *Scottsboro Citizen*, 28 Dec. 1882. On evangelicals' condemnations of profanity in the Civil War, see Faust, "Christian Soldiers," 79–80.

24. Luther McKinney, "Profanity," Box 2, Folder 16, Jeptha McKinney Papers, LSU; ADH to Sister, Harrisonburg, La., 28 Dec. 1878, ibid.; Jones, *Revival Sermons*, 132.

25. Mt. Moriah Fellowship Baptist Church Minutes, Jan. 1871, SBLA; Wheelers Baptist Church Minute Books, Apr. 1881, SHC; Black Creek Baptist Church Book, 14 May 1867, 36, typescript, USC.

26. Rorabaugh, *Alcoholic Republic*, 168–69.

27. Atkins, *It Can Be Done*, 11; *Morehouse Clarion*, 6 June 1884.

28. Sarah Morse Haynsworth to Children, Fairfield, S.C., 25 July 1868, Hayns-

worth Family Papers, SCHS; E. J. Larkin Diary, 15 Jan., 10 Mar. 1878, LSU; Jackson, *Vinegar Pie*, 33.

29. Durham, *Since I Was Born*, 160; Charles E. Dowman to John Davis Gray, Quincy, Fla., 1 Feb. 1875, Burge-Gray Family Papers, Emory; Powell, *I Can Go Home Again*, 14.

30. *Hinds County Gazette*, 5 June 1868; *Van Buren Press*, 19 Apr. 1870.

31. *Morehouse Clarion*, 9 Jan. 1880.

32. E. J. Larkin Diary, 25 Feb., 12 Mar., 2 June 1878, LSU; Isaac H. Hilliard, Jr., Diary, vol. 4, 19 Apr. 1871, Isaac H. Hilliard and Family Papers, LSU; E. J. Larkin Diary, 8 May 1878, LSU; Marcus Wayland Beck Diaries, 19 Dec. 1900, RBRL; Ayers, *Vengeance and Justice*, chap. 4.

33. Winston, *It's a Far Cry*, 52; E. J. Larkin Diary, 26 July 1878, LSU; *Oglethorpe Echo*, 8 Jan. 1875; *Calhoun County Courier*, 6 Oct. 1882; *Greeneville Herald*, 29 Dec. 1881.

34. Thetis Bush to Micajah Wilkinson, Collinsburg, La., 7 Apr. 1880, Micajah Wilkinson Papers, LSU; Jennie Samuel to Edward H. Samuel, Tuscaloosa, Ala., 25 Jan. 1871, Caroline Virginia Samuel Letters, LSU; David Schenck Diary, 25 Dec. 1872, SHC; Risden B. Gaddy to Fannie Bennett, Wadesboro, N.C., 25 Apr. 1869, Fannie (Bennett) Gaddy Papers, Duke.

35. *Hinds County Gazette*, 19 Nov. 1867; Street, *American Adventures*, 399; Bill Arp, quoted in Burton, *In My Father's House*, 297.

36. On this point, see Ryan, "Explosion of Family History," 185–86.

Chapter 3

1. Somers, "Leisure Revolution," 132–38.

2. Winston, *It's a Far Cry*, 46–47.

3. Twain, *Huckleberry Finn*, 120.

4. Isbell, *World of My Childhood*, 23; Thornburg, *Thread of My Life*, 15–16; Chamberlain, "Fifty Years Ago," 130, NCC; Shettles, *Recollections*, 43; Thomas Henry Briggs Diaries, 22 Oct. 1866, Willis Grandy Briggs Papers, SHC; Mattie to Anna Green, Midway, Ga., 11 Apr. 1866, Green-Cook Papers, UGA; Samuel A. Cook to Anna Green, Albany, Ga., 12 Nov. 1868, ibid.

5. *Rowan Record*, 7 Oct. 1909; Sally Randle Perry Diary, 16 Dec. 1867, ALDAH.

6. Evelyn Harden Jackson Diary, 27 Dec. 1875, Harden-Jackson-Carithers Collection, UGA; Winston, *It's a Far Cry*, 46; Mell Marshall Barrett Memoir, 14, GDAH. On the presence of blacks at circuses, see also Samuel A. Cook to Thomas F. Cook, Midway, Ga., 1 Nov. 1890, Green-Cook Papers, UGA; Rabinowitz, "From Exclusion to Segregation," 328.

7. Archibald C. McKinley Journal, 14 June 1869, UGA; Betty A. Gleaves Diary, 27 Apr. 1858, TNSLA; P. E. Roberts to Newton Morton Hale, Tyler, Tex., 1 May 1873, William George Hale Papers, LSU; Kirk, *Locust Hill*, 88.

8. See Isherwood, *Farce and Fantasy*, 44–48.

9. P. E. Roberts to Newton Morton Hale, Tyler, Tex., 1 May 1873, William George Hale Papers, LSU; *Hartwell Sun*, 9 May 1877; Winston, *It's a Far Cry*, 46; *Athens Post*, 31 July 1868.

10. *Chester Semi-Weekly News*, 2 Nov. 1915; Winston, *It's a Far Cry*, 46.

11. Dabney, *Across the Years*, 14; Hosch, *Nevah Come Back*, 193; *Jesup Sentinel*, 27 Oct. 1880.

12. *Athens Post*, 31 July 1868; Everard Green Baker Diary, 1:40–41 (8 Apr. 1857), SHC; Winston, *It's a Far Cry*, 47; Daniel, *Standing at the Crossroads*, 52–54.

13. Jordan, *White over Black*, 28–40.

14. Isherwood, *Farce and Fantasy*, 41. On children performing such stunts, see Wood, *Once Apunce a Time*, 104; Mattie to Anna Green, Midway, Ga., 11 Apr. 1866, Green-Cook Papers, UGA. See also Twain, *Tom Sawyer*, 133.

15. Dabney, *Across the Years*, 14; Hosch, *Nevah Come Back*, 192; Winston, *It's a Far Cry*, 46; Thigpen, *Boy in Rural Mississippi*, 47.

16. Harris, *Humbug*, 248.

17. Pierce, *Sermons and Addresses*, 288; Sermon Notes, Feb. 1871, V. V. Anderson Papers, Duke; Johnson, *Autobiographical Notes*, 219; Jeannie to R. T. DuBose, Athens, Ga., 19 Oct. 1879, DuBose Family Papers, UGA; William James Samford Diary, 30 Oct. 1899, Samford Diaries, SHC; Evelyn Harden Jackson Diary, 27 Dec. 1875, Harden-Jackson-Carithers Collection, UGA.

18. *Warren Record*, 22 Oct. 1897.

19. Jacob Henry Smith Diary, 7 Oct. 1867, 9 Oct. 1883, SHC; James Clarence Harper Diaries, 38 (9 Oct. 1867), SHC; W. Clinton Thompson to Ethel Bryson, Madison, Ga., 4 Nov. 1905, Bryson Family Papers, GDAH.

20. See for example, Hosch, *Nevah Come Back*; Thigpen, *Boy in Rural Mississippi*. See also several letters in Green-Cook Papers, UGA.

21. *Fayetteville Observer*, 25 Mar. 1869; *Marlboro Democrat*, 28 Oct. 1904; *Greensboro Herald*, 22 Nov. 1877.

22. Twain, *Huckleberry Finn*, 121; *Southwestern Press*, 5 June 1878.

23. Coffman, *Happy Years*, 17–18; Mollie A. Parham Diary, 24 (26 Oct. 1872), SHC. On *Ten Nights in a Barroom*, see Samuel Mills Meeks, Jr., Diaries, 26 Jan. 1886, Meeks Family Papers, UAL; Clark, *Deliver Us from Evil*, 40–43. For ministers' condemnations of the theater, see Lowber, *Devil in Modern Society*, 13–19; Lovejoy, *Mission of the Church*.

24. Mell Marshall Barrett Memoir, 37, GDAH; Roark, *Home Places*, 60; Long, *My Long Life*, 76; *Mansfield Enterprise*, 15 July 1911. For a description of the various traveling shows in the South, see Charles Reagan Wilson, "Traveling Shows," in Wilson and Ferris, *Encylopedia of Southern Culture*, 1247–49.

Chapter 4

1. Roark, *Masters without Slaves*; Woodward, *Origins of the New South*; Connelly and Bellows, *God and General Longstreet*; Osterweis, *Myth of the Lost Cause*; Wilson, *Baptized in Blood*; Friedman, *White Savage*.

2. Liddell, *With a Southern Accent*, 39.

3. Isaac, *Transformation of Virginia*, 80–114.

4. Ibid., 58–65.

5. Porter, *Straight Down a Crooked Lane*, 14; Scott, *Background in Tennessee*, 231–32.

6. Chamberlain, "Fifty Years Ago," 122–23, NCC; Poe, *My First Eighty Years*,

53; Jeptha McKinney to Ada McKinney, Oak Grove, La., 5 Sept. 1869, Jeptha McKinney Papers, LSU; Mary Eldridge to Mrs. Emmil, Americus, Ga., 21 Oct. 1882, Lewis Neale Whittle Papers, SHC.

7. Stowe, *Intimacy and Power*, 10.

8. Keen, *Chivalry*, 90.

9. Horton Branch to Robert R. Evans, Magnolia, Ga., 31 Aug. 1897, Branch Family Papers, SHC; Avary, *Dixie after the War*, 171–72; Ivey, *My Memoirs*, 56–57; Obear, *Old Winnsboro*, 96–97; Hiss, "Knights of the Lance," 341–42; Winston, *It's A Far Cry*, 51; *Weekly Columbus Enquirer*, 3 Nov. 1871; *Elberton Gazette*, 3 Dec. 1873.

10. Tate, *The Fathers*, 61–75 (quote, 64); Obear, *Old Winnsboro*, 96; Hiss, "Knights of the Lance," 341; Rice, *Eighteenth Century*, 76; Ella Gertrude (Clanton) Thomas Journal, 25 (3 Dec. 1868), Duke.

11. Avary, *Dixie after the War*, 172; Ella Gertrude (Clanton) Thomas Journal, 196 (13 Nov. 1870), Duke; *Charleston Daily Courier*, 11 Jan. 1872.

12. The names appear in Winston, *It's a Far Cry*, 51; See also [?] to Lucy Massenburg, Enberg, N.C., 3 Nov. 1869, Lucy C. Massenburg Papers, Duke; *Weekly Columbus Enquirer*, 5 Nov. 1872; Ella Gertrude (Clanton) Thomas Journal, 24–25 (3 Dec. 1868), 196 (13 Nov. 1870), Duke. See also Crooks and Crooks, *Ring Tournament*, 154–56.

13. Smith, *Boyhood Memories of Fauquier*, 125. Robert P. Ingalls describes tournaments in Tampa as examples of "classic southern romanticism" (*Urban Vigilantes*, 14).

14. "Mother" to "my darling child," Catawba Falls, S.C., 25 Oct. 1869, William Moultrie Reid Papers, USC; Obear, *Old Winnsboro*, 96; Smith, *Boyhood Memories of Fauquier*, 125; Ella Gertrude (Clanton) Thomas Journal, 196 (13 Nov. 1870), Duke. See also Long, *High Time*, 162; Clemson, *Rebel Came Home*, 93.

15. Ella Gertrude (Clanton) Thomas Journal, 196–97 (13 Nov. 1870), Duke; *Athens Post*, 11 Sept. 1868; Avary, *Dixie after the War*, 171.

16. Avary, *Dixie after the War*, 171.

17. Hiss, "Knights of the Lance," 340; Clemson, *Rebel Came Home*, 93; Long, *High Time*, 162.

18. Ella Gertrude (Clanton) Thomas Journal, 196 (23 Nov. 1870), Duke.

19. Long, *High Time*, 162; Risden B. Gaddy to Fannie Bennett, unspecified camp in Virginia, n.d. 1864/65, Fannie (Bennett) Gaddy Papers, Duke. See also Tate, *The Fathers*, 66–68; Hiss, "Knights of the Lance," 340–41.

20. John R. Polley to Newton Morton Hale, Hamilton, Tex., 6 Apr. 1874, William George Hale Papers, LSU; A. T. Henley to Tompkins, Macon Station, Ala., 25 May 1879, William S. Royston Papers, Duke; Obear, *Old Winnsboro*, 97; Winston, *It's a Far Cry*, 51; Ella Gertrude (Clanton) Thomas Journal, 26 (3 Dec. 1868), Duke; Invitation to tournament and coronation ball, Leaksville, N.C., 4 Dec. 1868, John R. Raine Letters and Papers, Duke.

21. John Dunningham to Calvin Henderson Wiley, Milton, N.C., 7 Sept. 1878, Calvin Henderson Wiley Papers, SHC; Washington S. Chaffin Journals, 27 Dec. 1871, Duke. Both ministers wrote texts that were delivered by laypersons.

22. Drury Lacy to Mrs. T. H. Dewey, Raleigh, N.C., 2 Dec. 1866, Drury Lacy Papers, SHC.

23. Ella Gertrude (Clanton) Thomas Journal, 26 (3 Dec. 1868), Duke; Ivey, *My Memoirs*, 57.

24. *Grit and Steel*, Sept. 1904, 26.

25. Geertz, "Deep Play."

26. W. J. Crittenden to James Gee Oakley, New Orleans, La., 3 Feb. 1900, James Gee Oakley Cockfighting Collection, UAL; *Grit and Steel*, May 1917, 57; ibid., July 1915, 48; Norman F. Harris to James Gee Oakley, New Orleans, La., 19 Mar. 1900, James Gee Oakley Cockfighting Collection, UAL; A. Burnett Rhett to Cleland K. Singleton, Charleston, S.C., 28 Jan. 1874, Singleton Family Papers, USC, W. W. Austen to James Gee Oakley, Atlanta, Ga., 4 Apr. 1900, James Gee Oakley Cockfighting Collection, UAL; Thomas Y. Henry to George L. F. Birdsong, Quincy, Fla., 23 Apr. 1867, George L. F. Birdsong Papers, Emory; *Histories of Game Strains*, 43.

27. Means, *Game Cock*, 33–34; McIntyre, *Game Fowl*, 39.

28. *Grit and Steel*, Mar. 1904, 11–12; J. S. Walden to James Gee Oakley, Lynchburg, Va., 8 Aug. 1900, James Gee Oakley Cockfighting Collection, UAL.

29. A. Burnett Rhett to Cleland K. Singleton, Charleston, S.C., 9 Jan. 1874, Singleton Family Papers, USC; Rhett to Singleton, Charleston, S.C., 14 Aug. 1872, ibid.; *Grit and Steel*, June 1905, 9; ibid., Feb. 1915, 17; ibid., Jan. 1902, 3.

30. McWhiney and Jamieson, *Attack and Die*; Means, *Game Cock*, 34; *Grit and Steel*, May 1902, 9; *Dixie Game Fowl*, Dec. 1902, 1; ibid., 2; *Grit and Steel*, Feb. 1905, 37.

31. *Grit and Steel*, Feb. 1902, 22. See also ibid., Dec. 1904, 15.

32. Ibid., May 1899, 9; ibid., Jan. 1902, 5. On mains and hackfights, see Means, *Game Cock*, 16.

33. W. J. White to James Gee Oakley, Eufaula, Ala., 25 Mar. 1894, James Gee Oakley Cockfighting Collection, UAL; Joseph H. Leech to George L. F. Birdsong, Verona, Miss., 19 Oct. 1868, George L. F. Birdsong Papers, Emory; *Grit and Steel*, Mar. 1902, 23; Joe Lloyd to James Gee Oakley, Meridian, Miss., 2 Dec. 1893, James Gee Oakley Cockfighting Collection, UAL; *Grit and Steel*, Nov. 1901, 5; ibid., Dec. 1901, 11; ibid., Feb. 1902, 2.

34. Wyatt-Brown, *Southern Honor*, 119–25.

35. *Grit and Steel*, Feb. 1905, 37; ibid., May 1902, 25.

36. See letters in the James Gee Oakley Cockfighting Collection, UAL; Means, Advertisements for Red Cuban Games, 1906, 1903, NCC.

37. Walker, *Art of Walking Cocks*, 12, 21.

38. Means, *Game Cock*, 96–97; Walker, *Art of Walking Cocks*, 39.

39. Hundley, *Social Relations*, 94; *Alabama Baptist*, 5 Jan. 1881, 1; Broughton, *Modern Prodigal*, 28–29; *Knoxville Tribune*, quoted in *Grit and Steel*, Feb. 1905, 20.

40. *Grit and Steel*, Nov. 1910, 31; Liddell, *With a Southern Accent*, 35; Beard, *My Own Life*, 37.

41. *Grit and Steel*, Jan. 1902, 5.

42. Hundley, *Social Relations*, 240; *Grit and Steel*, Jan. 1917, 39.

43. *Mobile Daily Register*, 17 Oct. 1873.

44. Joseph A. Leech to George L. F. Birdsong, Verona, Miss., 10 May 1869, George L. F. Birdsong Papers, Emory; Means, *Game Cock*, 103; *Grit and Steel*,

Sept. 1904, 26; Pridgen, *Courage*, 26.

45. *Grit and Steel*, Sept. 1904, 33; ibid., Apr. 1915, 52; McIntyre, *Game Fowl*, 148.

46. *Grit and Steel*, Aug. 1905, 32.

47. *Dixie Game Fowl*, 1 May 1904, 1; *Grit and Steel*, Aug. 1916, 43; ibid., Aug. 1905, 32–33.

48. McIntyre, *Game Fowl*, 149; *Grit and Steel*, Dec. 1916, 34. On more recent cockfighters' attempts to maintain an ethical element in their sport, see McCaghy and Neal, "Fraternity of Cockfighters."

Chapter 5

1. *Southern Cultivator and Dixie Farmer*, 15 Oct. 1901, 2; *Progressive Farmer*, Carolinas edition, 3 Nov. 1903, 8; Clark Berry Stewart Diary, 9 Nov. 1866, Clark Berry Stewart Papers, UGA.

2. Geertz, "Deep Play," 26. See also Frank Manning, "Cosmos and Chaos: Celebration in the Modern World," in Manning, *Celebration of Society*, 3–30.

3. Burke, *Popular Culture*, 185–91. The best theories on rituals of inversion are found in Gluckman, *Order and Rebellion*, 110–36; Turner, *Ritual Process*, 166–203. See also Caillois, *Man, Play, and Games*, 87–91.

4. Clemmons, *Great Time to Be Alive*, 41; *Oglethorpe Echo*, 30 Nov. 1874; *Greensboro Herald*, 1 Dec. 1876; Sarah B. Woods to Mollie Anderson, Strong Point, La., 28 Feb. 1886, Mollie E. Anderson Papers, LSU; Polly (Draper) Langford Diary, 1888, 28, TNSLA; Poe, *My First Eighty Years*, 10; Herring, *Saturday Night Sketches*, 146; Pamplin, *Scamps of Bucksnort*, 56; Wolf, *Life in the Leatherwoods*, 117; Craig, "Home Life in Rockingham County," 514; Shettles, *Recollections*, 19. See also Thigpen, *Ninety and One Years*, 35, 44; Rippy, *Bygones*, 19; Braden, *When Grandma Was a Girl*, 86; Hawks, *Distant Field*, 35–37; Smith, *Boyhood Memories of Fauquier*, 58–59; Bond, *I Had a Friend*, 16. Historical accounts appear in Hardeman, *Shucks, Shocks, and Hominy Blocks*, 40–45; Owsley, *Plain Folk*, 105–16.

5. Pamplin, *Scamps of Bucksnort*, 77; Hamrick, *Life Values*, 37; Herring, *Saturday Night Sketches*, 143; Puckett, *Snow White Sands*, 28–29. On corn shuckings, see also Hawks, *Distant Field*, 37. On cotton pickings, see also Hamrick, *Life Values*, 59. On fodder pullings, see also Herring, *Saturday Night Sketches*, 58.

6. Eleazar, *Dutch Fork Farm Boy*, 122; Owsley, *Plain Folk*, 113. See also Hawks, *Distant Field*, 37.

7. Hamrick, *Life Values*, 71; Stephens, *Echoes of a Passing Era*, 81. See also Pamplin, *Scamps of Bucksnort*, 56–67; Bond, *I Had a Friend*, 17.

8. Jelliffe, *For Dear Life*, 19; Shettles, *Recollections*, 15. See also Craig, "Home Life," 514; Campbell, *Arkansas Lawyer*, 29.

9. Hamrick, *Life Values*, 72; S. A. Morgan to Mollie Anderson, 19 Feb. 1883, Mollie E. Anderson Papers, LSU; McBroom, *Orange County Childhood*, 30; Garrett, *Horse and Buggy Days*, 87; Wolf, *Life in the Leatherwoods*, 117. See also Eleazar, *Dutch Fork Farm Boy*, 122; Stephens, *Echoes of a Passing Era*, 81–82; Pamplin, *Scamps of Bucksnort*, 77.

10. Hawks, *Distant Field*, 44. See also Coleman, *Five Petticoats*, 81; Drummond, *Hoot Owls and Orchids*, 37; Lee, *Recollections of Country Joe*, 58; McBroom, *Orange County Childhood*, 30; Pamplin, *Scamps of Bucksnort*, 66–67; Braden, *When Grandma Was a Girl*, 86. For quilts made from different family members' clothing, see Yabsley, *Texas Quilts*, 46–47. For the quilt made of Bible verses, see Ramsey and Waldvogel, *Quilts of Tennessee*, 48. For the names of different quilt patterns, see Yabsley, *Texas Quilts*, 17, 48; Ramsey and Waldvogel, *Quilts of Tennessee*, 6, 14, 28, 30, 50; Arkansas Quilter's Guild, *Arkansas Quilts*, 44, 48, 66, 84, 90, 98, 100, 106; Roberson, *North Carolina Quilts*, 21, 105, 106; Holstein and Finley, *Kentucky Quilts*, 21, 37, 54.

11. Bond, *I Had a Friend*, 17. See also Herring, *Saturday Night Sketches*, 63; McBroom, *Orange County Childhood*, 40; Wolf, *Life in the Leatherwoods*, 117, Drummond, *Hoot Owls and Orchids*, 37; Shettles, *Recollections*, 19; Puckett, *Snow White Sands*, 29.

12. Miller, "Improving School Grounds," 33.

13. Drummond, *Hoot Owls and Orchids*, 37; Pamplin, *Scamps of Bucksnort*, 67; Owens, "I Was There," 52; Puckett, *Snow White Sands*, 128.

14. Cox, *Hoot Owls*, 129–30; Pamplin, *Scamps of Bucksnort*, 68; Eleazar, *Dutch Fork Farm Boy*, 122. See also Hamrick, *Life Values*, 69–79; Clemmons, *Great Time to Be Alive*, 41; Owsley, *Plain Folk*, 112.

15. Pamplin, *Scamps of Bucksnort*, 77.

16. Darnton, *Great Cat Massacre*, 89–96.

17. Jennie Samuel to Edward H. Samuel, Tuscaloosa, Ala., 24 May 1866, Caroline Virginia Samuel Letters, LSU.

18. Silas F. Talbert to N. M. Hale, Keachi, La., 24 Apr. 1874, Benson Family Papers, LSU.

19. Pamplin, *Scamps of Bucksnort*, 67.

20. Abrahams, "Language of Festivals," 163; Burland, *Echoes of Magic*, 62–65; Forde, *Yakö Studies*, 241; Hose and McDougall, *Pagan Tribes of Borneo*, 1:112; Weiner, *Women of Value*, 131–36.

Chapter 6

1. Tryphena Holder Fox Diary, 3 May 1863, Tryphena Holder Fox Collection, MSDAH.

2. Ninety-Six Presbyterian Church Records, Apr. 1915, USC.

3. Coleman, *Five Petticoats*, 49; McDowall, *Cotton and Jasmine*, 11; English, *Family Religion*, 21. See also Wright, *Barefoot in Arcadia*, 165; Samuel Porter Jones, "Get There and Stay There," unpublished sermon, 75–76, Samuel Porter Jones Papers, Emory; Haygood, *Our Children*, 110–22; Lovejoy, *Mission of the Church*, 144; Rutherford, *Church Members' Guide*, 90–93; Hundley, *Social Relations*, 94–95.

4. Lathrop, *My Mother*, 115.

5. David Schenck Diary, 28 Aug. 1880, SHC; W. T. Bartlett Diary, 7 June 1879, Baber-Blackshear Collection, UGA; Newman, *Why I Am a Baptist*, 4. See also Wright, *Barefoot in Arcadia*, 165; Glenn, *I Remember*, 15.

6. Morrison, *Life Sketches and Sermons*, 25; Jane M. Jones Diaries, 31 Dec. 1856, TNSLA.

7. *Southern Methodist Home Altar*, May 1871, 25–26; Evelyn Harden Jackson Diary, 21 Aug. 1885, Harden-Jackson-Carithers Collection, UGA; Walter Edwin Tynes Diary, 21, MSDAH.

8. Yellow Creek Baptist Church Records, Jan. 1853, SBLA; Ebenezer Erskine Pressly Diaries and Commonplace Books, 24 Jan. 1909, Duke; James Gordon Diary, 25 May 1873, Robert and James Gordon Diaries, MSDAH; Mattie Johnston to Sister, Monroe, La., 3 Jan. 1892, Bennett Family Papers, LSU; Hatton-Lovejoy Memoirs, 20, UGA.

9. Coleman, *Five Petticoats*, 3; Twain, *Tom Sawyer*, 23; Wright, *Barefoot in Arcadia*, 25; Eleazar, *Fifty Years along the Roadside*, 22. See also Shettles, *Recollections*, 25.

10. Wright, *Barefoot in Arcadia*, 24; Cox, *Southern Sidelights*, 90; Russell, *Rare Pattern*, 26; McDowall, *Cotton and Jasmine*, 13; Long, *High Time*, 10; Rankin, *Story of My Life*, 47; Coleman, *Five Petticoats*, 3; Long, *High Time*, 11. See also Liddell, *With a Southern Accent*, 103; Hamrick, *Life Values*, 66; Sibley, "My Grandmother," 4, UGA.

11. Coleman, *Five Petticoats*, 5; Long, *High Time*, 10; Morrison, *Life Sketches*, 15; Faulkner, *Light in August*, 136–43. See also Rankin, *Story of My Life*, 47.

12. Cook, *Journal of a Milledgeville Girl*, 10, 25; Evelyn Harden Jackson Diary, 22 Mar. 1903, Harden-Jackson-Carithers Collection, UGA; James Hervey Greenlee Diary, 27 Mar. 1898, SHC.

13. Rebecca Sharp Clayton Diary, 25 Aug. 1878, TNSLA; Mrs. B. W. Brown to "Little Darling," Waynesville, Ga., 1 Mar. 1868, Hugh Lawson Papers, UGA; Mary Elizabeth Carter Rives Diary, 2 June 1865, LSU; Leila Callaway to Morgan Callaway, Cuthbert, Ga., 6 Sept. 1859, Morgan and Leila Callaway Collection, UGA. See also Cook, *Journal of Milledgeville Girl*, 13, 15; Coleman, *Five Petticoats*, 4.

14. John Jefferson Flowers Diary, 10 Mar. 1872, ALDAH; Elizabeth Baldwin Harris Diaries, 8 Dec. 1867, Duke; James F. Gwinnett Diary, 3 Jan. 1897, SHC; Elizabeth Eloise Wilkes Diary, 13 Oct. 1908, Elizabeth Eloise Wilkes Papers, GHS. On Sunday hunting, see Thetis Bush to Micajah Wilkinson, Collinsburg, La., 7 Apr. 1880, Micajah Wilkinson Papers, LSU; Davis, *The Stranger*, 27; Stockbridge, "Sacrilegious Possum."

15. Reid, *Life, Speeches, and Sermons*, 167.

16. Stacy, *Day of Rest*, 273; Clive Metcalfe Diary, 13 Jan. 1889, SHC.

17. William A. Gill to Tabitha Gill, Greensburg, La., 25 July 1862, Gill-Price Family Papers, MSDAH; Moore, *Dr. Tom*, 34; McBroom, *Orange County Childhood*, 59–60.

18. Mrs. Frank Robbins Diary, 21 Feb. 1897, TNSLA; William Wallace White Diary, 9 June 1907, SHC; James Gordon Diary, 30 Apr. 1876, MSDAH.

19. Jones, *Revival Sermons*, 134.

20. See John Potts Brown Notebook, LSU; Russell, *Rare Pattern*, 25–26; McDowall, *Cotton and Jasmine*, 13; Foust, *Horse and Buggy Days*, 68; Hatton-Lovejoy Memoirs, 15, UGA.

21. Smith-Rosenberg, "Female World of Love and Ritual," 10–13; Cashin, " 'Ties of Nature.' "

22. On this point, see Pederson, "Country Visitor."

23. Braden, *When Grandma Was a Girl*, 86; Wolf, *Life in the Leatherwoods*, 15; Coleman, *Five Petticoats*, 30.

24. Jackson, *Vinegar Pie*, 25–61.

25. Ibid., 61.

26. Ibid., 28, 34, 48.

27. Sallie Dickey to Bettie Scott, Atchafalaya, La., 1 Mar. 1874, Eva Scott and Family Papers, LSU; Mary Elizabeth Carter Rives Diary, 25 May 1868, LSU; Louisa Taylor Diary, 25–28 Mar. 1890, Calvin Taylor and Family Papers, LSU; Elizabeth Baldwin Harris Diaries, 26 June 1880, Duke.

28. Stanfield, *Sourwood Tonic*, 38.

29. Jelliffe, *For Dear Life*, 21; Mary E. Fries Diary, 11 (7 Oct. 1863), SHC; Emma L. Rankin Books, 42 (4 Dec. 1907), SHC; Sadie Gray to John Davis Gray, Pomaria, Ga., 30 July 1876, Burge-Gray Family Papers, Emory.

30. See Cott, *Bonds of Womanhood*; Smith-Rosenberg, "Female World of Love and Ritual."

31. Stanfield, *Sourwood Tonic*, 25; Jackson, *Vinegar Pie*, 34.

32. Mattie Johnston to Sister, Monroe, La., 18 Jan. 1892, Bennett Family Papers, LSU.

33. Merrick, *Old Times in Dixie Land*, 53; constitution of a sewing society, written on the back of an unidentified plantation diary entry, folder 13, Benson Family Papers, LSU. See also Saxon, *Southern Woman's War Time Reminiscences*, 32.

34. Mary Susan Kerr Diary, 25:296 (Feb. 1892), 25:297 (27 Feb. 1892), SHC. See also Mary E. Fries Diary, 11 (9 Oct. 1863), 20 (17 Nov. 1863), SHC.

35. Poe, *My First Eighty Years*, 53; Hawks, *Distant Field*, 85; Liddell, *With a Southern Accent*, 94.

36. *Nashville Banner*, 4 May 1903.

37. Chamberlain, "Fifty Years Ago," 123, NCC; Lovejoy, *Mission of the Church*, 215; First Baptist Church Minutes (Summit, Miss.), May 1904, MSDAH; Crocketts Creek Baptist Church Records, Dec. 1869, SBLA.

38. *Giles County Record*, 11 Dec. 1896.

39. Polk, *The Way We Were*, 172.

40. *Southern Lumber Journal*, 15 Apr. 1910, 68; William James Samford Diary, 31 Dec. 1895, Samford Diaries, SHC; Paul Welch Memoir, 86, TNSLA.

41. Henrietta Carroll Smith Diary, 13 Feb. 1897, GDAH.

42. Powell, *I Can Go Home Again*, 192–94; East Fork Baptist Church Minutes, Feb. 1884, MSDAH; First Baptist Church Minutes (Summit, Miss.), Apr.–May 1879, MSDAH; New Hope Baptist Church Records, Dec. 1883, SBLA; Amiable Baptist Church Records, Oct. 1875, SBLA.

43. First Baptist Church Records (Macon, Miss.), Jan. 1878, MSDAH.

44. Sermon Notes, Feb. 1871, V. V. Anderson Papers, Duke; Lovejoy, *Mission of the Church*, 214; Charles Jefferson Lewis Journal, 23, TNSLA; Nancy R. Willard to Micajah Wilkinson, Collinsburg, La., 30 Mar. 1876, Micajah Wilkinson Papers, LSU. See also Rutherford, *Church Members' Guide*, 163; Leftwich, *Duty of the Church*, 4–5; Thigpen, *Ninety and One Years*, 46.

45. Moore, *Dr. Tom*, 33–34; McBroom, *Orange County Childhood*, 64; ADH to Sister, Harrisonburg, La., 28 Dec. 1878, Jeptha McKinney Papers, LSU. See also

Lovejoy, *Mission of the Church*, 215; Charles Jefferson Lewis Journal, 23, TNSLA; Sermon Notes, Feb. 1871, V. V. Anderson Papers, Duke.

46. Johnson, *Highways and Byways*, 101; Craig, "Old Wentworth Sketches," 188; Powell, *I Can Go Home Again*, 93. I have found only one church that singled out Twistification as an offense worthy of church discipline. See Antioch Baptist Church Minutes, June 1887, SBLA. See also Botkin, "Play-Party in Oklahoma."

47. Hawks, *Distant Field*, 85; Betty A. Gleaves Diary, 27 Feb. 1859, TNSLA. See also Hatton-Lovejoy Memoirs, 15, UGA.

48. Sue Kilbourne to Susie Stone, Garner, Miss., 13 Sept. 1886, J. G. Kilbourne and Family Papers, LSU; Mother to Fanny Conner, Woodlands, Miss., 26 Dec. 1868, Lemuel Conner Family Papers, LSU; Mrs. Calvin Wiley to Calvin Henderson Wiley, Woodlawn, N.C., 29 Aug. 1867, Calvin Henderson Wiley Papers, SHC. See also Hundley, *Social Relations*, 99; Medford, *Finis and Farewell*, 113.

49. Braden, *When Grandma Was a Girl*, 72.

Chapter 7

1. Lizzie Diamond to Mary, Lafayette, Ala., 3 May 1870, James Diamond Family Papers, UGA; A. N. Ogden to Eliza Ogden, Port Gibson, Miss., 19 Oct. 1891, Ogden Family Papers, Tulane.

2. Dunbar Ogden to Eliza Ogden, Port Gibson, Miss., 21 Oct. 1891, Ogden Family Papers, Tulane; Daisy Lines to Jerome Reneau, Macon, Ga., 25 Sept. 1882, Akehurst-Lines Collection, UGA; Mittle D. to Bettie Scott, St. Francisville, La., Sept. 1874, Eva Scott and Family Papers, LSU.

3. Hawks, *Distant Field*, 85.

4. Thomas Henry Briggs Diaries, 26 Apr. 1866, Willis Grandy Briggs Papers, SHC; Sawyers Creek Baptist Church Records, 3:1, 1872, SHC; Brushy Creek Baptist Church Book, 1868, 182, USC.

5. Nancy R. Willard to Micajah Wilkinson, 5 Nov. 1876, Collinsburg, La., Micajah Wilkinson Papers, LSU.

6. Cook, *Journal of Milledgeville Girl*, 11, 102–3.

7. Ann Hassell to Caroline House, Williamston, N.C., 5 Dec. 1896, Sylvester S. Hassell Papers, SHC; Sallie Dobbins to Joe, Oakland, Ga., 22 Feb. 1863, John S. Dobbins Papers, Emory; Henrietta Carroll Smith Diary, 19 May 1897, GDAH; Clive Metcalfe Diary, 31 Mar. 1889, SHC.

8. Broadus, *Treatise*, 472–73; Roark, *Home Places*, 44. For a list similar to Broadus's, see Kern, *Ministry to the Congregation*, 488–89.

9. Sereno Taylor Diary, 11 July 1858, Sereno Taylor Papers, LSU; S. M. Goff to B. W. Pulliam, Kinston, N.C., 21 Feb. 1864, Solomon Hilary Helsabeck Papers, SHC.

10. Warner, *On Horseback*, 8; Allan-Olney, *New Virginians*, 1:199.

11. Thigpen, *Boy in Rural Mississippi*, 14; Hawks, *Distant Field*, 80; Brunner, *Church Life*, 50; Osmond, *Country Church in North Carolina*, 340. See also Braden, *When Grandma Was a Girl*, 76; Garrett, *Horse and Buggy Days*, 22–23; Hamrick, *Life Values*, 73; Masters, *Country Church in the South*, 15–21.

12. Broadus, *Treatise*, 499–500; Hurt, *This Is My Story*, 16; Rankin, *Story of My*

Life, 47; Hamrick, *Life Values*, 59; Paul Welch Memoir, 55–56, TNSLA; Fannie A. Tilley to "Cousin," Hillsboro, N.C., 29 June 1886, George Briggs Papers, Duke. See also Alexander, *Reminiscences*, 162; Smith, *Boyhood Memories of Fauquier*, 87; McGlothlin, *Vital Ministry*, 115–16; Thigpen, *Boy in Rural Mississippi*, 16–17.

13. According to an Arkansas Baptist in January 1910, "[T]here are many places where it is impossible to hold a meeting at this season of the year but not half so many as we often think" (*Baptist Advance*, 6 Jan. 1910, 1). See also Shettles, *Recollections*, 20.

14. Hosch, *Nevah Come Back*, 101; Chamberlain, *This Was Home*, 181. See also Alexander, *Reminiscences*, 180.

15. Henry W. Marston Diary, 1 Oct. 1876, Henry W. Marston and Family Papers, LSU; Long, *High Time*, 12; Roark, *Home Places*, 17. See also McBroom, *Orange County Childhood*, 59.

16. Anna Green to Samuel A. Cook, Milledgeville, Ga., 12 Dec. 1868, Green-Cook Papers, UGA; Edgar C. Haynsworth to Sister, Columbia, S.C., 19 Jan. 1885, Haynsworth Family Papers, SCHS; McGlothlin, *Vital Ministry*, 133; Robertson, *Red Hills and Cotton*, 103.

17. Faulkner, *Light in August*, 173; Samuel Porter Jones, "Why Should a Church Member Belong to the W.C.T.U.?" Samuel Porter Jones Papers, Emory.

18. For evidence that this was also the case in the antebellum period, see Mathews, *Religion in the Old South*, 102–6.

19. Samuel Porter Jones, "Why Should a Church Member Belong to the W.C.T.U.?" 1, Samuel Porter Jones Papers, Emory; Charles E. Dowman to John Davis Gray, Quincy, Fla., 17 Apr. 1876, Burge-Gray Family Papers, Emory; *Elm City Elevator*, 7 Nov. 1902. See also Jones, *Revival Sermons*, 138–39.

20. Johnson, *Autobiographical Notes*, 211.

21. A survey of twenty-seven churches revealed a total of 1,830 women and 1,159 men. Records located in SHC: Pleasant Union Christian Church Records, 1880; Wheelers Baptist Church Records, 1890. In USC: Cannon Creek Presbyterian Church Records, 1877; Central Methodist Church, South, Records, 1868; Concord Baptist Church Records, 1880; Liberty Chapel Methodist Church Register, 1871; New Allendale Baptist Church Records, 1906; New Providence Baptist Church Records, 1894; Smyrna Baptist Church Records, 1881. In GDAH: Cat Creek Primitive Baptist Church Records, 1897; Sharon Primitive Baptist Church Records, 1893. In MSDAH: Bethel Baptist Church Records, 1885; East Fork Baptist Church Records, 1868; First Baptist Church Records (Macon, Miss.), 1896; First Baptist Church Records (Pontotoc, Miss.), 1873; First Baptist Church Records (Summit, Miss.), 1874. In SBLA: Buffalo Baptist Church Records, 1890; Kiokee Baptist Church Records, 1869; Mountain Creek Baptist Church Records, 1907; Mt. Ararat Baptist Church Records, 1901; Mt. Zion Baptist Church Records, 1881; Shiloh Baptist Church Records, 1869; Yellow Creek Baptist Church Records, 1892. In Montreat: Bethany Presbyterian Church Records, 1874; Centre Ridge Presbyterian Church Records, 1892; Ebenezer Presbyterian Church Records, 1870; Mocksville Presbyterian Church Records, 1868.

22. Coolidge, *Growing Up with Chapel Hill*, 45; Welsh Neck Baptist Church Records, 2 Feb. 1867, USC; Central Methodist Church, South, Records, 1 Feb. 1895, USC.

23. Eleazar, *Fifty Years along the Roadside*, 23; Bond, *I Had a Friend*, 7; Hurt, *This Is My Story*, 16. See also Williams, "Memories," 19; Lipsey, "Memories," 34, TNSLA; Duncan H. Ogden to Mrs. Duncan H. Ogden, Meres, Miss., 10 Aug. 1903, Ogden Family Papers, Tulane.

24. Bond, *I Had a Friend*, 7; Shettles, *Recollections*, 21.

25. Coleman, *Five Petticoats*, 38; Hawks, *Distant Field*, 81; Long, *High Time*, 12; Hamrick, *Life Values*, 60; Lathrop, *My Mother*, 81; Allan-Olney, *New Virginians*, 1:199; Hurt, *This Is My Story*, 16.

26. Eleazar, *Fifty Years along the Roadside*, 23; Garrett, *Horse and Buggy Days*, 169–70; Braden, *When Grandma Was a Girl*, 75–76; Eleazar, *Fifty Years along the Roadside*, 23.

27. Eleazar, *Fifty Years along the Roadside*, 23; Vaughn, *Cotton Renter's Son*, 49.

28. Maria Dyer Davies Diary, 4 Sept. 1852, Duke; Allan-Olney, *New Virginians*, 1:199; Eleazar, *Fifty Years along the Roadside*, 23; Chamberlain, *This Was Home*, 180.

29. P. E. Roberts to Newton Morton Hale, Tyler, Tex., 1874, William George Hale Papers, LSU; *Hartwell Sun*, 27 Aug. 1881.

30. Camden Methodist Episcopal Church Minutes, 23 Sept. 1883, USC; *Conyers Examiner*, 8 July 1878; *Morehouse Clarion*, 20 May 1881; *Pearl River News*, 4 Dec. 1890.

31. Shettles, *Recollections*, 21; Eleazar, *Fifty Years along the Roadside*, 22–23; Moore, *Dr. Tom*, 35. See also Harris, *Circuit Rider's Wife*, 32; Faulkner, *The Hamlet*, 131.

32. James Daniel Frederick Diary, 3 June 1884, James Daniel Frederick Collection, UGA; Wright, *Barefoot in Arcadia*, 38.

33. Pearl, *Minnie Pearl*, 27; Roberts, *Highlights of My Life*, 2; *Morehouse Clarion*, 23 Sept. 1881.

34. The study examined charges regardless of whether a church member was found innocent or guilty. It studied only moral offenses and not trespasses of church polity such as nonattendance, joining other denominations, and nonpayment of church dues, nor did it include private disputes that the churches attempted to solve.

The study examined the minutes of forty-five Baptist churches, eight Primitive Baptist churches, thirty-five Presbyterian churches, two Cumberland Presbyterian churches, and seven Christian churches.

Baptist church minutes located in SBLA: Amiable Baptist Church; Antioch Baptist Church; Badin Baptist Church; Bethsaida Baptist Church; Brier Creek Baptist Church; Buffalo Baptist Church; Crocketts Creek Baptist Church; Cross Roads Baptist Church (Newberry County, S.C.); Cross Roads Baptist Church (Pickens County, S.C.); Durharts Baptist Church; First Baptist Church (Barnwell, S.C.); First Baptist Church (Hawthorne, Fla.); First Baptist Church (Jefferson, Ga.); First Baptist Church (Minden, La.); Longfield Baptist Church; Montevallo Baptist Church; Mt. Ararat Baptist Church; Mount Elon Baptist Church; Mt. Moriah Fellowship Baptist Church; Mt. Zion Baptist Church (Morgan County, Ala.); Mount Zion Baptist Church (Snellville, Ga.); Newburn Baptist Church; New Hope Baptist Church; New Light Baptist Church; Ocmulgee Baptist Church; Olive Chapel Baptist Church; Pleasant Grove Baptist Church (Anderson, S.C.); Pleasant

Grove Baptist Church (Greer, S.C.); Shiloh Baptist Church; Turkey Creek Baptist Church; Waco Baptist Church; Yellow Creek Baptist Church. In MSDAH: Bethel Baptist Church; East Fork Baptist Church; First Baptist Church (Macon, Miss.); First Baptist Church (Pontotoc, Miss.); First Baptist Church (Summit, Miss.); Leaf River Baptist Church; Zion Hill Baptist Church. In USC: Black Creek Baptist Church; Brushy Creek Baptist Church; Neal's Creek Baptist Church; New Providence Baptist Church; Welsh Neck Baptist Church. In SHC: Mount Carmel Baptist Church.

Primitive Baptist church minutes located in SHC: Globe Church. In GDAH: Beersheba Primitive Baptist Church; Bethel Primitive Baptist Church (Bulloch County, Ga.); Bethlehem Primitive Baptist Church (Gwinnett County, Ga.); Cat Creek Primitive Baptist Church/Friendship Primitive Baptist Church; Emmaus Primitive Baptist Church; Harmony Primitive Baptist Church; Sharon Primitive Baptist Church.

Presbyterian church minutes located in Montreat: Alabama Presbyterian Church; Barnwell Presbyterian Church; Bethany Presbyterian Church; Bethel Presbyterian Church; Bethesda Presbyterian Church (Ruffin, N.C.); Bethesda Presbyterian Church (Statesville, N.C.); Calvary Presbyterian Church; Carmel Presbyterian Church; Centre Ridge Presbyterian Church; Cornersville Presbyterian Church; Crabbottom Presbyterian Church; Ebenezer Presbyterian Church; First Presbyterian Church (Augusta, Ark.); First Presbyterian Church (Clinton, La.); First Presbyterian Church (Quincy, Fla.); Forest Grove Presbyterian Church; Green Springs Presbyterian Church; Hopewell Presbyterian Church; Jacksonville Presbyterian Church; Little Britain Presbyterian Church; Micanopy Presbyterian Church; Mocksville Presbyterian Church; Monticello Presbyterian Church; Morristown Presbyterian Church; New Bethel Presbyterian Church; Norcross Presbyterian Church; Richland Presbyterian Church; South Plains Presbyterian Church; Thyatira Presbyterian Church; Walnut Grove Presbyterian Church; Zion Presbyterian Church. In USC: Fishing Creek Presbyterian Church; Mt. Tabor Presbyterian Church; Ninety-Six Presbyterian Church; Pleasant Grove Presbyterian Church.

Cumberland Presbyterian church minutes located in TNSLA: McCains Cumberland Presbyterian Church; McKenzie Cumberland Presbyterian Church.

Christian church minutes located in GDAH: Black Springs Church of Christ; Galilee Christian Church. In TNSLA: Christian Chapel Church of Christ; Old Bildad Church of Christ. In DCHS: Edinburgh Christian Church; South Elkhorn Christian Church. In SHC: Pleasant Union Christian Church.

35. Jean E. Friedman has shown that a similar ratio existed in the antebellum South (*Enclosed Garden*, 14–17). E. William Monter suggests that men constituted a smaller majority of those accused of moral offenses at an important time in the Protestant past ("Women in Calvinist Geneva").

36. New Providence Baptist Church Minutes, 13 Mar. 1875, USC; Bethel Baptist Church Minutes, Jan. 1866, MSDAH; Turkey Creek Baptist Church Minutes, Oct. 1895, SBLA.

37. Taylor, *Travail and Triumph*, 141–45; Frazier, *Negro Church in America*, 35–51; Reimers, *White Protestantism*, 30–35; Williamson, *Crucible of Race*, 47, 250–51; Burton, *In My Father's House*, 309–10; Dvorak, "After Apocalypse, Moses."

38. Thigpen, *Boy in Rural Mississippi*, 14. Mary Kirkpatrick Tinsley Diary, 13 Nov. 1891, TNSLA; Mattie to Bettie Scott, St. Francisville[?], La., 9 Mar. 1876, Eva Scott and Family Papers, LSU; Lillie Boykin to Eva Scott, Bayou Current, La., 7 Feb. 1898, ibid.; Mary Bateman Diary, 35 (6 Apr. 1856), LSU. See also Thigpen, *Ninety and One Years*, 29.

39. Thigpen, *Boy in Rural Mississippi*, 15; Long, *High Time*, 167; Durham, *Since I Was Born*, 25–26. See also Shettles, *Recollections*, 3.

40. Durham, *Since I Was Born*, 26; Lathrop, *Comer Family Goes to Town*, 84; Mary Osborne Diary, 2 July 1905, J. F. Osborne Papers, SHC.

41. Long, *High Time*, 163.

42. Braden, *When Grandma Was a Girl*, 76; Thomas Dixon, in Crowe, "Southern Horizons," 202–3.

43. Isaac H. Hilliard, Jr., Diary, 12 Aug. 1866, Isaac H. Hilliard and Family Papers, LSU; Clive Metcalfe Diary, 21 Apr. 1889, SHC; John Ellis to Sallie Ellis, Jackson, La., 18 Sept. 1881, E. John and Thomas C. W. Ellis Family Papers, LSU; W. T. Sears to J. T. Pugh, Morrisville, N.C., 12 Jan. 1890, James Thomas Pugh Papers, SHC.

44. Doyle, *My Spiritual Life*, 35; Cook, *Journal of a Milledgeville Girl*, 70; Thomas Fitzgerald Cook to Julia Lee Nottingham, Midway, Ga., 4 June 1894, Green-Cook Papers, UGA. See also Newman, *Why I Am a Baptist*, 72.

45. Stephens, *Echoes of a Passing Era*, 15; Long, *High Time*, 163. See also Chamberlain, *This Was Home*, 181; Foust, *Horse and Buggy Days*, 60.

46. Mell Marshall Barrett Memoir, 12, GDAH; Chamberlain, "Fifty Years Ago," 128, NCC. See also Mary A. Gay to Mother, Ridgefield, La., 29 Oct. 1870, Andrew Haynes Gay and Family Papers, LSU; Eleazar, *Dutch Fork Farm Boy*, 93; Braden, *When Grandma Was a Girl*, 77; Wright, *Barefoot in Arcadia*, 16.

47. Johnson, *Highways and Byways*, 100.

48. Dunbar H. Ogden to Eliza Ogden, Port Gibson, Miss., 11 Nov. 1891, Ogden Family Papers, Tulane; *Franklin Times*, 20 June 1890; Hatton-Lovejoy Memoirs, 8, UGA.

49. Atkins, *It Can Be Done*, 62–63; Stuart, *Sermons*, 143; Powell, *Five Years*, 111–21.

Chapter 8

1. Hamrick, *Life Values*, 59.

2. George Gilman Smith Autobiography, 126, SHC.

3. Edwin Augustus Osborne Journal, 7 Apr. 1912, Edwin Augustus Osborne Papers, SHC.

4. Smith, *How the Spirit*, 14. See also Durham, *Since I Was Born*, 26; Lumpkin, *Making of a Southerner*, 162; Powell, *Five Years*, 60.

5. Hawks, *Distant Field*, 83; Thetis Bush to Micajah Wilkinson, Collinsburg, La., 18 Oct. 1881, Micajah Wilkinson Papers, LSU.

6. Ivey, *My Memoirs*, 44–45; Riley, "Story of a Camp Meeting," 7, DCHS; Rice, *Eighteenth Century*, 151. See also Hamrick, *Life Values*, 74; Wright, *Autobiography*, 67, 172; McElreath, *Walter McElreath*, 20.

7. Rice, *Eighteenth Century*, 151; Thomas Dixon, in Crowe, "Southern Horizons," 175; Wright, *Autobiography*, 67; Jones, *Reminiscences of North Carolina*, 3. See also Long, *High Time*, 167; Atkins, *It Can Be Done*, 9; Chamberlain, *This Was Home*, 180; Hamm, *From the Hills of Carolina*, 131; Hawks, *Distant Field*, 80; Lee, *Recollections of Country Joe*, 61; Hurt, *This Is My Story*, 19; Poe, *My First Eighty Years*, 50; Powell, *Five Years*, 60; Hatton-Lovejoy Memoirs, 28, UGA.

8. Sarah Grandy to Henry Briggs, Oxford, N.C., 27 Aug. 1873, Willis Grandy Briggs Papers, SHC; Nannie Prim to Mira Belle Prim, Silver City, N.C., 15 Sept. 1886, John M. Prim Papers, Duke; William A. Gill to Tabitha V. Tull, Greensburg, La., 3 Sept. 1860, Gill-Price Family Papers, MSDAH; Coleman, *Five Petticoats*, 139. See also Stephens, *Echoes of a Passing Era*, 15; Powell, *Five Years*, 59–61; Hosch, *Nevah Come Back*, 99; Hatton-Lovejoy Memoirs, 28, UGA.

9. J. W. Quillian, "Revivals," sermon preached in Newnan, Ga., 15 June 1906, Rev. J. W. Quillian Papers, GDAH.

10. Hubert, *Revivals of Religion*, 116–17; Rebecca Spencer to George W. Spencer, Oak Wood, N.C., 29 Aug. 1864, George W. Spencer Papers and Diary, Duke; Chamberlain, *This Was Home*, 285. See also Lumpkin, *Making of a Southerner*, 164; Goodard, *Modern Evangelism*, 38; Cox, *Hoot Owls*, 132.

11. Lizzie Woody to Susan Woody, Silver City, N.C., 27 Sept. 1906, Robert and Newton D. Woody Papers, Duke.

12. Ella Gertrude (Clanton) Thomas Journal, 22 Sept. 1882, Duke; Thomas Dixon, in Crowe, "Southern Horizons," 172; Ivey, *My Memoirs*, 47. See also Lipsey, "Memories," 9, TNSLA; Rankin, *Story of My Life*, 87.

13. Clemmons, *Great Time to Be Alive*, 18; Medford, *Finis and Farewell*, 78–79; Liddell, *With a Southern Accent*, 131; Morrison, *Life Sketches*, 29. See also McBroom, *Orange County Childhood*, 61; Wright, *Autobiography*, 198.

14. William H. Moore, sermon no. 14, William H. Moore Papers, Duke; Lipsey, "Memories," 9, TNSLA.

15. See Ivey, *My Memoirs*, 46; Powell, *Five Years*, 60.

16. Wolf, *Life in the Leatherwoods*, 111; Smith, *How the Spirit*, 15; Havner, *Three-Score and Ten*, 28; Long, *High Time*, 167; Lipsey, "Memories," 9, TNSLA.

17. Ella Gertrude (Clanton) Thomas Journal, 29 Aug. 1870, Duke; Norvell W. Wilson Diary, 3 Aug. 1964, Norwell W. Wilson Papers, SHC; Powell, *I Can Go Home Again*, 102. See also Moore, *Dr. Tom*, 35.

18. G. H. Snapp Diary, 30 Aug. 1863, Rev. G. H. Snapp Papers, Duke; Lumpkin, *Making of a Southerner*, 168; Feagin, *My Book*, 135; Charles E. Dowman to John Davis Gray, Quincy, Fla., 21 Feb. 1876, Burge-Gray Family Papers, Emory.

19. Joseph Hoomes Davis Diaries, 12 May 1872, Beale-Davis Papers, SHC; Smith, *How the Spirit*, 17.

20. Etheridge, *Threescore*, 23; Hubert, *Revivals of Religion*, 160–61.

21. Rebecca Sharp Clayton Diary, 19 Sept. 1878, TNSLA; Rankin, *Story of My Life*, 87.

22. Cox, *Hoot Owls*, 133–34; Henry W. Marston Diaries, 29 Oct. 1876, Henry W. Marston and Family Papers, LSU; *Weakley County Press and Martin Mail*, 2 Sept. 1921. See also Long, *High Time*, 168; Braden, *When Grandma Was a Girl*, 76; Solomon Hilary Helsabeck Diary, 28 Aug. 1894, SHC; Hutchins, *Red Clay*, 49.

23. Powell, *Five Years*, 66; Cornelius Miller Pickens Diary, 21 (29 Nov. 1892),

Duke; Lewis E. Oliver to Sylvester Hassell, Kenmore, Va., 10 Nov. 1897, Sylvester S. Hassell Papers, SHC; Samuel Mills Meeks, Jr., Diaries, 29 Apr. 1886, Meeks Family Papers, UAL.

24. *Clinton News Dispatch*, 12 Oct. 1916; *Yorkville Enquirer*, 29 Sept. 1886; *Siler City Grit*, 23 Sept. 1914; Thetis Bush to Micajah Wilkinson, Collinsburg, La., 26 Aug. 1880, Micajah Wilkinson Papers, LSU.

25. S. C. Ellington to John Jones, Washington, Ga., 22 Nov. 1879, Rev. John Jones Family Papers, UGA; J. F. Osborne Diaries, 15 Aug. 1909, SHC; Nannie Palmer to William Amos Snelling, Oconee, Ga., 3 Oct. 1878, William Amos Snelling Family Papers, Emory; Allen, *Autobiography*, 93. See also Goodard, *Modern Evangelism*, 8; Wright, *Autobiography*, 68; Richardson, *Lights and Shadows*, 215.

26. Powell, *Five Years*, 67; Mary M. Bethell Diary, 25 Aug. 1860, SHC.

27. Durham, *Since I Was Born*, 26; *Franklin Times*, 28 Nov. 1890; Long, *My Long Life*, 60.

28. *Lebanon Democrat*, 25 Aug. 1898; Lumpkin, *Making of a Southerner*, 172; Chamberlain, *This Was Home*, 288.

29. Topp, *Smile Please*, 66–67.

30. Nannie Prim to Mira Belle Prim, Silver City, N.C., 18 Sept. 1886, John M. Prim Papers, Duke; Wolf, *Life in the Leatherwoods*, 111; Etheridge, *Threescore*, 56–57.

31. Archelaus Madison Hughes Diary, 8 Aug. 1875, TNSLA; Williams, "Memories," 22. See also McElreath, *Walter McElreath*, 20; Poe, *My First Eighty Years*, 50; Havner, *Three-Score and Ten*, 26; Caldwell, *Deep South*, 12; Rippy, *Bygones*, 15; Morrison, *Life Sketches*, 14; Wright, *Autobiography*.

32. Cash, *Mind of the South*, 58.

33. Chamberlain, *This Was Home*, 286; Lipsey, "Memories," TNSLA.

34. Twain, *Huckleberry Finn*, 169.

35. See especially Turner, *Dramas, Fields, and Metaphors*, 166–230; Turner and Turner, *Image and Pilgrimage*, 1–39; Davies and Davies, *Holy Days and Holidays*.

36. Rice, *Eighteenth Century*, 151; *Walterboro News*, 22 Nov. 1873; Hutchins, *Red Clay*, 53; Hodges, "History of Balls Creek Camp Ground," 21, 14, NCC. See also Scott, *Background in Tennessee*, 235.

37. *McDuffie Weekly Journal*, 23 Aug. 1876; Ivey, *My Memoirs*, 53.

38. *Alabama Baptist*, 11 Oct. 1883, 2; Estelle Prim to Mira Belle Prim, Silver City, N.C., 21 Sept. 1886, John M. Prim Papers, Duke; John Prim to Mira Belle Prim, Salisbury, N.C., 27 Sept. 1892, ibid.; Solomon Palmer Diary, 13 (1873), Solomon Palmer Papers, ALDAH; *Arkansas Traveler*, 20 Sept. 1877. See also Powell, *Five Years*, 66; Hubert, *Revivals of Religion*, 49.

39. Lumpkin, *Making of a Southerner*, 164–65, 168; Wright, *Barefoot in Arcadia*, 25. See also Harris, *Circuit Rider's Wife*, 53.

40. Twain, *Tom Sawyer*, 134.

41. Johnson, *Frontier Camp Meeting*; Dulles, *America Learns to Play*.

42. James Mallory Diary, 20 July 1866, SHC.

Chapter 9

1. Loveland, *Southern Evangelicals*, 125.

2. Hahn, *Roots of Southern Populism*. See also the important contribution of Gavin Wright (*Old South, New South*, 39–43).

3. Gilbert Fite has placed the desire for consumer products at the heart of his interpretation of the southern economy, arguing that farmers wanted cash in order to enjoy the novelty and comfort promised by products in the general stores. James Turner and Edward L. Ayers have discussed the growth of railroads, towns, and stores and the new importance of mail-order catalogs. See Fite, "Agricultural Trap"; idem, *Cotton Fields No More*; Turner, "Understanding the Populists"; Ayers, "Toward a New Synthesis." See also Tang, *Economic Development*, 49–52, 98–104.

4. Thigpen, *Ninety and One Years*, 37.

5. See Foner, *Nothing but Freedom*; Woodward, *Strange Career of Jim Crow*; Williamson, *Crucible of Race*; Frederickson, *Black Image*, 256–82; Friedman, *White Savage*; Nolen, *Negro's Image*, 3–16; Kirby, *Darkness at the Dawning*.

6. On the limited objectives of early antidrinking movements, see Tyrrell, "Drink and Temperance"; Whitener, *Prohibition in North Carolina*, 21–32; Sellers, *Prohibition Movement in Alabama*, 14–18; Pearson and Hendricks, *Liquor and Anti-Liquor*, 55–110; Isaac, *Prohibition and Politics*, 4. On the limited objectives of the churches, see Farish, *Circuit Rider Dismounts*, chap. 9; Spain, *At Ease in Zion*, 174–97; Eighmy, *Churches in Cultural Captivity*, 49–56; Loveland, *Southern Evangelicals*, chap. 4.

7. Clark, *Deliver Us from Evil*, 57.

8. Scott, *Southern Lady*, 145–50; Friedman, *Enclosed Garden*, chap. 6; Bordin, *Women and Temperance*; Epstein, *Politics of Domesticity*; Sims, "'Sword of the Spirit'"; Clark, *Deliver Us from Evil*; Rorabaugh, *Alcoholic Republic*; Timberlake, *Prohibition and the Progressive Movement*; Carter, *Decline and Revival*, 31–45; Kerr, *Organized for Prohibition*.

9. See Sellers, *Prohibition Movement in Alabama*, 43–57; Isaac, *Prohibition and Politics*, 73–90.

10. Eubanks, *Ben Tillman's Baby*; Sellers, *Prohibition Movement in Alabama*, 86–100; Whitener, *Prohibition in North Carolina*, 116–30. On the rural emphasis of the movement, see Gould, *Progressives and Prohibitionists*.

11. See Sellers, *Prohibition Movement in Alabama*, 57–58; Isaac, *Prohibition and Politics*, 57, 147–49; Pearson and Hendricks, *Liquor and Anti-Liquor*, 153–54.

12. *Southwestern Press*, 6 Aug. 1880; Small, *Pleas for Prohibition*, 32; South Georgia Conference, Methodist Episcopal Church, South, Minutes, 1899, 62, UGA. See, for example, Mount Vernon Baptist Association Minutes, 1914, 14, UGA; Richardson, *Lights and Shadows*, 232.

13. White, "Prohibition," 9; Lochrane, *Address*, 15; Harrod C. Anderson Diary, 4 (27 Sept. 1887), Harrod C. Anderson Papers, LSU; Columbus Baptist Association Minutes, 1901, 4, UGA; Baptist Middle Association Minutes, 1890, 3, UGA; Charles E. Dowman to John Davis Gray, Quincy, Fla., 8 May 1877, Burge-Gray Family Papers, Emory; Mount Vernon Baptist Association Minutes, 1906, 5, UGA.

Dewey W. Grantham discusses the importance of racial conflict and concerns about animality for the rise of the prohibition movement (*Southern Progressivism*, 174–76). See also Tyrrell, "Drink and Temperance," 489–90.

14. Quoted in Ansley, *History of the Georgia Women's Christian Temperance Union*, 118–19, 213; *Weekly Columbus Enquirer*, 20 June 1870. See also Scott, *Southern Lady*, 147.

15. Arkansas, *Acts* (1873), no. 19, p. 27; Mississippi, *Code* (1822), chap. 64, p. 945; Florida, *Acts* (1881), chap. 3285, p. 87.

16. Quillian, *His Life and Sermons*, 62; Tennessee, *Acts* (1833), chap. 90, pp. 107–8; Alabama, *Acts* (1874–75), no. 153, p. 240; Arkansas, *Acts* (1859), no. 124, pp. 135–36; Florida, *Acts* (1909), chap. 5921, no. 52, pp. 64–65; Louisiana, *Acts* (1886), no. 31, pp. 40–41.

17. Louisiana, *Acts* (1886), no. 31, pp. 40–41; South Carolina, *Acts* (1894), no. 516, pp. 720–21; ibid. (1908), no. 456, p. 1033; Alabama, *Acts* (1885), no. 86, p. 142.

18. North Carolina, *Laws* (1913), chap. 40, p. 65; South Carolina, *Acts* (1894), no. 516, pp. 720–21; Georgia, *Acts* (1890–91), no. 222, p. 83; Alabama, *Acts* (1874–75), no. 177, p. 257; North Carolina, *Laws* (1907), chap. 470, p. 677; ibid. (1913), chap. 35, pp. 62–63.

19. Arkansas, *Acts* (1909), no. 30, pp. 73–74. See also ibid. (1859), no. 124, pp. 135–36; Alabama, *Acts* (1875–76), no. 153, p. 240.

20. Florida, *Acts* (1885), chap. 3620, pp. 61–62; North Carolina, *Laws* (1879), chap. 127, p. 231; South Carolina, *Acts* (1880), no. 362, pp. 447–48; Georgia, *Acts* (1882–83), no. 378, p. 131; Louisiana, *Acts* (1886), no. 31, p. 40.

21. Georgia, *Acts* (1897), no. 282, pp. 96–97.

22. Ibid. (1876), no. 306, p. 112; Louisiana, *Acts* (1890), no. 46, p. 39; Tennessee, *Acts* (1883), chap. 14, p. 18.

23. Tennessee, *Acts* (1891, extra sess.), chap. 14, p. 33; South Carolina, *Acts* (1893), chap. 21, p. 397; Louisiana, *Acts* (1890), no. 25, p. 19; Alabama, *Acts* (1870), no. 60, p. 51.

24. Laws forbidding specific sports: Mississippi, *Laws* (1880), chap. 31, pp. 157–60; Tennessee, *Acts* (1881), chap. 169, pp. 231–34; North Carolina, *Laws* (1881), chap. 368, pp. 609–12; Georgia, *Acts* (1889), no. 601, p. 164. Laws forbidding general cruelty to animals: Alabama, *Acts* (1882–83), no. 116, pp. 187–88; Arkansas, *Acts* (1879), no. 47, pp. 54–57; Georgia, *Acts* (1875), no. 61, p. 101; ibid. (1889), no. 601, p. 164; Florida, *Acts* (1901), chap. 4971, no. 87; Louisiana, *Acts* (1880), no. 44, pp. 43–44; Mississippi, *Laws* (1880), chap. 31, pp. 157–60; North Carolina, *Laws* (1881), chap. 368, pp. 609–12; South Carolina, *Acts* (1881–82), no. 455, p. 573; Tennessee, *Acts* (1881), chap. 169, pp. 231–34; Virginia, *Acts* (1877), chap. 7, no. 15, p. 304.

25. Arkansas, *Acts* (1879), no. 47, pp. 54–57; Georgia, *Acts* (1878–79), no. 352, pp. 183–84; Florida, *Acts* (1901), chap. 4971, no. 87; Louisiana, *Acts* (1888), no. 19, pp. 15–16; North Carolina, *Laws* (1881), chap. 368, pp. 609–12; Tennessee, *Acts* (1881), chap. 169, pp. 231–34.

26. Turner, *Reckoning with the Beast*; Louisiana State Society for the Prevention of Cruelty to Animals, Report, 1915, 48; *Abbeville Press and Banner*, 4 Oct. 1922.

27. Stacy, *Day of Rest*, 273.

28. Louisiana, *Acts* (1886), no. 18, p. 28; South Carolina, *Acts* (1874), no. 646, sec. 10; North Carolina, *Laws* (1876–77); chap. 38, pp. 83–84; Alabama, *Acts* (1903), no. 49, p. 64; Florida, *Acts* (1913), chap. 6516, sec. 4, p. 377.

29. Tennessee, *Acts* (1885), chap. 147, pp. 256–57; Florida, *Acts* (1905), chap. 5436, pp. 118–19; Alabama, *Acts* (1903), no. 326, p. 2812; Georgia, *Acts* (1898), no. 34, p. 107; Florida, *Acts* (1859), chap. 3289, pp. 89–90. See also Farish, *Circuit Rider Dismounts*, 335–40; Spain, *At Ease in Zion*, 150–51.

30. Wack, "Bob White," 868.

31. Flynn, *White Land, Black Labor*, 125–34; Hahn, *Roots of Southern Populism*, 58–63, 239–69. On fencing laws, see also McDonald and McWhiney, "South from Self-Sufficiency to Peonage," 1105–18; King, "Closing of the Southern Range." For a full discussion of class conflict in disputes between hunting for food and protecting game for sport in England, see Thompson, *Whigs and Hunters*.

32. Flynn, *White Land, Black Labor*, 128.

33. *Ansonian*, 10 Dec. 1907.

34. Robert Eugene Hale Recollections, 3, Robert Eugene Hale Papers, ALDAH.

35. Flynn, *White Land, Black Labor*, 124–28; Hahn, *Roots of Southern Populism*, 241–43.

36. Turner, *Reckoning with the Beast*, 129.

37. Alabama Department of Conservation, First Biennial Report, 1908, 6; idem, Second and Third Biennial Report, 1908–12, 9.

38. Ibid., Fourth Biennial Report, 1912–14, 124; idem, Second and Third Biennial Report, 1908–12, 35, 88; Audubon Society of South Carolina, First Annual Report, 1908, 15.

39. *Alabama Baptist*, 5 Jan. 1910, 8.

40. Audubon Society of South Carolina, Fifth Annual Report, 1915, 3; North Carolina Department of Conservation and Development, "Hunting in North Carolina," 11.

41. Audubon Society of North Carolina, Fourth Annual Report, 1906, 34–38; Shewey, *Shewey's Guide*; Leffingwell, *Happy Hunting Grounds*, 62–64; Audubon Society of South Carolina, Second Annual Report, 1909; Alabama Department of Conservation, First Biennial Report, 1908; ibid., "Game and Fish Laws of the State of Alabama," 1909; Louisiana Board of Commissioners for the Protection of Birds, Game, and Fish, "Game and Fish Laws of the State of Louisiana," 1909; Virginia Commission of Game and Inland Fisheries, First Annual Report, 1917; Arkansas State Game and Fish Commission, Second Annual Report, 1918.

42. Alabama Department of Conservation, First Biennial Report, 1908, 3; Audubon Society of North Carolina, Fifth Annual Report, 1907, 7. On the growth of enforcement agencies, see also Theodore S. Palmer, in *The South in the Building of the Nation*, 6:170–74. On the paucity of game laws in the antebellum South, see Gohdes, *Hunting in the Old South*.

43. Audubon Society of North Carolina, Sixth Annual Report, 1908, 10–11; Audubon Society of South Carolina, Second Annual Report, 1909, 24–25; Alabama Department of Game and Fish, Fourth Biennial Report, 1914, 159; Arkansas State Game and Fish Commission, Second Annual Report, 1918, 15; North Carolina Department of Conservation and Development, Third Biennial Report, 1930, 47.

44. *Macon Beacon*, 20 Feb. 1914; *Weakley County Press and Martin Mail*, 21 Jan. 1921; Wilson, *Backwoods America*, 107; Thomas Drake Samford Diary, 9 Mar. 1907, 7 Aug. 1909, Samford Diaries, SHC.

45. Sallie Colvin, in Louisiana Department of Agriculture, Farmers Institute Report, 1907, 15.

46. See *Progressive Farmer*, 16 Aug. 1906, 8; Zintheo, "Corn Harvesting Machinery," 7–8; *Southern Cultivator*, Aug. 1891, 383; Herring, *Saturday Night Sketches*, 64.

47. See Nourse, "Corn Husker and Fodder Cutter"; Zintheo, "Corn Harvesting Machinery," 33–41; Myers, "Husking Corn in the Field," 1; *Progressive Farmer*, 9 Aug. 1906, 5; ibid., 6 Sept. 1906, 9.

48. See *Southern Cultivator*, Dec. 1891, 608; Orr, "Butchering Hogs on the Farm," 5. For historical works, see Ransom and Sutch, *One Kind of Freedom*, 151–53; McDonald and McWhiney, "South from Self-Sufficiency to Peonage," 1116–18; Hahn, *Roots of Southern Populism*, 245–51; Wright, *Old South, New South*, 34–39.

49. According to the *Southern Lumber Journal*, "the cotton farmers and truck farmers in all the South Atlantic and Gulf States . . . are buying more lumber and making more building improvements about their premises than ever before" (15 Feb. 1910, 27). On the postbellum growth of the southern lumber industry, see Hickman, *Mississippi Harvest*.

50. Eleazar, *Dutch Fork Farm Boy*, 121; Wolf, *Life in the Leatherwoods*, 116. For similar recollections, see Coleman, *Five Petticoats*, 55; Eleazar, *Fifty Years along the Roadside*, 190–91; Hamrick, *Life Values*, 70. For a discussion of new agricultural techniques rendering traditional cultural events obsolete, see Weber, *Peasants into Frenchmen*, 125.

51. Abrahams, "Language of Festivals," 174.

52. On the same point, see Gates, "Modernization."

53. *Rural Carolinian*, Oct. 1873, 39. See particularly Scott, *Reluctant Farmer*, 16–17; Range, *Century of Georgia Agriculture*, 123.

54. Rubinow, "Fair Work in North Carolina," 4.

55. Georgia State College of Agriculture, "Farmers Institutes in Georgia." On the growth of the institutes, see Scott, *Reluctant Farmer*, 64–169.

56. Winterville Community Fair Program, 1924; Lafayette Parish Fair Premium List, 1916. See also Ormsby, "Community Fairs and Their Organization," 2.

57. *Weakley County Press and Martin Mail*, 21 Oct. 1921.

58. Louisiana Department of Agriculture, Farmers Institute Report, 1898, 86.

59. Tate, "Suggestions for County Fairs," 17; *Rock Hill Magazine*, Aug. 1916, 33–34; Martin County Fair Program, 1920, 69; Rubinow, "Score Cards," 18.

60. Chilton County Fair Premium List, 1915; Lafayette Parish Fair Premium List, 1916, 66–67.

61. *Progressive Farmer*, 7 Oct. 1911, 835. On canning contests, see Wilkes-Lincoln County Fair Premium List, 1914; *Alabama Farm Facts*, 1 July 1921, 6.

62. Wilkes-Lincoln County Fair Premium List, 1914; Talladega County Fair Premium List and Program, 1915. See also Lafayette Parish Fair Premium List, 1916, 45; Alachua County Fair Premium List, 1915, 16; Jefferson County Agricultural Exhibit Program, 1919.

63. Rubinow, "Score Cards"; Rubinow, "Score Card for Draft Horses." See also Francioni and LaCroix, "Lessons for Members," 26.

64. *Alabama Farm Facts*, 29 Nov. 1919, 6; ibid., 20 Nov. 1920, 9; ibid., 13 Nov. 1920, 1; Wilkes-Lincoln County Fair Premium List, 1914. See also Balic, "Organization of Boys' Pig Clubs," 4.

65. *Alabama Farm Facts*, 30 Oct. 1920, 12.

66. Balic, "Organization of Boys' Pig Clubs," 4.

67. *Progressive Farmer*, 14 Aug. 1920, 1460; Louisiana Department of Agriculture, Farmers Institute Report, 1898, 86.

68. Scott, *Reluctant Farmer*, 252; *Hickory Record*, quoted in *Progressive Farmer*, 27 Nov. 1915, 1104.

69. *Concord Times*, 4 Oct. 1926; East Alabama Fair Catalog and Premium List, 1915; Talladega County Fair Premium List and Program, 1915.

70. Kasson, *Amusing the Million*, 81–82. See also Caillois, *Man, Play, and Games*, 132–36.

71. East Alabama Fair Catalog, 1915; *Chester Semi-Weekly News*, 22 Sept. 1916. See also Fifth Annual Fair of the Haywood County Stock Raisers and Farmers Association Premium List, 1909, 5; Annual Fair of the Rutherford County Fair Association Premium List and Rules and Regulations, 1921, 4; Chilton County Fair Premium List, 1914.

72. Haywood County Fair Premium List, 1909, 5; Rutherford County Fair Premium List, 1921; East Alabama Fair Catalog, 1915; Middle Georgia Fair Official Premium List, 1929, 113.

73. East Alabama Fair Catalog.

74. Jones, *Revival Sermons*, 141.

75. First Baptist Church Records (Summit, Miss.), May 1890, MSDAH; Zion Hill Baptist Church Records, Aug. 1900, MSDAH; Longfield Baptist Church Records, 1900, SBLA. See also Spain, *At Ease in Zion*, 155.

76. *Progressive Farmer*, 26 Aug. 1911, 720.

Chapter 10

1. Alachua Baptist Association•Minutes, 1925, 16–17, SBLA.

2. Higham, "Reorientation of American Culture," 77–88; Kasson, *Amusing the Million*; Erenberg, *Steppin' Out*; Leonard, *Jazz and the White Americans*.

3. Jacobs, *Diary*, 364.

4. *Conyers Examiner*, 8 Feb. 1878; *Mountain Signal*, 31 Oct. 1879; Thigpen, *Boy in Rural Mississippi*, 47–48.

5. See Topp, *Smile Please*.

6. Eleazar, *Fifty Years along the Roadside*, 125.

7. *Waynesboro True Citizen*, 21 Apr. 1894; *Putnam County Herald*, 19 Mar. 1914. Also on religion in early movies, see Kirk, *Locust Hill*, 87; *Ansonian*, 24 Sept. 1907; *Asheboro Bulletin*, 28 Jan. 1914; Thomas Drake Samford Diary, 12 Aug. 1907, Samford Diaries, SHC.

8. *Ansonian*, 18 Feb., 3 Mar. 1908.

9. May, *Screening Out the Past*.

10. *Baptist Advance*, 26 May 1921, 5.

11. Cash, *Mind of the South*, 48; *Forest City Courier*, 20 Aug. 1925. On the South and air conditioning, see Arsenault, "End of the Long Hot Summer."

12. Cash, *Mind of the South*, 31; Welty, *One Writer's Beginnings*, 36.

13. *Putnam County Herald*, 18 Sept. 1919; *Etowah Enterprise*, 12 Dec. 1925; *Gaffney Ledger*, 1, 8 Mar., 19 May 1921.

14. May, *Screening Out the Past*. See also Sklar, *Movie-Made America*.

15. Plyler, *My Life as a Minister's Son*, 17; *Baptist Advance*, 27 Oct. 1921, 4; 20 Jan. 1921, 1; 10 Feb. 1921, 5. See also Bailey, *Southern White Protestantism*, 45–46; McDowell, *Social Gospel in the South*, 43–44.

16. Thomas Drake Samford Diary, 20 June 1907, Samford Diaries, SHC; Hamm, *From the Hills of Carolina*, 32; Faulkner, *As I Lay Dying*, 249, 248; Austin, *Beat Goes On*, 10.

17. Wood, *Once Apunce a Time*, 146–47.

18. Clark, *My South*, 65; Thomas Drake Samford Diary, 1 Jan. 1924, Samford Diaries, SHC.

19. Janice to Frank Drew, Jr., Live Oak, Fla., 17 Feb. 1909, Drew Collection, FSA; ibid., 21 Feb. 1909. On the significance of the automobile in Southern life, see Clark, *Emerging South*, 127.

20. Ebenezer Erskine Pressly Diaries and Commonplace Books, 24 Jan., 28 Feb., 6 June 1909, Duke; Robertson, *Changing South*, 216; William McGlothlin, in *Gaffney Ledger*, 8 Sept. 1921; *Etowah Enterprise*, 2 July 1925.

21. Masters, *Making America Christian*, 66; William McGlothlin, in *Gaffney Ledger*, 8 Sept. 1921.

22. Mell, *Corrective Church Discipline*, 22; First Baptist Church Minutes (Hawthorne, Fla.), Covenant, 1880, SBLA. For discussions that emphasize the corrective features of church discipline, see Mathews, *Religion in the Old South*, 42–46; Blanks, "Corrective Church Discipline," 91; Shore, "Church Discipline," 13.

23. Bethesda Presbyterian Church Session Records (Ruffin, N.C.), January 1874, Montreat.

24. Mell, *Corrective Church Discipline*, 21.

25. Kroll-Smith, "Transmitting a Revival Culture." On Baptists and community, see Mathews, *Religion in the Old South*, 22–28; Isaac, *Transformation of Virginia*, 161–77.

26. The Baptist church records examined were as follows. Located in SBLA: Amiable Baptist Church; Antioch Baptist Church; Badin Baptist Church; Bethsaida Baptist Church; Brier Creek Baptist Church; Buffalo Baptist Church; Crocketts Creek Baptist Church (Model, Tenn.); Cross Roads Baptist Church (Newberry County, S.C.); Cross Roads Baptist Church (Pickens County, S.C.); Durharts Baptist Church; First Baptist Church (Barnwell, S.C.); First Baptist Church (Hawthorne, Fla.); First Baptist Church (Jefferson, Ga.); First Baptist Church (Minden, La.); Kiokee Baptist Church; Longfield Baptist Church; Montevallo Baptist Church; Mountain Creek Baptist Church; Mt. Elon Baptist Church; Mt. Moriah Fellowship Baptist Church; Mt. Zion Baptist Church (Morgan County, Ala.); Mount Zion Baptist Church (Snellville, Ga.); New Hope Baptist Church; New Light Baptist Church; Ocmulgee Baptist Church; Olive Chapel Baptist Church;

Pleasant Grove Baptist Church (Greer, S.C.); Turkey Creek Baptist Church; Waco Baptist Church; Yellow Creek Baptist Church; Zion Hill Baptist Church. In MSDAH: East Fork Baptist Church; First Baptist Church (Macon, Miss.); First Baptist Church (Pontotoc, Miss.). In USC: Brushy Creek Baptist Church; New Providence Baptist Church. In SHC: Globe Church. In GDAH: Beersheba Primitive Baptist Church; Bethel Primitive Baptist Church (Bulloch County, Ga.); Bethlehem Primitive Baptist Church (Gwinnett County, Ga.); Cat Creek Primitive Baptist Church/Friendship Primitive Baptist Church; Emmaus Primitive Baptist Church; Harmony Primitive Baptist Church; Sharon Primitive Baptist Church.

27. Christian church records examined were as follows. In GDAH: Black Springs Church of Christ; Galilee Christian Church. In TNSLA: Christian Chapel Church of Christ; Old Bildad Church of Christ. In DCHS: Edinburg Christian Church; South Elkhorn Christian Church. In SHC: Pleasant Union Christian Church.

28. Presbyterian records examined were as follows. In Montreat: Alabama Presbyterian Church, Choudrant, La.; Bethany Presbyterian Church, Gloster, Miss.; Barnwell Presbyterian Church; Bethel Presbyterian Church; Bethesda Presbyterian Church (Ruffin, N.C.); Bethesda Presbyterian Church (Statesville, N.C.); Calvary Presbyterian Church; Carmel Presbyterian Church; Centre Ridge Presbyterian Church; Cornersville Presbyterian Church; Crabbottom Presbyterian Church; Ebenezer Presbyterian Church; First Presbyterian Church (Augusta, Ark.); First Presbyterian Church (Clinton, La.); First Presbyterian Church (Quincy, Fla.); Forest Grove Presbyterian Church; Green Springs Presbyterian Church; Hopewell Presbyterian Church; Jacksonville Presbyterian Church; Little Britain Presbyterian Church; Micanopy Presbyterian Church; Mocksville Presbyterian Church; Monticello Presbyterian Church; Morristown Presbyterian Church; New Bethel Presbyterian Church; Norcross Presbyterian Church; Richland Presbyterian Church; South Plains Presbyterian Church; Thyatira Presbyterian Church. In USC: Ninety-Six Presbyterian Church. In TNSLA: McCains Cumberland Presbyterian Church; McKenzie Cumberland Presbyterian Church.

29. Western Baptist Association Minutes, 1910, 10, UGA.

30. Haines, "Southern Baptist Church Discipline," 26.

31. Bethel Baptist Association Minutes, 1915, 23, UGA. For examples of new kinds of antialcohol sentiment, see North Bend Baptist Association, 1924, 13, SBLA; Magee's Creek Baptist Association, 1921, 8, SBLA; Alcorn County Baptist Association, 1923, 14, SBLA; *Wesleyan Christian Advocate*, 12 May 1922; *Christian Advocate*, 17 Apr. 1914, 29.

32. William McGlothlin, in *Gaffney Ledger*, 8 Sept. 1921; *Alabama Baptist*, 30 Sept. 1920, 3; *Christian Advocate*, 20 Mar. 1914, 13. See also *Baptist Advance*, 8 Mar. 1917, 1–2, on movements against dancing in schools.

33. Salisbury Ministerial Association Minutes, 1 June 1914, 5 Oct. 1914, 2 Nov. 1914, 14 Feb. 1921, Duke; Lincolnton Ministers' Conference Minutes, 13 Apr., Dec. 1914, 25 Jan. 1916, Duke; *Baptist Advance*, 20 Jan. 1921, 5; ibid., 13 Oct. 1921, 3.

34. Grantham, *Southern Progressivism*.

35. Flynt, "Southern Protestantism and Reform."

36. Among many possible examples, see Higham, "Integrating America" in *Send*

These to Me; Griffen, "Progressive Ethos"; Boyer, *Urban Masses and Moral Order*; idem, *Purity in Print*; Crunden, *Ministers of Reform*; Pivar, *Purity Crusade*; May, *Screening Out the Past*, chap. 3.

37. Pete Daniel has described such events as "domesticated violence" (*Standing at the Crossroads*, 172–79).

Bibliography

Manuscripts

Athens, Georgia
Richard B. Russell Library, University of Georgia
  Marcus Wayland Beck Diaries
Special Collections Division, University of Georgia Library
  Akehurst-Lines Collection
  Manning P. and Pellona David Alexander Letters
  Baber-Blackshear Papers
  Col. David C. Barrow Papers
  Annie Blount Diary
  Bower Family Papers
  William M. Browne Diary
  Morgan and Leila Callaway Collection
  Camak Collection
  Carlton-Newton-Mell Collection
  James Diamond Family Papers
  William J. Dickey Collection
  DuBose Family Papers
  James Daniel Frederick Collection
  Green-Cook Papers
  Harden-Jackson-Carithers Collection
  Safford Harris Gift
  Hatton-Lovejoy Memoirs
  George W. Howard Diary
  Rev. John Jones Family Papers
  Hugh Lawson Papers
  Archibald C. McKinley Journal
  Rhind-Stokes Collection
  Samuel Hale Sibley, "My Grandmother" (typescript)
  Stevens Family Papers
  Clark Berry Stewart Papers
  William Price Talmage Diary
  Tison Family Papers

Atlanta, Georgia
Georgia Department of Archives and History
  Mell Marshall Barrett Memoir
  Bryson Family Papers
  Robert F. Davis Collection

William E. Fort, "A Reminiscence: Christmas Eighteen Ninety-Six" (typescript)
Mary Raoul Millis Memoir
Mary Elizabeth Mangum Ozburn Family Papers
Shepard Ezekiel Perkins Diary
Rev. J. W. Quillian Papers
Henrietta Carroll Smith Diary
Rev. William R. Talley Autobiography
Ivy F. Thompson Diary
Wilkes Family Papers
Special Collections, Robert Woodruff Library, Emory University
John W. Baker Diaries
George L. F. Birdsong Papers
Burge-Gray Family Papers
John S. Dobbins Papers
Lucius H. Featherston Family Papers
Samuel Porter Jones Papers
Robert Watkins Lovett Papers
James V. Morris Diaries
Kate Whitehead Rowland Journals
William Amos Snelling Family Papers

Baton Rouge, Louisiana
Special Collections, Louisiana State University Library
O. P. Amacker Family Papers
Harrod C. Anderson Papers
Mollie E. Anderson Papers
Mary Bateman Diary (typescript)
George W. Bennett Account Books
Bennett Family Papers
Benson Family Papers
Audley Clark Britton and Family Papers
John Potts Brown Notebook
Lemuel Parker Conner and Family Papers
E. John and Thomas C. W. Ellis and Family Papers
Kate Garland Papers
Andrew Haynes Gay and Family Papers
J. M. Gould Diary
William George Hale Papers
Isaac H. Hilliard and Family Papers
J. G. Kilbourne and Family Papers
E. J. Larkin Diary
Jeptha McKinney Papers
Eliza L. Magruder Diary
Henry W. Marston and Family Papers
George C. Purvis and Family Papers
Mary Elizabeth Carter Rives Diary

Caroline Virginia Samuel Letters
Eva Scott and Family Papers
Rev. Joseph B. Stratton Diary
Calvin Taylor and Family Papers
Sereno Taylor Papers
Micajah Wilkinson Papers

Chapel Hill, North Carolina
North Carolina Collection, University of North Carolina
    Hope Summerell Chamberlain, "Fifty Years Ago, or 'Older Years than
        Fifty' " (typescript)
    J. E. Hodges, "A History of Balls Creek Camp Ground" (typescript)
    George W. Means, Advertisements for Red Cuban Games, 1903, 1906,
        1916
Southern Historical Collection, University of North Carolina
    Samuel A. Agnew Diary
    James Atkins Papers
    Mary E. Bailey Diary
    Everard Green Baker Diary (typescript)
    Henry Waring Ball Diary
    Beale-Davis Papers
    Taylor Beatty Diaries
    Mary M. Bethell Diary
    Launcelot Minor Blackford Diaries
    Emily Morrison Bondurant Reminiscences
    Branch Family Papers
    Willis Grandy Briggs Papers
    Bumpas Family Papers
    Julian Shakespeare Carr Papers
    Joseph Blount Cheshire Papers
    S. O. Deaver Diary
    William Porcher DuBose Reminiscences
    E. Walker Duvall, "Memories of E. Walker Duvall" (typescript)
    Mary E. Fries Diary (typescript)
    Gale and Polk Family Papers
    Leonidas C. Glenn Papers
    Pleasant Daniel Gold Papers
    James Hervey Greenlee Diary
    John Berkley Grimball Diary
    Edward Owings Guerrant Papers
    James F. Gwinnett Diary
    Francis Hanson Diary
    James Clarence Harper Diaries (typescript)
    Cushing B. Hassell Diary
    Sylvester S. Hassell Papers
    Solomon Hilary Helsabeck Papers and Diary
    Moses Young Henderson Diary

Julia E. Horner Papers
Robert P. Howell Memories
Hubbard Family Papers
Daniel R. A. C. Hundley Diary
Jones Family Papers
Mary Susan Kerr Diary (typescript)
Drury Lacy Papers
Emma Florence LeConte Journal
William P. McCorkle Papers
Francis McFarland Diary
John Bolivar McGinn Sermons
James Mallory Diary
James Pleasant Mason Diaries
Meares and de Rosset Family Papers
George A. Mercer Diary
Clive Metcalfe Diary
Eugene Morehead Diary
Edwin Augustus Osborne Papers
J. F. Osborne Diaries
Mollie A. Parham Diary (typescript)
William Nelson Pendleton Papers
P. H. Pitts Diary
William S. Powell Collection
James Thomas Pugh Papers
Olivia Kittredge Race Diary
Emma L. Rankin Books (typescript)
Joseph Rennie Papers
Roach and Eggleston Family Papers
William James Samford and Thomas Drake Samford Diaries
David Schenck Diary
George Gilman Smith Autobiography (typescript)
Jacob Henry Smith Diary
Alfred Taylor Diary
Thomas Cogdell Wetmore Papers
John Thomas Wheat Papers
William Wallace White Diary
Lewis Neale Whittle Papers
Calvin Henderson Wiley Papers
Nannie Haskins Williams Diary
Mary Ann Covington Wilson Papers
Norvell Winsboro Wilson Papers
Francis Donnell Winston Papers
George Munro Yoder Papers

Charleston, South Carolina
South Carolina Historical Society
    Thomas B. Chaplin Plantation Journal
    Cothran Family Papers

Haynsworth Family Papers
Louisa McCord Smythe Recollections
Maria Adelaide Whaley Recollections
Young Family Papers

Columbia, South Carolina
South Caroliniana Library, University of South Carolina
    John Montgomery Dubose Interview Transcript
    William Harleston Huger Letters
    James Washington Moore Diaries
    Porcher-Ford Family Papers
    Thomas Stephen Powell Journal
    William Moultrie Reid Papers
    Singleton Family Papers

Durham, North Carolina
Perkins Library, Duke University
    V. V. Anderson Papers
    Mary Beckham Diary
    Edward Earl Bomar Papers
    George Briggs Papers
    Charlton P. Brooke Diary
    Iveson L. Brookes Papers
    Abbie M. Brooks Diary
    John Caldwell Papers
    Washington S. Chaffin Journals
    Clement Claiborne Clay Papers
    Maria Dyer Davies Diary
    William Kearney Eborn Papers
    Fannie (Bennett) Gaddy Papers
    Elizabeth Baldwin Harris Diaries
    George Leonidas Lyon Papers
    Lucy C. Massenburg Papers
    William George Matton Papers
    William H. Moore Papers
    Cornelius Miller Pickens Diary (typescript)
    George T. Nichols, "Notes on Dogs and Hunting"
    Ebenezer Erskine Pressly Diaries and Commonplace Books
    John Ebenezer Pressly Papers
    John M. Prim Papers
    John R. Raine Letters and Papers
    William A. Roberts Papers
    William S. Royston Papers
    Joseph Belknap Smith Papers
    Rev. G. H. Snapp Papers
    George W. Spencer Papers and Diary
    Missouria H. Stokes Papers
    Ella Gertrude (Clanton) Thomas Journal (typescript)

Aaron Wilbur Papers
Sidney W. Wilkinson Papers
Robert and Newton D. Woody Papers

Jackson, Mississippi
Mississippi Department of Archives and History
  Tryphena Holder Fox Collection
  Gill-Price Family Papers
  Robert and James Gordon Diaries
  Daniel Washington McCormick Diary
  Walter Edwin Tynes Diary (typescript)

Montgomery, Alabama
Alabama Department of Archives and History
  Zillah (Haynie) Brandon Personal Reminiscences
  Samuel Walker Catts, "My Life, Era, and Incidents" (typescript)
  Kate Cumming Papers
  John Jefferson Flowers Diary
  Margaret Josephine Miles Gillis Diary
  Robert Eugene Hale Papers
  Jasper Ellis James Papers
  Joshua Burns Moore Diary
  Solomon Palmer Papers
  Sally Randle Perry Diary
  Marcus M. Smith Diaries
  Rev. Eldred Burden Teague Autobiography

Nashville, Tennessee
Disciples of Christ Historical Society
  Lilla Riley, "The Story of a Camp Meeting" (typescript)
Tennessee State Library and Archives
  Walter Chandler Personal Recollections
  Rebecca Sharp Clayton Diary
  John E. Duling Reminiscences
  Robert B. Freeman Diaries
  L. Virginia French War Journal
  Betty A. Gleaves Diary
  Archelaus Madison Hughes Diary
  Jane M. Jones Diaries
  Polly (Draper) Langford Diary
  Charles Jefferson Lewis Journal
  Plautus Iberus Lipsey, "Memories of His Early Life (1865–1888)"
    (typescript)
  William McClinchey Diary
  Mrs. Frank Robbins Diary
  Mary Kirkpatrick Tinsley Diary
  Paul Welch Memoir

New Orleans, Louisiana
Special Collections, Howard-Tilton Memorial Library, Tulane University
    William Ransom Hogan Collection
    Ogden Family Papers

Savannah, Georgia
Georgia Historical Society
    Gordon Family Papers
    Elizabeth Eloise Wilkes Papers
    Walter Wray Diaries

Tallahassee, Florida
Florida State Archives
    Drew Collection
    David and Nancy Mathews Family Papers
    Taylor Family Papers

Tuscaloosa, Alabama
William Stanley Hoole Special Collections Library, University of Alabama
    John Collier Foster Papers
    Cabot Lull Collection
    Meeks Family Papers
    James Gee Oakley Cockfighting Collection

Church Records

Athens, Georgia
Special Collections Division, University of Georgia Library
    Baptist Middle Association
    Bethel Baptist Association
    Columbus Baptist Association
    Mount Vernon Baptist Association
    South Georgia Conference, Methodist Episcopal Church, South
    Western Baptist Association

Atlanta, Georgia
Georgia Department of Archives and History
    Beersheba Primitive Baptist Church, Locust Grove, Ga.
    Bethel Primitive Baptist Church, Bulloch County, Ga.
    Bethlehem Primitive Baptist Church, Gwinnett County, Ga.
    Black Springs Church of Christ, Baldwin County, Ga.
    Cat Creek Primitive Baptist Church/Friendship Primitive Baptist
        Church, Lowndes County, Ga.
    Emmaus Primitive Baptist Church, Upson County, Ga.
    Galilee Christian Church, Jackson County, Ga.
    Harmony Primitive Baptist Church, Pike County, Ga.
    Sharon Primitive Baptist Church, Monroe County, Ga.

Chapel Hill, North Carolina
Southern Historical Collection, University of North Carolina
  Globe Church, Caldwell County, N.C.
  Mt. Carmel Baptist Church, Orange County, N.C.
  Pleasant Union Christian Church, Harnett County, N.C.
  Sawyers Creek Baptist Church, Belcross, N.C.
  Wheelers Baptist Church, Person County, N.C.

Columbia, South Carolina
South Caroliniana Library, University of South Carolina
  Black Creek Baptist Church, Beaufort County, S.C.
  Brushy Creek Baptist Church, Greenville County, S.C.
  Camden Methodist Episcopal Church, Camden, S.C.
  Cannon Creek Presbyterian Church, Newberry County, S.C.
  Central Methodist Church, South, Newberry County, S.C.
  Concord Baptist Church, Barnwell County, S.C.
  Fishing Creek Presbyterian Church, Chester County, S.C.
  Liberty Chapel Methodist Church, Florence County, S.C.
  Mt. Tabor Presbyterian Church, Greer, S.C.
  Neal's Creek Baptist Church, Anderson County, S.C.
  New Allendale Baptist Church, Barnwell County, S.C.
  New Providence Baptist Church, Hartsville, S.C.
  Ninety-Six Presbyterian Church, Ninety-Six, S.C.
  Pleasant Grove Presbyterian Church, Chester County, S.C.
  Smyrna Baptist Church, Allendale, S.C.
  Welsh Neck Baptist Church, Society Hill, S.C.

Durham, North Carolina
Perkins Library, Duke University
  Lincolnton Ministers' Conference, Lincolnton, N.C.
  Salisbury Ministerial Association, Salisbury, N.C.

Jackson, Mississippi
Mississippi Department of Archives and History
  Bethel Baptist Church, Slate Springs, Miss.
  East Fork Baptist Church, Smithdale, Miss.
  First Baptist Church, Macon, Miss.
  First Baptist Church, Pontotoc, Miss.
  First Baptist Church, Summit, Miss.
  Leaf River Baptist Church, Smith County, Miss.
  Zion Hill Baptist Church, Amite County, Miss.

Montreat, North Carolina
Historical Foundation of the Presbyterian and Reformed Churches
  Alabama Presbyterian Church, Choudrant, La.
  Barnwell Presbyterian Church, Barnwell, S.C.
  Bethany Presbyterian Church, Gloster, Miss.

Bethel Presbyterian Church, Walhalla, S.C.
Bethesda Presbyterian Church, Ruffin, N.C.
Bethesda Presbyterian Church, Statesville, N.C.
Calvary Presbyterian Church, Johnsville, Ark.
Carmel Presbyterian Church, Piedmont, Ala.
Centre Ridge Presbyterian Church, Richmond, Ala.
Cornersville Presbyterian Church, Cornersville, Tenn.
Crabbottom Presbyterian Church, Highland County, Va.
Ebenezer Presbyterian Church, Clinton, Ala.
First Presbyterian Church, Augusta, Ark.
First Presbyterian Church, Clinton, La.
First Presbyterian Church, Quincy, Fla.
Forest Grove Presbyterian Church, Leake County, Miss.
Green Springs Presbyterian Church, Abingdon, Va.
Hopewell Presbyterian Church, Vaiden, Miss.
Jacksonville Presbyterian Church, Jacksonville, Ala.
Little Britain Presbyterian Church, Rutherford County, N.C.
Micanopy Presbyterian Church, Micanopy, Fla.
Mocksville Presbyterian Church, Mocksville, N.C.
Monticello Presbyterian Church, Monticello, Fla.
Morristown Presbyterian Church, Morristown, Tenn.
New Bethel Presbyterian Church, Piney Flats, Tenn.
Norcross Presbyterian Church, Norcross, Ga.
Richland Presbyterian Church, Westminster, S.C.
South Plains Presbyterian Church, Albermarle County, Va.
Thyatira Presbyterian Church, Jefferson County, Ga.
Walnut Grove Presbyterian Church, Walnut Grove, Ga.
Zion Presbyterian Church, Tupelo, Miss.

Nashville, Tennessee
Disciples of Christ Historical Society
 Edinburg Christian Church, Edinburg, Va.
 South Elkhorn Christian Church, Lexington, Ky.
Southern Baptist Library and Archives
 Alachua Baptist Association, Alachua, Fla.
 Alcorn County Baptist Association, Alcorn County, Miss.
 Amiable Baptist Church, Glenmora, La.
 Antioch Baptist Church, Lafayette, Ala.
 Badin Baptist Church, Badin, N.C.
 Bethsaida Baptist Church, Fayette County, Ga.
 Brier Creek Baptist Church, Wilkes County, N.C.
 Buffalo Baptist Church, Rutledge, Tenn.
 Crocketts Creek Baptist Church, Model, Tenn.
 Cross Roads Baptist Church, Newberry County, S.C.
 Cross Roads Baptist Church, Pickens County, S.C.
 Durharts Baptist Church, Louisville, Ga.
 First Baptist Church, Barnwell, S.C.

First Baptist Church, Hawthorne, Fla.
First Baptist Church, Jefferson, Ga.
First Baptist Church, Minden, La.
First Baptist Church, Winchester, Tenn.
Kiokee Baptist Church, Columbia County, Ga.
Longfield Baptist Church, Anderson County, Tenn.
Magee's Creek Baptist Association, Magee's Creek, La.
Montevallo Baptist Church, Montevallo, Ala.
Mountain Creek Baptist Church, Anderson, S.C.
Mt. Ararat Baptist Church, Darden, Tenn.
Mt. Elon Baptist Church, Lydia, S.C.
Mt. Moriah Fellowship Baptist Church, Mt. Moriah, Ala.
Mt. Zion Baptist Church, Morgan County, Ala.
Mount Zion Baptist Church, Snellville, Ga.
Newburn Baptist Church, Green County, Ala.
New Hope Baptist Church, Lawrence County, Ark.
New Light Baptist Church, near Wake Forest, N.C.
North Bend Baptist Association, North Bend, Ky.
Ocmulgee Baptist Church, Ocmulgee, Ala.
Olive Chapel Baptist Church, Apex, N.C.
Pleasant Grove Baptist Church, Anderson, S.C.
Pleasant Grove Baptist Church, Greer, S.C.
Shiloh Baptist Church, Bernice, La.
Turkey Creek Baptist Church, Abbeville County, S.C.
Waco Baptist Church, Waco, N.C.
Yellow Creek Baptist Church, Spring City, Tenn.
Zion Hill Baptist Church, Buford, Ga.
Tennessee State Library and Archives
Christian Chapel Church of Christ, Henderson County, Tenn.
McCains Cumberland Presbyterian Church, Maury County, Tenn.
McKenzie Cumberland Presbyterian Church, McKenzie, Tenn.
Old Bildad Church of Christ, Keltonburg, Tenn.

Newspapers

Abbeville Press and Banner (S.C.)
Almanac Gleaner (Graham, N.C.)
Ansonian (Wadesboro, N.C.)
Anson Times (Wadesboro, N.C.)
Arkansas Traveler (Conway, Ark.)
Arkansas Tribune (Harrisburg, Ark.)
Asheboro Bulletin (N.C.)
Athens Post (Tenn.)
Atlanta Constitution (Ga.)
Brunswick Weekly Advertiser (Ga.)
Calhoun County Courier (Leary, Ga.)

Carthage Herald (Tenn.)
Carthagian (Carthage, Miss.)
Central Georgian (Sandersville, Ga.)
Charleston Daily Courier (S.C.)
Charlotte Observer (N.C.)
Chester Semi-Weekly News (S.C.)
Clayton Bud (N.C.)
Clinton News Dispatch (N.C.)
Concord Register (N.C.)
Concord Times (N.C.)
Conyers Examiner (Ga.)
Copiah Signal (Hazlehurst, Miss.)
Crawfordville Democrat (Ga.)
Eastern Courier (Hertford, N.C.)
Eaton Messenger (Ga.)
Elberton Gazette (Ga.)
Elberton Star (Ga.)
Elm City Elevator (N.C.)
Etowah Enterprise (Tenn.)
Fayetteville Observer (Tenn.)
Forest City Courier (N.C.)
Forest News (Jefferson, Ga.)
Franklin Times (Louisburg, N.C.)
Gaffney Ledger (S.C.)
Giles County Record (Pulaski, Tenn.)
Greeneville Herald (Tenn.)
Greensboro Herald (Ga.)
Greer Citizen (S.C.)
Harnett County News (Lillington, N.C.)
Hartwell Sun (Ga.)
High Point Review (N.C.)
Hinds County Gazette (Raymond, Miss.)
Jackson News (Ga.)
Jesup Sentinel (Ga.)
King's Weekly (Greenville, N.C.)
Kinston Journal (N.C.)
Lancaster Ledger (S.C.)
Lebanon Democrat (Tenn.)
Littleton News Reporter (N.C.)
Lumberton Argus (N.C.)
McDuffie Weekly Journal (Thomson, Ga.)
Macon Beacon (Miss.)
Mansfield Enterprise (La.)
Marlboro Democrat (Bennetsville, S.C.)
Mississippi Democrat (Hazlehurst, Miss.)
Mobile Daily Register (Ala.)
Morehouse Clarion (Bastrop, La.)

Moultrie Daily Observer (Ga.)
Mountain Signal (Dahlonega, Ga.)
Nashville Banner (Tenn.)
Newnan Herald and Advertiser (Ga.)
Oglethorpe Echo (Crawford, Ga.)
Orangeburg Times and Democrat (S.C.)
Pearl River News (Columbia, Miss.)
Putnam County Herald (Cookeville, Tenn.)
Rockingham Rocket (N.C.)
Rome Daily Tribune (Ga.)
Rowan Record (China Grove, N.C.)
Salisbury Tri-Weekly Examiner (N.C.)
Sandersville Gazette (Ga.)
Savannah Courier (Tenn.)
Scottsboro Citizen (Ala.)
Shelby Guide (Columbiana, Ala.)
Siler City Grit (N.C.)
Southwestern Press (Washington, Ark.)
Sumner Free-Trader (Ga.)
Van Buren Press (Ark.)
Vass Pilot (N.C.)
Walterboro News (S.C.)
Warren Record (Warrenton, N.C.)
Waynesboro True Citizen (Ga.)
Weakley County Press and Martin Mail (Tenn.)
Weekly Columbus Enquirer (Ga.)
Yorkville Enquirer (S.C.)

Periodicals and Trade Publications

Alabama Baptist, selected issues.
Alabama Farm Facts, selected issues.
Alachua County Fair. Premium List. Gainesville, Fla., 1915.
Annual Fair of the Rutherford County Fair Association. Premium List and
    Rules and Regulations. Rutherford County, N.C., 1921.
Audubon Society of North Carolina. Annual Reports, 1903–9.
Audubon Society of South Carolina. Annual Reports, 1908–15.
Baptist Advance (Little Rock, Ark.), selected issues.
Buie's Creek Community Fair. Advertisement. Buie's Creek, N.C., 1917.
Chilton County Fair. Premium List. Clanton, Ala., 1914–15.
Christian Advocate, selected issues.
Commerce Four County Fair. Premium List. Commerce, Ga., 1917.
Cumberland County Fair. Premium List. Fayetteville, N.C., 1909.
East Alabama Fair. Catalog and Premium List. Alexander City, Ala., 1915.
Dixie Game Fowl, selected issues.
Field and Stream, selected issues.

Fifth Annual Fair of the Haywood County Stock Raisers and Farmers Association. Premium List. Waynesville, N.C., 1909.

Forest and Stream, selected issues.

Francioni, B., and M. M. LaCroix. "Lessons for Members of Boys and Girls Pig Clubs." Louisiana State University and Agricultural and Mechanical College, Agricultural Extension Division Circular no. 45, February 1921.

Greenville County Fair. Premium List. Greenville, S.C., 1923.

Grit and Steel, selected issues.

Haywood County Fair. Premium List. Waynesville, N.C., 1909.

Home Monthly, The (Nashville, Tenn.), selected issues.

Jefferson County Agricultural Exhibit. Program. Fayette, Miss., 1919.

Lafayette Parish Fair. Premium List. Lafayette, La., 1916.

Martin County Fair. Program. Williamston, N.C., 1920.

Middle Georgia Fair. Official Premium List. Milledgeville, Ga., 1929.

Nourse, David O. "Corn Husker and Fodder Cutter." Virginia Agricultural and Mechanical College, Agricultural Experiment Station, Bulletin no. 33, October 1893.

Outing, selected issues.

Pee Dee Agricultural and Mechanical Fair. Premium List. Cheraw, S.C., 1876.

Pender County Community Fair. Premium List. Pender County, N.C., 1919.

Progressive Farmer, selected issues.

Randolph County Fair. Premium List. Asheboro, N.C., 1922.

Rock Hill Magazine (York County, S.C.), 1916

Rural Carolinian, selected issues.

Rutherford County Fair. Premium List. Rutherford County, N.C., 1921.

Shelby County Fair. Program. Montevallo, Ala., 1915.

Sky-Land Magazine, selected issues.

Southern Cultivator, selected issues.

Southern Lumber Journal (Norfolk, Va.), selected issues.

Southern Methodist Home Altar, a Guide to Christian Perfection (McMinnville, Tenn.), selected issues.

Talladega County Fair. Premium List and Program. Sylacauga, Ala., 1915.

Tate, W. K. *Suggestions for County Fairs and Field Days*. Columbia: South Carolina Department of Education, 1913.

Wesleyan Christian Advocate, selected issues.

Wilkes-Lincoln County Fair. Premium List. Washington, Ga., 1914.

Winterville Community Fair. Program. Winterville, Ga., 1924.

Public Documents

Alabama Department of Conservation. Biennial Reports, 1908–14.

Alabama Department of Game and Fish. Biennial Reports, 1908–14.

Arkansas State Game and Fish Commission. Annual Report, 1918.

Louisiana Board of Commissioners for the Protection of Birds, Game, and Fish. "Game and Fish Laws of the State of Louisiana," 1909.

Louisiana Department of Agriculture. Farmers Institute Reports, selected years.

Louisiana Department of Conservation. "Wild Life Resources of Louisiana, Their Nature, Value, and Protection." Bulletin no. 10, 1921.

Louisiana State Society for the Prevention of Cruelty to Animals. Report, 1915.

Miller, E. A. "Improving School Grounds and Athletics." In *Agricultural and Industrial Education*. Alabama Department of Agriculture Bulletin, 1909.

Mississippi Agricultural and Mechanical College, Extension Department. "Agricultural Fairs," 1919.

Moran, J. Sterling. "The Community Fair." United States Department of Agriculture, Farmers' Bulletin no. 870, 1917.

Myers, Kenneth H. "Methods and Costs of Husking Corn in the Field." U.S. Department of Agriculture, Farmers' Bulletin no. 1715, 1933.

North Carolina Department of Conservation and Development. "Hunting in North Carolina." Bulletin no. 36, 1928.

———. Third Biennial Report, 1930.

Orr, A. W. "Butchering Hogs on the Farm." Missouri State Board of Agriculture Bulletin, September 1910.

Rubinow, S. G. "How Cooperative Fair Work Is Carried on in North Carolina." North Carolina Department of Agriculture Bulletin no. 254, 1919.

———. "Score Card for Draft Horses." North Carolina Agricultural Extension Service Circular no. 100, 1919.

———. "Score Cards for Judging at Fairs." North Carolina Agricultural Extension Service Circular no. 92, 1919.

———. "Some Results of Fair Work in North Carolina." North Carolina Agricultural Extension Service Circular no. 94, 1919.

Tate, W. K. "Suggestions for County Fairs and Field Days." South Carolina Department of Education Bulletin, 1913.

Virginia Commission of Game and Inland Fisheries. Report, 1917.

Zintheo, C. J. "Corn Harvesting Machinery." U.S. Department of Agriculture, Office of Experiment Stations, Bulletin no. 173, 1907.

The published acts and laws of various states are cited by state name, abbreviated title, and year (Arkansas, *Acts*, 1867).

Published Works

Abrahams, Roger D. "The Language of Festivals: Celebrating the Economy." In Victor Turner, ed., *Celebration: Studies in Festivity and Ritual*. Washington, D.C.: Smithsonian Institution Press, 1982.

Agee, James, and Walker Evans. *Let Us Now Praise Famous Men*. Boston: Houghton Mifflin, 1941.

Alexander, John Brevard. *Reminiscences of the Past Sixty Years*. Charlotte, N.C.: Ray Printing Co., 1908.

Allan-Olney, Mary. *The New Virginians*. 2 vols. Edinburgh: William Blackwood and Sons, 1880.

Allen, Frank G. *Autobiography of Frank G. Allen, Minister of the Gospel*. Cincinnati, Ohio: Guide Printing and Publishing Co., 1887.

———. *The Old-Path Pulpit: A Book of Original Doctrinal Sermons*. Covington, Ky.: Guide Printing and Publishing Co., 1886.

Altherr, Thomas L. "The American Hunter-Naturalist and the Development of the Code of Sportsmanship." *Journal of Sport History* 5 (Spring 1978): 7–22.

Andrews, Eliza Frances. *The War-Time Journal of a Georgia Girl*. New York: D. Appleton, 1908.

Andrews, Sidney. *The South since the War: As Shown by Fourteen Weeks of Travel and Observation in Georgia and the Carolinas*. Boston: Ticknor and Fields, 1866.

Ansley, Mrs. J. J. *History of the Georgia Women's Christian Temperance Union, from Its Organization, 1883 to 1907*. Columbus, Ga.: n.p., 1914.

Anthony, Bascom. *Fifty Years in the Ministry*. Macon, Ga.: J. W. Burke, 1937.

Anthony, J. D. *Life and Times of Rev. J. D. Anthony*. Atlanta, Ga.: C. P. Byrd, 1896.

Ariès, Philipe. *Western Attitudes toward Death: From the Middle Ages to the Present*. Translated by Patricia Ranum. Baltimore, Md.: Johns Hopkins University Press, 1974.

Arkansas Quilter's Guild. *Arkansas Quilts: Arkansas Warmth*. Paducah, Ky.: American Quilter's Society, 1987.

Arnold, Eddy. *It's a Long Way from Chester County*. Old Tappan, N.J.: Hewitt House, 1969.

Arsenault, Raymond. "The End of the Long Hot Summer: The Air Conditioner and Southern Culture." *Journal of Southern History* 50 (November 1984): 597–628.

Atherton, Lewis. *Main Street on the Middle Border*. Chicago: Quadrangle Books, 1954.

Atkins, R. A. *It Can Be Done: The Autobiography of Rev. R. A. Atkins*. N.p., 1970.

Auld, William Muir. *Christmas Traditions*. New York: Macmillan, 1933.

Austin, Bill Joe. *The Beat Goes On and On and On*. Benson, N.C.: Godwin Printing Co., 1976.

Avary, Myrta Lockett. *Dixie after the War*. Boston: Houghton Mifflin, 1937.

Avirett, James Battle. *The Old Plantation: How We Lived in Great House and Cabin before the War*. New York: F. Tennyson Neely, 1901.

Ayers, Edward L. "Toward a New Synthesis of the New South." Paper presented at the annual meeting of the Organization of American Historians, Reno, Nev., March 1988.

―――. *Vengeance and Justice: Crime and Punishment in the Nineteenth-Century American South*. New York: Oxford University Press, 1984.

Babcock, Havilah. *My Health Is Better in November: Thirty-Five Stories of Hunting and Fishing in the South*. New York: Holt, Rinehart and Winston, 1947.

Bailey, Kenneth. *Southern White Protestantism in the Twentieth Century*. New York: Harper and Row, 1964.

Balic, W. H. "Organization of Boys' Pig Clubs." Louisiana State University and Agricultural and Mechanical College, Agricultural Extension Division Circular no. 2, June 1915.

Barr, Basil D. *Big Game Hunting in Alaska, Arizona, and North Carolina*. Johnson City, Tenn.: Overmountain Press, 1982.

Barth, Gunther. *City People: The Rise of Modern City Culture in Nineteenth-Century America*. New York: Oxford University Press, 1980.

Bazemore, Thomas Jefferson. *Words of Comfort*. Atlanta: Foote and Davies, n.d.

Beard, Ida May. *My Own Life, or, a Deserted Wife*. Raleigh, N.C.: Edwards and Broughton, 1900.

Bertelson, David. *The Lazy South*. New York: Oxford University Press, 1967.

Blackman, Marion Cyrenus. *Look Away! Dixie Land Remembered*. New York: McCall Publishing Co., 1971.

Blanks, W. D. "Corrective Church Discipline in the Presbyterian Churches of the Nineteenth Century South." *Journal of Presbyterian History* 44 (June 1966): 89–105.

Bode, Frederick A. *Protestantism and the New South: North Carolina Baptists and Methodists in Political Crisis, 1894–1903*. Charlottesville: University Press of Virginia, 1975.

Boles, John B. *The Great Revival, 1787–1805*. Lexington: University Press of Kentucky, 1972.

Bond, Willard F. *I Had a Friend*. Kansas City, Mo.: E. L. Mendenhall, 1958.

Bordin, Ruth. *Women and Temperance: The Quest for Power and Liberty, 1873–1900*. Philadelphia: Temple University Press, 1981.

Botkin, B. A. "The Play-Party in Oklahoma." In J. Frank Dobie, ed., *Follow de Drinkin' Gou'd*, 7–24. 1928. Reprint. Dallas, Tex.: Texas Folklore Society, 1965.

Bounds, Edward M. *Heaven a Place, a City, a Home*. Grand Rapids, Mich.: Baker Book House, 1975.

Boyer, Paul S. *Purity in Print: The Vice-Society Movement and Book Censorship in America*. New York: Scribner's, 1968.

————. *Urban Masses and Moral Order in America, 1820–1920*. Cambridge, Mass.: Harvard University Press, 1978.

Braden, Beulah Brummett. *When Grandma Was a Girl*. Oak Ridge, Tenn.: The Oak Ridger and The Clinton Courier-News, 1976.

Bradshaw, DeEmmett. *My Story, the Autobiography of DeEmmett Bradshaw*. Omaha, Neb.: Omaha Printing Co., 1941.

Breen, T. H. "Horses and Gentlemen: The Cultural Significance of Gambling among the Gentry of Virginia." *William and Mary Quarterly* 34 (April 1977): 239–57.

————. "Looking Out for Number One: Conflicting Cultural Values in Early Seventeenth-Century Virginia." *South Atlantic Quarterly* 78 (Summer 1979): 342–60.

Brents, T. W. *Gospel Sermons*. Nashville, Tenn.: Gospel Advocate Publishing Co., 1981.

Broadus, John A. *A Treatise on the Preparation and Delivery of Sermons*. New York: A. C. Armstrong and Son, 1870.

Brooks, Aubrey Lee. *A Southern Lawyer: Fifty Years at the Bar*. Chapel Hill: University of North Carolina Press, 1950.

Broughton, Len. G. *The Modern Prodigal: A Series of Practical Talks to Young People*. Atlanta, Ga.: Foote and Davies, 1890.

―――. *Old Wine in New Bottles.* Cleveland, Ohio: F. M. Barton, 1904.

―――. *Talks on Home.* Roanoke, Va.: Stone Printing and Manufacturing Co., 1894.

―――. *Up from Sin: The Fall and Rise of a Prodigal.* Chicago: Fleming H. Revell, 1901.

―――. *Where Are the Dead?* Atlanta, Ga.: Phillips-Boyd Publishing Co., 1914.

Bruce, Dickson D., Jr. *And They All Sang Hallelujah: Plain-Folk Camp-Meeting Religion, 1800–1845.* Knoxville: University of Tennessee Press.

―――. *Violence and Culture in the Antebellum South.* Austin: University of Texas Press, 1979.

Brunner, Edmund de Schweinitz. *Church Life in the Rural South: A Study of the Opportunity of Protestantism Based upon Data from Seventy Counties.* New York: George H. Doran, 1923.

Buckingham, Nash. *De Shootingest Gent'man.* New York: G. P. Putnam's Sons, 1934.

Bumgarner, Andrew Monroe. *Autobiography of Andrew Monroe Bumgarner, or, the Little Book.* Charlotte, N.C.: Observer Printing House, n.d.

Burge, Dolly Sumner (Lunt). *The Diary of Dolly Lunt Burge.* Edited by James I. Robertson, Jr. Athens: University of Georgia Press, 1962.

Burke, Peter. *Popular Culture in Early Modern Europe.* New York: Oxford University Press, 1978.

Burland, C. A. *Echoes of Magic: A Study of Seasonal Festivals through the Ages.* London: Peter Davies, 1972.

Burleigh, William. *Sermons That Stirred a City.* Pennington Gap, Va.: Sun Publishing Co., 1915.

Burton, Orville Vernon. *In My Father's House Are Many Mansions: Family and Community in Edgefield, South Carolina.* Chapel Hill: University of North Carolina Press, 1985.

Butler, Bion H. "The Sportsman's Paradise." *Sky-Land Magazine* 2 (September 1914): 397–400.

Butler, Jon. "The Future of American Religious History: Prospectus, Agenda, Transatlantic Problématique." *William and Mary Quarterly* 42 (April 1985): 167–83.

Caillois, Roger. *Man, Play, and Games.* Translated by Meyer Barasch. New York: Free Press of Glencoe, 1958.

Calder, Jenni. *The Victorian Home.* London: Batsford, 1977.

Caldwell, Erskine. *Deep South: Memory and Observation.* Brown Thrasher Books. Athens: University of Georgia Press, 1980.

Campbell, Tom W. *Arkansas Lawyer: Reminiscences of a Lifetime.* Little Rock, Ark.: Pioneer Publishing Co., 1952.

Carmer, Carl Lawson. *Stars Fell on Alabama.* New York: Farrar and Rinehart, 1934.

Carson, Jane. *Colonial Virginians at Play.* Williamsburg, Va.: Colonial Williamsburg Foundation, 1965.

Carter, Jimmy. *Why Not the Best?* Nashville, Tenn.: Broadman Press, 1975.

Carter, Paul A. *The Decline and Revival of the Social Gospel: Social and*

Political Liberalism in American Protestant Churches, 1920–1940. Ithaca, N.Y.: Cornell University Press, 1954.

Cash, James I. *Autobiography and Sermons*. Spring Hill, Tenn.: n.p., 1934.

Cash, W. J. *The Mind of the South*. New York: Vintage Books, 1941.

Cashin, Joan. " 'The Ties of Nature': Kinship in the Antebellum South." Paper presented at the annual meeting of the Southern Historical Association, Houston, Tex., 15 November 1985.

Cason, Clarence. *Ninety Degrees in the Shade*. Chapel Hill: University of North Carolina Press, 1935.

Cavallo, Dominick. *Muscles and Morals: Organized Playgrounds and Urban Reform, 1880–1920*. Philadelphia: University of Pennsylvania Press, 1981.

Censer, Jane Turner. *North Carolina Planters and Their Children, 1800–1860*. Baton Rouge: Louisiana State University Press, 1984.

Chamberlain, Hope Summerell. *This Was Home*. Chapel Hill: University of North Carolina Press, 1938.

Clark, G. Dewey. *My South*. New York: Carlton Press, 1970.

Clark, Norman H. *Deliver Us from Evil: An Interpretation of American Prohibition*. New York: Norton, 1976.

Clark, Thomas D. *The Emerging South*. New York: Oxford University Press, 1961.

———. *Pills, Petticoats, and Plows: The Southern Country Store*. Norman: University of Oklahoma Press, 1944.

Clayton, Washington Lafayette. *Olden Times Revisited: W. L. Clayton's Pen Pictures*. Edited by Minrose Clayton Gwin. Jackson: University Press of Mississippi, 1982.

Clemmons, T. Elbert. *A Great Time to Be Alive: An Autobiography*. Stuart, Fla.: Southeastern Press, 1968.

Clemson, Floride. *A Rebel Came Home*. Edited by Charles M. McGee, Jr., and Ernest M. Lander, Jr. Columbia: University of South Carolina Press, 1961.

Clinton, Catherine. *The Plantation Mistress: Woman's World in the Old South*. New York: Pantheon, 1982.

Coffman, Edward. *Happy Years: An Autobiography*. Nashville, Tenn.: Parthenon Press, 1964.

Coleman, Caroline S. *Five Petticoats on Sunday*. Greenville, S.C.: Hiott Press, 1962.

Connelly, Thomas L., and Barbara L. Bellows. *God and General Longstreet: The Lost Cause and the Southern Mind*. Baton Rouge: Louisiana State University Press, 1982.

Cook, Anna Maria. *The Journal of a Milledgeville Girl, 1861–1867*. Edited by James C. Bonner. Athens: University of Georgia Press, 1964.

Coolidge, Jane Toy. *Growing Up with Chapel Hill*. Chapel Hill, N.C.: Chapel Hill Historical Society, 1977.

Cooper, William J. *The South and the Politics of Slavery, 1828–1856*. Baton Rouge: Louisiana State University Press, 1985.

Cott, Nancy F. *The Bonds of Womanhood: "Woman's Sphere" in New England, 1780–1835*. New Haven, Conn.: Yale University Press, 1977.

Cox, C. Waldo. *Hoot Owls, Honeysuckle, and Hallelujah.* New York: Vantage Press, 1966.

Cox, William E. *Southern Sidelights: A Record of Personal Experience.* Raleigh, N.C.: Edwards and Broughton, 1942.

Craig, Alberta Ratcliffe. "Home Life in Rockingham County in the 'Eighties and 'Nineties," edited by Marjorie Craig. *North Carolina Historical Review* 33 (October 1956): 510–28.

_____. "Old Wentworth Sketches." *North Carolina Historical Review* 11 (July 1934): 185–204.

Craig, Marjorie. "Survivals of the Chivalric Tournament in Southern Life and Literature." M.A. thesis, University of North Carolina, 1935.

Crooks, Esther J., and Ruth W. Crooks. *The Ring Tournament in the United States.* Richmond, Va.: Garrett and Massie, 1936.

Crowe, M. Karen. "Southern Horizons: The Autobiography of Thomas Dixon. A Critical Edition." Ph.D. diss., New York University, 1982.

Crunden, Robert M. *Ministers of Reform: The Progressives' Achievement in American Civilization, 1889–1920.* New York: Basic Books, 1982.

Cumming, Joseph B. *Reminiscences of Joseph B. Cumming, 1893–1983, an Oral History.* Edited by Arthur Ray Rowland. Augusta, Ga.: Richmond County Historical Society, 1983.

Dabney, Virginius. *Across the Years: Memories of a Virginian.* Garden City, N.Y.: Doubleday, 1978.

Daniel, Pete. *Standing at the Crossroads: Southern Life since 1900.* New York: Hill and Wang, 1986.

Daniels, Josephus. *Tar Heel Editor.* Chapel Hill: University of North Carolina Press, 1939.

Dannenbaum, Jed. *Drink and Disorder: Temperance Reform in Cincinnati from the Washington Revival to the WCTU.* Urbana: University of Illinois Press, 1984.

Darnton, Robert. *The Great Cat Massacre and Other Episodes in French Cultural History.* New York: Basic Books, 1984.

Davidoff, Leonore, and Catherine Hall. *Family Fortunes: Men and Women of the English Middle Class, 1780–1850.* Chicago: University of Chicago Press, 1987.

Davies, Horton, and Marie-Hélène Davies. *Holy Days and Holidays: The Medieval Pilgrimage to Canterbury.* London: Associated Presses for Bucknell University Press, 1982.

Davis, Marcellus L., with Henry P. Davis and C. T. Davis. *The Stranger.* Philadelphia: n.p., 1938.

Davis, Natalie Zemon. "The Sacred and the Body Social in Sixteenth-Century Lyon." *Past and Present* 90 (February 1981): 40–70.

Dawson, Sarah Morgan. *A Confederate Girl's Diary.* Boston: Houghton Mifflin, 1913.

DeCanio, Stephen J. *Agriculture in the Postbellum South: The Economics of Production and Supply.* Cambridge, Mass.: MIT Press, 1974.

Demos, John. *A Little Commonwealth: Family Life in Plymouth Colony.* New York: Oxford University Press, 1970.

Dodson, W. R. "Co-operative Extension Work in Agriculture and Home Economics." Louisiana State University and Agricultural and Mechanical College. Agricultural Extension Circular, January 1917.

Donner, Sam. *Giving the Devil His Dues, and Other Sermons.* Union, S.C.: n.p., 1926[?].

Douglas, Ann. *The Feminization of American Culture.* New York: Alfred A. Knopf, 1977.

———. "Heaven Our Home: Consolation Literature in the Northern United States, 1830–1880." In David E. Stannard, ed., *Death in America*, 49–68. Philadelphia: University of Pennsylvania Press, 1975.

Douglas, John Jordan. "Quail Shooting in the South." *Field and Stream* (October 1904): 548.

Doyle, Adna M. *My Spiritual Life.* Zebulon, N.C.: privately printed, 1978.

Drummond, Hattie McFadden. *Hoot Owls and Orchids.* San Antonio, Tex.: Naylor Co., 1956.

Dulles, Foster Rhea. *America Learns to Play: A History of Popular Recreation, 1607–1940.* New York: D. Appleton-Century, 1940.

Dunbar, Mary Conway. *My Mother Used to Say: A Natchez Belle of the Sixties.* Edited by Elizabeth Dunbar Murray. Boston: Christopher Publishing House, 1959.

Dunn, Floyd. *Swimmin' Holes 'n' Fishin' Poles: Tales from Brushy Creek.* Chattanooga, Tenn.: Brushy Creek Press, 1979.

Durham, Robert Lee. *Since I Was Born.* Edited by Marshall William Fishwick. Richmond, Va.: Whittet and Shepperson, 1953.

Dvorak, Katharine L. "After Apocalypse, Moses." In John B. Boles, ed., *Masters and Slaves in the House of the Lord: Race and Religion in the American South.* Lexington: University Press of Kentucky, 1988.

Edmonston, Catherine Devereux. *"Journal of a Secesh Lady": The Diary of Catherine Ann Devereux Edmonston.* Edited by Beth G. Crabtree and James W. Patton. Raleigh, N.C.: North Carolina Division of Archives and History, 1979.

Eighmy, John Lee. *Churches in Cultural Captivity: A History of the Social Attitudes of Southern Baptists.* Knoxville: University of Tennessee Press, 1972.

Eleazar, J. M. *A Dutch Fork Farm Boy.* Columbia: University of South Carolina Press, 1952.

———. *Fifty Years along the Roadside.* Anderson, S.C.: Independent Publishing Co., 1968.

Eliade, Mircea. *The Sacred and the Profane: The Nature of Religion.* Translated by Willard R. Trask. New York: Harper and Row, 1959.

English, T. R. *Family Religion: A Sermon.* Richmond, Va.: Whittet and Shepperson, 1889.

Epstein, Barbara Leslie. *The Politics of Domesticity: Women, Evangelism, and Temperance in Nineteenth-Century America.* Middletown, Conn.: Wesleyan University Press, 1981.

Erenberg, Lewis A. *Steppin' Out: New York Nightlife and the Transformation of American Culture, 1890–1930.* Westport, Conn.: Greenwood Press, 1981.

Etheridge, Paul S. *Threescore and Eleven.* New York: Hobson Book Press, 1945.

Eubanks, John. *Ben Tillman's Baby: The Dispensary System of South Carolina, 1892–1915.* N.p., 1950.

Farish, Hunter Dickinson. *The Circuit Rider Dismounts: A Social History of Southern Methodism, 1865–1900.* Richmond, Va.: Dietz Press, 1938.

Faulkner, William. *As I Lay Dying.* New York: Vintage Books, 1957.

_____. *The Hamlet.* New York: Random House, 1940.

_____. *Intruder in the Dust.* New York: Vintage Books, 1949.

_____. *Light in August.* New York: Random House, 1932.

Faust, Drew Gilpin. "Christian Soldiers: The Meaning of Revivalism in the Confederate Army." *Journal of Southern History* 58 (February 1987): 63–90.

Feagin, Mabel Lightner. *My Book.* Nashville, Tenn.: Baird-Ward Printing Co., 1964.

Filene, Peter. *Him/Her/Self: Sex Roles in Modern America.* 2d ed. Baltimore, Md.: Johns Hopkins University Press, 1986.

Finsterbush, C. A. *Cock Fighting All Over the World.* Gaffney, S.C.: Grit and Steel, 1929.

Fite, Gilbert C. "The Agricultural Trap in the South." *Agricultural History* 60 (Fall 1986): 38–50.

_____. *Cotton Fields No More: Southern Agriculture, 1865–1980.* Lexington: University Press of Kentucky, 1984.

Flynn, Charles L., Jr. *White Land, Black Labor: Caste and Class in Late Nineteenth-Century Georgia.* Baton Rouge: Louisiana State University Press, 1983.

Flynt, J. Wayne. "Dissent in Zion: Alabama Baptists and Social Issues, 1900–1914." *Journal of Southern History* 35 (November 1969): 523–42.

_____. "Southern Protestantism and Reform, 1890–1920." In Samuel S. Hill, ed., *Varieties of Southern Religious Experience,* 135–57. Baton Rouge: Louisiana State University Press, 1988.

Foner, Eric. *Nothing but Freedom: Emancipation and Its Legacy.* Baton Rouge: Louisiana State University Press, 1983.

Forde, Daryll. *Yakö Studies.* London: Oxford University Press, 1964.

Foster, Gaines. *Ghosts of the Confederacy: Defeat, the Lost Cause, and the Emergence of the New South, 1865–1913.* New York: Oxford University Press, 1987.

Foust, Clora McNeill. *Horse and Buggy Days in "the State of Wilkes."* Greensboro, N.C.: privately printed, 1969.

Fox-Genovese, Elizabeth. *Within the Plantation Household: Black and White Women of the Old South.* Chapel Hill: University of North Carolina Press, 1988.

Franklin, John Hope. *The Militant South, 1800–1861.* Cambridge, Mass.: Belknap Press, 1956.

Frazier, E. Franklin. *The Negro Church in America.* New York: Schocken Books, 1963.

Frederickson, George M. *The Black Image in the White Mind: The Debate on Afro-American Character and Destiny, 1817–1914.* New York: Harper and Row, 1971.

Friedman, Jean E. *The Enclosed Garden: Women and Community in the Evangelical South, 1830–1900.* Chapel Hill: University of North Carolina Press, 1985.

Friedman, Lawrence J. *The White Savage: Racial Fantasies in the Postbellum South.* Englewood Cliffs, N.J.: Prentice-Hall, 1970.

Gallman, Robert E. "Self-Sufficiency in the Cotton Economy of the Antebellum South." *Agricultural History* 44 (January 1970): 5–23.

Garrett, Mitchell B. *Horse and Buggy Days on Hatchet Creek.* University: University of Alabama Press, 1957.

Gaston, Paul M. *The New South Creed: A Study in Southern Mythmaking.* New York: Alfred A. Knopf, 1970.

Gates, Warren J. "Modernization as a Function of an Agricultural Fair: The Great Grangers' Picnic at Williams Grove, Pennsylvania, 1873–1916." *Agricultural History* 58 (July 1984): 262–79.

Geertz, Clifford. "Deep Play: Notes on the Balinese Cockfight." *Daedalus* 101 (Winter 1972): 1–38.

Gelber, Steven M. "Working at Playing: The Culture of the Workplace and the Rise of Baseball." *Journal of Social History* 16 (Summer 1983): 3–22.

Georgia State College of Agriculture. "Farmers Institutes in Georgia." *Bulletin of the University of Georgia,* 1910.

Glenn, Layona, with Charlotte Hale Smith. *I Remember, I Remember.* Old Tappan, N.J.: Fleming H. Revell, 1969.

Glenn, Reverend and Mrs. Wilbur. *A Life Sketch.* Atlanta, Ga.: Foote and Davies Co., 1913.

Gluckman, Max. *Order and Rebellion in Tribal Africa.* London: Cohen and West, 1963.

Gohdes, Clarence Lewis Frank, ed. *Hunting in the Old South: Original Narratives of the Hunters.* Baton Rouge: Louisiana State University Press, 1967.

Goodard, O. E. *Modern Evangelism on Fundamental Lines.* Nashville, Tenn.: Cokesbury Press, 1924.

Gordon, Elizabeth Biddle. *Days of Now and Then.* Philadelphia: Dorrance and Co., 1945.

Gordon, Jan, and Cora J. Gordon. *On Wandering Wheels: Through Roadside Camps from Maine to Georgia in an Old Sedan Car.* New York: Dodd, Mead, 1928.

Gorn, Elliott J. " 'Gouge and Bite, Pull Hair and Scratch': The Social Significance of Fighting in the Southern Backcountry." *American Historical Review* 90 (February 1985): 18–43.

Gould, Lewis L. *Progressives and Prohibitionists: Texas Democrats in the Wilson Era.* Austin: University of Texas Press, 1973.

Grantham, Dewey W. *Southern Progressivism: The Reconciliation of Progress and Tradition.* Knoxville: University of Tennessee Press, 1983.

Greaves, Robert L. *Society and Religion in Elizabethan England.* Minneapolis: University of Minnesota Press, 1981.

Green, John W. *Autobiographical Sketch.* N.p., n.d.

Greenberg, Kenneth S. *Masters and Statesmen: The Political Culture of American Slavery.* Baltimore, Md.: Johns Hopkins University Press, 1985.

Greven, Philip. *The Protestant Temperament: Patterns of Child-rearing, Religious Experience, and the Self in Early America.* New York: Meridian, 1977.

Griffen, Clyde. "The Progressive Ethos." In Lorman Ratner and Stanley Coben, eds., *The Development of an American Culture.* 2d ed. New York: St. Martin's Press, 1983.

Hackney, Sheldon. "Southern Violence." *American Historical Review* 74 (February 1969): 906–25.

Hahn, Steven A. *The Roots of Southern Populism: Yeoman Farmers and the Transformation of the Georgia Upcountry, 1850–1890.* New York: Oxford University Press, 1983.

Haines, Stephen M. "Southern Baptist Church Discipline, 1880–1939." *Baptist History and Heritage* 20 (April 1985): 14–27.

Hall, James Hamilton. *The Exodus from Death.* Nashville, Tenn.: Press of Marshall and Bruce, 1903.

Hamm, Thomas B. *From the Hills of Carolina: The Life of Thomas B. Hamm.* Indian Rocks Beach, Fla.: Books Unlimited, 1970.

Hamrick, Wiley Cicero. *Life Values in the New South.* Gaffney, S.C.: Observer Printing House, 1931.

Hantover, Jeffrey P. "The Boy Scouts and the Validation of Masculinity." In Elizabeth H. Pleck and Joseph H. Pleck, eds., *The American Man.* Englewood Cliffs, N.J.: Prentice-Hall, 1980.

Hardeman, Nicholas P. *Shucks, Shocks, and Hominy Blocks: Corn as a Way of Life in Pioneer America.* Baton Rouge: Louisiana State University Press, 1981.

Hardy, Stephen. *How Boston Played: Sports, Recreation, and Community, 1865–1915.* Boston: Northeastern University Press, 1982.

Harris, Corra. *A Circuit Rider's Wife.* Philadelphia: Henry Altemus, 1910.

Harris, Nathaniel E. *Autobiography: The Story of an Old Man's Life with Reminiscences of Seventy-Five Years.* Macon, Ga.: J. W. Burke, 1925.

Harris, Neil. *Humbug: The Art of P. T. Barnum.* Chicago: University of Chicago Press, 1973.

Havner, Vance. *Three-Score and Ten.* Old Tappan, N.J.: Fleming H. Revell, 1943.

Hawks, Elizabeth H. *A Distant Field: Memoirs of a Nonagenarian.* Warrenton, N.C.: n.p., ca. 1947.

Hawks, Joanne V., and Sheila L. Skemp, eds. *Sex, Race, and the Role of Women in the South.* Jackson: University Press of Mississippi, 1983.

Haygood, Atticus P. *Close the Saloons.* Macon, Ga.: J. W. Burke, 1880.

––––––. *Our Children.* New York: Nelson and Phillips, 1876.

_____. *A Plea for Prohibition*. Macon, Ga.: J. W. Burke, 1881.

Herring, J. L. *Saturday Night Sketches: Stories of Old Wiregrass Georgia*. Boston: Gorham Press, 1918.

Hickman, Nollie. *Mississippi Harvest: Lumbering in the Longleaf Pine Belt, 1840–1915*. University: University Press of Mississippi, 1962.

Higginson, A. Henry, and Julian Ingersoll Chamberlain. *The Hunts of the United States and Canada: Their Masters, Hounds, and Histories*. Boston: Frank L. Wiles, 1908.

Higham, John. "The Reorientation of American Culture in the 1890s." In *Writing American History: Essays on Modern Scholarship*. Bloomington: Indiana University Press, 1970.

_____. *Send These to Me: Immigrants in Urban America*. Rev. ed. Baltimore, Md.: Johns Hopkins University Press, 1984.

Hill, Samuel S. *Southern Churches in Crisis*. New York: Holt, Rinehart and Winston, 1967.

Hill, Samuel S., Edgar T. Thompson, Anne Firor Scott, Charles Hudson, and Edwin Gaustad. *Religion and the Solid South*. Nashville, Tenn.: Abingdon Press, 1972.

Hill, Walter B. *The Necessity of Education and Enforcement as Aids to Prohibition*. Macon, Ga.: J. W. Burke, 1886.

Hiss, Hanson. "The Knights of the Lance in the South." *Outing* (January 1889): 338–44.

Histories of Game Strains. Gaffney, S.C.: Grit and Steel, 1928.

Hobbs, Thomas Hubbard. *The Journals of Thomas Hubbard Hobbs*. Edited by Faye Acton Axford. University: University of Alabama Press, 1976.

Holmes, N. J. *Life Sketches and Sermons*. Royston, Ga.: Press of the Pentescostal Holiness Church, 1920.

Holmes, Sarah Katherine (Stone). *Brokenburn: The Journal of Kate Stone, 1861–1868*. Edited by John Q. Anderson. Baton Rouge: Louisiana State University Press, 1972.

Holstein, Jonathan, and John Finley. *Kentucky Quilts, 1800–1900: The Kentucky Quilt Project*. New York: Pantheon, 1983.

Horn, Pamela. *The Changing Countryside in Victorian and Edwardian England and Wales*. London: Athlone Press, 1984.

Horton, Laurel, and Lynn Robertson Myers, eds. *Social Fabric: South Carolina's Traditional Quilts*. Columbia, S.C.: McKissick Museum, 1985.

Hosch, Clarence Robert. *Nevah Come Back No Mo': Boyhood Memories of the Foothills of North Georgia*. New York: Exposition Press, 1968.

Hose, Charles, and William McDougall. *The Pagan Tribes of Borneo*. New York: Barnes and Noble, 1966.

Hubert, Thomas S. *Revivals of Religion*. Nashville, Tenn.: Publishing House, M. E. Church, South, 1895.

Hundley, Daniel R. *Social Relations in Our Southern States*. New York: Henry B. Price, 1860.

Hurt, John Jeter. *This Is My Story*. Atlanta: privately printed, 1957.

Hunter, Alexander. *The Huntsman in the South*. New York: Neale Publishing Co., 1908.

Hutchins, Myldred Flanigan. *Red Clay*. Lakemont, Ga.: Copple House Books, 1981.

Ingalls, Robert P. *Urban Vigilantes in the New South, Tampa, 1882–1936*. Knoxville: University of Tennessee Press, 1988.

Isaac, Paul E. *Prohibition and Politics: Turbulent Decades in Tennessee, 1885–1920*. Knoxville: University of Tennessee Press, 1965.

Isaac, Rhys. *The Transformation of Virginia, 1740–1790*. Chapel Hill: University of North Carolina Press, 1982.

Isbell, Robert L. *The World of My Childhood*. Edited by Kearney C. Pierce. Hudson, N.C.: W and H Graphics, 1955.

Isherwood, Robert M. *Farce and Fantasy: Popular Entertainment in Eighteenth-Century Paris*. New York: Oxford University Press, 1986.

Ivey, J. B. *My Memoirs*. Greensboro, N.C.: Piedmont Press, 1941.

Jackson, Nannie Stillwell. *Vinegar Pie and Chicken Bread: A Woman's Diary of Life in the Rural South, 1890–1891*. Edited by Margaret Jones Bolsterli. Fayetteville: University of Arkansas Press, 1982.

Jacobs, William Plumer. *Diary of William Plumer Jacobs*. Edited by Thornwell Jacobs. Oglethorpe, Ga.: Oglethorpe University Press, 1937.

James, E. O. *Seasonal Feasts and Festivals*. New York: Barnes and Noble, 1961.

Jelliffe, Belinda. *For Dear Life*. New York: Charles Scribner's Sons, 1936.

Jenkins, Winchester. *Wild Life in Mississippi from Forty-five Years Experience*. Natchez, Miss.: Reporter Printing Co., 1933.

Johnson, Ashley S. *Evangelistic and Expository Sermons*. Knoxville, Tenn.: S. B. Newman and Co., 1896.

Johnson, Charles A. *The Frontier Camp Meeting: Religion's Harvest Time*. Dallas, Tex.: Southern Methodist University Press, 1955.

Johnson, Clifton. *Highways and Byways of the South*. New York: Macmillan, 1904.

Johnson, John Lipscomb. *Autobiographical Notes*. N.p.: Crawford Toy Johnson, Jr., and Allen Acree Johnson, 1958.

Jones, Claude C. *Reminiscences of North Carolina*. N.p.: North Carolina Disciples of Christ Historical Commission, 1954.

Jones, Plummer F. "Turkey-Hunting in the Old Dominion." *Field and Stream* (December 1905): 751–52.

Jones, Sam S. *Sam Jones' Revival Sermons*. New York: Fleming H. Revell, 1912.

———. *Sermons and Sayings*. Nashville, Tenn.: Southern Methodist Publishing House, 1885.

Jordan, Winthrop D. *White over Black: American Attitudes toward the Negro, 1550–1812*. Chapel Hill: University of North Carolina Press, 1968.

Kane, Harnett T. *The Southern Christmas Book, the Full Story from Earliest Times to the Present: People, Customs, Conviviality, Carols, Cooking*. New York: D. McKay, 1958.

Kasson, John. *Amusing the Million: Coney Island at the Turn of the Century*. New York: Hill and Wang, 1978.

Kearney, Belle. *A Slaveholder's Daughter*. New York: Abbey Press, 1900.

Keen, Maurice. *Chivalry*. New Haven, Conn.: Yale University Press, 1984.

Kenan, William R., Jr. *Incidents by the Way: Lifetime Recollections and Reflections*. N.p.: privately printed, 1946.

Kern, John A. *The Ministry to the Congregation: Lectures on Homiletics*. Nashville, Tenn.: Publishing House, M. E. Church, South, 1901.

Kerr, K. Austin. *Organized for Prohibition: A New History of the Anti-Saloon League*. New Haven, Conn.: Yale University Press, 1985.

King, Edward. *The Great South: A Record of Journeys*. Hartford, Conn.: American Publishing Co., 1875.

King, J. Crawford. "The Closing of the Southern Range: An Exploratory Study." *Journal of Southern History* 48 (February 1982): 53–70.

Kingsdale, Jon M. "The Poor Man's Working-Class Saloon." *American Quarterly* 25 (October 1973): 472–89.

Kirby, Jack Temple. *Darkness at the Dawning: Race and Reform in the Progressive South*. Philadelphia: J. B. Lippincott, 1972.

———. *Rural Worlds Lost: The American South, 1920–1960*. Baton Rouge: Louisiana State University Press, 1987.

Kirk, Mary Wallace. *Locust Hill*. University: University of Alabama Press, 1972.

Kroll-Smith, J. Stephen. "Transmitting a Revival Culture: The Organizational Dynamic of the Baptist Movement in Colonial Virginia, 1760–1777." *Journal of Southern History* 50 (November 1984): 551–68.

Kulikoff, Allan. *Tobacco and Slaves: The Development of Southern Cultures in the Chesapeake, 1680–1800*. Chapel Hill: University of North Carolina Press, 1986.

Lamar, J. S. *First Principles and Perfection, or the Birth and Growth of a Christian*. Cincinnati, Ohio: Standard Publishing Co., 1891.

Lanier, Charles D. "On the Trail of the Wild Turkey." *Harper's New Monthly Magazine* (November 1894): 882.

Lathrop, Sallie B. Comer. *The Comer Family Goes to Town*. Birmingham, Ala.: Birmingham Printing Co., 1942.

———. *My Mother*. Birmingham, Ala.: Birmingham Printing Co., 1942.

Lee, S. E. *Recollections of Country Joe*. Gretna, La.: Pelican Publishing Co., 1976.

Leffingwell, William Bruce. *The Happy Hunting Grounds, also Fishing, of the South*. Chicago: Southern Railway Co., 1895.

Leftwich, J. T. *The Duty of the Church in View of the Law and the Testimony against the Sin of Social Dancing*. Atlanta: James P. Harrison, 1878.

Leigh, Frances Butler. *Ten Years on a Georgia Plantation since the War*. London: Richard Bentley and Son, 1883.

Lentz, Henry Jackson. *The Diary of Henry Jackson Lentz (1819–1869)*. N.p.: Northeast Mississippi Historical and Genealogical Society, 1983.

Leonard, Neil. *Jazz and the White Americans: The Acceptance of a New Art Form*. Chicago: University of Chicago Press, 1962.

Leonard, R. B. L. *Some Personal Experiences of My First Ninety Years*. Lexington, N.C.: privately printed, 1967.

Liddell, Viola Goode. *With a Southern Accent*. Norman: University of Oklahoma Press, 1948.

Lochrane, O. A. *Address of Judge O. A. Lochrane on Prohibition.* Atlanta, Ga.: James P. Harrison, 1885.

Long, Augustus White. *Son of Carolina.* Durham, N.C.: Duke University Press, 1939.

Long, Huey P. *Every Man a King.* New Orleans: National Book Co., 1933.

Long, Mary Alves. *High Time to Tell It.* Durham, N.C.: Duke University Press, 1950.

Long, Nat G. *My Long Life.* Conyers, Ga.: T.H.P., 1978.

Lovejoy, W. P. *The Mission of the Church.* Nashville, Tenn.: Publishing House, M. E. Church, South, 1894.

Loveland, Anne C. *Southern Evangelicals and the Social Order, 1800–1860.* Baton Rouge: Louisiana State University Press, 1980.

Lowber, J. W. *The Devil in Modern Society.* Cincinnati, Ohio: Standard Publishing, 1906.

Lumpkin, Katharine DuPre. *The Making of a Southerner.* Brown Thrasher Books. Athens: University of Georgia Press, 1981.

McBroom, Ruth Gates. *An Orange County Childhood.* N.p.: Betsy Holloway, 1983.

McCaghy, Charles H., and Arthur G. Neal. "The Fraternity of Cockfighters: Ethical Embellishments of an Illegal Sport." *Journal of Popular Culture* 8 (Winter 1974): 557–69.

McCall, Sol P. *Conditioning Cocks Correctly.* Gaffney, S.C.: Grit and Steel, 1926.

McCravy, Edwin Parker. *Memories.* Greenville, S.C.: Observer Printing Co., 1941.

McDonald, Forrest, and Grady McWhiney. "The South from Self-Sufficiency to Peonage: An Interpretation." *American Historical Review* 85 (December 1980): 1095–1119.

McDowall, Sue Ellen Price. *Cotton and Jasmine: A Southern Mosaic.* New York: Vantage Press, 1956.

McDowell, John Patrick. *The Social Gospel in the South: The Women's Home Mission Movement in the Methodist Episcopal Church, South, 1886–1939.* Baton Rouge: Louisiana State University Press, 1982.

McElreath, Walter B. *Walter McElreath, An Autobiography.* Edited by Albert B. Saye. Macon, Ga.: Mercer University Press, 1984.

Macfarlane, Alan. *Marriage and Love in England: Modes of Reproduction, 1300–1840.* Oxford: Basil Blackwell, 1986.

McGaffney, Ernest. "How They Hunt Deer in Arkansas: Where Still Hunting Is Fraught with Insurmountables and Hounding Legitimate," *Field and Stream* (November 1905): 648–52.

———. "Hunting Wildcats with Hound and Rifle: Exciting Times in the Arkansas Wilderness, When the Days Are Very Short." *Field and Stream* (December 1905): 770–74.

McGlothlin, W. J. *A Vital Ministry: The Pastor of To-Day in the Service of Man.* New York: Fleming H. Revell, 1913.

McIlhenny, Edward A. *The Wild Turkey and Its Hunting.* Garden City, N.Y.: Doubleday, 1914.

McIntyre, R. A. *The Game Fowl: Its Origins and History.* Gaffney, S.C.: Grit and Steel, 1904.

McKoy, Henry Bacon. *Wilmington, North Carolina—Do You Remember When?* Greenville, S.C.: Keys Printing Co., 1957.

Macrae, David. *The Americans at Home.* Glasgow: John S. Marr and Sons, 1875.

McWhiney, Grady. *Cracker Culture: Celtic Ways in the Old South.* University: University of Alabama Press, 1988.

McWhiney, Grady, and Perry D. Jamieson. *Attack and Die: Civil War Military Tactics and the Southern Heritage.* University: University of Alabama Press, 1982.

Malcolmson, Robert W. *Popular Recreations in English Society, 1700–1850.* Cambridge: Cambridge University Press, 1973.

Mangan, J. A., and James Walvin, eds. *Manliness and Morality: Middle-Class Masculinity in Britain and America, 1800–1940.* New York: St. Martin's Press, 1987.

Manning, Frank, ed. *The Celebration of Society: Perspectives on Contemporary Cultural Performance.* Bowling Green, Ohio: Bowling Green University Popular Press, 1983.

Marriott, McKim. "The Feast of Love." In Milton Singer, ed., *Krishna: Myths, Rites, and Attitudes.* Honolulu: East-West Press, 1966.

Marsden, George M. *Fundamentalism and American Culture: The Shaping of Twentieth-Century Evangelicalism, 1870–1925.* New York: Oxford University Press, 1980.

Masters, Victor I. *Country Church in the South.* Atlanta: Home Mission Board of the Southern Baptist Convention, 1916.

————. *Making America Christian.* Atlanta, Ga.: Home Mission Board of the Southern Baptist Convention, 1921.

Mathews, Donald G. *Religion in the Old South.* Chicago: University of Chicago Press, 1977.

Mathews, John. *Peeps into Life.* Nashville, Tenn.: C. H. Hawkins, 1904.

May, Lary L. *Screening Out the Past: The Birth of Mass Culture and the Motion Picture Industry.* New York: Oxford University Press, 1980.

Means, George W. *The Game Cock from the Shell to the Pit: A Comprehensive Treatise on Gameness, Selecting, Mating, Breeding, Walking, and Conditioning.* Gaffney, S.C.: Grit and Steel, 1911.

Medford, W. Clark. *Finis and Farewell.* Waynesville, N.C.: Miller Printing, 1969.

Mell, Patrick Hughes. *Corrective Church Discipline.* Athens, Ga.: E. D. Stone Press, 1912.

Meriwether, Elizabeth Avery. *Recollections of Ninety-two Years, 1824–1916.* Nashville, Tenn.: Tennessee Historical Commission, 1958.

Merrick, Carolina Elizabeth. *Old Times in Dixie Land: A Southern Matron's Memories.* New York: Grafton Press, 1901.

Mikell, I. Jenkins. *Rumbling of the Chariot Wheels.* Columbia, S.C.: The State Co., 1923.

Miles, Clement A. *Christmas in Ritual and Tradition Christian and Pagan.*

1921. Reprint. Detroit: Gale Publishing Co., 1968.

Miller, Nora. *The Girl in the Rural Family*. Chapel Hill: University of North Carolina Press, 1935.

Miyakawa, T. Scott. *Protestants and Pioneers: Individualism and Conformity on the American Frontier*. Chicago: University of Chicago Press, 1964.

Monter, E. William. "Women in Calvinist Geneva (1550–1800)." *Signs* 6 (Winter 1980): 189–209.

Montgomery, John Dexter. *Reminiscences of John Dexter Montgomery*. N.p., n.d.

Montgomery, Lizzie Wilson. *Sketches of Old Warrenton, North Carolina: Traditions and Reminiscences of the Town and People Who Made It*. Raleigh, N.C.: Edwards and Broughton, 1924.

Moore, Arthur K. *The Frontier Mind: A Cultural Analysis of the Kentucky Frontiersman*. Lexington: University Press of Kentucky, 1957.

Moore, J. Thomas. *Dr. Tom*. Nashville, Tenn.: Parthenon Press, 1957.

Morgan, Edmund Sears. *The Puritan Family: Essays on Religion and Domestic Relations in Seventeenth-Century New England*. Boston: Trustees of the Public Library, 1944.

Morrison, H. C. *Life Sketches and Sermons*. Louisville, Ky.: Pentecostal Publishing Co., 1903.

Mrozek, Donald J. *Sport and American Mentality, 1880–1910*. Knoxville: University of Tennessee Press, 1983.

Myers, Charlie Herbert. *This Is My Life*. LaGrange, Ga.: Smedley Printing Co., 1969.

Myers, Robert. *Celebrations: The Complete Book of American Holidays*. Garden City, N.Y.: Doubleday, 1972.

Neely, Wayne Caldwell. *The Agricultural Fair*. New York: Columbia University Press, 1935.

Newman, Louie Devotie. *Why I Am a Baptist*. New York: Thomas Nelson and Sons, 1957.

Noland, Julia Tignor, and Blanche Connelly Saucier. *Confederate Greenbacks: Mississippi Plantation Life in the 70's and 80's*. San Antonio, Tex.: Naylor Co., 1940.

Nolen, Claude H. *The Negro's Image in the South: The Anatomy of White Supremacy*. Lexington, Ky.: University Press of Kentucky, 1967.

Norbeck, Edward. "African Rituals of Conflict." *American Anthropologist* 65 (December 1963): 1254–79.

Norwood, James. *Are You Seeking the Best? Then Try These for They Are War Horses and Crosses and Never Fail to Give Good Account of Themselves in the Pit*. Durham, N.C.: Seeman Printery, 1901.

Novak, Daniel A. *The Wheel of Servitude: Black Forced Labor after Slavery*. Lexington: University Press of Kentucky, 1978.

Oakes, James. *The Ruling Race: A History of American Slaveholders*. New York: Vintage Books, 1982.

Obear, Katharine Theus. *Through the Years in Old Winnsboro*. Columbia, S.C.: R. L. Bryan, 1940.

Obelkovich, James. *Religion and Rural Society: South Lindsey, 1825–1875*.

New York: Oxford University Press, 1976.

Olds, F. A. "A Christmas Morning in Carolina." *Outing* (January 1899): 383–84.

Ormsby, A. A. "Community Fairs and Their Organization." Louisiana State University Agricultural and Mechanical College, Agricultural Extension Circular, 1921.

Osmond, Jessie Marvin. *The Country Church in North Carolina: A Study of the Country Churches in North Carolina in Relation to the Material Progress of the State.* Durham, N.C.: Duke University Press, 1931.

Osterweis, Rollin G. *The Myth of the Lost Cause, 1865–1900.* Hamden, Conn.: Archon Books, 1973.

Owen, William Russell. *The Song at Sunrise.* New York: Fleming H. Revell, 1923.

Owens, George W. *"I Was There . . .": An Autobiographical Sketch of Educational, Legislative, and Rehabilitation Experiences during the Changing Systems of Government in Mississippi.* Pontotoc, Miss.: Itawamba County Times, 1973.

Ownby, Ted. "The Defeated Generation at Work: White Farmers in the Deep South, 1865–1890." *Southern Studies* 23 (Winter 1984): 325–47.

Owsley, Frank L. *Plain Folk of the Old South.* 1949. Reprint. Chicago: Quadrangle Books, 1965.

Ozment, Steven. *When Fathers Ruled: Family Life in Reformation Europe.* Cambridge, Mass.: Harvard University Press, 1983.

Pamplin, Lila May. *The Scamps of Bucksnort: Memories of a Nineteenth-Century Childhood in Rural Tennessee.* New York: Exposition Press, 1962.

Pearl, Minnie, with Joan Drew. *Minnie Pearl, an Autobiography.* New York: Simon and Schuster, 1980.

Pearson, C. C., and J. Edwin Hendricks. *Liquor and Anti-Liquor in Virginia, 1619–1919.* Durham, N.C.: Duke University Press, 1967.

Pederson, Jane Marie. "The Country Visitor: Patterns of Hospitality in Rural Wisconsin, 1880–1925." *Agricultural History* 58 (July 1984): 347–64.

Peiss, Kathy. *Cheap Amusements: Working Women and Leisure in Turn-of-the-Century New York.* Philadelphia: Temple University Press, 1986.

Percy, William Alexander. *Lanterns on the Levee: Recollections of a Planter's Son.* New York: Alfred A. Knopf, 1941.

Pierce, Lovick. *Bishop Pierce's Sermons and Addresses.* Nashville, Tenn.: Publishing House, M. E. Church, South, 1896.

Pivar, David. *Purity Crusade: Sexual Morality and Social Control, 1868–1900.* Westport, Conn.: Greenwood Press, 1973.

Plyler, Marion T., Jr. *My Life as a Minister's Son.* N.p., n.d.

Poe, Clarence. *My First Eighty Years.* Chapel Hill: University of North Carolina Press, 1963.

Polk, Mary. *The Way We Were.* Winston-Salem, N.C.: John F. Blair, 1962.

Porter, Martha Byrd (Spruill). *Straight Down a Crooked Lane.* Richmond, Va.: Dietz Press, 1945.

Powell, Arthur G. *I Can Go Home Again.* Chapel Hill: University of North Carolina Press, 1943.

Powell, Theophilus Schuck. *Five Years in South Mississippi*. Cincinnati, Ohio: Standard Publishing Co., 1889.

Pridgen, Tim. *Courage: The Story of Modern Cockfighting*. Boston: Little, Brown, 1938.

Puckett, Martha Mizell. *Snow White Sands*. Douglass: South Georgia College, 1975.

Quillian, William F. *His Life and Sermons*. Atlanta: Foote and Davies, 1907.

Rabinowitz, Howard N. "From Exclusion to Segregation: Southern Race Relations, 1865–1890." *Journal of American History* 43 (September 1976): 325–50.

Ralph, Julian. *Dixie, or Southern Scenes and Sketches*. New York: Harper and Brothers, 1876.

Ramsey, Bets, and Merikay Waldvogel. *The Quilts of Tennessee: Images of Domestic Life prior to 1930*. Nashville, Tenn.: Rutledge Hill Press, 1986.

Range, Willard. *A Century of Georgia Agriculture, 1850–1950*. Athens: University of Georgia Press, 1954.

Rankin, George Clark. *The Story of My Life*. Nashville, Tenn.: Smith and Lamar, 1912.

Ransom, Roger, and Richard Sutch. *One Kind of Freedom: The Economic Consequences of Emancipation*. Cambridge: Cambridge University Press, 1977.

Reid, Numa F. *Life, Speeches, and Sermons*. New York: E. S. Hale and Son, 1874.

Reiger, John F. *American Sportsmen and the Origins of Conservation*. New York: Winchester Press, 1975.

Reimers, David M. *White Protestantism and the Negro*. New York: Oxford University Press, 1965.

Rice, James Henry, Jr. *Glories of the Carolina Coast*. Columbia, S.C.: R. L. Bryan, 1925.

Rice, John Andrew. *I Came Out of the Eighteenth Century*. New York: Harper and Brothers, 1942.

Richardson, Simon Peter. *The Lights and Shadows of Itinerant Life*. Nashville, Tenn.: Publishing House, M. E. Church, South, 1900.

Rippy, J. Fred. *Bygones I Cannot Help Recalling: The Memoirs of a Mobile Scholar*. Austin, Tex.: Steck-Vaughn, 1966.

Rivers, R. H., and H. C. Morrison. *Arrows from Two Quivers*. Nashville, Tenn.: Publishing House, M. E. Church, South, 1890.

Roark, James Larry. *Masters without Slaves: Southern Planters in the Civil War and Reconstruction*. New York: Norton, 1977.

Roark, Joseph Bruce, with Nancy Roark Ruiz. *Home Places: Stories of a Carolina Boyhood*. N.p.: Joseph Bruce Roark and Nancy Roark Ruiz, 1977.

Roberson, Ruth Haislip, ed. *North Carolina Quilts*. Chapel Hill: University of North Carolina Press, 1988.

Roberts, B. W. C. "Cockfighting: An Early Entertainment in North Carolina." *North Carolina Historical Review* 42 (July 1965): 306–14.

Roberts, Cyrus Tapscott. *Some Oaks Grow Small*. Fulton, Miss.: Itawamba County Times, 1961.

Roberts, T. P. *Highlights of My Life and Ministry in Old Time Revivals.* Wilmore, Ky.: n.p., 1952.

Robertson, Ben. *Red Hills and Cotton: An Upcountry Memory.* Columbia: University of South Carolina Press, 1963.

Robertson, William J. *The Changing South.* New York: Boni and Liveright, 1927.

Roosevelt, Theodore. *Hunting Trips of a Ranchman: Sketches of Sport on the Northern Cattle Plains.* New York: Current Literature Publishers, 1907.

_____. *Outdoor Pastimes of an American Hunter.* New York: Scribner's, 1905.

_____. *The Wilderness Hunter: An Account of the Big Game of the United States and Its Chase with Horse, Hound, and Rifle.* New York: G. P. Putnam's Sons, 1893.

Rorabaugh, W. J. *The Alcoholic Republic: An American Tradition.* New York: Oxford University Press, 1979.

Rosenberg, Charles E. "Sexuality, Class, and Role in Nineteenth-Century America." *American Quarterly* 25 (May 1973): 131–53.

Rosengarten, Theodore. *Tombee: Portrait of a Cotton Planter.* New York: William Morrow, 1986.

Rosenzweig, Roy. *Eight Hours for What We Will: Workers and Leisure in an Industrial City, 1870–1920.* Cambridge: Cambridge University Press, 1983.

Rotundo, E. Anthony. "Body and Soul: Changing Ideals of American Middle-Class Manhood, 1770–1920." *Journal of Social History* 16 (Summer 1983): 23–38.

_____. "Learning about Manhood: Gender Ideals and the Middle-Class Family in Nineteenth-Century America." In J. A. Mangan and James Walvin, eds., *Manliness and Morality: Middle-Class Masculinity in Britain and America, 1800–1940.* New York: St. Martin's Press, 1987.

Roubin, Lucienne. "Male Space and Female Space within the Provençal Community." Translated by Patricia M. Ranum. In Robert Forster and Orest Ranum, eds., *Rural Society in France,* 152–80. Baltimore, Md.: Johns Hopkins University Press, 1977.

Ruffer, Jonathan Garnier. *The Big Shots: Edwardian Shooting Parties.* New York: Viking, 1977.

Russell, Lucy Phillips. *A Rare Pattern.* Chapel Hill: University of North Carolina Press, 1957.

Rutherford, William. *Church Members' Guide for Baptist Churches.* Atlanta, Ga.: James P. Harrison, 1885.

Rutledge, Archibald. *An American Hunter.* New York: J. B. Lippincott, 1937.

_____. "My Greatest Thrill." *Field and Stream* (August 1930), 19, 63, 70.

_____. *Plantation Game Trails.* Boston: Houghton Mifflin, 1921.

_____. "That Hunt at Jasper Hill: The Pursuit of a Big Stag on a Carolina Plantation." *Field and Stream* (December 1919): 896–97, 914–15.

_____. *Those Were the Days.* Richmond, Va.: Dietz Press, 1955.

Ryan, Mary P. *Cradle of the Middle Class: The Family in Oneida County, New York, 1790–1865.* New York: Cambridge University Press, 1981.

————. "The Explosion of Family History." In Stanley I. Kutler and Stanley N. Katz, eds., *The Promise of American History*, 181–95. Baltimore, Md.: Johns Hopkins University Press, 1982.

Salley, A. S., Jr. *The Happy Hunting Ground: Personal Experiences in the Low-Country of South Carolina.* Columbia, S.C.: The State Co., 1926.

Sampey, John R. *Memoirs of John R. Sampey.* Nashville, Tenn.: Broadman Press, 1947.

Saum, Lewis. "Death in the Popular Mind of Pre–Civil War America." In David E. Stannard, ed., *Death in America*, 30–48. Philadelphia: University of Pennsylvania Press, 1975.

Saxon, Elizabeth Lyle. *A Southern Woman's War Time Reminiscences.* Memphis, Tenn.: Pilcher Printing Co., 1905.

Schama, Simon. *The Embarassment of Riches: An Interpretation of Dutch Culture in the Golden Age.* Berkeley: University of California Press, 1988.

Scott, Anne Firor. *The Southern Lady: From Pedestal to Politics, 1830–1930.* Chicago: University of Chicago Press, 1970.

Scott, Evelyn. *Background in Tennessee.* 1937. Reprint. Knoxville: University of Tennessee Press, 1980.

Scott, Roy Vernon. *The Reluctant Farmer: The Rise of Agricultural Extension to 1915.* Urbana: University of Illinois Press, 1970.

Sellers, James Benson. *The Prohibition Movement in Alabama, 1702 to 1943.* Chapel Hill: University of North Carolina Press, 1943.

Shettles, Elijah L. *Recollections of a Long Life.* Edited by Archie P. McDonald. Nashville, Tenn.: Blue and Gray Press, 1973.

Shewey, Arista C. *Shewey's Guide to the Happy Hunting Grounds of Missouri and Arkansas.* St. Louis, Mo.: privately printed, 1892.

Shingleton, Royce Gordon. "The Utility of Leisure: Game as a Source of Food in the Old South." *Mississippi Quarterly* 25 (Fall 1972): 429–45.

Shipp, J. E. D. *Total Prohibition the Remedy.* Sumter County, Ga.: Sumter County Prohibition Club, 1902.

Shore, George E. "Church Discipline in Ten Baptist Churches in Wake County, North Carolina, 1850–1915." Th.M. thesis, Southeastern Baptist Theological Seminary, 1955.

Sims, Anastatia. " 'The Sword of the Spirit': The WCTU and Moral Reform in North Carolina, 1883–1933." *North Carolina Historical Review* 64 (October 1987): 394–415.

Singleton, Royce Gordon. "The Utility of Leisure: Game as a Source of Food in the Old South." *Mississippi Quarterly* 25 (Fall 1972): 429–45.

Skinner, Thomas D. *Sermons, Addresses, and Reminiscences.* Raleigh, N.C.: Edwards and Broughton, 1894.

Sklar, Robert. *Movie-Made America: A Social History of American Movies.* New York: Random House, 1975.

Small, Sam W. *Pleas for Prohibition.* Atlanta, Ga.: Sam W. Small, 1890.

Smith, Bertha. *How the Spirit Filled My Life.* Nashville, Tenn.: Broadman Press, 1973.

Smith, Presley A. L. *Boyhood Memories of Fauquier.* Richmond, Va.: Old Dominion Press, 1926.

Smith-Rosenberg, Carroll. "The Female World of Love and Ritual: Relations between Women in Nineteenth-Century America." *Signs* 1 (Autumn 1975): 1–30.

Somers, Dale. "The Leisure Revolution: Recreation in the American City, 1820–1920." *Journal of Popular Culture* 5 (Summer 1971): 125–47.

———. *The Rise of Sports in New Orleans, 1850–1900.* Baton Rouge: Louisiana State University Press, 1972.

Somers, Robert. *The Southern States since the War, 1870–1871.* London: Macmillan, 1871.

South in the Building of the Nation, The. 12 vols. Richmond, Va.: Southern Historical Publication Society, 1909.

Spain, Rufus B. *At Ease in Zion: Social History of Southern Baptists, 1865–1900.* Nashville, Tenn.: Vanderbilt University Press, 1967.

Stacy, James. *Day of Rest: Its Obligations and Advantages.* Richmond, Va.: Whittet and Shepperson, 1885.

Stanfield, Mattie Cole. *Sourwood Tonic and Sassafras Tea: Memories of Rural Life in Northern Alabama at the Turn of the Century.* New York: Exposition Press, 1963.

Stannard, David E., ed. *Death in America.* Philadelphia: University of Pennsylvania Press, 1975.

———. *The Puritan Way of Death: A Study in Religion, Culture, and Social Change.* New York: Oxford University Press, 1977.

Stearns, Peter N. *Be a Man! Males in Modern Society.* New York: Holmes and Meier, 1979.

———. "Men, Boys, and Anger in American Society, 1860–1940." In J. A. Mangan and James Walvin, eds., *Manliness and Moralty: Middle-Class Masculinity in Britain and America, 1800–1940.* New York: St. Martin's Press, 1987.

Stephens, J. Harold. *Echoes of a Passing Era (Down Memories Lane).* Orlando, Fla.: Daniels Publishers, 1971.

Stockbridge, H. E. "A Sacrilegious Possum." *Field and Stream* (December 1904): 166–70.

Stone, Lawrence. *The Family, Sex, and Marriage in England, 1500–1800.* Abr. ed. New York: Harper and Row, 1979.

Stowe, Steven M. *Intimacy and Power in the Old South: Ritual in the Lives of the Planters.* Baltimore, Md.: Johns Hopkins University Press, 1987.

Street, Julian. *American Adventures.* New York: Century Co., 1917.

Stuart, George R. *Sermons.* Philadelphia: Pepper Publishing Co., 1904.

Sweeney, John S. *Sweeney's Sermons.* Nashville, Tenn.: Gospel Advocate Publishing Co., 1893.

Sydnor, Charles S. *American Revolutionaries in the Making: Political Practices in Washington's Virginia.* New York: Free Press, 1965.

Tang, Anthony M. *Economic Development in the Southern Piedmont, 1860–1950: Its Impact on Agriculture.* Chapel Hill: University of North Carolina Press, 1958.

Tate, Allen. *The Fathers.* New York: G. P. Putnam's Sons, 1938.

Taylor, Arnold H. *Travail and Triumph: Black Life and Culture in the South since the Civil War.* Westport, Conn.: Greenwood Press, 1975.

Taylor, J. M. *Hunting Grounds in Virginia and North Carolina.* New York: C. G. Crawford, 1894.

Thigpen, Julia Arledge. *Ninety and One Years.* Picayune, Miss.: S. G. Thigpen, 1965.

Thigpen, S. G. *A Boy in Rural Mississippi and Other Stories.* Picayune, Miss.: S. G. Thigpen, 1966.

Thomason, Philip. "The Men's Quarter of Downtown Nashville." *Tennessee Historical Quarterly* 41 (Spring 1982): 48–66.

Thompson, E. P. *Whigs and Hunters: The Origins of the Black Act.* London: Allen Lante, 1975.

Thornburg, Miles O. *The Thread of My Life.* Charlotte, N.C.: William Loftin, 1958.

Timberlake, James. *Prohibition and the Progressive Movement, 1900–1920.* Cambridge, Mass: Harvard University Press, 1963.

Topp, Mildred Spurrier. *Smile Please.* Boston: Houghton Mifflin, 1948.

Turner, James. *Reckoning with the Beast: Animals, Pain, and Humanity in the Victorian Mind.* Baltimore, Md.: Johns Hopkins University Press, 1980.

———. "Understanding the Populists." *Journal of American History* 67 (September 1980): 354–73.

Turner, Victor. *Dramas, Fields, and Metaphors: Symbolic Action in Human Society.* Ithaca, N.Y.: Cornell University Press, 1974.

———. *The Ritual Process: Structure and Anti-Structure.* Chicago: Aldine Publishing Co., 1969.

Turner, Victor, and Edith Turner. *Image and Pilgrimage in Christian Culture: Anthropological Perspectives.* New York: Columbia University Press, 1978.

Twain, Mark [Samuel Clemens]. *The Adventures of Huckleberry Finn.* Edited by Sculley Bradley, Richmond Croom Beatty, E. Hudson Long, and Thomas Cooley. New York: Norton, 1977.

———. *The Adventures of Tom Sawyer.* New York: Harper and Row, 1965.

Tyrrell, Ian. "Drink and Temperance in the Antebellum South: An Overview and Intepretation." *Journal of Southern History* 48 (November 1982): 485–510.

Van de Wetering, Maxine. "The Popular Concept of 'Home' in Nineteenth-Century America." *Journal of American Studies* 18 (April 1984): 5–28.

Vaughn, G. L. *The Cotton Renter's Son.* Wolfe City, Tex.: Henington Publishing Co., 1967.

Wack, Henry Wellington. "Bob White, 'Coon, and 'Possum, with Something about the Beautiful Country Where the Sportsman Can Find All Three." *Field and Stream* (Feb. 1909): 868.

Walker, Ewing A. *The Art of Walking Cocks.* Gaffney, S.C.: Grit and Steel, n.d.

Warner, Charles Dudley. *On Horseback: A Tour in Virginia, North Carolina, and Tennessee.* Boston: Houghton Mifflin, 1889.

Wayne, Michael. *The Reshaping of Plantation Society: The Natchez District, 1860–1880.* Baton Rouge: Louisiana State University Press, 1983.

Weber, Eugen. *Peasants into Frenchmen: The Modernization of Rural France, 1870–1914.* Stanford, Calif.: Stanford University Press, 1978.

Weiner, Annette B. *Women of Value, Men of Renown: New Perspectives in*

Trobriand Exchange. Austin: University of Texas Press, 1976.

Weisberger, Bernard A. *They Gathered at the River: The Story of the Great Revivalists and Their Impact upon Religion in America.* Boston: Little, Brown, 1958.

Welter, Barbara. "The Cult of True Womanhood, 1820–1860." *American Quarterly* 18 (Summer 1966): 151–74.

Welty, Eudora. *One Writer's Beginnings.* Cambridge, Mass.: Harvard University Press, 1984.

Whitaker, R. H. *Whitaker's Reminiscences, Incidents, and Anecdotes.* Raleigh, N.C.: Edwards and Broughton, 1905.

White, John E. "Prohibition: The New Task and Opportunity of the South." *South Atlantic Quarterly* 7 (April 1908): 130–42.

Whitener, Daniel Jay. *Prohibition in North Carolina, 1715–1945.* Chapel Hill: University of North Carolina Press, 1945.

Whitney, Casper W. "Fox-Hunting in the United States." In Frederick H. Curtiss, ed., *Hunt Clubs and Country Clubs in America.* Boston: privately printed, 1928.

Wiebe, Robert. *The Search For Order, 1877–1920.* New York: Hill and Wang, 1967.

Wiener, Jonathan. *Social Origins of the New South: Alabama, 1860–1885.* Baton Rouge: Louisiana State University Press, 1978.

Wilentz, Sean. *Chants Democratic: New York City and the Rise of the American Working Class, 1788–1850.* New York: Oxford University Press, 1984.

Wilkinson, Andrew. "Southern Sportswomen: Hunting Quail on Horseback over the Finest Grounds in Dixie." *Field and Stream* (December 1905): 775–78.

Williams, Dora Proffitt. "Memories of Dora Proffitt Williams." In Jerry Wear, Mary Teague, and Lynn Alexander, eds., *Lost Communities of Sevier County Tennessee: Greenbrier.* Sevierville, Tenn.: Sevierville Heritage Committee, 1985.

Williamson, Joel. *The Crucible of Race: Black-White Relations in the American South since Emancipation.* New York: Oxford University Press, 1984.

Wills, David. *Idols of the Age.* Macon, Ga.: Telegraph Messenger Steam Printing House, 1870.

Wilson, Charles Morrow. *Backwoods America.* Chapel Hill: University of North Carolina Press, 1934.

Wilson, Charles Reagan. *Baptized in Blood: The Religion of the Lost Cause, 1865–1920.* Athens: University of Georgia Press, 1980.

———, ed. *Religion in the South.* Jackson: University Press of Mississippi, 1985.

Wilson, Charles Reagan, and William Ferris, eds. *Encyclopedia of Southern Culture.* Chapel Hill: University of North Carolina Press, 1989.

Wilson, Peter Mitchell. *Southern Exposure.* Chapel Hill: University of North Carolina Press, 1927.

Winston, Robert Watson. *It's a Far Cry.* New York: Henry Holt, 1937.

Wolf, John Quincy. *Life in the Leatherwoods.* Edited by John Quincy Wolf, Jr. Memphis, Tenn.: Memphis State University Press, 1974.

Wood, Maude Talmadge. *Once Apunce a Time*. Athens, Ga.: Classic Press, 1977.

Woodward, C. Vann. *American Counterpoint: Slavery and Racism in the North-South Dialogue*. Boston: Little, Brown, 1971.

———. *Origins of the New South, 1877–1913*. Baton Rouge: Louisiana State University Press, 1951.

———. *The Strange Career of Jim Crow*. New York: Oxford University Press, 1955.

Wright, A. B. *Autobiography of Rev. A. B. Wright*. Edited by J. C. Wright. Cincinnati, Ohio: Cranston and Curts, 1896.

Wright, Gavin. *Old South, New South: Revolutions in the Southern Economy since the Civil War*. New York: Basic Books, 1986.

———. *The Political Economy of the Cotton South: Household Markets and Wealth in the Nineteenth Century*. New York: Norton, 1978.

Wright, Louis B. *Barefoot in Arcadia: Memories of a More Innocent Era*. Columbia: University of South Carolina Press, 1974.

Wyatt-Brown, Bertram. *Southern Honor: Ethics and Behavior in the Old South*. New York: Oxford University Press, 1982.

———. *Yankee Saints and Southern Sinners*. Baton Rouge: Louisiana State University Press, 1985.

Yabsley, Suzanne. *Texas Quilts, Texas Women*. College Station: Texas A&M University Press, 1984.

Index

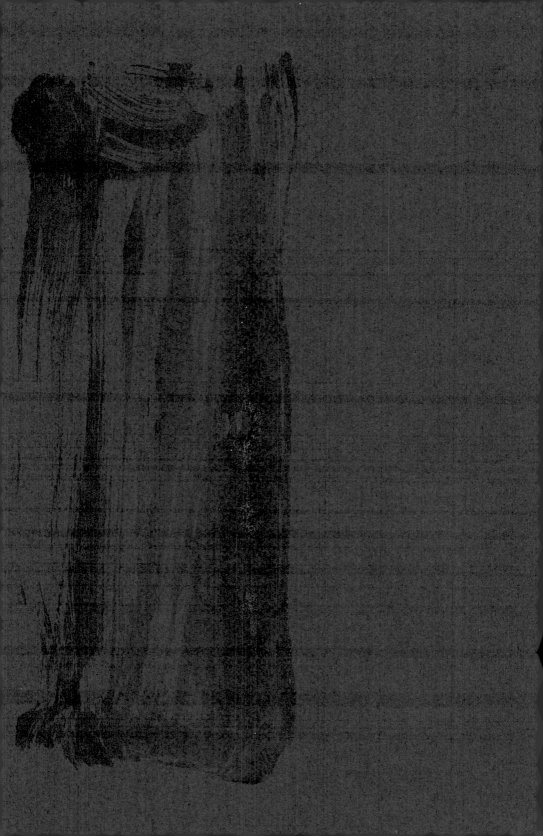